Cricket's Rich Heritage

A HISTORY OF
RHODESIAN AND ZIMBABWEAN
CRICKET
1890-1982

by
JONTY WINCH

BOOKS OF ZIMBABWE
Bulawayo
1983

ALSO BY JONTY WINCH

Rhodesia Rugby
A History of the National Side
1898-1979

Since the advent of Zimbabwe's Independence in 1980 a number of place names of former Rhodesia have been changed, e.g. Salisbury to Harare, Umtali to Mutare, Gwelo to Gweru, Fort Victoria to Masvingo. This being a work of history, covering the period 1890-1982, the names in the text are those that were in use at the time of the events described.

ISBN 0 86920 256 1

Published and bound by
BOOKS OF ZIMBABWE PUBLISHING CO.
(PVT.) LTD.
137A Rhodes Street
Bulawayo
Zimbabwe

Photoset in Baskerville by
BOOKSET (PVT.) LTD.
Bulawayo

Printed by
PUBLICATIONS C.A. (PVT.) LTD.
Bulawayo

Contents

Acknowledgements

The Zimbabwe Cricket Union, together with the Mashonaland Cricket Association, wishes to record its grateful thanks to the following companies for their support which has helped to make this record of cricket in Zimbabwe.

A.A. Mutual Insurance Association Ltd.

AFIA Insurance Company S.A. — N.V.

C.T. Bowring and Associates (Pvt.) Ltd.

C.U. Fire, Marine and General Insurance Company Ltd.

Eagle Insurance Company Ltd.

Export Credit Insurance Corporation Ltd.

Gerling-Global Reinsurance Company of S.A. Ltd.

NEM Insurance Company (Zimbabwe) (Pvt.) Ltd.

Norwich Union Fire Insurance Society Ltd.

Old Mutual Fire & General Insurance Company (Pvt.) Ltd.

Pearl General Insurance Company (Pvt.) Ltd.

Phoenix Prudential Assurance of Zimbabwe Ltd.

Royal Insurance Zimbabwe (Pvt.) Ltd.

Shield of Zimbabwe Insurance Company Ltd.

Willis Faber Syfrets (Pvt.) Ltd.

Zimnat Insurance Company Ltd.

Research has relied largely on newspapers and in particular back copies of *The (Rhodesia) Herald, The (Bulawayo) Chronicle* and *The Sunday Mail.* Here mention might be made that close reference has been paid to the cricket reports in the early years of Louis Duffus, the doyen of South African cricket writers, as well as to the work of the former Springbok, Len Brown, during the 1950s and 1960s and in more recent times to that of Glen Byrom. The National Archives were most helpful in obtaining the necessary material.

Of those who have helped to trace photographs, grateful acknowledgement is due to past players, to Brian Bassano, to the staff of the photographic sections of *The Star, Natal Daily News, Natal Mercury, The Chronicle, The Herald* and in particular to the Sports Editor of *The Herald*, Hugh Eley.

Past and present cricketers and administrators have read over the various chapters and have made invaluable comments and criticisms. In this regard the assistance provided by Messrs. A. "Jock" Holden, David Lewis and Rex McCulloch has been appreciated.

The majority of the statistics of the Rhodesian cricket period 1903-1979 have been based on the comprehensive records maintained by the former R.C.U. Hon. Secretary, Mr. K. G. Mockler.

The caricatures are the work of Mrs. Joan Dunstan whose talents in this field were for many years well received in the local Press.

The most onerous task in a book of this nature is the typing of the original manuscripts and special thanks are due to my wife for undertaking the assignment.

Finally, Mr. David Ellman-Brown, who managed the 1982 Zimbabwe tour to England, kindly provided the report on the highly successful ICC Trophy campaign.

— AUTHOR

Photo Credits

The kindly co-operation of the following photographic sources is gratefully acknowledged. As the origins of many of the pictures used could not be traced it was not possible to give all the credits due. Thanks are extended to all contributors including those not named.

The Argus: Pages 116 top, 122 bottom, 126 top and bottom.

Central Press Photographs: Page 184 top.

The Chronicle: Pages 35 left, 49, 51 — 3 pictures, 68, 69, 70 top (Mike Boutall), 80, 81, 84 top and bottom, 114 (Andrew Hendry), 121 top (Roy Reed), 121 bottom and 122 top (Andrew Hendry), 140 top (Andrew Hendry), 145 and 146 (Andrew Hendry), 159 (Costa Manzini), 160 (Stephen Sibanda), 186, 192 bottom, 195 bottom left (Andrew Hendry), 196 bottom, 197 top right (Costa Manzini).

Daily Press: Page 34.

Green, Wally: Page 24.

The Herald: Pages 8 bottom, 60, 71 top (David Paynter), 77 top, 85, 90 top (Ken Potter), 90 bottom (David Paynter), 94, 98 top and bottom (Vic Wasserfall), 101 top and bottom (Roger Bull), 103 top (Alan Murdoch), 103 bottom (Peter Winterbach, 115 right (Jim Tampin), 117 (Roger Bull), 129 top (Jim Tampin), 129 bottom, 131 top, 132 top (Simon McBride), 133 (Vic Wasserfall), 134 (Simon McBride), 135 top (Alan Murdoch), 135 bottom (Simon McBride), 136 (Roy Reed), 140 bottom (Paddy Hartdegen), 142 top, 142 bottom (Paddy Hartdegen), 143 top, 144 (Chris Dehon), 147, 148 top and bottom (Chris Dehon), 150 bottom (Roger Bull), 151 (Jack White), 152, 153 (Jack White), 154 (Allyson Brooks), 156 (Allan Gray), 157, 163 (Jack White), 164 and 165 (Peter Winterbach), 166 and 189 bottom (Allan Gray), 192 top (Jim Tampin), 193 right (Chris Dehon), 193 top (Michael Rushworth).

Herald Sun, Sydney: Page 74.

Kelly, Ken, Birmingham: Pages 169-180 inclusive — 13 photos.

Marylebone Cricket Club: Page 2.

McGeorge: Pages 161, 168, 198.

Ministry of Information: Pages 112 top, 188.

Natal Daily News: Pages 40, 194 top.

Natal Mercury: Pages 78 top, 197 top left.

National Archives: Cecil John Rhodes and Sir Murray Bissett, Introduction; pages 3, 4 bottom, 6 — 3 photos, 7, 11 bottom left.

Payne's Studios Ltd.: Page 42.

Photo and Travel: Page 109.

Pretoria News: Page 57, 195 bottom right.

Robal Studio: Page 37, insets 61.

Royal Air Force Photographic Section: Page 33 bottom.

Russell & Sons, Southsea: Page 5.

Sport and General: Pages 15, 39, 48, 59, 76, 78 bottom, 92, 93 top, 104.

The Star: Pages 35 right, 71 bottom, 73 bottom, 75, 107 (Geoff Paxton), 118, 139 (Dave Pughe-Parry), 150 top (Clive Lloyd), 193 left (Pat McKechnie).

Wesson, Noel: Page 66.

Windsor Studios: 128, 131 bottom, 190.

Foreword

THE GAME OF CRICKET has a rich history in many nations around the world. It is fitting, therefore, that the catalogue of cricketing events of our country, which have on previous occasions been recorded by others, should be researched afresh and extended up to the present day. It is also fitting that this latest history of the game in Zimbabwe should have been undertaken when we, as an independent nation, have taken our first giant step towards the main entrance to the Test cricket arena by handsomely winning, at the first attempt, the International Cricket Conference Trophy. This win places Zimbabwe on the road to the Prudential Cup in 1983 which in turn, with luck and hard work, will form the gateway to full Test status. Consequently, Zimbabwe cricket stands breathtakingly on the threshold of an exciting future from which point it may gaze out, in high anticipation but also with the necessary sense of proportion, at the potential glories and hopes which are attendant upon Test cricket.

It is fitting, too, that the person who already has to his credit a history of the game of rugby in this country, namely Jonty Winch, should be the author of this splendid publication, reflecting as it does a comprehensive survey of cricket in Zimbabwe to the modern day.

Cricket has shaped nations, events and people and those who have been its adherents, in whatever form, have reason to be grateful for the role it has played in their lives — friends and memories accumulated; character and sportsmanship developed; travel and opportunity presented — these are only some of the factors which it has brought and will continue to bring to those who embrace it.

All of these things are portrayed in this work to which I have been honoured to be asked, amongst many more suited to the task, to provide the Foreword. Jonty Winch is to be sincerely congratulated on his production and thanked for the painstaking research he has so obviously undertaken. It will be a valuable and intriguing addition to any sportsman's library, well supported as it is by a wide range of photographs.

This record of events traverses in interesting form down the years, the actions, successes and, naturally, the failures of players and administrators alike and the reader will be captivated by the narration.

Let us hope that in contributing to the past and the present, this book will also inspire the future because if we are to achieve our goal of Test cricket status, we will need to add to the obvious quality of administrator and player that we already have, a great deal more depth in the number of player participants since without that depth we would not sustain, for long into the future, any hard-won Test status that may be attained.

D. J. LEWIS

Introduction

THE EARLY EUROPEAN pioneers of this country somehow found space for cricket bats and balls in their rumbling ox-wagons as they infiltrated a new land which was to be known as Rhodesia. Even before they had reached Fort Salisbury the members of the historic Pioneer Column of 1890 had played their first cricket match in the shadow of the hills that overlook the Providential Pass near Fort Victoria. And by 1894, Bulawayo was in the position to issue a bold challenge to Salisbury for an inter-town contest. Such was the game's progress in the new Colony that in 1898, the Rhodesian Cricket Union was formed and soon afterwards the first English touring side arrived to play two matches.

Cricket was fortunate in that a number of the influential figures in power at that time gave the game their support. Cecil John Rhodes himself had been a keen cricketer as a youngster and had played for the Bishop's Stortford cricket XI of 1869 — the team photograph is preserved at Rhodes House. He gave the game much needed financial support in Rhodesia on several occasions, and was instrumental in the appointment of Sir William Milton, the former South African cricket captain, as the Colony's first Administrator in 1901. Milton's part in helping to spread the domain of cricket across Rhodesia is reflected by a comment in G. H. Tanser's book *A Scantling of Time*: 'Where previously one had to be a member of the la-di-da class to get a job in the Civil Service, now you had to beat the hide off a ball.

Many of the legendary figures in South Africa's early cricket history crossed the Limpopo and made their homes in Rhodesia. They became valued mentors of Rhodesian cricket and did much to promote the game. Herbert Castens, who captained the first South African team on tour to England in 1894, was a noted barrister in Rhodesia and ultimately a member of the Legislative Council. His vice-captain on the English tour, Godfrey Cripps, settled in Bulawayo and was a prominent figure in the town's league cricket. Murray Bisset, who led the second South African side to England, became Chief Justice of Southern Rhodesia, was knighted in 1928, and was acting Governor of the Colony when he died in 1931. Percy Sherwell, who was to play a leading role in the growth of Bulawayo's cricket and became a Rhodesian selector, was one of South Africa's greatest captains and led the first touring team to Australia. The Taberer brothers, (Henry captained the first South African side to play a home Test against Australia) both held high positions in the Native Affairs Department. "Sonny" Taberer, who became Chief Native Commissioner for Mashonaland, was said to have recruited new members to his department for their athletic ability and, if they should fail at a week-end match, he would shake his finger and say: 'You are for Gutu, my lad, if you do that again.'

Close links were always maintained with 'Home' and several players with county experience bolstered Rhodesia's cricket ranks. A number of the earlier cricketers had learnt the game at Oxford and Cambridge Universities. Walter Forbes, Captain Foley, H. J. Mordaunt and Herbert Keigwin spent their formative cricket years at Cambridge whilst the South Africans, Henry Taberer and Herbert Castens, played for Oxford. Many years later, Rhodesia was to repay the debt by supplying both universities with a crop of exciting young players and, indeed, five Rhodesians were to captain Oxford in succession.

In the early years numbers were an obvious problem and demands by the various sporting bodies were great on the time of the more talented individuals. Before the turn of the century the total European population for the Colony was estimated at between 8 000 and 10 000 but it was scattered and Salisbury's figure had not yet reached 1 000. Nevertheless, several fine sportsmen had already come to the fore and they set a proud standard which would be difficult to emulate in future years. Outstanding, of course, was the unassuming Freddie Brooks who, apart from being the star batsman of his era, won twenty-one national tennis titles including the singles on six occasions, finished first in several events at the Rhodesian Athletics Championships and captained Mashonaland at football and Rhodesia at rugby. But his greatest moment came whilst holidaying in England when he was chosen to play on the wing against Paul Roos's 1906-07 Springboks and scored a vital try which enabled England to draw the match.

This book traces the story of the national side which effectively began with the visit of Lord Hawke's English team in 1898-99, although first-class cricket started with the Colony's Currie Cup debut in 1904-05. However, mention is made for the most part of the notable deeds at lower levels such as the outstanding performances in the Logan Cup which for many years

CECIL JOHN RHODES.

was the cornerstone of the country's cricket. An attempt has also been made to recall the deeds of some of the many colourful personalities who have adorned the country's rich cricket heritage.

Throughout its history, the development of the game in Rhodesia (now Zimbabwe) has obviously been governed by the major political events. During the First World War, cricket languished on a somewhat limited scale, whilst the Second World War halted all first-class cricket. (Nevertheless, the game at league level in this country was kept very much alive during the latter war despite Southern Rhodesia contributing more fighting men in proportion to its population than any other Commonwealth country.)

Northern Rhodesian players first gained selection for the national side in 1938-39, but following the advent of an annual clash between the two Rhodesias in 1948-49, their performances thereafter warranted more attention than they had previously received. Yet, although they beat their southern counterparts on one occasion, few Northern Rhodesian cricketers earned selection for the full national side, and from 1954-55 they played their fixtures against Southern Rhodesian provincial teams.

Federation in 1953 hardly affected the Rhodesian team's composition in that Nyasaland did not participate in the existing cricket structure. When the breakup of the Federation occurred ten years later, and Zambia gained its independence, Southern Rhodesia continued alone, again as Rhodesia. However, there were additional developments and U.D.I. in 1965 resulted in international isolation with Rhodesia's cricket being further affected by the political pressure which caused South Africa to be expelled from the Test fold. The International Wanderers' tours in the mid-70s provided the only real link with the outside world for over a decade and Rhodesia became increasingly reliant on the Currie Cup competition.

For a short period during 1979, the cumbersome title Zimbabwe Rhodesia came into operation prior to the Lancaster House conference. It was temporarily then changed back to Rhodesia but on 18 April 1980, Zimbabwe was born, marking the severance of a 76-

year-old link with South African cricket. At the same time it opened up new horizons and to date, tours have been entertained from English County, Kenyan, West Indian and Pakistani sides. The inclusion of Zimbabwe in the World Cup is an exciting stage of a bright, new era for cricket in this country.

In 1962, a team of Rhodesian schoolboys known as the Fawns had embarked on a tour to England and made a tremendous impact, returning undefeated. The Mashonaland Country Districts ventured on a similar visit two years later and again gave an excellent account of this country's cricket strength. The following year, in 1965, the grandson of an 1894 Pioneer was one of the big drawcards of the English season and the crowds flocked to watch him in action. Television cameras and hordes of spectators were in attendance at Canterbury as Colin Bland gave an impressive demonstration of knocking down stumps from all angles — feats he repeated with breathtaking brilliance in the Test arena. Recently a team of home-grown players mounted Zimbabwe cricket's greatest challenge to date and toured England. The side returned triumphant, having won the International Cricket Conference Trophy in a most convincing manner.

Jock Thompson, in his book *A History of Sport in Southern Rhodesia, 1889-1935*, quoted a visiting Transvaal cricketer in 1913 as saying: 'The sporting spirit is to be found everywhere. It is in the air.' The comment was an apt one to have been made about cricket in this country which is played all year round. The summer season, during which the provincial and national leagues plus all first-class matches are staged, lasts from September to March whilst the flourishing Mashonaland Country Districts competition is played during the remaining months because summer is the busy time of the year for the tobacco growers. Climatically, winter is possibly the best time to play the game — a trifle cold occasionally, but nearly always free from rain. Within the untamed veld and in the most remote outposts of the country, picturesque cricket grounds, splendidly equipped, have sprung up. Since 1944, the district sides have competed for the coveted Lilthurbridge Cup — the title being taken

SIR MURRAY BISSET.

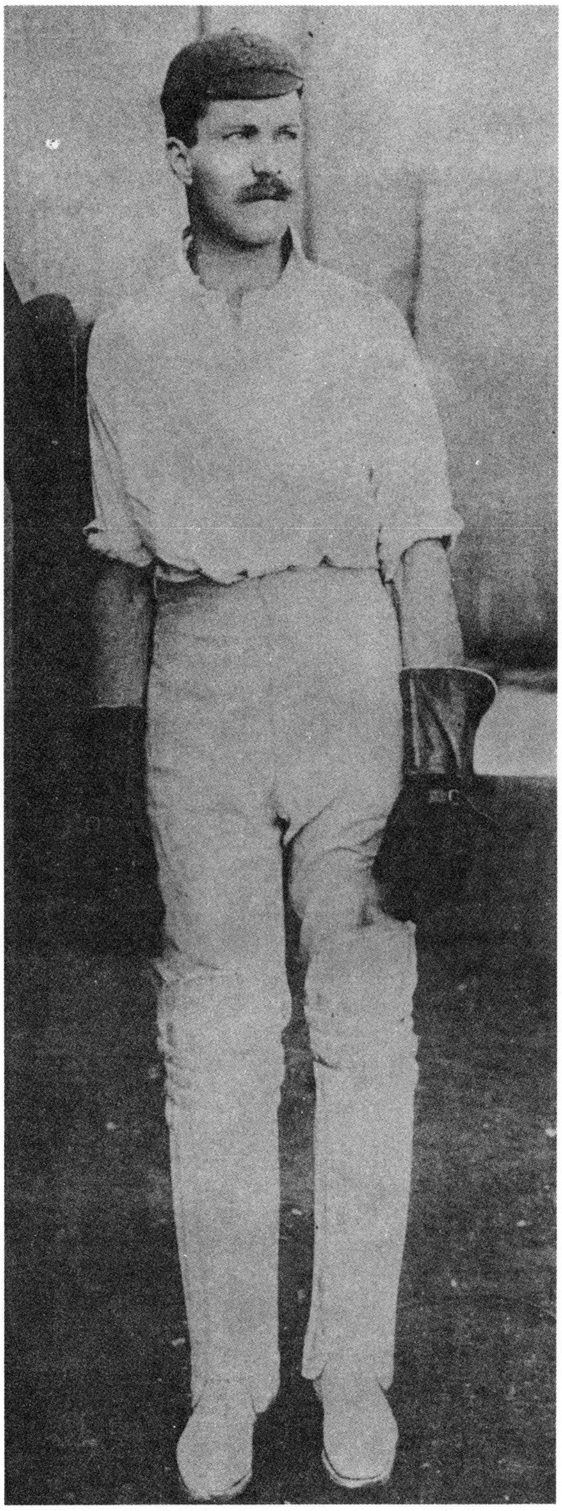

PERCY SHERWELL.

from the first syllables of the names of the three gentlemen who presented it — D. C. Lilford of Norton, R. W. O. Thurburn of Trelawney and E. T. Bridges of Bindura.

Cricket should prosper in Zimbabwe and standards must improve as the players are given the opportunity of testing their mettle against world-wide competition. The Z.C.U. are fully aware of the vast reservoir of untapped raw material in this country and coaching projects are well underway in new, untried areas. The Stragglers Cricket Club has undertaken in recent years the task of spreading the word amongst the African people and its achievements have been heartening. The inclusion of African players in the Zimbabwe Schools Cricket Week towards the end of 1981 represents an important breakthrough and paves the way for further honours. Their participation at senior level is eagerly anticipated and will further enhance the already vibrant and progressive atmosphere pervading Zimbabwean cricket.

CHAPTER ONE
The Pioneers

THE GAME of cricket arrived with the legendary Pioneer Column, which trekked into this country in 1890, and raised the Union Jack at Fort Salisbury on 12 September of that year. It is recorded that sport had been an important criteria in the enlisting of the pioneers selected to embark on the great adventure, as it made for sound constitutions. It can also be added that because of the large percentage of Englishmen participating, cricket inevitably featured prominently in the party's interests.

Such was their enthusiasm for the game that, when the members of the Column grouped together in Johannesburg, it did not take them long to organize a cricket match. Adrian Darter, who was originally from the Cape, wrote in his book, *The Pioneers of Mashonaland*: 'The Johannesburg contingent challenged us to cricket and gave us a tremendous drubbing due chiefly to the savage relish they took in my bowling, and the unmerciful manner in which they punished it. Wimble and Bowden were the chief offenders — to me — both played splendid innings. We contested this match in the neighbourhood of Otta's Hoek, and in the vicinity are the Malmani goldfields.'

Members of the Pioneer Corps played again in Mafeking as they wended their way northwards and "Skipper" Hoste in his book, *Gold Fever*, wrote: 'On Thursday the 15th May we took the day off from drill and played a match — Home-born versus Colonials. I played for Home-born and was in for two hours with one of our men, Pocock, during which time he piled up 60 runs. I also managed to pile up quite a score, consequently by the time I was bowled I felt as though I had been cooked to a turn.'

Before crossing into the new colony it seems possible that the pioneers continued their cricket contests at Fort Macloutsie with E and D Troops who already occupied the camp. The company commander, Major A. G. Leonard, wrote in his book, *How We Made Rhodesia*, that cricket helped to 'while away many a weary hour'.

On 16 August the first game of cricket in this country took place approximately four weeks before the Pioneer Column reached its destination. The match is recorded in a narrative by "Skipper" Hoste who commanded B Troop. On 14 August the Column had laagered 'about a mile from the pass and a spot was selected on which to build a fort to guard the pass, the fort to be named after H.M. Queen Victoria (the present town of Fort Victoria, now Masvingo)'. After a visit to the Zimbabwe Ruins, Hoste and his men returned to laager in the forenoon of 16 August and he continued: 'In the afternoon the first cricket match ever played in the country was played. The sides were A Troop (Pioneers) versus B and C Troops (Pioneers). I forget who won. It was probably A Troop as they had several outstanding cricketers, notably Monty Bowden, the celebrated Surrey wicket-keeper.'

It is an almost fairy-tale introduction to the country's cricket history that an England cricket captain should have been a member of the A Troop of the Pioneer Column. Montagu Parker Bowden, a Surrey cricketer during the years 1883-88, had been a wicket-keeper/batsman during the first English cricket tour of South Africa in 1888-89. He achieved the distinction of being England's youngest-ever captain, when at 23 years 144 days he skippered the side in the second official Test between the two countries, won convincingly by the visitors to the tune of an innings and 202 runs. Bowden had then settled in Johannesburg as a stockbroker and played for Transvaal against Kimberley in April 1890, scoring the second-ever century in Currie Cup cricket — 126 not out. A man of an intensely adventurous spirit, he attested into the Pioneer Corps soon afterwards, in May 1890. Adrian Darter wrote of him: ' "Monty" Bowden, England's fine amateur cricketer, had resided some time in Johannesburg and thrown in his lot with us. Tall, handsome, dark and charming, "Monty" was a fine type of England's best. His wicket-keeping was a revelation to South Africans, and his late cut, over the off stump, crisp as a blown kiss as he wafted the ball away with a flick to the boundary — the game of a blown kiss knows no limit once caught on the wave.'

On the demobilization of the Pioneer Corps, Bowden went into partnership in a trading business in Old Umtali. He supplied this store by travelling the treacherous route to Beira and returning with the goods carried on the heads of African porters, as tsetse fly prevented animals being used for much of the route. Malaria and blackwater fever were also rife and in October 1891, Cecil John Rhodes on his way to Umtali came across Bowden in poor health in Mozambique. Rhodes gave the sick man a bottle of whisky and a horse which enabled him to struggle to Umtali where the pioneer nurses cared for him in their primitive hospital. Interestingly, Darter claimed that 'the fevers of the low-lying country of the Pungwe route' killed Bowden, whilst a nominal roll of pioneers prepared in 1930 recorded that Bowden had died through being 'crushed by a wagon near Umtali'. Both explanations might have been contributary factors towards the unfortunate Bowden's death but the accepted account appears to have been that given by the pioneer nurses, Blennerhassett and Sleeman, in their book *Adventures in Mashonaland*. The two nurses wrote:

> The first case we lost in New Umtali was Mr. Montagu Bowden, the well-known cricketer. He was singularly handsome, popular and with every chance of success in trading and prospecting enterprises.
>
> In February 1892, while travelling from Salisbury to Umtali, he was thrown from his cart but was apparently uninjured. The day after his arrival he played in a cricket match and it was observed that he was in bad form. The next day but one he had an epileptic seizure and was conveyed to the hospital.

M.P. "MONTY" BOWDEN.

> His temperature rose to 107 and he passed away peacefully on the fourth day after his admittance. On account of the heat it was necessary to keep the doors and windows of the room where he lay, wide open, and a man with a loaded revolver sat there all night to protect the corpse from wild beasts.
>
> Next day he was buried, the whole community attending his funeral. With great difficulty owing to the scarcity of wood, a coffin had been made out of whisky cases. It was covered with dark blue limbo. A card, bearing his name and age, was nailed to the lid. Beneath it we placed a large cross of flowers. The remains were carried across the compound to a bullock-cart, and the melancholy procession started. We lingered to watch it wind across the plain, until it disappeared from view, and then with sad steps returned to the wards.

There were other useful cricketers amongst the pioneer contingent. Darter, himself a Western Province rugby player, had played inter-college cricket in Cape Town, along with fellow pioneer, Alick Halkett. Louis Vintcent, brother of the Springbok cricketer, and Bentley Wimble, 'one of the best bats of the Wanderers', were noted players, whilst the Scottish rugby international, Edward Pocock, had captained B Troop in that first cricket match.

With the large number of cricket enthusiasts amongst the early settlers it is not surprising that the game flourished in the various provinces soon after the Column's arrival in Salisbury. Although it is not possible to ascertain exact dates of the first matches there are numerous references to these early games. "Skipper" Hoste referred to a match between Police and The World, played in Salisbury on 4 April 1891, in his book *Gold Fever*. He had just returned from Umtali and wrote: 'Biscoe and I rode ahead of the wagons and reached the Fort in time to see the tail-end of one of the most popular relaxations in those early days — a cricket match.'

There is also a newspaper record of a match held in Salisbury between the Police and the Civilians to celebrate Occupation Day on 12 September 1891. The article implied that cricket had been played since the earliest days as the report stated that 'cricket is not dead but has been sleeping'. And less than a month after this match a meeting for the formation of a cricket and athletic club was held and the Salisbury Cricket Club was constituted on 10 October. One hundred pounds had already been collected to secure a good cricket kit and the Cricket Club Committee then called for tenders to clear and level an area a hundred feet square. The piece of ground selected ran parallel to Pioneer Street on the south side of Manica Road.

Until the new ground was ready matches were played in the enclosure of Messrs. Frank Johnson & Co. Ltd. and there were some interesting contests. A popular combination at the time was the Public School Old Boys and so strong was the 'Old School Tie' feeling that the name of the school that each Old Boy had attended was recorded in the score sheet. "Skipper" Hoste (Haileybury) and Captain Pocock (Clifton) were keen players for this side, whilst the popular Venerable Archdeacon Upcher (Haileybury and Cambridge) was a well-known figure on the cricket fields in this period. On one particularly memorable occasion The World beat the Public School Old Boys by 4 runs, aided somewhat by the fact that their side scored 46 extras — due largely to the nature of the pitch rather than poor wicket-keeping.

Testimony of the organization and enthusiasm at this time was that as early as 1893-94 Percy Craven became the first batsman to score 1 000 runs in a season in league cricket. He compiled 1 006 runs in 40 innings (average 26,47) with a highest score of 82. It was not until the arrival of the Taberer brothers that centuries were scored with any regularity.

Inevitably there were many interesting incidents arising from these early matches. On one famous occasion, during a match between All Comers against Colonials in September 1895, Judge Vintcent and Henry Taberer were enjoying an unbeaten stand of 77 for Colonials when according to a Press report, 'the match came to an unexpected termination owing to the ball bursting'.

Perhaps the most incredible tale was recorded by Cecil Hulley who wrote *Where Lions Once Roamed*.

Writing about the early 1890s in Umtali when the main street was also used as a cricket field he recalled: 'Cricket was a zealous affair, exciting considerable feeling. This was made evident when the Newcomers played the Veterans and a batsman for the Newcomers was playing havoc with the bowling. A spectator somewhat inebriated and very much on the side of the Veterans, staggered on to the "field" waving his revolver, and threatening to shoot the batsman if he did not stop scoring! All efforts to persuade him to leave the "field" failing, the captain of the Veterans shot him in the leg. The injured man was taken to hospital and the match resumed.'

Cricket in Bulawayo also progressed rapidly and by 1894 three club sides — Queens, B.A.C. and the Matabeleland Mounted Police — had been established. The 7th Hussars provided a fourth team because they had a camp near the Old Nic Mine. Visiting teams travelled there by bicycle or mule-cart and Col. J. de L. Thompson mentioned in his book *The Story of Rhodesian Sport: 1899-1935* that after matches 'there was royal entertainment in the Officers' Mess'.

Baragwanath, who scored 65 and on the strength of his performance was included in the team.

The side set off armed with two cases of "mixed" whisky, presents from the Masonic and Hatfield Hotels 'to keep out the fever'. Team captain was Henry Melville Taberer who was described in *The Bulawayo Chronicle* as 'the best amateur cricketer in South Africa'. Taberer, who had represented Oxford, Essex and Natal, had been sent to Rhodesia by Cecil Rhodes in 1895 as Chief Commissioner for Natives and held this position until 1901. He was subsequently transferred to the position of Native Commissioner of the Central Districts of the Transvaal and in the 1902-03 season captained South Africa in the First Test at the Wanderers cricket ground against the touring Australians in his one and only Test appearance.

Although a little out of practice for the Bulawayo game as he had only just recovered from a severe illness, Taberer batted, bowled and fielded with great success. Said *The Bulawayo Chronicle* reporter: 'I shudder to think what sort of show Salisbury would have made if they had been minus his services.'

A match between 7th Hussars and Old Buffers staged in 1896 at the 7th Hussars Camp near Bulawayo.

Towards the end of 1894, the "upstart" town (as Salisbury considered Bulawayo) challenged Salisbury to a cricket match. Herman Bezuidenhout (who combined farming with transport-riding) came forward immediately with an offer to transport the team of thirteen men for a round sum of £200. The offer, however, was not accepted — the cricketers expressing the opinion that 'the preservation of life and limb, not to mention comfort, was preferable to the honour of representing the town'.

After a year Bezuidenhout's contract was withdrawn and Doel Zeederberg introduced his American spring coaches. Salisbury took advantage of this new link between the two towns in 1895 to travel the round trip of nearly 600 miles in order to play three matches. Bulawayo offered free accommodation and Zeederberg agreed to take the team at the reduced rate of £300. Subsequently a trial match was held between Salisbury regulars and eighteen newcomers — the batting was dominated by a young man, Orlando

The Mashonas beat Queens, went down to B.A.C. in a hard-fought encounter and in the final game against Bulawayo were thrashed by an innings. In this last match Salisbury were given a lesson in batsmanship by Godfrey Cripps who hit a fine 98 and won the presentation bat. A dashing right-hand batsman, Cripps had an impressive cricketing background as he had played in one Test against W. W. Read's England team for South Africa in 1891-92 and was vice-captain of the first South African team to tour the United Kingdom in 1894.

There was at the same time a reason for Salisbury's dismal final performance as interest in cricket had almost disappeared when the news came on 29 December that Dr. Jameson and his raiders had gone on their ill-starred venture to Johannesburg. With the town full of rumours, Taberer suddenly found to his disgust that he was without two of his bowlers and Baragwanath because they were busy trying to get

SALISBURY v. QUEENS CLUB, 1895.
Back: R. Sidgreaves, G. Tucker, H. Christian, H. Mordaunt, O. Ogilvie, J. Purcell, H. Galt, D. Dollar, C. Gill, O. Baragwanath, H. Farquhar (Scorer).
Seated: Backhouse, H. Taberer, G. Cripps, E. Sharp, Money, A. Bramwell, C. Southey.
Front: G. Hill, P. Craven, A. Hill, H. Douslin, S. Goldsmith, Fergusson, Macdonald, Macfarlane.

enrolled in the force which was to follow and support the raiders.

A cricket visit was a hazardous exercise at this time and sadly the troubles were not yet over for the Salisbury cricketers. On their return journey their coach was bogged down numerous times, the rivers were flooded and the team was continuously delayed. Two of the players decided when the coach was some twenty miles south of Fort Charter, to walk home and arrived several days before the others.

SCORES: The 1895 Tournament at Bulawayo (Matches not first-class).

Queens — 53 (G. A. Tucker 5/4, H. M. Taberer 3/9) and 150 (A. B. Bramwell 36, H. J. Mordaunt 30; C. S. Gill 5/22)

Salisbury — 185 (E. C. Sharpe 58, G. Hill 39) and 20-1

Salisbury won by 9 wickets.

B.A.C. — 197 (D. Ingham 42, G. Cripps 37) and 122 (H. M. Taberer 5/15)

Salisbury — 136 (H. M. Taberer 79; A. Hill 4/24) and 141 (H. M. Taberer 49; S. J. Goldsmith 5/44)

B.A.C. won by 42 runs.

Bulawayo — 241 (G. Cripps 98, H. J. Mordaunt 42; C. S. Gill 4/72)

Salisbury — 34 (S. J. Goldsmith 6/9) and 124 (H. M. Taberer 31; H. J. Mordaunt 6/53)

Bulawayo won by an innings and 83 runs.

Undoubtedly the greatest motivating factor for Salisbury cricket and ultimately the national team in those days was the arrival of William "Joey" Milton in 1896. Later to become the Administrator of Southern Rhodesia and eventually Sir W. H. Milton, K.C.M.G., K.C.V.O., he was also an English rugby international (1874-75) but declared once that, next to his home and his work, cricket was the only thing for which he cared.

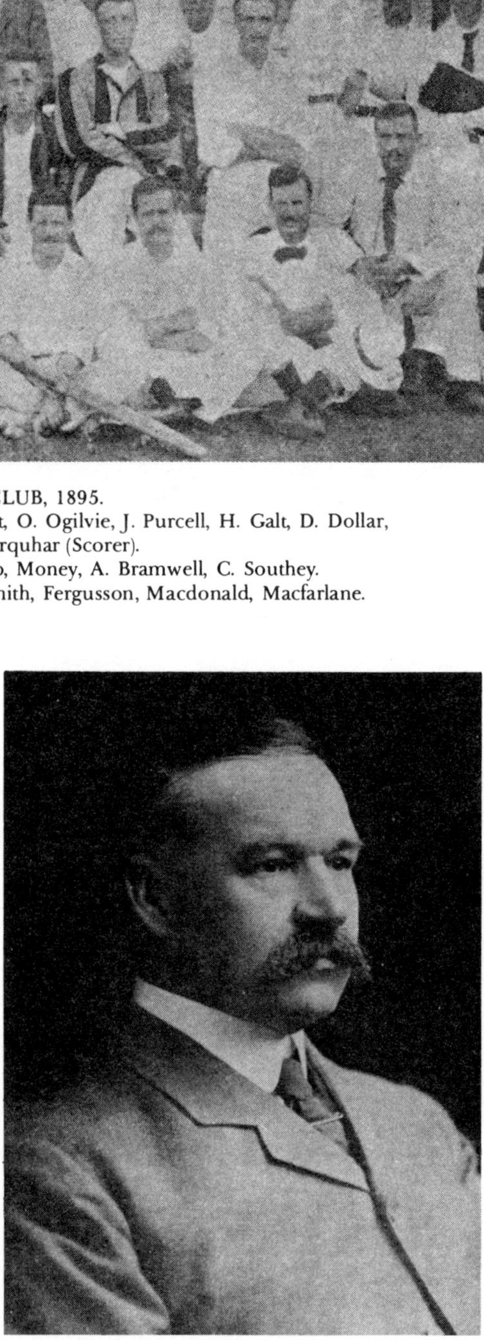

W.H. "JOEY" MILTON.

It was owing to his energy and enthusiasm that the first English cricket team visited South Africa in 1888-89; and against this side he had captained the Western Province XXII, the Cape Colony XV and South Africa. When the Western Province played England only 10 of the 44 innings reached double figures and Milton was top scorer with 36 and 40. He also captained South Africa against the English in 1891-92 — Milton (21 and 16) and Frank Hearne were the only South Africans to make double figures in both innings of the one Test that was played.

In Rhodesia, Milton set about reorganizing the Civil Service and brought to the country men who were experienced civil servants and good sportsmen — names such as Colin Duff, "Sonny" Taberer and Freddie Brooks. At a meeting of the Salisbury Cricket Club, Milton expressed his dislike of the nomenclature of the teams in the Salisbury area such as All Comers, New Chums and The World as well as teams chosen by individuals and in particular sides selected by the ladies with the titles Beautiful and Hideous. He suggested that the Kopje Club, which, with the Police Club and the Salisbury Club had formed an association football league, should once again provide a cricket team. This was done and the Kopje Club began to develop its field on the race course.

Further, by this stage the Salisbury Cricket Club had moved its ground to the Cecil Square which was levelled and improved as a playing-field, but Milton was not satisfied and looked for a more spacious setting. A move was made to the site of the present Harare Sports Club ground with Milton being responsible for the grant of free title to the ground in favour of the Salisbury Cricket Club on 7 May 1897, ahead of the other applications. Milton soon had the site cleared while all players about to begin any game were ordered to bring a badza and use it for half an hour before any match could commence. The first match was played on 7 August 1897 and the pitch consisted of a piece of coir matting put down between the creases. White shirts and trousers were worn, whilst braces, though not debarred, were thought not to be good form. Some of the senior members, however, still played their games wearing bow-ties.

MAJOR R.M. POORE.

Incidentally, in this first match, H.E. Rushton, the secretary of Salisbury Sports Club, achieved the distinction of taking a hat-trick.

A Sports Carnival was organized in September 1897, in honour of both Queen Victoria's Diamond Jubilee and the end of the Mashona War. It was hoped that cricket teams from Bulawayo, Fort Victoria and Umtali would journey to Salisbury for the cricket tournament but only the first named were able to travel. However, the 7th Hussars, who had arrived in Salisbury to aid the Police in the battle against Matshayangombi and the Mashonas, agreed to delay their departure in order to participate in the Carnival. Their commander, Captain Robert Montagu Poore, had been posted to South Africa from India as a lieutenant in the British Army in 1895 and had soon made his mark in Natal cricket. His innings of 112 for the Maritzburg XV against Lord Hawke's English side of 1895-96, was the first century recorded against a touring team. He repeated this feat in the following match for the Natal XV by rattling up 107 not out. These achievements led to Lord Hawke inviting him to play for his team, but Poore's commanding officer agreed to grant him leave of absence only if he were selected to represent South Africa. He took part in all three Tests, having the unique distinction of being the only cricketer to have been invited to play for both sides in a Test series. Later Poore, who ended his military career as a Brigadier-General, scored 1551 runs (average 91,23) including 7 centuries for Hampshire in 1899, and topped the English season averages.

Even stopping off in Gwelo for two matches could not lessen the uncomfortable and wearisome five-day coach journey which the Bulawayo team suffered. The players arrived a mere two hours before the start of the match, lost the toss and were made to field. "Joey" Milton and the two Taberers then climbed into the bowling and with each recording half-centuries, Salisbury were able to total 331. That fine all-rounder, W.S. "Sonny" Taberer, who had hit a competent 51 for a King William's Town XXII against Lord Hawke's 1895-96 team, proceeded to trouble all the Bulawayo batsmen with his bowling and thereby enabled Salisbury to win by an innings and seven runs.

The Bulawayo side had better fortune against the soldiers, winning narrowly on the first innings largely due to having Captain Poore run out for 18. Reg (later Sir Reginald) Blanckenberg of the well-known cricket family then hit a second-innings century to give Bulawayo a big lead but Poore's batting foiled their victory hopes in the Regiment's second knock and *The Rhodesia Herald* commented: 'Captain Poore's 75 not out was a splendid exhibition of cricket, combining sound defence with resolute hitting; his placing and timing were marvellously accurate.' Six feet four inches tall and of large frame, Poore's drive was one of the most powerful the game has known.

In the final match of the tournament Bulawayo gained sweet revenge by thrashing Salisbury by an innings and 9 runs. An outstanding all-round performance by Leo Robinson, who was stationed at Umzingwane, and used to cycle 16 miles into Bulawayo for his games of cricket over the week-ends, saw the visitors comfortably in charge throughout. At the end of the game Bulawayo were presented with the I.H. Hirschler Cup which, because it was not a floating trophy, became the Bulawayo First League Cup.

W.S. "SONNY" TABERER.

HENRY TABERER.

REG BLANCKENBERG.

SCORES: The 1897 Tournament in Salisbury (Matches not first-class).

Bulawayo — 143 (A.E. Fitzgerald 45, G.T.B. Hepburn 44; W.S. Taberer 6/46)
and 181 (L.G. Robinson 70; W.S. Taberer 6/40)

Salisbury — 331 (W.S. Taberer 65, W.H. Milton 60, H.M. Taberer 54)

Salisbury won by an innings and 7 runs.

Bulawayo — 142 (A.E. Fitzgerald 53, W. Jackson 50)
and 294-3 dec. (R.A. Blanckenberg 118, L.G. Robinson 83)

7th Hussars — 126 (L.G. Robinson 5/42)
and 146-2wkts. (Capt. R.M. Poore 75*)

Match drawn.

Bulawayo — 271 (A.E. Fitzgerald 80*, L.G. Robinson 58; Gleeson 4/52)

Salisbury — 81 (L.G. Robinson 4/28, M.G. Linnell 4/31)
and 181 (W.S. Taberer 55; L.G. Robinson 6/54)

Bulawayo won by an innings and 9 runs.

The tournament certainly reflected abundant talent and it appeared as if Rhodesian cricket was now ripe to accept outside challenge.

It seemed remarkable that less than nine years after the hoisting of the Union Jack in Fort Salisbury, Rhodesia should be hosting Lord Hawke's M.C.C. team. Two matches, both in Bulawayo, were arranged — the first against a Bulawayo XVIII followed by an encounter against a Rhodesia XV. The visit aroused tremendous interest and, through local endeavour, £500 was raised in order to guarantee the fixtures. In addition, the local Chamber of Commerce declared two public holidays in order to provide every facility for the public to support the games.

Lord Hawke's 1898-99 touring side was the second team which the Yorkshire and England cricket captain had brought to southern Africa. Strict but fair, he is remembered as having done much to improve the lot of the professional cricketer and under his captaincy Yorkshire won the English County Championship eight times. A *Bulawayo Chronicle* reporter found him a fascinating man to talk to because he was interested in such a wide range of subjects and much of the interview was taken up with the prospects of Rhodesia and the character of its gold formations. Interestingly, however, Lord Hawke did remark, 'Yes, I like the country but I am afraid the professionals will find it rather dull.'

The division between Gentlemen and Players was very much adhered to in those days. The Gentlemen, for example, stayed at the Grand Hotel whilst the Players were put up at the less plush Palace Hotel — a surprising separation but seemingly in accordance with the prevailing practice. To further emphasize this fact was that on the rest day the Gentlemen were invited to Cecil John Rhodes's estate at Sauerdale whilst the professionals were entertained to a luncheon with various entertainments at the Umgusa Hotel. But in this regard *The Bulawayo Chronicle* was quick to point out that the professionals found their programme, which included foot and horse-races as well as a variety of shooting competitions and a boxing contest, 'far from dull'.

On the day of the opening fixture *The Bulawayo Chronicle* reported that the ground was in first-class condition whilst a member of the touring party later wrote in a journal called *The African Review* that the ground was composed of 'sandy soil devoid of grass but dead level'. At that time turf outfields were unheard of in the Colony but the visitor did add that there was 'a good pavilion with spacious luncheon room, quite equal to many grounds in England where an occasional county game is played'.

The Bulawayo XVIII put up a sterling performance against Lord Hawke's XII and J. Bissett's bowling figures of 9/59 in 33 overs with 12 maidens were particularly commendable. Ultimately the Bulawayo side did lose outright by nine wickets but their efforts were most encouraging against a side which had recorded fifteen victories and two draws from seventeen matches in South Africa. In the tourists' line-up were Pelham Warner, J.T. Tyldesley, Schofield Haigh, Frank Mitchell, Frank Milligan and Albert Trott — all great names in world cricket. The legendary Trott, a medium-paced bowler with a wide variety of deliveries, represented Australia against England in 1894-95 and after scoring 205 runs in 5 innings with 2 not outs in addition to bowling well, was omitted from the side which toured the United Kingdom in 1896. No doubt upset, he left his native land to play for Middlesex and became the only man to hit a six over the pavilion at Lord's. But his greatest feat occurred during his benefit match which he wrecked somewhat by taking four wickets in four balls and a hat-trick in the same match.

A Rhodesian XV took on the tourists in their second encounter and an article in *The Bulawayo Chronicle* said: 'Today the local team have a harder task to see what they can do against Lord Hawke's team with fifteen players. On the other hand they have the advantage of playing five good Salisbury men, that is if the journey has not sent them off colour.'

There had been a long drought that year and the rains did not start in earnest until February but when they did, they created havoc on the primitive roads. By March the Zeederberg coaches were being bogged down or held up at rivers and were taking ten to twelve days, instead of the usual four, to reach Salisbury. The five Salisbury cricketers — Henry Taberer, Eric Sharpe,

One of the many hazards of early transport — a Zeederberg coach is bogged down in a drift.

Colin Duff, R.B. Beatson and G. Finch — allowing themselves a fortnight for the journey, set off in hope but found the Hunyani in heavy flood. It was thought, however, that if the coach was lightened it might be able to cross, drawn by the swimming mules.

G.H. Tanser records in his book *A Scantling of Time*:

> The only way for the men to cross was by establishing communications with the other side, for the wire rope which carried a skip had been broken. Taberer, who it was said could throw a cricket ball a hundred yards while standing in a barrel, overcame the difficulty by hurling a ball, to which a cord had been nailed, across the river. Then a stronger cord was passed over, then a rope and finally a wire rope to which a skip could be attached. Each player, with his cricket gear, then pulled himself across. When the coach attempted the passage the mules were washed down away from the drift, and the driver had to struggle to get them to the bank. Wet and miserable, the cricketers had to wait until the Bulawayo coach arrived, when it was turned around and set off on the return journey. At Enkeldoorn the coach became so deeply bogged down that three spans (thirty-six oxen), were needed to pull it out. During much of the journey the players had to remain alert, ready to jump out and put their shoulders to the wheel to help the straining animals to keep the coach moving.

The five men arrived in Bulawayo on the morning of the match shortly before play started. Their determination to make the game so impressed Mr. J.D. Logan, a member of the Cape Legislative Council and one of cricket's most liberal patrons, that he asked Lord Hawke to buy a cup on his return to England for inter-town competition. In due course the trophy arrived and, as the Logan Cup, is still competed for by the various provinces.

Appearing to shrug off any after-effects of the nightmare journey, Taberer bowled superbly to take the wickets of Mitchell, Tyldesley, Cuttell, Milligan and Wilson for 62 runs in 38 immaculate overs. Rated by "Plum" Warner as the quickest bowler the English had faced on tour, Taberer was also outstanding in the field setting a splendid example. His marvellous throwing arm — he held the Natal cricket ball-throwing record of 126 yards — constantly drew rounds of applause.

Unfortunately for Rhodesia, the bowling of Haigh and Trott proved too good and between them they accounted for twenty-one of the wickets to fall. A fine innings of 52 by H. Hallward highlighted Rhodesia's first knock whilst Colin Duff was top scorer in their second dismal effort.

SCORES: Lord Hawke's English Tour, 1898-99.

At Bulawayo, 1, 2 and 3 March (Not first-class).

Bulawayo XVIII — 124 (H.G. Board 29, Dollar 21*; C.E.M. Wilson 7/27, F.W. Milligan 5/29)
and 180 (L.G. Robinson 28, R.A. Blanckenberg 22, M.H. Routledge 20; S. Haigh 11/44, A.E. Trott 5/55)

England — 172 (S. Haigh 52, J.T. Tyldesley 51; J. Bissett 9/59)
and 135-1 wkt. (P.F. Warner 54*, F. Mitchell 45)

England won by 9 wickets.

At Bulawayo, 4, 6 and 7 March (Not first-class).

England — 275 (P.F. Warner 80, J.T. Tyldesley 71, C.E.M. Wilson 32; H.M. Taberer 5/62, J. Bissett 4/85)

The Logan Cup was presented in 1899 and the first contest was staged in 1903-04. The name Grimmer appeared in the Mashonaland side that played in the inaugural fixture and some 75 years later Cecil Grimmer became the third generation of the same family to be selected for a Logan Cup side.

CECIL GRIMMER.

Rhodesia XV — 121 (H. Hallward 52, J. Bissett 21; S. Haigh 9/36, A.E. Trott 5/35)
and 89 (C.E. Duff 27; S. Haigh 4/8, F.W. Milligan 4/23, A.E. Trott 3/31)

England won by an innings and 65 runs.

Six years later the Rhodesians further tested their cricket progress when they visited Johannesburg to take part in the Currie Cup tournament. They had been automatically accepted into the competition at the semi-final stage against Transvaal.

The team, consisting of five players from Salisbury, one from Gwelo and six from Bulawayo, journeyed for the first part of their long haul by train. However, it was then necessary to travel by coach from Mafeking to Potchefstroom, as there was no connecting link between the Cape and Johannesburg lines. Unfortunately for the Rhodesians, they discovered that there had been some heavy rains and travelling conditions were hazardous with muddy roads and swollen rivers.

Yet the team could not afford to be delayed. Urged on by the players, the drivers of the mules — the drivers and animals changed every ten miles — took some frightening risks. Even in the day-time when the good-humoured A.H. Tummell perched precariously on top of the coach in the pelting rain and tried to give some guidance to the driver, there was always the chance the coach might go into a washed-out hole and be capsized. In crossing rivers there was also the possibility that the swimming mules might lose their direction and allow the vehicle to float downstream.

At night those dangers were increased. Time and again the cricketers had to sit with water swirling around their feet whilst sleep was impossible. For twenty-six hours the coach battled against the elements before, wet and exhausted, the team boarded the train at Potchefstroom, finally reaching the field of play an hour before the match was due to start. The Johannesburg spectators, having learnt of the efforts of the Rhodesians, gave the players a hearty welcome as they went out to field in clothes borrowed from their hosts, their own still being rain-sodden.

Heavy rain in Johannesburg had continued until 8.30 that morning when the weather cleared sufficiently to permit play. Winning the toss, the Rhodesian skipper, Leo Robinson, had sent Transvaal in to bat on a wicket which the rain, if anything, had rendered easy. Yet by bundling out five of the top order Transvaal batsmen for 123 the visitors nevertheless appeared to have justified their captain's decision. Sadly, it was a case of dropped catches which allowed J.J. Slatem to compile 154 at a rapid rate that let Transvaal off the hook and when rain stopped play in the late afternoon the home side had put together a healthy 340.

Play was held up the next day after heavy rain all night but, with the weather clearing, the Rhodesians went in at 11.15 a.m. Through Freddie Brooks batting superbly they were 109-5 at lunch (Brooks 59 not out). Unfortunately Brooks was out shortly after the break having only added two runs to his total and the innings crumbled dramatically, forcing the Rhodesians to follow on, 225 runs behind.

Opening the second innings with Brooks, the Rhodesians suffered a further set-back when their star batsman was bowled first ball by a beauty from R.W. Norden. Never recovering from this shock, the visitors were bundled out for an inept 55 that afternoon to give Transvaal a huge innings victory.

As the Currie Cup match was over in two days the Rhodesians played against the Wanderers — a side which included eight of the Transvaal players who left for Cape Town that evening to compete in the Currie Cup final against Western Province. The start of this one-day friendly fixture was characterized by some sensational bowling by George Anderson who clean bowled the famous Springboks, Jimmy Sinclair and William Shalders, with the first two balls of the innings. Anderson aided by Colin Duff continued to run through the remaining batsmen backed up by superb fielding. In little over an hour the star-studded line-up (six present or future Springboks) was all out for 42, a total the Rhodesians passed comfortably, largely through a steady knock by "Sonny" Taberer.

SCORES: First Currie Cup Entry, 1904-05.

At Johannesburg, 15 and 16 March.

Transvaal — 340 (J.J. Slatem 154, J.H. Sinclair 57, M. Hathorn 43; G. Anderson 7/91)

Rhodesia — 115 (F.G. Brooks 61; R.W. Norden 4/21, R.O. Schwarz 4/29)
and 55 (R.W. Norden 8/12)

Transvaal won by an innings and 170 runs.

At Johannesburg, 17 March (Not first-class).

Wanderers — 42 (G. Anderson 5/24, C.E. Duff 5/15) and 121-4 wkts. (L.J. Tancred 52*)

Rhodesia — 91 (W.S. Taberer 30)

Rhodesia won on first innings by 6 wickets.

After this brief Currie Cup interlude Rhodesian cricket was to wait for twenty-five years before entering South Africa's premier competition again. For the national side, fixtures were therefore limited to infrequent tours from South African and English sides during the intervening period. Cricket nevertheless remained a popular pastime and many sterling battles were fought. In Mashonaland Mr. E. Vigne presented a handsome trophy in 1899 for inter-club competition and during the first fifteen years of its existence Salisbury Club won it on thirteen occasions. Among the records of these early times is one of William Blanckenberg taking all ten wickets in an innings for 17 runs for All-comers against Home-born — in the second innings he nearly repeated the feat by taking a further eight wickets. The highest score achieved was Salisbury's 450 for 5 wickets against Kopje and in this match Colin Duff, that great sportsman who batted, bowled and fielded in his white sun-helmet, recorded a new individual highest by compiling 250 not out. A Bulawayo First-League record was set up by A.H. Tummell (226) beating Mark Linnell's previous mark of 176 not out.

The Logan Cup, chosen by Lord Hawke, arrived in Rhodesia in 1899 and remained in Bulawayo for four years until the first contest was held in 1904. The trophy, costing one hundred guineas, is a huge silver cup on an ebony stand, two feet six inches in height. It bears the following inscription: 'Presented by the Hon. J.D. Logan, M.L.C., to the Rhodesian Cricket Association in commemoration of the first visit of an English team of Lord Hawke's, March 1899.'

The first Logan Cup match was a semi-final between the home side, Bulawayo, and the visiting Salisbury team in 1903-04. In a match which saw a remarkable change of fortune, Salisbury led by 199 runs on the first innings but lost outright by 54 runs. Freddie Brooks narrowly failed to become the first Logan Cup century-maker when he scored 99 in Salisbury's first innings — the honour ultimately went to Mark Linnell who hit 127 the same season against Gwelo, helping Bulawayo to a convincing innings victory.

Leo Robinson, who had played for Natal as a schoolboy, visited England in 1907 whilst Percy Sherwell's team was touring that country, actually taking part in the English Trials, in which he scored 95. The Springbok selection committee jumped at the opportunity of strengthening their Test team by playing him, and he was actually selected but, so it was said, was kept out of the side by his brother, the Rev. Cyril D. Robinson, who was vice-captain of the touring team. The Rev. Robinson claimed that it would not be the correct procedure and so a disappointed Leo Robinson never gained the distinction of playing Test cricket.

LEO ROBINSON.

Finance again proved an important factor when H. D. G. Leveson-Gower's touring English side visited in 1910. The South African Cricket Union initially asked for a guarantee of £800 but on representations being made to them, reduced the figure to £600. This was also considered too heavy a sum and the whole scheme was therefore dropped. Subsequently, however, the captain of the M.C.C. tourists, H. D. G. Leveson-Gower, himself wrote to the Rhodesian Cricket Union, stating that his team was keen to visit the Colony and he suggested a guarantee of £450 with matches in Bulawayo and Salisbury. The R.C.U. agreed and soon efforts were under way towards raising the money. The Bulawayo Town Council immediately voted £100 for the purpose whilst their Salisbury counterparts agreed to £50. The Chartered Company and that generous cricket benefactor, Abe Bailey, then stepped in and the amount was ensured.

Unfortunately, owing to the stress of English cricket engagements, it was necessary for all but six of the team to leave for England immediately after the Test matches in South Africa were concluded. In these circumstances it was thought at first by the Chartered Company and the R.C.U. that the guarantee should be withdrawn. But, with some well-known South African players making up the tour party, a powerful side made its way from Cape Town to Bulawayo.

It was a pity that Jack Hobbs, on his way to becoming the finest batsman in the world, Herbie Strudwick the great 'keeper, Wilfred Rhodes the famous all-rounder, and Frank Woolley, the majestic left-hander, were unable to tour. But the Rhodesian cricket fraternity, starved of outside competition, nevertheless gave Leveson-Gower's side a royal welcome, the highlight of their trip being a visit to the Victoria Falls.

The short tour began at the Queens ground, Bulawayo, with G.H. Simpson-Hayward, who was regarded as something of a secret weapon, sending down his lobbed, underarm deliveries. The Rhodesians scored quickly but lost wickets regularly. "Sonny" Taberer with a lusty 45 and Keigwin with 35, in spite of suffering from a fever, were the only batsmen to master the bowling for any length of time.

All out for 164, Rhodesia had Leveson-Gower's side 69-3 before John Zulch and A.E. Cook came together in a partnership of 190. Both gave chances, with Cook, at 42, hitting the ball to cover point where Norman Henwood spilled the catch. Disillusioned, Henwood rolled the ball along the ground to the stumps, not realizing that Cook and Zulch in the course of a misunderstanding, were stranded in the same crease.

Percy Sherwell added a whirlwind 43 to enable Leveson-Gower to declare 272 runs ahead. It is interesting to note that Sherwell, who had the distinction of being the first South African captain to lead a winning team, later returned to Southern Rhodesia to live, and became involved in Bulawayo cricketing circles. To digress a little further Sherwell had the honour of hitting the winning runs during a nerve-racking last wicket partnership of 48 which took South Africa to a dramatic-one wicket victory over the 1905-06 M.C.C. side.

Following on, Rhodesia were never in the picture, save for another fighting knock from Taberer, and received a huge innings battering from Leveson-Gower's tourists. Perhaps the failure was a little inevitable, considering the Rhodesians' lack of experience against top-class cricketers but they did have a second crack at the tourists in Salisbury, in which to make amends.

In the meantime Leveson-Gower's side stopped off in Gwelo to play against a Midlands XVIII. Host Bradley guaranteed £50 for the game and made the visitors his guests at his hotel. He entertained both teams to a champagne dinner, whilst a local farmer, Hugh Williams, who possessed stables, placed saddle-horses at the disposal of the cricketers. Mule races and

FREDDIE BROOKS.

show-jumping competitions created much excitement amongst the tourists.

Midlands performed creditably with Arthur Bailey, an Australian, bowling outstandingly well whilst "Chin" Bradley had a good first knock. In fact the tourists struggled to get the 60 runs to win in 65 minutes and surprise was expressed thereafter that no Gwelo players were invited to play in Salisbury.

The Rhodesia Herald reported that cricket 'had been for weeks the sole topic in sporting circles' in Salisbury. As expected, a big crowd greeted the tourists on the first day's play and they were treated to some fine batting with George Hopley and "Lobster" Simpson-Hayward adding 100 in a hurricane partnership lasting 42 minutes. George Anderson, who had bowled so well in Johannesburg five years earlier, returned the

HERBERT KEIGWIN.

COLIN DUFF.

very creditable figures of 7/78 out of a total of 379.

Leo Robinson and Herbert Keigwin demonstrated that the Rhodesians were well up to the task of chasing the runs by giving the innings a solid start with an opening stand of 75. Robinson's 95 was a chanceless knock which lasted three hours but the lower order batsmen did not take advantage of his priceless foundation work and the last five wickets fell for 20 runs — Rhodesia followed on 172 runs in arrears.

Freddie Brooks opened with Keigwin in the second innings and the pair put on 94 in 70 minutes before Brooks fell a victim to Simpson-Hayward's lobs, attempting to score off a "wrong 'un" which should have been left alone. Robinson replaced Brooks and with Keigwin added 128 (the Colony's first 100 partnership) to take the score to 222 before the second wicket fell.

The tall, fair and very athletic Herbert Stanley Keigwin went on to become Rhodesia's first-ever century-maker, reaching three figures in 197 minutes and hitting thirteen fours. Also a Rhodesian rugby player, the talented Keigwin had completed an M.A. at Cambridge before joining the Mines Department in Bulawayo in 1902, transferring to Native Affairs the following year. He progressed to Director of Native Development after the 1914-18 War, and it was he who made the first suggestion that a dam should be built across the Zambezi at Kariba — he wrote that a ball could be thrown across the gorge.

Thanks to their great start and aided by "Sonny" Taberer weighing in with an undefeated 44 (including eight fours) Rhodesia were able to declare in their second knock but they left Leveson-Gower's side an impossible target. The tourists never even contemplated going for the 133 required in just over half an hour but there were a few fireworks as Colin Duff snapped up 4 wickets for 11 runs.

SCORES: H.D.G. Leveson-Gower's XI Tour, 1909-10.

At Bulawayo, 22, 23, 24 March.

Rhodesia — 164 (W.S. Taberer 45, H.S. Keigwin 35) and 152 (W.S. Taberer 42)

Leveson-Gower's XI — 436 (J.W. Zulch 168, A.E. Cook 101, R.O. Schwarz 63, P.W. Sherwell 43*; G.M. Stephenson 5/104)

Leveson-Gower's XI won by an innings and 120 runs.

At Gwelo, 27 March (Not first-class).

Midlands XVIII — 104 (A.J. Bradley 31; R.O. Schwarz 7/25, G.H. Simpson-Hayward 6/17)
and 99 (R.L. Juul 26)

Leveson-Gower's XII — 144 (J.W. Zulch 44; A. Bailey 8/81)
and 60-7 wkts. (Collier 4/20, A. Bailey 3/36)

Leveson-Gower's XII won by 3 wickets.

At Salisbury, 31 March, 1 and 2 April.

Leveson-Gower's XI — 379 (F.L. Fane 103, A.E. Cook 72, G. Hopley 55, G.H. Simpson-Hayward 49, R.O. Schwarz 48; G. Anderson 7/78)
and 22-4 wkts. (C.E. Duff 4/11)

Rhodesia — 207 (L.G. Robinson 95, H.S. Keigwin 34; G.H. Simpson-Hayward 6/38)
and 304-5 dec. (H.S. Keigwin 111, L.G. Robinson 57, F.G. Brooks 51, W.S. Taberer 44*)

Match drawn.

The next visiting side to Rhodesia was I. D. Difford's Transvaal team in 1912-13 which was captained by the veteran Springbok, Ernest Halliwell, and included two other Test players, William Ling and Lionel "Doodles" Tapscott. They played seven matches, winning four, drawing two and losing to Salisbury where George Anderson had match figures of 12/70. This was the first side to make a general tour of Rhodesia (as well as visiting Beira) and their visit was most beneficial.

CHAPTER TWO
Rebuilding the Challenge

THE FIRST WORLD WAR resulted in a suspension of all senior sport in the Colony, although schools and women kept the various games continuing. Outside the Colony newspaper mention was made of Rhodesians being involved in "pick-up" matches. In the early part of the War a lull in the fighting would give the 2nd Rhodesia Regiment an extended rest near the British East African border at Voi where cricket would be played whatever the season. Teams were composed of officers and men and games were played between different platoons and between regiments.

Captain R.W.M. Langham, M.C., of Murray's Column, recalled, in his *Memories of the 1914-18 Campaign* of Rhodesians playing cricket at Mbamba Bay on Lake Nyasa towards the end of the War: 'Someone produced a "composition" cricket ball, so the carriers were put on fatigue to sew sacks together to make a "matting" cricket pitch. The askari came to the rescue again by carving solid bats from the lightest native timber they could find. The handles were bound with twine made from unravelled sacking. Driving a composition ball with a solid bat gave one the sensation of touching a "live" electric wire. All the same, we managed to arrange some interesting matches. The only one we couldn't organize was "married" versus "single" as there were no married men in the Column. Rhodesians didn't seem to be so keen on getting married before the first War as they do now.'

Cricket was soon in full swing again in 1919 in both Mashonaland and Matabeleland, with the former raising three leagues and the latter two. With many new players being enrolled cricket prospects were bright and therefore great interest was focused on the Green Point Club's tour in February 1922. The tour was a success in that the visitors were a good test for the provincial sides. Mashonaland did in fact beat them but the tourists gained their revenge by thrashing the complacent home side by an innings in their second encounter. The most notable achievement by a local player in the course of the tour was probably Tom Bourdillon's century for Matabeleland.

The following season a strong Transvaal side toured containing Springboks Charlie Frank, Bob Catterall, Douglas Meintjies and Nevil Lindsay. Frank might be remembered for his great match-saving 152 against

Tom Bourdillon makes his way towards the pavilion having scored a century against Green Point Club in 1921-22.

the 1921-22 Aussies when he batted for eight and a half hours, battered and bruised, against the legendary attack of McDonald and Gregory to save the Springboks from certain defeat. Catterall, in his second season of first-class cricket, and Meintjies were fresh from playing Tests against the 1922-23 M.C.C. touring side whilst Nevil Lindsay had represented South Africa against the 1921-22 Australians.

Opening their tour against Matabeleland in Bulawayo, Transvaal won the toss and elected to bat. The innings began sensationally with their first four batsmen — Springboks Catterall, Frank, Lindsay and Meintjies — back in the pavilion with only 15 runs on the board. In two hours they were all out for 99 but bounced right back into the game by having Bulawayo six wickets down for 40. However, George Hopley 46 and Gerald Ledeboer 15 not out, aided by the other tail-enders, saw Matabeleland pass the Transvaal score to be all out 37 runs ahead. In the limited time left Transvaal showed what might have happened by hitting 103 for no wickets in 65 minutes (Catterall 69 not out).

The dashing Catterall continued his good form against Mashonaland by hitting 95, being run out by a smart throw from Frank Brooks. The latter's brother Fred top-scored with 49 in reply but the game petered out in a similar manner to the Matabeleland fixture through lack of time.

It was a pity that Freddie Brooks, through illness, had to withdraw from the Rhodesian team that played the Transvaalers in Salisbury. But his replacement, younger brother Frank, took advantage of the opportunity and on a difficult wicket attained a top score of 28 in Rhodesia's rain-marred innings of 118. An indication of the uncertainties of the pitch was even better illustrated in the Transvaal innings when Phil Rabinson had both Charlie Frank and Bob Catterall back in the pavilion in the space of seven balls with the latter brilliantly caught one-handed in the slips by Austin Cooper. Meintjies guided the Transvaalers to 53 before he was trapped leg before by Rabinson and then the little Midlander, Fred Morgan, broke the back of the visitors' batting and at one stage had three wickets for three runs. In failing light, the Transvaalers gamely agreed to bat on and lost their eighth wicket with a miraculous catch by "Chin" Bradley off what seemed a certain six. Shortly afterwards the match was called off, Transvaal 24 runs behind and two wickets remaining.

The visitors thereafter travelled back to Bulawayo, stopping off to play in Gwelo at the Gymkhana ground against Midlands, who were well beaten in an entertaining match. Charlie Frank was at last amongst the runs in this match, with a confidence-restoring 64. He was certainly thankful to be seeing the ball better because in the tourists' next match against Rhodesia in Bulawayo he found himself at the wicket sooner than he had anticipated with the scoreboard showing Transvaal two wickets down in two overs. Phil Rabinson, repeating his Salisbury feat, dismissed E.C. Murray and Bob Catterall in a dramatic opening spell. Frank stood his ground stolidly whilst wickets fell at regular intervals before he, too, went with the score at 223-8 wickets. At this stage Nevil Lindsay, who was batting well, was joined by the number 10 batsman G.R. McCubbin. An incredible 221 runs later — a record which still stands for the South African ninth wicket — McCubbin was caught by Bourdillon off a tired Rabinson for 97. Lindsay remained undefeated with 160 and Transvaal's score had leapt to 444.

A somewhat shell-shocked Rhodesian side was never again in the game. In their first innings, eight batsmen reached double figures without any of them making a substantial total whilst Douglas Meintjies clean-bowled six of his victims in the Rhodesian second innings to ensure a huge Transvaal victory.

The Transvaal side agreed to play an additional match against a combined Bulawayo Schools XI after their sight-seeing trip to the Victoria Falls. Unfortunately the return train was held up and less than three hours cricket was possible which merely allowed the schoolboys to gain some invaluable batting experience against the Transvaalers. Although the young Milton batsman, Victor Hepker, made top score (26*), the visitors' manager, Mr. Algy Frames, decided to present a bat to Jock Thompson (also Milton) for his dogged 18 in the early stages of the innings. It was a generous gesture on Transvaal's part not only to present the award but to partake in the match — *The Bulawayo Chronicle* remarked: 'They are surely the most sporting crowd of players Rhodesians have ever had the pleasure of entertaining.'

SCORES: Transvaal Tour, 1922-23.

At Bulawayo, 6 and 7 March (Not first-class).
Transvaal — 99 (V.L. Robinson 3/4)
and 103-0 wkts. (R.H. Catterall 69*)
Matabeleland — 136 (G.C. Hopley 46)
Match drawn.

At Salisbury, 10 and 11 March (Not first-class).
Transvaal — 230 (R.H. Catterall 95; C.E. Duff 3/42)
and 68-2 wkts.
Mashonaland — 140 (F.G. Brooks 49; A. Kennedy 5/39)
Match drawn.

At Salisbury, 12 and 13 March.
Rhodesia — 118 (E.C. Murray 5/22)
Transvaal — 94-8 wkts. (P. Rabinson 4/23, F.H. Morgan 3/25)
Match drawn.

At Gwelo, 15 and 16 March (Not first-class).
Midlands — 110
and 128 (X.X. Skottowe 5/25)
Transvaal — 208 (C.N. Frank 64; L.D. Elworthy 3/46, Sewell 3/46)
and 31-1 wkt.
Transvaal won by 9 wickets.

At Bulawayo, 17, 18 and 19 March.
Transvaal — 444-9 dec. (N.V. Lindsay 160*, G.R. McCubbin 97, C.N. Frank 63; P. Rabinson 6/89)
Rhodesia — 204 (G. Gemmell 34, A.C. Curle 34)
and 107 (D.J. Meintjies 8/63)
Transvaal won by an innings and 133 runs.

At Bulawayo, 24 March (Not first-class).
Combined Bulawayo Schools XI — 110-6 wkts. (V. Hepker 26*)
Match abandoned.

With the M.C.C. touring Australia in 1924-25, Solly Joel, a South African mining magnate, sponsored a tour to South Africa by what was virtually an England second team. Captained by the Hon. Lionel Tennyson, who had represented England before and after the War, the side included a number of famous names who had or later were to play Test cricket such as Ernest Tyldesley, George Geary, Percy Holmes, Alex Kennedy and Jack Russell.

The good news for Rhodesia was that Bob Catterall, the batting success of the 1924 Springbok tour to the United Kingdom where he headed the averages, was living in Bulawayo. Catterall had in fact led Matabeleland during the 1923-24 season and had hit a scintillating 156 for Raylton against the touring Rhodes

R.H. "BOB" CATTERALL.

University College side. He was a brilliant all-round sportsman and Louis Duffus commented on the versatile manner in which he had '. . . spread his natural gifts through most provinces of South Africa as well as Rhodesia. An outstanding schoolboy soccer player and athlete, which led to his becoming an arresting figure when fielding on the boundary, he captained Natal at cricket and represented it in soccer and hockey although he starred with Transvaal in the Currie Cup. He once held the men's doubles title in the Free State, was more than an average golfer, played baseball for Springs and excelled at billiards.'

Catterall was named as the Rhodesian skipper for their match against Solly Joel's England XI, taking over from Tom Bourdillon. It is interesting to note, though, that Bourdillon had the honour of playing against an English touring team for the second time having been selected for both matches against Leveson-Gower's side in 1909-10. Also in the team were two further great all-round sportsmen — Freddie Morgan, who was Rhodesia's greatest Bisley marksman and a Rhodesian soccer player, and George Gemmell, who had played for Aston Villa and was regarded as one of the best centre forwards of his day in England.

Tremendous excitement was created in Bulawayo with employers allowing their staff a half-holiday and buses being laid on to the Raylton ground from the Post Office at one shilling a head. *The Bulawayo Chronicle* also made a special appeal to farmers on the question of the weather: 'The whole game is at the moment in the hands of our unreliable climate and it is hoped that for the next few days the farmers will cease from their prayers and so enable the match to be played to a finish, for after all if defeat is to be our portion that is a much more desirable end than that anathema of the cricketer: "Match abandoned owing to rain." '

Rhodesia began well with slow left-hander, Austin Cowper, at one stage having the figures of 4/26 off eleven overs as England slumped to 92-7. Ted Bowley, who was batting well, was then joined by Capt. Jackson and the pair proceeded to add 168 and avert disaster for England. Nevertheless both of them had huge slices of luck. Freddie Morgan had the mortification of seeing Jameson dropped at 2 by Gloak although the latter was unlucky enough to suffer from a split hand in the attempt. A dropped catch, however, is part of the game but it is not often that a batsman is bowled but still lives to continue his innings. An unusual incident occurred when Cowper hit Bowley with a short ball in the face and the ball then hit the Sussex man's off-stump. From there it rebounded off wicket-keeper Arnold's pads back on to the wicket. Bowley was just about to leave his crease when Arnold appealed for a stumping but the square leg umpire replied, 'Not out.' The bowler appealed at his end for bowled but unfortunately, he had obscured the umpire's view and the appeal was therefore not upheld.

In reply to the England XI's 294, Rhodesia made a poor start and even Catterall looked uneasy in his 38 before he hit a ball hard on to his pads and it trickled on to his wicket to bowl him. George Geary who did most of the damage in this innings of 121 continued to trouble the Rhodesians in their second knock when they followed on 173 runs behind. The home side, however, made a determined bid to prolong the game with Morgan scoring 50 in 98 minutes whilst 17-year-old Hamish Campbell-Rodger, Bill Wood and Dr. Aidan Campbell also batted confidently. With the aid of several other contributions Rhodesia forced England to bat again although the tourists were able to knock off the required 40 runs in seven overs for the loss of only two wickets.

SCORES: versus Solly Joel's England XI, 1924-25.

At Bulawayo, 5, 6 and 8 December.

Rhodesia — 121 (R.H. Catterall 38)
and 212 (F.H. Morgan 50; G. Geary 5/70)

England XI — 294 (E.H. Bowley 131, T.O. Jameson 90*; S.A. Cowper 4/65, F.H. Morgan 3/85)
and 42-2 wkts.

England XI won by 8 wickets.

Adding spice to local cricket throughout the 1920s were three tours by Rhodes University College touring teams. On each tour the teams were captained by a Rhodesian — I. Campbell-Rodger (1923), A.G.E. "Jock" Speight (1925) and H.B. Dugmore (1928). The visitors were keen to see as much of the country as possible and travelled far and wide on each occasion — they also played good cricket and the 1925 side was unbeaten in 13 matches. Their most noted performer was probably the future Rhodesian opening bat, A.H. "Pat" Pattison (1923 and 1925) who made two centuries amid some prolific run-making and took wickets regularly.

Jock Thompson told of an unusual incident related to the 1928 team which occurred at Umtali: 'A Rhodes batsman who was suffering from a leg-strain drove a ball which disappeared in some grass inside the boundary. The fielder, after some searching, discovered the Wisden down an ant-bear hole. He summoned aid but no arm was long enough to get the ball. Meanwhile the batsmen ran eight runs at which stage the lame one refused to go on! Eventually another ball was requisitioned to allow the game to continue.'

In 1928, Transvaal made a return visit organized by Rhodesia's staunch friend in the South African cricket world, Algy Frames, who also managed and captained the side. They played against provincial sides as well as the national team and also made a trip to Livingstone.

Once again Matabeleland gave the Transvaalers a tough start, amassing 281 with eight players scoring over 20. They then bundled Transvaal out 81 runs behind, although the visitors improved greatly in their second innings but ran out of time in their bid to get the 238 runs required to win. Langebrink, who hit 102 not out for Transvaal in their chase for runs, narrowly missed a second century in the two-day fixture against the Matabeleland Schools.

At this stage a young schoolboy, Jack Hayward, was making a name for himself in Matabeleland circles and after scores of 29, 28* and 23 against Transvaal he was selected for the Rhodesian side in the three-day encounter in Bulawayo. Making his debut in first-class cricket the youthful Milton captain top-scored with a splendid 72 and in so doing provided the backbone of the Rhodesian total of 303. Hamish Campbell-Rodger and E.C. Arnold were also in a punishing run-scoring mood that day with scores of 47 and 57 respectively. Surprisingly, the Transvaal batting collapsed in reply against the tight bowling of Arnold Hyde and Frank Dollar and they were all out for 205.

Rhodesia's second innings was built on two partnerships with little other support. Fletcher and Thompson gave the innings a solid start through a partnership of 58 whilst Wood batting most responsibly with Arnold, added 80 for the sixth wicket. Rhodesia were all out for 184 — James Christy who wrapped up the innings in six overs with 3 wickets for 13 then proceeded to carve the home side's attack apart as he smote 103 and added 173 for the second wicket with Langebrink. Transvaal set to make 283 won a thrilling encounter by three wickets and moved on to Salisbury.

Another schoolboy prodigy was to star in Transvaal's match against Mashonaland when the visitors scraped a draw through appealing against the light ten minutes from the end with only one wicket in hand and 177 runs in arrears. Bob Crisp, the young Prince Edward all-rounder, hit 57 not out to help lift Mashonaland from 134-7 in their second innings to 249 and a comfortable overall lead of 265. Crisp, who was later to gain international honours as a fiery opening bowler, added 69 in a little under half an hour with Arnold Hyde and delighted the crowd by launching his 50 with a huge 6.

Transvaal's appeal against the light was severely

RHODESIA v. TRANSVAAL, 1927-28 (BULAWAYO).
Back: E. Munnik (Umpire), E. Arnold, G. Fletcher, J. Rackham (12th Man), J. Hayward, H. Campbell-Rodger, T. Hancock (Umpire).
Seated: R. Tomlinson, J. Thompson, A. Hyde, C. Ridgway (Captain), W. Wood, F. Dollar, D. Tomlinson.

criticized by the Sports Editor of *The Star* (Johannesburg) who wrote: 'Transvaalers are there primarily to teach a weaker province and to assist in building up the game which is confronted with many handicaps up North, where visiting teams are rarely seen and the keen young Rhodesian cricketers, with every bit as much natural ability as the sons of the more favoured provinces, suffer from want of opportunity. The Salisbury team seemed to have well earned a victory which would have done a world of good and harmed nobody, and it seems a pity that a team making a social and missionary tour should have stooped to calling a technical point to their aid to save them from an imminent and deserved defeat.'

Escaping ignominious defeat at the hands of Mashonaland, the Transvaalers proceeded to vent their feelings in slaughtering Rhodesia in the last game of their tour. A great 175 by Christy enabled Transvaal to win by an innings against a depleted home side that was weakened by Hyde, unable to bat in the first innings, and Saunders in the second. Hyde, after throwing himself around the field during a long Saturday as the Transvaalers pulverized the Rhodesian bowling to the tune of 423, turned up to box against the visiting Rand University boxing team that night. Not surprisingly Hyde was not at his best and a punch from his opponent in the welterweight division, to whom he was giving nearly a stone, opened an old wound and put him out of action. The score-card for the Rhodesian first innings subsequently read: 'A. Hyde — indisposed, did not bat.'

SCORES: Transvaal Tour, 1927-28.

At Bulawayo, 24 and 25 March (Not first-class).
Matabeleland — 281 (E.C. Arnold 40, J.A. Thompson 39, W. Wood 38, C.R. Ridgeway 37)
and 156-6 dec. (W. Wood 51*)
Transvaal — 200 (A.S. Frames 56; H. Campbell-Rodger 5/55)
and 190-2 wkts. (A.C. Langebrink 102*, J.A. Christy 67)
Match drawn.

At Bulawayo, 26 March (Not first-class).
Transvaal — 255-4 dec. (A.C. Langebrink 98, B. Mitchell 68*)
Matabeleland Schools — 113 (C.J.R. Hayward 28*, S.L.R. Jackson 21)
and 130 (C.J.R. Hayward 23, S.R. McPhee 20)
Transvaal won by an innings and 12 runs.

At Bulawayo, 31 March, 1 and 2 April.
Rhodesia — 303 (C.J.R. Hayward 72, E.C. Arnold 57, H. Campbell-Rodger 47, G.E. Fletcher 31)
and 184 (W. Wood 60*, G.E. Fletcher 51)
Transvaal — 205 (B. Mitchell 54; F. Dollar 4/46, A. Hyde 3/34)
and 283-7 wkts. (J.A. Christy 103, A.C. Langebrink 68)
Transvaal won by 3 wickets.

At Salisbury, 4 and 5 April (Not first-class).
Mashonaland — 175 and 249 (R.J. Crisp 57*; D.P. Conyngham 5/51, B. Mitchell 3/61)
Transvaal — 159 (J.A. Christy 61; R.N. Tomlinson 5/19, Q.A. Austin 3/9)
and 88-9 wkts. (Reid Rowland 3/20)
Match drawn.

At Salisbury, 7, 8 and 9 April.
Transvaal — 423 (J.A. Christy 175, D.P. Conyngham 63; D.S. Tomlinson 4/105)
Rhodesia — 135.
and 129 (R.N. Tomlinson 44*)
Transvaal won by an innings and 159 runs.

At the end of the Transvaal tour, Algy Frames urged the Rhodesians to enter a team in the Currie Cup remarking that the Colony's cricket had improved a hundred per cent on the 1923 standard. He thought Rhodesia had every prospect of doing well in South Africa and although a trip would be expensive with players having to dip into their own pockets he felt such expense would be really worthwhile. He further singled out Jack Hayward as being one of the best schoolboy batsmen he had seen whilst also paying tribute to the all-round ability of Bill Wood and the wicket-keeper/batting skills of E.C. Arnold.

Louis Duffus, a prominent member of the Transvaal team at that time, wrote of the tour years later in his autobiography *Play Abandoned*: 'One of the joys of the game that has never faded was to visit Rhodesia for a series of matches in a strong team led by Algy Frames. It was like tales you read of games in old outposts of Empire such as Singapore and Hong Kong with the Governor present, an Askari band playing on the fringe of the field at Livingstone and ending up with a ball of social importance. I had several enjoyable cricket trips but none equalled the attraction of Rhodesia. The wide streets of Bulawayo and Salisbury, bedecked with spectacular displays of jacarandas and flaming flamboyants gave the tours such distinctive backgrounds.'

Less than two years after the Transvaal visit, Rhodesia followed the advice of Mr. Algy Frames and made their second entry into the Currie Cup. The public responded generously to Rhodesia's first venture south in twenty-five years and raised £500 towards the costs. The R.C.U. presented each member of the team, which was captained by Dr. Aidan Campbell, with a cricket cap in the Rhodesian colours — dark green with the white lion badge.

The actual tour of twenty-three days was occupied by twelve days' cricket, two days of rest and nine days' travel in which the players covered 2,655 miles by train. The programme obviously was not conducive to good cricket but despite being well beaten in each of the four three-day fixtures the team learnt much about the game.

An incredible start was made to the tour in Kimberley when Rhodesia had Griqualand West three wickets down for three runs (all extras) only to allow the game to slip and watch the home side compile a total of 602. Despite dropping a number of catches the Rhodesians never gave up trying and their batting reflected this determined attitude. In their two totals of over 300, nine players scored more than 30 in at least one of their two knocks whilst Arnold Hyde, who hit 80 in the first innings, and T.P. "Simmie" Syminton, 84 in the second, were the top scorers. The *Diamond Fields Advertiser* singled out Arnold Hyde for his batting and fielding at cover point:' . . . he saved boundary after boundary. His throwing in, too, was exceptionally accurate and in his batting he did not give the semblance of a chance. Throughout he was master and he scored all round the wicket with cleverly executed shots.'

But the greatest back-to-the-wall display occurred when Pat O'Reilly and E. Sim took Rhodesia's second innings total from 201-9 to 307 and thereby forced Griquas to bat again. This magnificent fight-back, which followed Dr. Campbell and Syminton's earlier stand of 94, produced a record partnership for the tenth wicket of 106 which still stands today.

The promising start was followed by some disappointing performances. Against the Orange Free State, at the Ramblers ground, two poor batting displays ruined any hope of success that had been brought about by some steady bowling. Only Hayward withstood the Free State attack in two defiant knocks of 56 and 86 as Rhodesia went down by 184 runs.

Sadly, when Hayward failed in the following match against Border, which was lost by 162 runs, the brittleness of the Rhodesian batting was woefully exposed. Possibly the change to sea-level and the heavier atmosphere affected the Rhodesians but there was little to fear in the modest Border bowling attack. At this stage "Stumper" wrote in *The Bulawayo Chronicle*: 'There is no gainsaying the fact that our Currie Cup team's performance against Border has cast something akin to gloom over local cricketers. Old players are shaking their heads and murmuring that they do not know what to make of it; young players are equally at a loss to offer any feasible excuse for the team. One reason might be that our local bowling is so weak that our batting strength is liable to be over-estimated. Three-day cricket is also different to Saturday afternoon and Sunday morning local league — an example of this is the normally brilliant Hyde dropping two catches late in the day against Griqualand West.'

Seemingly more acclimatized, the Rhodesians performed better in their last tour fixture against Eastern Province despite losing heavily again. Leading run scorer on tour, the young Jack Hayward (286 runs) weighed in with a face-saving 73 in the first innings whilst the consistent "Simmie" Syminton (257 runs on tour) made runs along with Arnold Hyde and Bill Wood in the second knock.

With regard to the bowling, the Rhodesian attack could be admired in the manner in which it pluckily stuck to its task with the bowlers rarely wilting despite lengthy spells. O'Reilly (20 wickets at 24,80 runs apiece), Wood (15 wickets at 21,40) and Sim (14 wickets at 24,29) bore the brunt of the attack, came in for "stick" at times but also made vital breakthroughs and returned some good figures.

RHODESIAN TOURING TEAM, 1929-30.
Back: W. Strachan (Scorer), J. Hayward, T. Syminton, J. Thompson, R. Tomlinson, F. Dollar, W. Wood, C. Ridgway (Manager).
Seated: D. Fowler, J. Dickinson, F. Morgan, A. Campbell (Captain), A. Hyde, E. Sim, P. O'Reilly.
Front: J. Willing, L. Roberts.

SCORES: Currie Cup Tour, 1929-30.

At Kimberley, 9, 10 and 11 January.

Griqualand West — 602 (X.C. Balaskas 206, C.D. McKay 85, J.L. Daly 70, R. Henderson 62, J. McNally 61, F. Nicholson 50; H.J. O'Reilly 6/166) and 43-1 wkt.

Rhodesia — 334 (A. Hyde 80, W. Wood 49, R.N. Tomlinson 35, J. de L. Thompson 34) and 307 (T.P. Syminton 84, E.S. Sim 61, Dr. A. Campbell 37, H.J. O'Reilly 37*, C.J.R. Hayward 34)

Griqualand West won by 9 wickets.

At Bloemfontein, 13, 14 and 15 January.

Orange Free State — 225 (P. Withers 62, M. Francis 55, S. Barry 51; F. Dollar 3/40, H.J. O'Reilly 3/58) and 325 (J.C. Newton 67; W. Wood 5/67, E.S. Sim 3/48)

Rhodesia — 156 (C.J.R. Hayward 56) and 210 (C.J.R. Hayward 86, F.H. Morgan 31)

Orange Free State won by 184 runs.

At King William's Town, 17, 18 and 20 January.

Border — 155 (F. Goldschmidt 50; H.J. O'Reilly 3/28, J.W. Willing 3/50) and 189 (L. Miles 66; H.J. O'Reilly 5/44, W. Wood 3/52)

Rhodesia — 122 (T.P. Syminton 34; J.G. Phillips 6/16) and 60 (K. Muzzell 5/14)

Border won by 162 runs.

At Port Elizabeth, 23, 24 and 25 January.

Eastern Province — 295 (H.E. Pagden 80, H.B. Cameron 67; E.S. Sim 4/50, W. Wood 3/58) and 289-7 dec. (H.E. Pagden 91*, R.A. Mardon 75; E.S. Sim 4/76)

Rhodesia — 158 (C.J.R. Hayward 73; W. Boltman 5/53) and 260 (A. Hyde 51, W. Wood 45, T.P. Syminton 44, F.H. Morgan 36)

Eastern Province won by 166 runs.

Overall the results were disappointing but "Rhodesian" had this to say in partial defence of the side in *The Bulawayo Chronicle*: 'Perhaps the local supporters of the Rhodesian team expected too much and had visions of our men blazing a trail of glory through the Union and spectacularly re-entering the Currie Cup competition with victory at every turn. Naturally they were disappointed.

'Without, however, making excuses for a team that had shown itself capable of better things, I would like our sterner critics to remember certain considerations. Rhodesia is a province in size but not in population, and the mere fact that Rhodesia is able to send a team at all is worthy of credit. A single town like Port Elizabeth alone contains nearly as many people as there are in Rhodesia while the Orange Free State team represented five times the population of Rhodesia. Our team also lacked experience of touring long distances and playing three-day matches in different climates and at different altitudes, without being long enough in any one place to become acclimatized. Such conditions are disturbing, especially to so young a team as ours. It shouldn't be so of course, but unless a team learns by experience (even at the expense of victory) the difficulties and the sustained strain of travelling thousands of miles between matches, they will never learn. So without pretending to defend the quality of our team's cricket I would suggest that their tour has had its uses. It has shown us our limitations and has proved one rung in the ladder of experience. Just as we have to fall off a horse three times good and solid before we can call ourselves competent equestrians, so must we get a few good, hard bumps before we can call ourselves Currie Cup cricketers.'

Team manager, Mr. C.R. Ridgeway, endorsed this report when he said: 'Reviewing the tour it is the considered opinion of those who had the opportunity of seeing the cricket — the good, the bad and the indifferent — that good results must accrue. Although our men lost their matches they learnt a good deal, both on and off the field, and the experience they have thus gained will be passed on to their colleagues in local cricket with most beneficial results.'

In time both "Rhodesian" and Mr. Ridgeway were going to be rewarded for their faith in the national side but they still had to bear another heavy defeat in the last match of the 1929-30 season. Transvaal, captained by South Africa's master batsman, Herby Taylor, visited Rhodesia and Bulawayo was given the honour of staging the country's first Currie Cup encounter. Several changes were made to the Rhodesian team with Victor Robinson and Denis Tomlinson returning, Bob Crisp and Bill Napier making their debuts and former Natal player, W. J. Lee, taking over the captaincy.

Rhodesia made their now customary good start with Crisp taking two wickets in successive balls in his first over but thereafter the game was firmly in Transvaal's control. Herby Taylor (139) expectedly reached the three-figure mark although he was overtaken in the run race by W.H. Foley (153). Transvaal were eventually all out for 417 with Bill Wood mopping up the tail in seven overs and five balls by taking 4/38.

In reply Rhodesia were out twice within the Transvaal total and only a determined Arnold Hyde looked happy in notching two invaluable half-centuries. In no uncertain terms it was another humiliating defeat. But at the same time the first seven batsmen in the Rhodesian line-up all had at least one innings of over 20 to their credit in the course of the game yet, Hyde apart, failed to build on their initial grafting.

SCORES: versus Transvaal, 1929-30 (Currie Cup).

At Bulawayo, 29, 30 and 31 March.

Transvaal — 417 (W.H. Foley 153, H.W. Taylor 139; W. Wood 4/38, R.J. Crisp 3/88)

Rhodesia — 194 (A. Hyde 60, W.J. Lee 30) and 212 (A. Hyde 55, W.A. Napier 38, C.J.R. Hayward 32)

Transvaal won by an innings and 11 runs.

Perhaps Rhodesian cricket fans were to an extent consoled by the words of encouragement from Herby Taylor who felt that if 'the plenty of fine material' in the Colony was guided in the right direction Rhodesia could beat such sides as Eastern Province, Free State, Border and Griqualand West. He also singled out Denis Tomlinson and Bob Crisp as outstanding prospects despite their modest performances.

As it turned out, Taylor's predictions were to be proved correct on all accounts. Better days were just around the corner.

In December 1930, Percy Chapman's powerful M.C.C. side visited Rhodesia and great players such as Bob Wyatt, Wally Hammond, Maurice Leyland, Ian Peebles, Maurice Tate and Bill Voce took on the young and comparatively inexperienced Rhodesian side at the Queens ground in Bulawayo.

Crowds poured in from all parts of Rhodesia on a hot Saturday as Jock Speight won the toss and put the M.C.C. in to bat. It was a decision which was criticized at lunch because the tourists were comfortably placed at 64 for no wicket. However, Denis Tomlinson who had come on five minutes before the interval had White leg before wicket in his first over after the resumption of play. And then he claimed one of his greatest wickets when he tossed one up to Hammond who swung wildly well down the track to be smartly stumped by wicket-keeper, Nigel Boast. At this stage the M.C.C. began treating Tomlinson with respect whilst Moll, O'Reilly and Crisp gave good support in economical spells.

Thanks to a slow but invaluable 78 from Wyatt, a typically hard hit 48 by Chapman and useful contributions from the tail-enders, the M.C.C. tallied 278 near the end of the first day. Losing a wicket before nightfall set the Rhodesians back but on the second day Hayward held the innings together with a chanceless 95 and with "Simmie" Syminton (60) added a fine 110 for the fourth wicket. The two left-handers withstood a varied attack as Chapman tried seven bowlers including Voce bumping the ball in fiery spells with four slips and Peebles flighting his deliveries in a contrasting but equally menacing manner. Hayward's knock, which was the highest against the M.C.C. up to that stage, finally ended to a brilliant catch in the slips by Chapman off Voce after 225 minutes at the crease. Boast helped out in a lively, undefeated 33 and Rhodesia ended up with a creditable 248.

The game, which had reached an interesting stage, unfortunately then dragged out into a tame draw mainly through a rain stoppage and the depleted state of the M.C.C. team. With so many men *hors de combat* there was hardly a team to take the field if the position had so arisen but the situation did give Leyland the chance to make amends for his first innings failure with a brilliant 169 which included twenty-five fours and a six. The seriousness of the Englishmen's plight, though, was illustrated by the tourists having no further batsmen when Leyland was out at 322-8. Because of the spreading illness (five out of action) Bob Crisp was called into the M.C.C. side for their scheduled game in Northern Rhodesia. The young Rhodesian fast bowler was in fact hardly needed as the M.C.C. thrashed the local side by nine wickets on the first innings but he did, nevertheless, take one wicket for three runs in the three overs he bowled.

SCORES: versus M.C.C., 1930-31.

At Bulawayo, 6, 8 and 9 December.

M.C.C. — 278 (R.E.S. Wyatt 78; D.S. Tomlinson 5/106, H.J. O'Reilly 3/49)
and 322 (M. Leyland 169; R.J. Crisp 3/64)

Rhodesia — 248 (C.J.R. Hayward 95, T.P. Syminton 60, N.I. Boast 33*; I.A.R. Peebles 6/57)

Match drawn.

Rhodesia's third Currie Cup entry was by far the Colony's most successful season to date. After the encouraging points made towards the end of the 1929-30 season there were high hopes for the side but at the same time there were several factors counting against the success of the 1931-32 venture. The Rhodesians

DENIS TOMLINSON.

were without key performers such as Pat O'Reilly, "Simmie" Syminton, that fine wicket-keeper Jack Dickinson, his promising replacement 'keeper against the M.C.C., Nigel Boast, and the exciting fast bowling 'find' Bob Crisp.

The last-named was undoubtedly the greatest loss. Debonair and good-looking, twice Victor Ludorum at Prince Edward, he went on to perform outstandingly for Western Province, toured England with the 1935 Springboks and represented South Africa again in 1935-36 against the visiting Australians. He became the only player in cricket history to have twice taken four wickets in four balls — feats achieved in Currie Cup matches against Griqualand West in Johannesburg in 1931-32 and against Natal in Durban in 1933-34. In fact Crisp nearly did it on three occasions as he also took four wickets in five balls against Transvaal in the 1931-32 tournament. But Crisp will not only be remembered as a great fast bowler: he represented Mashonaland at rugby; won several Rhodesian athletics titles; ran against American university athletes in an unofficial Test at Cape Town; climbed Kilimanjaro twice in two weeks; attempted a motor dash from Cape Town to Nairobi in 1936; became a reporter with the London *Daily Express*; ran a duck farm; as a tank commander in the Western Desert he was wounded and awarded the D.S.O. and M.C.; published a book about his wartime experiences; and then while living in England "opted out" and went to live a hermit-like life on a Greek island supposedly suffering from an incurable disease. A great character, he never lacked guts — in the 1935 Test at Trent Bridge, when Maurice Leyland and Bob Wyatt were in command at the crease in a record stand, Crisp limped off the field with a foot inflamed from a blood blister. The doctor warned him not to bowl again that day but with "Sandy" Bell acting as a decoy to lure the doctor out of the dressing-room, he returned to take the wickets of both batsmen.

An interesting selection in the 1931-32 Rhodesian touring side was that of "Jackie" Grant who had captained the West Indies on their 1930-31 tour to Australia. Although the West Indies were outplayed in the first four Tests, Grant established a reputation as an astute captain and his judgement was particularly vindicated when he declared twice in the Fifth Test to win a splendid but narrow victory by 30 runs. Grant in fact headed the averages in that series with 255 runs (average, 42,50). It might also be mentioned that he captained the West Indies in England in 1933 and then in 1934-35 played an important role in the West Indies winning a home series 2-1 against the touring English.

Grant provided welcome experience to a Rhodesian side that was a happy blend of young and old, under the aggressive leadership of Hamish "Bronte" Campbell-Rodger. The team's wicket-keeper, Jock Thompson, wrote: 'It was with feelings of mingled trepidation and confidence that Rhodesia proceeded to Johannesburg at the end of 1931. The Colony had fared so badly in the previous tournament that it was felt the other provinces could hardly consider the Rhodesians as much of an opposition. On the other hand most of the

G.C. "JACKIE" GRANT.

RHODESIA v. M.C.C., 1930-31.
Back: T. Syminton, R. Crisp, N. Boast, J. Hayward, H. Moll, D. Tomlinson.
Seated: A. Hyde, J. Thompson, J. Speight (Captain), P. O'Reilly, W. Napier.
Front: D. Morris (12th Man).

R.J. "BOB" CRISP.

lessons learnt in 1930 had been assimilated and fairly creditable performances against the visiting Transvaalers and the M.C.C. showed that Rhodesia would never again be the "wooden spoonists".'

After the previous tour the Rhodesians had much to avenge and they showed little mercy in thrashing the Orange Free State by 209 runs to record the Colony's first-ever cricket victory. Rhodesia however, began quietly and A.H. "Pat" Pattison in particular, had difficulty judging the fast deliveries rising viciously off the pitch. The first 45 minutes yielded a mere 21 runs but the Rhodesians stuck to their task and a useful first innings total was built on Pattison's carefully compiled innings (128). His hundred came up in 225 minutes and he was involved in two useful partnerships with Tomlinson and Moll whilst Campbell-Rodger's lightning 22 included a gigantic six over the Pirates' ground fence and into the railway yard.

Opening bowler Mike Quinn and left-arm spinner "Scotty" Adamson then provided a formidable partnership to give Rhodesia a useful first innings lead of 153 which was not squandered. Carefully building on this total, Rhodesia eventually set Free State an almost impossible target of 383 largely due to a second innings partnership of 98 between the adventurous Campbell-Rodger and the in-form Pattison. Given a total to which he could bowl against, Tomlinson did the rest in creating the breakthrough to set up the historic victory.

The strong Transvaal side which included those two great but controversial Springboks, Bob Catterall and "Buster" Nupen, provided sterner opposition. Batting first, Rhodesia lost Pattison for 3 but Thompson and Grant dug in to put on a valuable 60. Both fell quickly in close succession and then Victor Hyde was bowled by Nupen without scoring. Campbell-Rodger was joined by Hayward at 63-4 but seemingly unconcerned with the position the powerful Rhodesian captain proceeded to annihilate the bowling, reaching his 50 in 48 minutes and his 100 in 90 minutes. A newspaper report from Johannesburg stated: 'Seldom has more brilliant pulling and driving been seen on the Rand', in its admiration of Campbell-Rodger's 108. He had added 185 with Hayward for the fifth wicket and team manager, J.R.C. MacKay, commented: 'Campbell-Rodger made a brilliant, aggressive effort when he had terrific responsibility on his shoulders and Hayward magnificently responded to his skipper's efforts to complete an outstanding wicket stand at a crucial time.'

The Rhodesian efforts however were brushed aside by the Transvaalers who established a lead of 104 and then dismissed the visitors for 188 in their second visit to the wicket. Campbell-Rodger and Hayward again batted well whilst Arnold Hyde made a useful contribution but "Buster" Nupen, the blonde Springbok of Norwegian stock, had the final say and his dangerous armoury of vicious off-breaks, leg cutters and devastating yorkers resulted in match figures of 13/102.

From Nupen, regarded as South Africa's greatest matting pitch bowler since the hey-day of Ernie Vogler, the Rhodesians faced a new evil in their next Currie Cup encounter. Jock Thompson recorded that the Rhodesians 'felt far from happy at the prospect of playing the next day on turf. But on a wicket slightly dampened by the overnight dew, Quinn, helped by Tomlinson, rattled out the opposition.' After initial apprehension about playing on turf the Rhodesians did not look back in chalking up a second victory with Victor Robinson emerging as the batting hero whilst "Scotty" Adamson claimed four inexpensive wickets in Border's second innings.

Adamson again bowled well the following day and was largely responsible for dismissing Griqualand

HAMISH CAMPBELL-RODGER.

VICTOR ROBINSON.

West cheaply (126) but the Rhodesians in reply failed miserably (107). The Griqua batsmen proceeded to rub in this slender advantage and the Rhodesians were set a huge fourth innings target of 305 in six hours. All hopes seemed to fade as they started badly, losing 3 wickets for 32 with Hayward tragically run out but Pattison and Grant gave their side a great boost in a fourth wicket stand of 127. Heavy rain during the tea interval added to the suspense and held up play for a short period. Useful totals by Campbell-Rodger, Thompson and Robinson then helped the score creep over the 250 mark but the ninth wicket fell at 278 — 26 runs behind the Griqua aggregate. Quinn joined Adamson and was dropped off a hard catch whilst the latter lived dangerously. The atmosphere verged on the hysterical as runs were scrambled together and the deficit was whittled down as Griquas strained every sinew for the one wicket which would give them the match.

Jock Thompson recalled: '. . . during alternate moments of cheering and tense silence this pair got the runs somehow and the Rhodesians won by one wicket. Whew! Those last minutes were a nerve-racking period!' Incredibly Rhodesia had scored their last 80 runs in 55 minutes and in so doing had become the first provincial side in South Africa to succeed in winning a match after being left to score over 300 in the last innings.

Eastern Province proved an easy hurdle in the last fixture — the rampant Rhodesians were in fine form in amassing 437 and then dismissing their opponents twice within that total. Denis Tomlinson hit a maiden first-class century and bowled well to wrap up Province's second innings whilst Campbell-Rodger registered his second three-figure score of the tournament. But overall it was another fine team performance which ensured Herby Taylor's shrewd predictions had become a reality.

SCORES: Currie Cup Tour, 1931-32 (Johannesburg).

At Pirates' ground, 21 and 22 December.
Rhodesia — 277 (A.H. Pattison 128, H. de V. Moll 45; L. de Villiers 6/56)
and 230 (H. Campbell-Rodger 58, A.H. Pattison 48, V.L. Robinson 42; L. de Villiers 6/52)
Orange Free State — 124 (M. H. Quinn 5/23, J.A. Adamson 3/34)
and 174 (D.S. Tomlinson 5/55)
Rhodesia won by 209 runs.

At Old Edwardians, 23 and 24 December.
Rhodesia — 272 (H. Campbell-Rodger 108, C.J.R. Hayward 86, G.C. Grant 40; E.P. Nupen 7/77)
and 188 (H. Campbell-Rodger 49, A. Hyde 39, C.J.R. Hayward 35*; E.P. Nupen 6/25)
Transvaal — 376 (R.H. Catterall 91, M.J. Susskind 64, D.I.E. Anderson 63; M.H. Quinn 4/60)
and 85-1 wkt. (M.J. Susskind 60*)
Transvaal won by 9 wickets.

At Pirates' ground, 26 and 28 December.
Border — 108 (M.H. Quinn 5/25, D.S. Tomlinson 3/35)
and 121 (J.A. Adamson 4/19)
Rhodesia — 151 (V.L. Robinson 59)
and 80-4 wkts. (G.C. Grant 33, V.L. Robinson 32)
Rhodesia won by 6 wickets.

At Wanderers, 29 and 30 December.
Griqualand West — 126 (J.A. Adamson 5/38, M.H. Quinn 3/31)
and 285 (G.E. Bock 78; H. Campbell-Rodger 3/41)
Rhodesia — 107 (C.J.R. Hayward 45*; J. McNally 7/35)
and 307-9 wkts. (G.C. Grant 68, A.H. Pattison 65, J. de L. Thompson 47, H. Campbell-Rodger 35)
Rhodesia won by one wicket.

At Wanderers, 1 and 2 January.
Eastern Province — 222 (D.S. Tomlinson 3/36, H. Campbell-Rodger 3/47)
and 134 (D.S. Tomlinson 4/19)
Rhodesia — 437 (D.S. Tomlinson 109, H. Campbell-Rodger 105, C.J.R. Hayward 65, V.L. Robinson 34)
Rhodesia won by an innings and 81 runs.

Rhodesia emerged from the tournament as joint runners-up on eight points — one behind Western Province. However if points had been allotted on the basis of an outright win counting more than a win on the first innings the Rhodesians would have won the tournament. The first three positions in the log were as follows:

	OUTRIGHT			1st INNS			
	P	W	L	W	L	D	PTS
Western Province	5	1	0	3	0	1	9
Rhodesia	5	4	1	0	0	0	8
Transvaal	5	3	0	1	1	0	8

There were a number of reasons for the success of the 1931-32 Rhodesian side but none was more relevant than that it had been a centralized tournament and therefore the burden of travelling between fixtures fell away. In addition one cannot discount the fact that the cream of South African cricket was touring Australia, save Catterall and Nupen who had been left behind for 'reasons other than cricketing ability'.

Victor Robinson, the Rhodesian vice-captain, made some interesting comments on his team's return and singled out three members of the successful touring side. He felt that the presence of Grant had had a great moral effect on the side; that Quinn, who had had the ability to make an early breakthrough in practically every match was one of the best opening bowlers of the tournament; and that Campbell-Rodger's hitting had been an absolute "eye-opener". Robinson also mentioned that Bob Catterall had remarked that Hayward's batting was the best the veteran Springbok had seen by a left-hander against Nupen. But amid the success Robinson warned that if Rhodesia was to do well in the future Currie Cup tournaments, turf wickets would have to be introduced: 'Even if we could only put down a practice turf pitch at first that would be something.'

In October 1932 a side from Nyasaland visited Salisbury and played against a local combination. Contact with Nyasaland had been established three years earlier when a Salisbury side was thrashed by an innings and 57 runs at Limbe. In their second clash Salisbury gained ample revenge at home by an innings and 66 runs with Ken Austin (89) leading the run riot as Salisbury raced to 446. Former Springbok Syd Pegler commanded respect from the home side throughout their innings and finished with 6 for 77, but the Nyasaland batsmen were not up to the task which confronted them and were bowled out twice for scores of 144 and 236.

RHODESIAN TOURING TEAM, 1931-32.
Back: J. Grant, J. Hayward, D. Tomlinson, J. Thompson, V. Hyde, M. Quinn, J. Adamson, H. Moll.
Seated: A. Hyde, A. Pattison, H. Campbell-Rodger (Captain), V. Robinson, R. Forbes.

CHAPTER THREE

Farewell to Matting

UP UNTIL the early 1930s the main object in the maintenance of the grounds was to keep the playing area devoid of veld grass to provide a smooth red earth surface. However, the season of 1930-31 had seen South Africa stage Test matches on turf for the first time and the second match at the Wanderers during that series was the last Test to be played on matting. A major step had been taken to ensure that the Springbok teams would be better equipped to handle conditions abroad. All provinces were, therefore, encouraged to follow suit but the transition in Rhodesia was a slow one. In fact there seemed to be a certain reluctance in Rhodesian cricket circles to encourage turf wickets.

The problems and pressures for turf wickets received considerable attention in the Press during the 1920s and it was obvious that efforts at least should be made towards turf outfields. One article in *The Bulawayo Chronicle* mentioned that 'slippery mud made it difficult for the fieldsmen to move' but many still argued that the sparse rainfall would not support grass survival. Further it was stressed that because fields would also be used for rugby and football the grass simply would not take the punishment. Nevertheless an experiment was made at the Raylton ground in Bulawayo and when the turf outfield was completed in January 1934, *The Bulawayo Chronicle* said that the cricket was 'certainly pleasanter to watch and is less of a strain on one's eyes than the brown fields of Queens, B.A.C. and Defence Force'.

In March 1934, Raylton went one step further when a turf wicket was completed for the first time in Rhodesia. The achievement was that much more noticeable because the wicket had been set down in arid Matabeleland and the undertaking was described at the time as a herculean task. The first game on turf was played on 17 March and the biggest attraction of this unique match was the fact that A.J. "Sandy" Bell, the Springbok opening bowler, was performing. Bell, who had earned a big reputation in England and Australia on turf wickets, was full of praise for the Raylton Club's efforts and provided some constructive criticism which was reported in *The Bulawayo Chronicle*: 'In brief he thought that on the wicket the grass was too long and that the soil did not "bind" enough. The turf on the pitch was nearly two inches long and it had queer effects on the bowling. For the pace bowlers the short ball "bit" into the pitch and "stood up" while the half-volley was inclined to "skid" through. The length of the grass aided the spin bowlers who got a tremendous amount of "work" on the ball. Batting under these conditions made for an excess of back-play whereas under normal turf wicket conditions forward play is generally the rule.'

Sadly, Bulawayo then made no further progress and was eventually overtaken by Salisbury. The latter tasted the initial unpredictable problems of a turf wicket for the first time in February 1935, at the Police Camp, and by late 1937, had two turf pitches and one in preparation whilst Bulawayo had none. However, the 1938-39 M.C.C. still played on matting and many mourned its passing after the Second World War because it demanded a high standard of batsmanship and helped bowlers who cut and spun the ball.

There were other interesting innovations during the 1930s. For the first time in southern Africa it was decided that numbers would be used on the backs of cricketers in the course of a Logan Cup match between Mashonaland and Matabeleland in March 1934. *The Bulawayo Chronicle* saw it as '... an experiment in which there is a lot of sense. Salisbury players are not seen in Bulawayo so often that they are recognizable from the stands when fielding, and scoreboards in the Colony are not the large, informative type.' Lance Roberts, later a Rhodesian selector, told an amusing tale of his experience during that match. He was the opening batsman and number 1 in the Mashonaland side but was not at the wicket long enough to make any material difference to the score. As he wended his way disconsolately back to the pavilion a beery voice from the refreshment tent shouted, 'Hey you ... are you sure there shouldn't be another 1 in front of that 1 on your back?'

A different method of identifying players was adopted when the 1935-36 Australians toured. A broadcasting apparatus with a microphone was placed in the Press tent at which an official of the R.C.U. presided and informed the crowd of the names of the batsmen, bowlers and fielders, as it was known that many of the spectators found difficulty in recognizing the players. Eric Scholl who was travelling with the Australian team on behalf of an Australian broadcasting company was an amusing and interesting announcer. Here it might be noted that the first 'live' cricket broadcast to be made in Rhodesia was by E.W. Swanton during the 1938-39 M.C.C. visit.

But perhaps the most important breakthrough for

Rhodesia during the 1930s was the selection of the first Rhodesian-born Springbok — Denis Tomlinson. Rhodesia had played no games since their successful 1931-32 Currie Cup entry but two former Prince Edward schoolboys were selected for the 1935 England tour. Bob Crisp and Umtali-born Denis Tomlinson, who had been the star bowlers of a cricket festival at the Cape in 1932-33 were both chosen after the Springbok trials in December 1934. Tomlinson had in fact been the "find" of the Cape Town festival and the *Cape Argus* reported: 'No matter how long any batsman might have been at the wicket it was apparent that they were never able to play mechanically at Tomlinson's deliveries, so well did he mix them, and the stroke had frequently to be made hurriedly because until the ball had pitched the direction of the spin was not discernible. Nor did the Rhodesian representative mind being hit; there were times when he "fed" the batsman with a four and completely beat and bowled him with the next ball.' Denis Tomlinson had come a long way since January 1925, when, hailed as a bowling prodigy, he had taken 3/31 as a 14 year-old for Mashonaland in a Logan Cup match against Midlands.

Denis Tomlinson — Rhodesia's first Springbok.

A.J. "Sandy" Bell pictured during the 1931-32 Springbok tour to Australasia.

Bob Crisp was, of course, at this stage a Western Province player but "Sandy" Bell, who was also selected for the England tour, was registered with the South African Cricket Board as a Rhodesian club representative. His arrival in Rhodesia had been a quiet one and his selection for the 1935 Springbok tour to England was based on his performances for B.A.C. in the Bulawayo league although his reputation was such that he would have been difficult to overlook. A big-hearted and aggressive pace bowler with a sharp in-swinger, Bell was first selected for South Africa on their 1929 tour to England. It was in the Third Test at Headingley on that tour that he hit the headlines with "Tuppy" Owen-Smith by adding 103 for the last wicket in 65 minutes. However, it was as a bowler that Bell continued to serve South Africa and he took 23 wickets in the 1931-32 Australian series which was as many as the next two on the list put together.

The 1935 Springboks made history in becoming the first South African side to win both a Test match and a series in England. It was a strenuous programme of forty matches — thirty-one of them first-class — and the Springboks emerged with twenty-one victories and only two defeats. Crisp took 107 wickets on the tour which also included a match against the Netherlands at The Hague whilst Tomlinson and Bell each claimed 52 wickets. Sadly the tour also had its tragic side when "Jock" Cameron contracted enteric fever on the voyage home and died at the early age of thirty. Denis Tomlinson was also ill with the same fever after the tour which put him out of action whilst an injury to "Sandy" Bell's right elbow ended his career for several years.

When a Rhodesian side next took the field they were, therefore, without their two Springboks — Bell and Tomlinson. More's the pity, because the 1935-36 Australian side's visit followed immediately on the heels of the Springboks' tour to the United Kingdom. And in spite of the non-availability of Don Bradman, the Aussies, under Victor Richardson, had a powerful side. They arrived in Bulawayo with eleven victories in twelve games — only the South Africans in the Second Test had escaped with a draw,

The experienced Rhodesian wicket-keeper, Jock Thompson, was named as captain of the side which included only three other "old hands", Arnold Hyde, Henry Moll and Jack Hayward. There were seven newcomers to the team — Jack Charsley, Bill Parry, Mark Napier, Jimmy Fuller, Tommy Pattinson, Ronnie Michell and A. "Sonny" Den.

The first glimpse which the awaiting Rhodesians had of this awesome touring side after their long, dusty journey up from Kimberley was that of two pyjama-clad players jumping off a moving train on to Bulawayo platform in order to get first use of the station bathrooms. The initial meeting was in itself a brief one as the Aussies were merely passing through Bulawayo on their way to Victoria Falls.

On their return the Australians found the Bulawayo Raylton ground in fine condition for this long-awaited encounter. The green grass outfield with the fine Raylton Institute building at one end and the white marquees and the stands on the borders of the oval, made for an attractive setting for the match, although the ominous black clouds served as a reminder that it could rain at any moment. The big surprise, though, for the visitors, was that Jock Thompson, captaining Rhodesia for the first time, put them in to bat.

Unfortunately, only seventy-five minutes play was possible on the opening day due to rain. In fact the game began in intermittent drizzle, with heavy rain driving the players and spectators for cover after

JACK HAYWARD.

Bob Crisp and Denis Tomlinson enjoy a golf break during the 1935 Springbok tour to England.

Col. J. deL. ("Jock") Thompson in later years.

twenty minutes, whilst a gang of ground labourers dashed out with tarpaulins to preserve the wicket. It was one of the season's heaviest showers, imprisoning people in their shelters and in a very short time the field was flooded with parts of the ground being entirely under water. A gutter between the reserved tent and the Raylton clubhouse became a small lake which no one could cross until duck-boards had been laid down. However the sun which followed the downpour kept up the hopes of the crowd whilst the Raylton groundsmen, helped by Boy Scouts, worked hard to repair damage done to the field. After inspections at 4 o'clock, play began and it was not long before there was a burst of excitement. Opening batsman Morris Sievers took a mighty swing at a loose ball from Arnold Hyde. Eyes moved towards the boundary in anticipation of a six but it did not get there as Tommy Pattinson 'leapt a yard into the air to take a magnificent one-handed catch'. This brought out the great Stan McCabe, captaining the visitors in place of Richardson who had gone through to Salisbury to see some friends. The crowd buzzed with excitement — Australia's batting genius had made scores of 149 and 189 in the first two Tests against South Africa — but they were quickly stunned into silence. A shout went up with Hyde's first ball and McCabe was caught, flashing outside the off-stump, by Jock Thompson.

There was no play on the morning of the second day but that afternoon the Australians chased the bowling to score a further 280 runs in 210 exhilarating minutes. Equally memorable, though, was the catching of the Rhodesian fielders. Henry Moll snapped up Ben Barnett (33), inches from the ground at mid-off and then with a neat pick-up and return was instrumental in running out Arthur Chipperfield (3). Ronnie Michell stretched out and had Len Darling (108) held well above his head at short square leg and when Jack Fingleton (28) struck at a ball outside the off-stump, Pattinson stuck out his left hand for Charsley to complete a spectacular catch at first slip. Admittedly Bill Brown (97) was dropped off a stinging chance in the slips before he had reached double figures but Mark Napier took a great catch at deep mid-on to get rid of the swashbuckling Aussie after a cavalier 85 minutes at the wicket. Finally Jack Hayward, who had produced the very creditable figures for a novice bowler of 4 for 34 in 11,5 overs, took a fine catch at short third man to send Bert Oldfield back to the pavilion.

On a hot third day with no indication of rain other than a few light wispy clouds, Rhodesia set after the Australian total of 357. An unfortunate start was made when Fuller was bowled off his pads and just dislodged his bails but thereafter, Parry and Jock Thompson refused to be rattled. Bill O'Reilly set his famous leg trap but the Rhodesians were unperturbed and it was not until the score had reached 73 that Parry was out after hitting 47 in 94 minutes. Thompson went 10 runs later and then Hayward and Napier came together and took the score past the 150 mark. At this stage the rain began to fall and during the shower Ernie McCormick came on to bowl a wild over at Hayward bumping two over his head. Napier went in the next over and tea was taken before another heavy downpour resulted in the game being abandoned.

SCORES: versus Australia, 1935-36.

At Bulawayo, 8, 10 and 11 February.

Australia — 357 (L.S. Darling 108, W.A. Brown 97; C.J.R. Hayward 4/34, H. de V. Moll 3/56)

Rhodesia — 157-4 wkts. (W.J. Parry 47, M. Napier 38, C.J.R. Hayward 33*, J. de L. Thompson 31)

Match drawn.

The 1936-37 and 1937-38 seasons were somewhat disappointing — firstly at the non-entry of Rhodesia into the Currie Cup tournament, then the last-minute decision of the Griqualand West side not to tour in 1936-37 and finally the cancellation of the Transvaal visit the following season. One national game was played when Rhodesia travelled to Johannesburg in December 1936, to play against the Transvaal and were ingloriously defeated.

Taking a side with six new caps, the Rhodesians collapsed in the face of Transvaal's total of 262 and at one stage totalled 19 with nine wickets down. At this point the only two members of the team who had played Transvaal in that memorable game in December 1931, came together in a determined rearguard fight. Last man, Henry Moll, joined his skipper, Jack Hayward, and added a gallant 64 for the tenth wicket. Hayward even had the confidence to smash a ball from Balaskas into the grandstand for six. Sadly the Rhodesians did little better in their second knock and were thrashed by an innings and 73 runs. The chief reason given for the pathetic batting displays — inexperience on a turf wicket!

SCORES: versus Transvaal, 1936-37.

At Johannesburg, 16, 17 and 18 December.

Transvaal — 262 (T.W.T. Baines 79, A. Melville 70; J.H. Charsley 6/92)

Rhodesia — 83 (C.J.R. Hayward 37*; S.C. Parkyns 5/32)
and 106 (M. Mansell 34)

Transvaal won by an innings and 73 runs.

The *Wisden Cricketers' Almanack* reports that during the 1936-37 season M.I. Yusuf scored 412 not out for the Government Indian Schools Cricket Club against Star Club at Bulawayo. This has been recorded as the highest individual score in all grades of cricket to have been made in southern Africa. Yusuf who was formerly a Natal Indian league player captained Bulawayo Indians at this time and on another memorable occasion scored a century in an hour against Salisbury Indians in a Nagrani Cup match.

Another interesting occurrence was the arrival in December 1936, of a Hercules troop-carrier which brought a cricket team representing the South African Air Force. This was the first time that air travel had been used in the staging of a cricket match. For the record, the South African Air Force XI were defeated by a team from the 2nd Battalion Rhodesia Regiment.

In October 1937, Alec Tait scored 260 for Old Hararians against Raylton to break Colin Duff's Rhodesian record for the highest first league score. Tait put on 318 for the second wicket with Harry Chittenden to help their side to a first innings total of 466-5 declared. Both these tallies were new league records whilst Raylton's defeat by an innings and 285 runs had in itself never been bettered.

Keeping the Bulawayo flag flying, Jimmy Fuller scored a faultless 188 in a Logan Cup semi-final match for Matabeleland against Midlands at Gwelo in December 1937. This eclipsed R.J. Oliver's previous record score of 159 set during the 1932-33 season.

One of the most sensational performances in the history of the Logan Cup occurred during the 1938-39 season when Don Giles took a hat-trick in his opening over for Mashonaland against Matabeleland in the final, played at Bulawayo.

In 1938-39 the M.C.C. visited this country again with a strong combination captained by Wally Hammond — the only notable absentee being Denis Compton who was engaged in professional soccer with Arsenal. The Rhodesian Cricket Union, realising the uphill task ahead of them, decided to hold a trial in early January 1939, to select a side to play against the tourists. Hayward's XI, thanks to a fine 96 by Percy Mansell, comfortably defeated Tomlinson's XI. There were also competent displays from two Northern Rhodesians, Tommy and Frank Davidson. They had been practising assiduously in the nets for some weeks prior to the trial and thoroughly deserved to become the first Northern Rhodesian players to be selected for a Rhodesian cricket team. Tommy Davidson, who was given a large sundowner party by the Roan Antelope Mine in honour of his selection, had represented Border and Western Province in his earlier years.

Another encouraging sign in 1938 had been that "Sandy" Bell was back and bowling well. An inspired spell of 7/28 against Manicaland in a Logan Cup semi-final ensured him of a place in the national side to play against the tourists. More good news was the fact that the country's other Springbok, Denis Tomlinson, returned to the team after some useful bowling performances throughout the season.

It is worth noting that Matabeleland had six representatives, as well as 12th man Mark Napier, to Mashonaland's two — hardly surprising considering the former's overwhelming ten-wicket victory in the

The 1938-39 Rhodesian side at Bulawayo as Richard Lee saw them.

1937-38 Logan Cup final. In Percy Mansell, Jimmy Fuller and Jack Hayward they had three players who were having terrific seasons in League and Logan Cup matches, whilst wicket-keeper Harry Evans was already being acclaimed as a player of great potential despite his 'unorthodox stance with feet wide apart'.

Rain again featured in the Bulawayo game against the M.C.C. and only 94 minutes' play was possible on the first day. In that time the visitors scored 152 runs for the loss of two wickets with Len Hutton and Eddie Paynter rapidly adding 115 for the second wicket. Although unable to stem the tide, the Rhodesian fielding was often brilliant on a slippery, treacherous field with Jack Charsley making a superb one-handed catch in the slips to dismiss Hedley Verity.

No play was possible on the second day and on the third, the game became very much a one innings affair. The M.C.C. declared at 307 for 5 — Len Hutton making 145. Wrote Louis Duffus: 'Hutton is so richly endowed with cricket ability that it doubtless makes little difference to him whether the wicket is grass, matting or just an appropriated strip of a Pudsey highway. With the ball rising high he exploited some daring hook shots. Once in an ambitious stroke he nearly pulled a ball from Bell on to his wicket from outside the off-stump. A cardinal trait was the smooth timing of his batting.'

The most prolific run-maker so far on the M.C.C.'s southern African tour had been the slightly-built left-hander, Eddie Paynter — the man who, following a dreary train trip, described Rhodesia as 'miles and miles of nowt'. Louis Duffus wrote of his innings of 53: 'Paynter was a little confused at the start of his innings especially as one or two short-pitched balls from Bell bumped up head-high. Tomlinson's big break also caused him some embarrassment but as the attack was liberally sprinkled with full tosses he was very soon hitting boundaries, stealing outrageously short runs and giving the 1 500 spectators an idea of the aggressive tactics that have made him one of the most successful batsmen of the tour.'

It was not really a suitable day to judge the bowling. Both Charsley, who was most accurate, and Bell, who was not as fast as he used to be, were handicapped by the slow pitch. Tomlinson did make the ball turn sharply but the matting was lifeless and his few overs were expensive.

The Rhodesian batting, however, was most encouraging in putting together a creditable 242 — Mansell 62 and Fuller 46 being the top scorers. Again Louis Duffus's remarks are worth recording: 'Both the young players, Fuller and Evans did much to justify their rosy reputations and Mansell who is only eighteen showed an all-round ability that should lead to his being one of Rhodesia's leading cricketers of the future. It is often dangerous to judge wicket-keepers on one performance. A conservative opinion of Evans is that he is a zealous young wicket-keeper of considerable promise. His methods are not all polished but he possesses considerable skill. Fuller is an opening bat with a wide command of strokes. He hooked and pulled effectively and among other good shots drove one ball through the covers with a power and technique that could scarcely have been bettered by Hammond and Hutton. He had the misfortune to tread on his wickets while two other batsmen, Noble and Frank Davidson, each played on.'

What a pity the weather had destroyed so much of a great game — all concerned prayed the elements would be kinder in Salisbury as the M.C.C. players boarded the train in Bulawayo. The tourists had made a great impact and scores of small boys stood around Hutton's compartment in particular at Bulawayo station, lavishing on him blatant hero worship. And as the train moved off towards Salisbury a diminutive Boy Scout ran alongside to ask the great batsman, 'Can I write to you?'

Two hours of hectic cricket were crammed into another rain-affected opening day in Salisbury. In that time England were 162-9, adding a further 18 the following day to be all out for 180. Jack Charsley finished with 6/58, swinging the ball away effectively and bowling with great accuracy. He was aided by two fine slip catches by Jack Hayward to get rid of the opening batsmen Paul Gibb and Doug Wright, and added Wally Hammond's wicket to his bag which already included Hutton caught by Bell in Bulawayo. Tomlinson, pitching his leg breaks and googlies with success claimed 3/87.

Getting the visitors out for so few runs was a tremendous achievement but it must be remembered that they were the last overseas side to play on a matting wicket and for most of them it was a novel experience. Their batsmen, accustomed to the pace of turf wickets, played forward too soon and invariably hit the ball hazardously into the air. Even skipper Hammond saw the best tactics being to thrash the innings back to line and security and his 43 which contained two huge sixes was inevitably fraught with peril.

Rhodesia opened responsibly with Fuller (22) and Tomlinson (27) providing a solid opening partnership. However, a hat-trick by Tom Goddard sent the home side's innings toppling from its promising position. The Rhodesians had some difficulty in distinguishing between Goddard's off-break and straight ball through his deceptive finger action. The experienced Arnold Hyde (11 not out) did his best to keep an end intact, watching helplessly as his team-mates came and went to be all out for 96. Duffus described Hyde as seeing the ball 'as a regulation-sized, hand-sewn round object and not the matchbox shaped article of destruction which appeared to the other Rhodesian batsmen when it left the hand of Goddard'.

Going in a second time, the M.C.C. made amends and rattled up 174-2 wickets — Bill Edrich 101 not out — giving them an overall lead of 258. But heavy rain once again intervened and play seemed remote at 2.00 p.m. on the last afternoon. It was only an ingenious idea on the part of the organizing committee, who were certainly made of stern stuff, which made play possible again at 3.15 p.m. They poured about forty gallons of petrol on the pitch and set it alight! The blaze expedited the resumption of play so quickly that fielders had to be called from billiards, squash rackets and table tennis and an England fast bowler was roused from the lounge in the middle of a post-prandial nap. His comment on being told what had happened was that he knew of many other pitches more deserving of being made into a bonfire.

Goddard was again menacing in the second innings but the Rhodesians battled hard to stave off defeat. Fuller (22), Napier (24) and Hayward (15 not out) played determinedly and the home side ultimately earned another draw.

SCORES: M.C.C. Tour, 1938-39.

At Bulawayo, 4, 6 and 7 February.

M.C.C. — 307-5 dec. (L. Hutton 145, E. Paynter 53)

Rhodesia — 242 (P.N.F. Mansell 62, J.H.F. Fuller 46, A. Hyde 37; D.V.P. Wright 4/64)

Match drawn.

At Salisbury, 10, 11 and 13 February.

M.C.C. — 180 (J.H. Charsley 6/58, D.S. Tomlinson 3/87)
and 174-2 dec. (W.J. Edrich 101 not out)

Rhodesia — 96 (T.W. Goddard 6/38)
and 95-6 wkts.

Match drawn.

Despite the cricket being limited to an extent by the weather, the visit by the M.C.C. had built up tremendous interest and this is well illustrated in a short article by Louis Duffus. He wrote: 'If those who have watched the cricket of this English team for the past four months were apt to become jaded they could scarcely fail to respond to the refreshing enthusiasm with which Rhodesians are following these matches. Lovers of cricket have journeyed long distances from outposts of the Colony to see in the flesh, players like Hammond and others whose names have appeared so frequently, even in the headlines that reach lonely bush settlements. Enthusiasts drove hundreds of miles by motor car over treacherous, wet roads to see the M.C.C. play at Bulawayo.

'One of the players, Tommy Davidson, travelled some 1,600 miles for his day's play. No doubt when he returns to his police post in the Copperbelt he will reflect with satisfaction for many summers that he once hit a ball from Len Hutton for six.'

The shadows of war were already gathering when Wally Hammond's team returned home and it was to be some years before a Rhodesian side took the field again.

In the early days of the Second World War, cricket played an important part in the off-duty activities of the members of the forces and received considerable Press coverage. A couple of fixtures played by Rhodesian contingents were labelled as "Rhodesia" matches and when considering the representative talent involved this was hardly surprising.

In November 1939 at Kumasi, a match was played between the Gold Coast and Rhodesia. A report of the game stated: 'The Gold Coast team were impressed by the fine all-round work of Denis Tomlinson, by the stubborn defence of Clarence in both innings and by the promise of Chittenden for whom they prophesy a great future.'

SCORES: (Not first-class).

Gold Coast — 126 (J.H. Charsley 3/34, D.S. Tomlinson 3/41)
and 116 (D.S. Tomlinson 7/48)

Rhodesia — 147 (D.S. Tomlinson 46)
and 97-7 wkts.

Rhodesia won by 3 wickets.

Another report from the Gold Coast stated: 'The cricket activities of the two Tomlinsons who have now made big scores in several different centres have given the sporting public here the impression that there are at least twelve brothers of that name now serving with the regiment.'

In Nigeria, the Rhodesian troops played the rest of Zaria on a tarmac pitch — owing to the heat it was only possible to play after 5 o'clock in the afternoon. The visitors followed their "Test" triumph at Kumasi with a resounding victory.

SCORES: (Not first-class).

Rhodesia — 182-5 dec. (C. Harvey 72, J. Evershed 30*, H. Streak 20)

Zaria — 82 (C. Harvey 4/21)

Rhodesia won by 100 runs.

An extract from *The Springbok*, the official paper for the Sixth Division, reported that a cricket "Test" match was held at the Alamein Club, Cairo, on 15 and 16 July 1944 between the United Kingdom and the Rest of the Empire. Forbes McDonald (Eiffel Flats) and Lance Roberts (Salisbury) played in this fixture for the Rest XI. McDonald, who had represented South Africa at hockey and Eastern Province at cricket before the War, came in to bat with his side struggling at 46-5. Unperturbed, he hit 84 in 154 minutes to help build the score up to 279 before he was caught and bowled by the Yorkshire colt, Jim Laker.

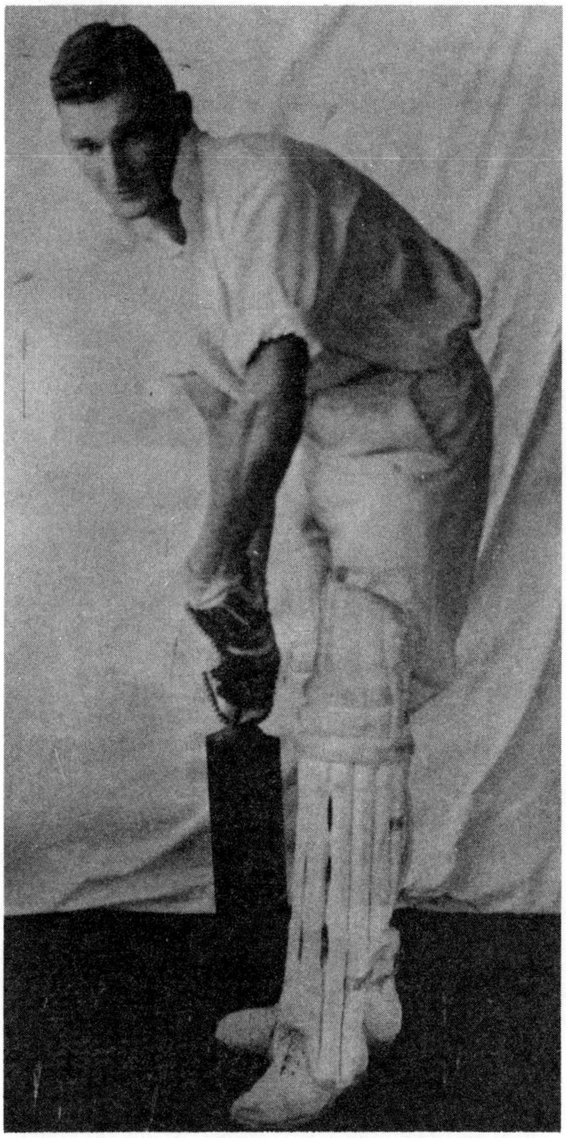

ARNOLD HYDE.

In Rhodesia, the game was kept alive during the War by the Rhodesian Air Training Scheme. This Group provided organized cricket for its members with local sports clubs making their grounds available and where possible fielding civilian teams. A Ladies XI played for the first years, captained by Lila Franklin, Rhodesia's triple title tennis champion. Other sides over the years included various R.A.F. combinations, the Light Battery, Police, R.A.R., Signallers, Old Hararians, Raylton, Vacuum Oil Company, Postals, Alexandra, Municipality, Old Crocs, Combined Printers, Salisbury Sports Club, Nondescripts and Norton. Teams would also visit Salisbury from Umtali and in the Bulawayo region, Air Force (Kumalo), Air Force (Guinea Fowl), B.A.C., Raylton, Army, Queens, Ramblers and I.T.W. fielded sides. At times, representative teams were selected such as a combined Air Force XI playing the Rest of Salisbury and in the course of these periodic major matches, collections would be taken to aid Air Force charities and local war funds.

There were a number of outstanding achievements during these years. "Sandy" Singleton (R.A.F. Cranborne) took all 10 wickets in an innings and had match figures of 15/75 against Headquarters in 1940-41. That season, Ronnie Michell (R.A.F. Belvedere) made a string of centuries and T. McCormick (Police) took over 100 wickets — a feat he repeated in 1941-42. After taking 9 wickets in an innings on several occasions, McCormick had the distinction of taking all ten for 37 against Mount Hampden in October 1944. In 1941-42 Hamish Campbell-Rodger made a lot of runs characterized by some big hitting — he captained the Army XI in the highlight match of the season, beating an Air Force side which contained several county players by 22 runs. In December 1943, "Sandy" Bell led a team of Norton farmers and he played a number of other matches including taking 12/68 for the Rest against the R.A.F. In April 1944, the Salisbury Air Training Group played Heany in the RATG cricket championships in Bulawayo — Denis Tomlinson had match figures of 14/26 to give Salisbury an easy victory. The same month, however, a Matabeleland side took Mashonaland on for the first time since the War broke out, and thanks to good bowling from Henry Moll beat them by 52 runs.

The finale to six years of keenly contested wartime cricket was played in Salisbury in March 1945. It was a contest between the Royal Air Force and Rhodesia and stimulated great interest at the time. His Excellency the Governor, Vice-Admiral Sir Campbell Tait and Lady Tait watched the encounter and later lunched with the teams at Salisbury Sports Club.

The game ended amid much excitement with the Air Force, captained by Geoff Ellman-Brown, narrowly forcing a draw as their last two batsmen played out several overs of tense cricket. Yet such is cricket that the match began with both sides showing little discretion and runs were scored at a fast and furious pace whilst wickets tumbled regularly. Nigel Boast, Jock Holden, Edgar Morris and John Johnson all batted well in both their knocks for Rhodesia, whilst the Air Force batting was in contrast disappointingly brittle. Indeed it was a pity that Tom Thornton, who was rated by a *Rhodesia Herald* correspondent as being 'a batsman without a peer in the Colony,' did not come off in what were two of his last innings before he returned to his native Yorkshire at the end of 1945.

Of interest, Cecil "Sam" Cook, whose left-arm slow bowling was responsible for five wickets in the match for Air Force also returned to England, and in 1947 was selected to play against South Africa in the Trent Bridge Test of that series.

SCORES: (Not first-class).

Rhodesia — 192 (E.D. Morris 44*, J.B.C. Johnson 35, A. Holden 33; C. Cook 3/62)
and 207-8 dec. (J.B.C. Johnson 46, A. Holden 34, E.D. Morris 33*, N.I. Boast 32)

R.A.F. — 127 (D. Austin 50*; E.D. Morris 4/33)
and 162-9 wkts. (R.J. Oliver 57; W. Sunter 3/24)

Match drawn.

Cricket returned to normality in the 1945-46 season although it was dampened by the alarming news that cricket in Manicaland had folded up. A telegram from the Manicaland secretary, "Binks" Holland, to the Rhodesian Cricket Union read: 'Unless you can advise where cricket bats and balls can be purchased we are unable to continue.'

As a result, the reintroduction of Logan Cup saw a three-way competition with Mashonaland taking on Midlands in the first game. The Mashonas, led by "Trods" Hards won comfortably by 86 runs although they were held up for some time by McCormick who hit a gallant 73 for the Midlands. Top scorer with 71 for the winners was veteran Arnold Hyde and to further demonstrate that he had lost little of the old touch he slammed 91 not out in the final against Matabeleland.

Another old-timer, Ken Austin, who had two good knocks for Mashonaland in their Logan Cup triumph was deservedly named Rhodesian captain for their first post-War first-class match — a friendly, against Transvaal. Under him he had a fairly experienced combination particularly when one considers the lack of top class cricket during the War. Austin, himself, and Arnold Hyde had made their debuts for Rhodesia during the 1927-28 season whilst Denis Tomlinson (1935) and Bob Newson (1930-39) were both Springboks. The latter, a talented all-rounder, had represented South Africa against the 1930-31 and the 1938-39 M.C.C. touring sides. The wily "Bucky" Buchanan was an experienced campaigner from the Eastern Province and Percy Mansell, Jack Charsley, Harry Evans and Reg Noble had all played for Rhodesia before the War. New caps were John Johnson and Edgar Morris.

Rhodesia struggled in their return to first-class cricket to dismiss Transvaal for 342 with all the visiting batsmen, bar number 11, reaching double figures. However, the Rhodesians batted determinedly in reply for their 260 runs, with Johnson (64) top scoring, and if Tomlinson and Noble had not both been run out they might well have reached the visitors' score. Noble's dismissal was most unfortunate — the bowler appealed for an lbw decision which was refused but while awaiting the umpire's verdict Noble was standing out of his crease and the slip fielder threw the wicket down.

An interesting end to this game at one stage appeared possible when Transvaal set Rhodesia 214 to score in 155 minutes. Unfortunately, rain prevented Rhodesia going out to bat a second time and the game

Q.A. "KEN" AUSTIN.

was abandoned. A disappointing end but the Transvaal stayed on in the country for two further matches.

The first of these games was a drawn match against a Rhodesia Junior XI in which several local youngsters showed up well. The Rhodesian Junior captain, Cecil Harris, batted exceptionally well in the first innings for his 72 out of 155 whilst a fine partnership of 84 between Denis O'Connell-Jones and Connie Pretorius kept the experienced Transvaal attack at bay in the second innings. Of the others, Peter Johnson and Benny Chimowitz bowled impressively and commanded respect throughout — the latter being rewarded with a full Rhodesian cap against Transvaal in Bulawayo in place of the unavailable Newson.

The young Gatooma-born Chimowitz top scored (49) in his first-class debut, delighting in particular with hard-hit, scoring shots off the back foot. But Rhodesia's 200 was quickly placed into insignificance as Transvaal nonchalantly passed it for the loss of three wickets and proceeded to amass a huge first innings score. Austin used ten bowlers in his desperation to curb the mounting score — his ordeal only ended when Transvaal declared 189 ahead. To make matters worse, Denis Tomlinson and Jack Charsley were unable to take any further part in the match but Transvaal's skipper, Ken Viljoen, sportingly came to the depleted Rhodesian side's aid in a unique move. He allowed the two substitutes, David Lewis and Robert Kennedy, to bat in the second innings, but his move made little difference to the final outcome. Only Reg Noble and Arnold Hyde in a third wicket partnership of 111 were prepared to use their feet against the Transvaal spinners as Rhodesia collapsed to be all out for 157.

SCORES: Transvaal tour, 1945-46.

At Salisbury, 16, 17 and 18 March.

Transvaal — 342 (S. Lacey 102; D.S. Tomlinson 3/95) and 131-4 dec.

Rhodesia — 260 (J.B.C. Johnson 64, P.N.F. Mansell 37, J.H. Charsley 35)

Match drawn.

At Gwelo, 19 and 20 March (Not first-class).
Rhodesia Junior XI — 155 (C.M. Harris 72)
and 161-7 wkts. (C.J. Pretorius 59, D.B. O'Connell-Jones 35)

Transvaal — 236-9 dec. (L.S. Brown 64*, K.G. Viljoen 63; B.L. Chimowitz 4/70)

Match drawn.

At Bulawayo, 23, 24 and 25 March.
Rhodesia — 200 (B.L. Chimowitz 49, J.B.C. Johnson 30, E.D. Morris 30*; X.C. Balaskas 5/87)
and 157 (R.J. Noble 69, A. Hyde 47; X.C. Balaskas 5/71)

Transvaal — 489-8 dec. (K.G. Viljoen 124, R. Somers-Vine 119, L. Sadler 85, S. Lacey 73)

Transvaal won by an innings and 132 runs.

RHODESIA XI v. R.A.F., 1945.
Back: H. Pichanick (Secretary, R.C.U.), G. Ledeboer (Umpire), H. Hards, N. Boast, E. Morris, R. Oliver, E. Cutter, J. Johnson, Swann, C. Cook, A. Hyde, W. Soloman (Umpire), G. Laing.
Seated: H. Broad, T. Thornton, W. Best, A. Holden, T. Pattinson (Captain, Rhodesia XI), E. Watson, (Chairman, M.C.A.), G. Ellman-Brown (Captain, R.A.F.), A. Morris, D. Austin, W. Lee.
Front: H. Chittenden, Semmans, A. Candler, R.A.F. 12th Man, W. Sunter, K. Austin.

CHAPTER FOUR

The Captaincy Search

WHEN UNINTERRUPTED cricket resumed after the Second World War, Rhodesia's initial problem seemed to be to find a cricket captain on a regular basis. The search continued as Rhodesia re-entered the Currie Cup competition and captains were chopped and changed regularly until David Lewis took over at the beginning of the 1953-54 season. During this earlier period some of the most respected and talented cricketers to have graced the country's fields were given the opportunity to lead the national side and indeed did so with distinction. But the responsibility of captaincy never remained in any of these capable hands long enough for that individual to have a marked influence on the course of Rhodesian cricket.

Immediately after the War, Rhodesia had called upon the experience of Ken Austin to tide them over the opening friendlies against Transvaal and the following year (1946-47), Bob Newson took the side on tour. The same season Lee Walkden stepped into the fold for one match when Newson was unavailable for the home Currie Cup encounter against Transvaal. He, in turn, was succeeded by "Sandy" Singleton in the season's last fixture, a friendly against the same Transvaal visitors. Singleton, whose credentials were impressive, having captained Oxford University and Worcestershire, had the distinction of leading Rhodesia to their first victory over Transvaal. During the 1946 English season, Singleton scored 1 778 runs and took 43 wickets and might have been chosen for the M.C.C. tour of Australasia had he been available.

In recognition of his achievements, Singleton retained the leadership in 1947-48. Denis Tomlinson was named as vice-captain but a gesture in true sporting fashion occurred when Singleton went off the field during the course of that season. Tomlinson asked Syd Martin to take over from him — a tribute to the unlimited cricket knowledge of the former Worcestershire and Natal player.

The 40-year-old Martin, who twice achieved the English first-class double of 1 000 runs and 100 wickets during his ten seasons in county cricket, took over as captain of the side in the clashes against the M.C.C. in 1948-49 and against the Australians in 1949-50 before deciding to call it a day.

"Bebe" Franklin captained Rhodesia in the first match of 1950-51 but found himself 12th man in the side's next fixture against Transvaal, a sad relegation for the batsman who brought the following comment from John Arlott during the 1948-49 M.C.C. visit: 'This boy's timing is quite the best I have seen on the tour.'

Percy Mansell succeeded Franklin and kept the captaincy for the three-match tour but on the team's return withdrew from the side to play against Border because of a strained muscle and Johnny Leibbrandt took over for this game. Mansell, one of Rhodesia's greatest cricketers, was always reticent about captaining a cricket side and was never to lead Rhodesia again.

In 1951-52 there was a new skipper for the opening match against Free State but Ronnie Hayes found himself omitted from the team in the next game following a controversial selection. For the remainder of the season and for 1952-53 David Rees filled the role with a certain amount of success. Rees, who had led his club side Alma in the Western Province League

A.P. "SANDY" SINGLETON.

Syd Martin, in later years as the Matabeleland coach, demonstrates to Andre Nel.

and later became captain of Bulawayo Queens, was in charge of the Rhodesian team for eleven matches, winning six and drawing two.

In the 1946-47 season, the Currie Cup competition was resumed and with a tour organized to South Africa, a north versus south trial was held at the Salisbury Sports Club. Reg Noble scored a fine hundred, whilst youngsters "Bunny" de Grandhomme and Connie Pretorius, ensured selection with useful half-centuries. Bob Newson was named as captain of the touring side which included two other Springboks, Denis Tomlinson and new arrival Len Brown, who had toured Australasia in 1931-32 with Jock Cameron's South Africans. The experienced Jimmy Fuller was named vice-captain and two wicket-keepers were selected — Cecil Harris and the 1941 South African Schools representative, Norman Dyer.

Rhodesia had been suddenly faced with a wicket-keeping crisis because the season had opened with the tragic death of regular wicket-keeper, Harry Evans, who had collapsed during a Mashonaland versus Combined Districts match in September. Also a Rhodesian hockey player, the following tribute was paid to him at the time: 'He had a happy knack of making a batsman feel at home even though he rarely missed a chance of sending him back to the pavilion — by his friendly chatting and cordial praise for a good stroke.'

The tour comprised of three matches, beginning against North-Eastern Transvaal at Brakpan in a match in which Rhodesia so nearly pulled off a deserved victory. So tight was the finish that there was talk at the time that Rhodesia should claim an extra eight minutes play for delay caused by a civic luncheon on the first day. However, a newspaper report of the game probably best reflected the general feeling when it said: 'Many must have been glad that this was not done. If the Rhodesian side had not gained the Currie Cup points they had at least gained a terrific moral victory.'

In this match Mark Napier celebrated his return to the side with a fine 97 not out in Rhodesia's first innings total of 277. Unfortunately, dropped catches allowed North-Eastern Transvaal to reach 321 in reply and in order to stand a chance of winning, Rhodesia were forced to score quick runs in their second batting display. Reg Noble (84) dominated the early part of the innings whilst newcomer, Forbes McDonald, and the experienced Newson added 112 for the sixth wicket. Set a winning target of 277, North-Easterns started badly as Brown captured two early wickets and then struck again to get rid of future Springboks Ken Funston and Johnny Lindsay. But time was not on Rhodesia's side as Newson grabbed the ninth wicket with the last ball of the day and North-Easterns 55 runs behind.

Moving on to Cape Town to face a strong Western Province side, Rhodesia were given a great opening start of 123 by Harris and Fuller 'playing sedate, correct cricket and taking no chances at all against bowling that was always steady'. Sadly, the rest did not take advantage of this start and off-spinner Martin Hanley captured the remaining eight wickets as Rhodesia tumbled to 225 all out. Obviously peeved at this collapse, Newson reacted in determined fashion and a report from Cape Town said: 'Bob Newson, with the wind behind his back, produced the fastest spell of bowling seen at Newlands since that of the late Ken

LEN BROWN.

Farnes of the 1938-39 M.C.C. team.' He sent back the opening pair at a cost of only eleven runs and then learning from Hanley's success, brought on Tomlinson. Flighting the ball well, Tomlinson broke the back of the Province innings and by the end of the second day Rhodesia were 308 ahead with two second innings wickets in hand. In an incredible finish they lost. A fine 90 not out by the young schoolboy, Clive van Ryneveld, guided the home side to a great four-wicket victory.

In Kimberley, apart from Len Brown, the Rhodesians bowled and fielded badly during the first two days against Griqualand West. In contrast, the home side, largely through the Waddingtons, bowled tightly and thereby gained an eighty-run first innings lead. Going in a second time, Griquas proceeded to build on this run difference and eventually set Rhodesia a mammoth target of 421. It was expectedly out of reach for the Rhodesians but there was nevertheless some magnificent cricket. Coming in at number three, skipper Newson proceeded to carve the Griqua attack apart in a magnificent innings. He reached his century in a record 65 minutes with fourteen fours and four sixes and went on to make 114 in 73 minutes before skying a ball to be well held by McNamara. Harris stayed with him to add 102 for the second wicket but thereafter Rhodesia collapsed to be 186-8. Mansell fought back and in a gallant undefeated knock of 90 added 53 with Brown and 70 with Carew for the 9th and 10th wickets respectively to take the score to 309 — 112 behind.

SCORES: Currie Cup Tour, 1946-47.

At Brakpan, 29, 30 November, 2 December.

Rhodesia — 277 (M. Napier 97*, R. Noble 40)
and 320-7 dec. (R. Noble 84, F. McDonald 72, E.S. Newson 62)

N.E. Transvaal — 321 (R.S. Martin 62, J.D. Lindsay 51; L.S. Brown 3/85, A.S. Carew 3/37)
and 221-9 wkts. (A. Steyn 73; L.S. Brown 4/60)

Match drawn.

At Cape Town, 6, 7 and 9 December.

Rhodesia — 225 (C.M. Harris 73, J.H.F. Fuller 49; M.A. Hanley 8/55)
and 222 (P.N.F. Mansell 57, C.M. Harris 47, F. McDonald 45, J.H.F. Fuller 35)

Western Province — 136 (D.S. Tomlinson 6/56)
and 313-6 wkts. (C. van Ryneveld 90*, S. Kiel 75, A.D. Keen 63; D.S. Tomlinson 3/107)

Western Province won by 4 wickets.

RHODESIAN TOURING TEAM, 1946-47.
Back: C. Bartles (Manager), C. Pretorius, C. Harris P. Mansell, E. Newson (Captain), D. Tomlinson, N. Dyer, A. Carew, R. Noble, H. Pichanick (Secretary).
Seated: F. McDonald, H. de Grandhomme, L. Brown, J. Fuller (Vice-Captain), M. Napier.

At Kimberley, 13, 14 and 16 December.

Griqualand West — 300 (D.H. Buckley 72, N. Cartwright 61, L.E. McNamara 54; L.S. Brown 6/94)
and 341-8 dec. (L.E. McNamara 94, D.H. Buckley 80, D.S. Tomlinson 3/65)

Rhodesia — 220 (P.N.F. Mansell 57, F. McDonald 41*, M. Napier 40; A. Waddington 5/52)
and 309 (E.S. Newson 114, P.N.F. Mansell 90*, C.M. Harris 35; J.E. Waddington 7/110)

Griqualand West won by 112 runs.

Returning home the Rhodesians began their encounter against Natal in Salisbury on New Year's Day. It was to be a great start to 1947 as well, because in front of a crowd of 3 000 the Rhodesians humbled a powerful Natal side after skipper Dudley Nourse had opted to bat. Denis Tomlinson was in great form and *The Rhodesia Herald* said: 'He was unplayable at times and had the batsmen fumbling for the ball.' A side that contained eight present or future Springboks was back in the pavilion with 166 on the board but the Rhodesians in turn struggled against Ian Smith — Arnold Hyde made three runs in eighty minutes. The home side were in fact sixteen runs behind when their last wicket pair, Forbes McDonald and Alan Carew, came together. Said *The Rhodesia Herald*: 'Salisbury virtually deserted business for an hour and a half yesterday morning to see the last wicket put on 50 runs in an electric finish to the innings which gave Rhodesia a lead of 34 runs. It was the most joyous exhibition seen for many years, including veteran-like batting by number eleven batsman, Carew, who is number eleven in his league team.'

Rain unfortunately ended the match prematurely with Rhodesia 30-2 chasing 245 to win. The Rhodesians had put up a brave battle but could not repeat this effort in Bulawayo where they were annihilated by an innings and 119 runs. The selectors had taken the opportunity to "blood" youngsters in this return "friendly" but some were out of their depth. An exception was the young left-arm spin bowler Peter Johnson who impressed Dudley Nourse in that he retained his length throughout and bowled consistently to his field.

SCORES: versus Natal, 1946-47.

At Salisbury, 1, 2 and 3 January (Currie Cup).

Natal — 166 (D.S. Tomlinson 6/87)
and 278-8 dec. (A.D. Nourse 70, S.H. Martin 69; A.S. Carew 4/69, L.S. Brown 4/86)

Rhodesia — 200 (J.H.F. Fuller 41, F. McDonald 38*; V.I. Smith 5/59)
and 30-2 wkts.

Match drawn.

At Bulawayo, 5, 6 and 7 January.

Rhodesia — 156 (F. McDonald 48)
and 134 (P.N.F. Mansell 34; H.J. Tayfield 6/27)

Natal — 409-6 dec. (D. Fell 161, J.C. Watkins 71, D.V. Dyer 61, S.H. Martin 56)

Natal won by an innings and 119 runs.

A month after the Natal visit, Transvaal arrived to play two matches. The first, a Currie Cup encounter played in Bulawayo, resulted in a draw. Several features of the game are worthy of mention: Lee Walkden, who replaced the unavailable Bob Newson, was also entrusted with the captaincy in his one and only appearance for his country; Ken Austin, described by "Onlooker" in *The Rhodesia Herald* as remaining 'a model for many of the younger generation,' was

RHODESIA v. TRANSVAAL, 1946-47.
Back: J. Buchanan, C. Harris, P. Mansell, A. Carew, K. Curran (12th Man), F. McDonald, M. Napier, R. Hayes.
Seated: Q. Austin, L. Walkden (Captain), D. Tomlinson, J. Fuller.

recalled to the side that he had first represented twenty years previously; and of the game Jimmy Fuller batting at number 6 struck his maiden first-class century.

The second match, although a "friendly" was perhaps more significant in Rhodesia's cricket history as it marked the country's first victory over the Transvaal. With five changes from the Currie Cup combination and "Sandy" Singleton assuming the captaincy, it was a new-look side that saw 300 runs on the board in 275 minutes. Singleton, Fuller, McDonald and Mansell, with a superb 111 not out, all made runs but the excitement had only just begun.

In a totally unexpected manner, the Transvaalers led by Springbok captain, Alan Melville, were routed by the home side for 99 and forced to follow on. Jolted somewhat by the humiliation, the Transvaalers then proceeded to hammer the Rhodesian attack to all parts of the ground and rattled up 410-6 before Melville made what could have been interpreted as a token declaration; 153 runs were required in 85 minutes.

To the delight of the crowd the Rhodesians took up the challenge despite losing their seasoned campaigners, Singleton and Tomlinson, for 12 runs. Forbes McDonald and Percy Mansell plundered the bowling with a daring array of attacking strokes and sent up the 50 in 30 minutes, then accelerated, and the 100 was hoisted in 50 minutes. Mansell celebrated his personal 50 with a six over the leg boundary but at 134 he departed and Hayes and Fuller followed, all having a go, but McDonald was still at the helm.

McDonald and Noble took Rhodesia into the last over with the situation not only exciting but unwittingly a little confusing. The umpires believed incorrectly that Rhodesia required 151 runs but the crowd realised that the target was 153. To the bewilderment therefore of all in the ground the umpires pulled up the stumps after two balls had been bowled in the final over. So back they went, passed the Transvaal total, batted on and Noble skied a playful full toss from Heaney to be caught.

"Thirteenth Man" writing in *The Rhodesia Herald* was most distressed: 'It is to be hoped that the result of the match, being ranked as a first-class game, will not go into *Wisden* and the South African and Rhodesian cricket histories in the form in which the result was apparently accepted here. It is recognized by all recorders and historians of the game that nothing which happens after a match has been completed finds a place in the official records. The last over was an unhappy one and by creating a sense of anticlimax detracted from a magnificent afternoon's cricket. As I saw the picture when Melville declared, the scoreboard showed 408-6 and presumably the umpires took that as the basis of their calculations. It was also the score which was broadcast.'

SCORES: versus Transvaal, 1946-47.

At Bulawayo, 1, 2 and 3 February. (Currie Cup)

Rhodesia — 200 (C.M. Harris 46, R. Hayes 44, F. McDonald 33; L. Heany 6/45)
and 303-7 dec. (J.H.F Fuller 107*, D.S. Tomlinson 50*, P.N.F. Mansell 30)

Transvaal — 221 (A. Melville 69, L. Sadler 50; D.S. Tomlinson 3/62, P.N.F. Mansell 3/24)
and 185-5 wkts. (C. Jones 57, L. Sadler 52; Q.A. Austin 4/51)

Match drawn.

At Salisbury, 7, 8 and 9 February.

Rhodesia — 357 (P.N.F. Mansell 111*, A.P. Singleton 72, F. McDonald 65, J.H.F. Fuller 53; L. Heany 6/69)
and 156-5 wkts. (F. McDonald 72*, P.N.F. Mansell 65)

Transvaal — 99 (A.P. Singleton 4/20, D.S. Tomlinson 4/41)
and 410-6 dec. (A. Melville 74 rt. inj., R. Harrison 73*, B. Shaw 60, R. Wooler 51*; A.P. Singleton 3/84)

Rhodesia won by 5 wickets.

The 1947-48 season began with the arrival in Bulawayo of a side described as a team of "mystery cricketers". Captained by former Rhodesian Nuffield batsman and national rugby player, Bernard Carew, it was in fact a Northern Rhodesian combination that had arrived on tour to play against three of the Southern Rhodesia provincial sides. They were saved by rain with only one wicket standing and after being 121 runs in arrears against Matabeleland, and were well beaten by Midlands and Mashonaland. In the Midlands game they chased leather as they were unable to contain Forbes McDonald who hit a tremendous 180 not out, whilst former Natalian, Hugh Tayfield, returned match figures of 10/91 for Mashonaland.

Tayfield also bowled well in taking 6/25 in the final Rhodesian trial to select the Currie Cup touring team. "Sandy" Singleton was named as the Rhodesian captain with Denis Tomlinson his deputy. The tour party included only six "pukka" Rhodesians in a party of thirteen — Denis Tomlinson, Connie Pretorius, Forbes McDonald, Cecil Harris, Jimmy Fuller and Mark Napier. "Sandy" Singleton came from Britain, Ronnie Hayes was born in Cairo and the remainder were from South Africa. Bob Newson was unfortunately unavailable but a welcome replacement was Syd Martin. Martin had been appointed a Land Development Officer near Enkeldoorn, nearly 100 miles from the nearest cricket centre. A *Rhodesia Herald* report said of the country's latest cricketing addition: 'When he arrived to take up his position he found that only five other Europeans lived in the area and the most educated of the native inhabitants thought that "e-clicket" was essentially an insect. Undismayed, Martin set about doing something about it. With the help of a gang of Africans he levelled out a plot in the bush, laid a foundation of ant heap and ordered a coir mat.' Aided by some rather unorthodox assistants a new game made its appearance in the remote Enkeldoorn district.

Opening the tour in Johannesburg the Rhodesian bowling attack stuck determinedly to their task in their match against Transvaal and limited a powerful batting line-up including seven Springboks — to 305. Unfortunately the visiting batsmen could not match their bowlers' efforts and it was only a battling 28 not out from Jimmy Fuller that helped them to limp to 106. In their defence the pitch did take a lot of spin and the world-rated off-spinner, Athol Rowan, in particular, made the ball lift sharply and turn dangerously. It might have been a rather disheartening situation for the Rhodesians to be in but kind words were issued by Louis Duffus at this stage of the game: 'The team's unfailing zest in the field was one of the best things about the Rhodesian cricket. Other features which struck were Singleton's imaginative generalship, the bowling of ex-Natalians, Martin and Tayfield, and the smooth, efficient wicket-keeping of the 23-year-old Cecil Harris. Martin fell at once into rhythm with accurate seam bowling as though he were in the middle of a pre-War season with the Worcestershire cricket eleven. For the couple of thousand holiday spectators, Martin produced a spell of steady bowling that is perfected by the best professionals in England, but rarely seems acquired by South African bowlers.'

Asked to follow on, the Rhodesians produced an improved second innings display thanks to a defiant partnership between Connie Pretorius and Hugh Tayfield which helped stem the tide after the visitors were 83-6 at lunch. The pair added 130 in 96 minutes for the seventh wicket — Pretorius taking 148 minutes for his century with one six and nine fours. Denis Tomlinson weighed in with an undefeated 31 and Transvaal were forced to bat a second time in order to score the required runs.

A fine win was recorded in Rhodesia's next encounter against North-Eastern Transvaal following a modest start. A face-saving partnership of 139 in their second innings by Syd Martin and Forbes McDonald and two fine bowling performances by Johnny Leibbrandt ensured victory. Set to get 248 to win the match at a run-a-minute, North-Easterns were all out for 211 — a report from Pretoria stating: 'Leibbrandt getting some work on the ball on a wicket which began to show signs of wear was almost unplayable at times. Concentrating on the leg stump, and bowling to a close field of four behind that stump he repeatedly beat both bat and wicket.'

Rhodesia's unpredictable batting unfortunately let them down badly against Border. The varied Rhodesian bowling attack with Tayfield and Singleton prominent, saw the home side bowled out twice reasonably cheaply and Rhodesia required a mere 179 runs in the end. After a terrific 4½-hour duel the Rhodesians fell short by 12 runs although Brown and Tomlinson for a time looked as though they might pull it off whilst adding 44 for the ninth wicket.

In their final tour fixture Rhodesia never recovered after losing three early wickets to Natal's fiery teenage opening bowler, Cuan McCarthy. The Rhodesians were bundled out twice in reply to Natal's 353 and lost by an innings and 43 runs. Once again it was an inability on the part of the batsmen to score runs and it is significant to point out that on tour no more than three batsmen ever came off in the same match.

Tour post-mortems revealed four major problems for the failures:

1) Poor fielding through wild returns to wicket and dropped catches — only against Transvaal were the Rhodesians on their toes.

2) Although the opening bowlers kept a good line and length and were economical, they only once succeeded in breaking up an opening partnership.

3) The team had little opportunity for net practices on account of the unsuitable state of the wickets as the result of rain which obviously militated against the success of certain batsmen.

4) Impetuosity on the part of the batsmen accounted for too many failures.

HUGH TAYFIELD.

On the brighter side were Singleton's excellent captaincy and bowling; the model exhibitions of stroke play by Martin; Leibbrandt and Tayfield's bowling; the first-class arrangements throughout the tour where entertainment, transport and accommodation were concerned. Summing up, the manager Jack Elsworth, said: 'The time has definitely come when we should start building up our team for the future.'

SCORES: Currie Cup Tour, 1947-48.

At Johannesburg, 1, 2 and 3 January.
Transvaal — 305 (D.W. Begbie 80, G.W.A. Chubb 54; H.J. Tayfield 5/94, S.H. Martin 3/47)
and 76-0 wkts. (E.A.B. Rowan 50*)
Rhodesia — 106 (A.M.B. Rowan 7/40)
and 272 (C.J. Pretorius 104, H.J. Tayfield 48, D.S. Tomlinson 31*)
Transvaal won by 10 wickets.

At Pretoria, 5, 6 and 7 January.
Rhodesia — 188 (C.J. Pretorius 67, F. McDonald 38)
and 285-8 dec. (S.H. Martin 87, F. McDonald 68)
North-Eastern Transvaal — 226 (J. Seccombe 114; J.M. Leibbrandt 4/43)
and 211 (H. Jordaan 67; J.M. Leibbrandt 5/56)
Rhodesia won by 36 runs.

At East London, 10, 12 and 13 January.
Border — 180 (G. Wienand 51; H.J. Tayfield 6/47, A.P. Singleton 3/20)
and 208 (M. Adey 53, K.N. Kirton 50*; A.P. Singleton 3/40, H.J. Tayfield 3/47)

RHODESIAN TOURING TEAM, 1947-48.
Back: J. Leibbrandt, J. Buchanan, R. Hayes, C. Harris, L. Brown, F. McDonald, M. Napier, J. Fuller, D. Tomlinson, C. Pretorius.
Front: S. Martin, A.P. Singleton (Captain), J. Elsworth (Manager), B. Brand (Assistant Manager).

Rhodesia — 210 (S.H. Martin 78, A.P. Singleton 44, C.J. Pretorius 39)
and 167 (L.S. Brown 44*, C.M. Harris 30; D. Woods 5/54)

Border won by 11 runs.

At Durban, 17, 18 and 19 January.

Natal — 353 (W.W. Wade 107, D. Dowling 71, A.D. Nourse 58; A.P. Singleton 5/58, H.J. Tayfield 3/66)

Rhodesia — 129 (L.A. Markham 5/40)
and 181 (S.H. Martin 55, A.P. Singleton 43)

Natal won by an innings and 43 runs.

On the Rhodesian side's return from South Africa they were pitched straight into the Logan Cup semi-finals and at the Raylton ground, Bulawayo, 19-year-old Kevin Curran beat Jimmy Fuller's Logan Cup record of 188 by scoring 201 not out for Matabeleland against Midlands in an innings of seasoned restraint. His reward was a place in the Rhodesian side to play against Western Province in their end-of-season Currie Cup fixture in Salisbury. Mashonaland's Bob Newson also made a welcome return to the national team after humbling the Manicaland side by registering match figures of 13/26.

At the Salisbury Sports Club on an easy-paced wicket, Rhodesia made a poor start against Western Province and were 42-5 before Connie Pretorius and Kevin Curran brightened up proceedings in a partnership of 104. Newcomer Curran was left undefeated on 52 with Rhodesia all out for 173 — a meagre score which suddenly jumped in value as Province were dismissed for 165. Unfortunately the Rhodesians did not take full advantage of their unexpected lead, despite another fighting knock by Curran in their second innings, and lost by three wickets in bad light with only two minutes of play left. The fun really began at five o'clock when 48 runs were needed in the last 35 minutes — said a *Rhodesia Herald* report: 'The fielders also had a difficult time. There were many occasions when they did not see the ball until it had passed them in the poor light.'

Western Province stayed on to play a Combined Mashonaland/Manicaland Farmers XI but even though 'an attempt was made to continue playing although the players should have been wearing rain-coats' the match was finally abandoned in the early afternoon.

SCORES: Western Province Tour, 1947-48.

At Salisbury, 5, 6 and 8 March (Currie Cup).

Rhodesia — 173 (C. Pretorius 72, K.P. Curran 52*; E. Witte 5/70)
and 187 (A.P. Singleton 36, K.P. Curran 35)

Western Province — 165 (J. M. Leibbrandt 3/54) and 198-7 wkts. (J.M. Leibbrandt 4/78, E.S. Newson 3/46)

Western Province won by 5 wickets.

At Salisbury, 9 March (Not first-class).

Western Province — 234 (B. Crews 73, I. Burmeister 54; I. Grimmer 3/58)

Farmers XI — 13-3 wkts.

Match drawn.

To serve as a trial to select players for the matches against the visiting 1948-49 M.C.C. tourists, a Southern Rhodesian team travelled by train to Nkana to play Northern Rhodesia and unexpectedly were given a fright by their northerly neighbours. Only a fighting second innings partnership of 135 by Theo Passaportis and Hugh Tayfield, plus good bowling by the latter, saw the Southerners to a 54-run win in the end.

SCORES: versus Northern Rhodesia, 1948-49.

At Nkana, 20 and 21 October (Not first-class).

Southern Rhodesia — 157 (O. Harrison 68) and 250 (T.L. Passaportis 97*, H.J. Tayfield 73)

Northern Rhodesia — 213 (B.J. Carew 92*, D. Borland 65; T. Anderson 5/91, H.J. Tayfield 3/79) and 140 (B.J. Carew 67; H.J. Tayfield 6/61)

Southern Rhodesia won by 54 runs.

Connie Pretorius, who had been unavailable for this match, indicated to the selectors that he was in fine form when he beat Kev Currans's newly set Logan Cup record for the highest individual score, compiling 206 not out for Mashonaland against Manicaland. Demonstrating the Mashonas' superiority was the fact that they blasted 434 runs on the Saturday afternoon in 220 minutes.

Syd Martin was elected as the new Rhodesian captain against the M.C.C. at the end of January in Bulawayo. Under him he had a side that batted down to number 11 — in order it read: Singleton, Harris, Martin, Carew, Pretorius, Newson, McDonald, Curran, Franklin, Mansell and Tayfield. The only newcomer was Bernard Carew, who had clinched his selection with two fine innings for Northern Rhodesia against their southern counterparts.

Prior to their first match in Bulawayo, the M.C.C. visited the Victoria Falls where they were given a noon-day garden party by Sergeant Stonier of the B.S.A.P. Revelling in the holiday atmosphere they sat about the party in Tarzan-like costumes having earlier in the day tramped through the Rain Forest and experienced the thrill of being paddled across to Cataract Island on the brink of the chasm in canoes. Said one excited cricketer: 'When I learned about the Zambezi at school I never thought I'd go across it in a canoe.'

Louis Duffus who accompanied the team wrote vividly of the trip: 'They ate mangoes, sunbathed on the lawn, took pictures and relaxed with refreshment. This visit in which they have resembled the exuberance of schoolboys should remain the most memorable of field experiences of their tour. The day before, after laughter and competitive pushing of the railway trolley, they went seven and a half miles up the river by launch, saw crocodiles, a very distant view of hippos, inspected the flying boat that had just touched down on its way to England and fed monkeys on Kandahar Island.'

In Bulawayo there was a crowd of 6 000 to greet George Mann's side when they took to the field. Surrounding rainstorms only encroached once to cause a brief interruption but after a useful opening partnership of 52 by Singleton and Harris the Rhodesian batsmen came and went at regular intervals although the bowling was never venomous. Towards the end Kevin Curran (16 not out) kept one end intact whilst "Bebe" Franklin (26) and Percy Mansell (17) hit out to see Rhodesia to 174.

The illustrious visiting batting line-up also found run-making difficult. Chiefly due to the dynamic bowling of the 38-year-old Bob Newson who delivered the ball with great pace and used a rain-affected pitch to good effect, Rhodesia succeeded in dismissing the M.C.C. for the lowest total so far on their tour (193). In fact in a spell of four overs Newson dismissed five of the tourists for five runs before Jenkins and Gladwin

RHODESIA v. M.C.C., 1948-49 (BULAWAYO).
Left to right: S. Martin (Captain), B. Newson, H. Tayfield, C. Pretorius, A. Singleton, B. Franklin, C. Harris, T. Lange (12th Man), B. Carew, P. Mansell, F. McDonald, K. Curran.

Kevin Curran walks out to bat against the M.C.C. at Bulawayo, 1948-49.

consolidated in a rescue eighth wicket partnership of 73.

With the match in an intriguing position the Rhodesians battled in their second innings to set the tourists a reasonable target. Jack Young was difficult to get away — he conceded a mere 29 runs in 27 eight-ball overs — whilst Denis Compton "bought" wickets from the other end. The promising Kevin Curran made top score of 36 in a total of 166 which meant the M.C.C. had the whole of the last afternoon to make 148. But their efforts were to no avail as heavy downpours ruined any chance of a result.

The rain continued in Salisbury and limited play on the first day to 2½ hours during which Len Hutton scored a polished 67 not out. He was dropped early by Cecil Harris but the highly rated Rhodesian 'keeper made up for it the following day by catching the great Yorkshireman on 79 and had a hand in four other dismissals. He caught Denis Compton off Singleton for 34, Alan Watkins off Newson for 14, stumped skipper, George Mann, off Martin for 32 and then gave Godfrey Evans a dose of his own medicine by stumping him, again off Martin, for a "duck". Rhodesia treated a second-day crowd of 8 000 to some great cricket in restricting the M.C.C. to 228 with Syd Martin returning the outstanding analysis of 28-9-49-6.

Sadly, a lamentable batting display followed and only Martin in an undefeated captain's knock of 27 offered any serious resistance to Alec Bedser who produced one of the finest exhibitions of fast-medium bowling ever seen in this country. The perplexed Rhodesians were just not up to the task as the famous Surrey man tore the heart out of their batting. Their meagre 61 was the lowest total score made against the M.C.C. on tour and they were forced to follow on, 167 runs behind.

With no play possible until three o'clock on the last afternoon, Rhodesia batted out the remaining 155 minutes and to an extent redeemed themselves by adding another 174 runs to their overnight total of 17-1. Kevin Curran and Connie Pretorius put on 110 for the third wicket with the latter's 75 including two sixes, both off Jack Young, and six fours. It was a greatly improved display against an English side that went through their southern African tour unbeaten in a 23-match programme and won the Test series 2-0.

Despite rain interference the M.C.C. visit to Rhodesia generated enormous enthusiasm for the game and Louis Duffus wrote after the Salisbury match: 'There is an air of enterprise and progress about this part of Rhodesia and if it should be granted a Test match, the zeal of Mashonaland would ensure its success. If I had to select the most pleasant atmosphere outside of Newlands in which the M.C.C. have played their matches I would choose this Salisbury Sports Club ground, where bronzed farmers and red-coated schoolboys sat around the green between tall trees; where no one shouted "how's that?" because a bowler appealed too often but instead asked each other, "How's your crop?"; where spectators could inspect the pitch with impunity; where flags and marquee tents and a scoreboard modelled in miniature on the telegraph of Ellis Park made it a setting to remember with relish.'

Alec and Eric Bedser also mentioned the avid interest in cricket in the capital city in their book *Our Cricket Story*: 'The Rhodesians treated us grandly, and Salisbury — a town which has doubled its European population in ten years — was in the grip of cricket fever. Harry Pichanick, the Rhodesian secretary, spared no effort to make the M.C.C.'s visit memorable and the hospitality reached a new high level. All the government offices were closed and the non-cricket-minded citizens (of whom there seemed to be few) gave up all thoughts of business while the M.C.C. were there.'

SCORES: M.C.C. Tour, 1948-49.

At Bulawayo, 29 and 31 January and 1 February.

Rhodesia — 174 (A.P. Singleton 38; J.A. Young 4/39, R. Jenkins 4/78)
and 166 (K.P. Curran 36, S.H. Martin 32; J.A. Young 4/29, D.C.S. Compton 4/51)

M.C.C. — 193 (D.C.S. Compton 60; E.S. Newson 5/54, A.P. Singleton 3/29)
and 117-2 wkts.

Match drawn.

At Salisbury, 4, 5 and 7 February.

M.C.C. — 228 (L. Hutton 79; S.H. Martin 6/49, E.S. Newson 3/108)

Rhodesia — 61 (S.H. Martin 27*; A.V. Bedser 6/17, C. Gladwin 4/37)
and 191-5 wkts. (C.J. Pretorius 75, K.P. Curran 37)

Match drawn.

In the last match of the 1948-49 season, Bob Newson achieved the outstanding all-round "double" in Mashonaland League cricket. In an encounter between Mashonaland and The Rest, Newson had Alex Tait caught behind by wicket-keeper, Billy Kidd, to notch his hundredth wicket, having already scored 1 000 runs. He won a bat as a prize for his performance which at the end of the game stood at 1 069 runs (average 56,26) and 102 wickets (average 11,00).

As did their predecessors fourteen years before, the 1949-50 Australians strode undefeated through their tour, winning four of the Tests with one drawn. The Rhodesians, realizing the momentous task ahead, assembled in Bulawayo several days prior to their encounter with the tourists. It was perhaps with the famous Australian opening bowler Ray Lindwall in mind that the Rhodesian selectors saw it advisable to include a fair sprinkling of opening batsmen in the team. Six were included — Harris, Singleton, De Grandhomme, Martin, Baldwin and Leibbrandt — with the first two named doing duty.

By the end of the opening day the Australians were in command — 86-0 wickets chasing Rhodesia's 166 all out. Louis Duffus commented: 'Most of the Rhodesians playing in the match against the Australian cricket tourists here today were either overawed or grossly underrated their batting ability.

'The sponge in the wicket absorbed all the life from the bowling of Lindwall and Walker and though its

"Bebe" Franklin walks out to bat against the M.C.C. at Salisbury, 1948-49.

brittle edges gave the ball plenty of spin, particularly from the hand of Colin McCool, it came off too slowly to worry good batsmen. In fact this was the most unsympathetic of the tour pitches the Australians have bowled on.

'Sandy Singleton and John Wallace showed the best class of batsmanship. Both are stylish players generously equipped with strokes, and Singleton revived in the adventures and certainty of his shots some of the skill of the years when his cricket reached full bloom on Worcester's mellow field beside the River Severn. Like many batsmen before him and others who will follow, he played too soon to Ian Johnson's subtly delayed flight and was whipped away like a hotel's morning marmalade, just when you had a taste for some more.

'Wallace went on to make top score of 38 not out with graceful, correct strokes. Judged by Australian standards he is perhaps too correct. It would be harsh to chide young Jeremy Baldwin for taking nearly two hours to score 16 in his first provincial match but he is too good a bat to treat so many loose balls, as he did, with leniency. The whole tone of the innings was tempered by too much soft pedal. All the conditions — the dead wicket, the moderate bowling, and the high temperature — cried out for a swashbuckler, someone with venturesome feet to take a few risks and his life in his hands.

'Now that the Australians have been revealed as human and fallible it may be different in the second innings.'

Rhodesia's fortunes did not improve and they had to wait until the Australians' score reached 210 before they claimed their first wicket. Test openers, Arthur Morris and Jack Moroney, both made centuries and Sam Loxton and skipper, Lindsay Hassett, played useful supporting knocks. Mansell nevertheless bowled well and claimed 6/89 in the Australian total of 398.

Many felt Rhodesia erred in their second innings by not placing Newson (number 9) and Leibbrandt (number 10 — 20 not out) higher up in the order. One was left with the impression that nothing would have been lost if these two had been sent in earlier to attempt to hit the grip out of the bowling. Duffus said of the towering Leibbrandt, who used to be considered a batsman for Eastern Province: 'He employed his long reach to move out to the ball, played drives in classic style, hit a terrific six and was wasted at number 10.'

All out for 71 in their second innings, Rhodesia found the skills of Ian Johnson and Colin McCool on the crumbling clay too much for them, although a number of the batsmen contributed to their own downfalls through a fateful urge to play back. Duffus wrote: 'A couple were bowled without making strokes at the ball, a third hit his wicket, and finally Sandy Singleton dismissed himself through a gesture that smacked of ethics learned at Shrewsbury and Oxford. Given not out from the bowler's end he asked the square leg umpire if the ball was caught at slip and that official raised his finger. Technically the decision should have been up the wicket, but there was no doubt that it was correct.'

SCORES: versus Australia, 1949-50.

At Bulawayo, 11 and 12 November.

Rhodesia — 166 (J.H.A. Wallace 38*, S.H. Martin 30) and 71 (I. Johnson 5/24)

Australia — 398 (A.R. Morris 104, J.M. Moroney 104, S.J.E. Loxton 76, A.L. Hassett 66*; P.N.F. Mansell 6/89)

Australia won by an innings and 161 runs.

Later in the week a South African XI played against the Australians in Salisbury giving Rhodesians an opportunity of seeing some of southern Africa's top young cricketers in action against the tourists. Interest in this match like the previous one was tremendous and made the Australian visit very worthwile. In Bulawayo 7 800 people watched the two days — gate receipts were £1 400 and, despite the loss of a day, a profit of nearly £600 was made. In Salisbury 20 000 people paid over £3 700 with the Saturday crowd of 10 000 being an all-time record.

Arthur Mailey, the former Australian Test player, made these sketches during the 1949-50 match at Bulawayo.

Two Rhodesians, Kev Curran and Cecil Harris, were named in the South African XI whilst Louis Duffus noted John Wallace and Percy Mansell as being unlucky not to have been chosen. However, Wallace and Mansell both gained selection in South African XIs that played the Australians later in the season. It might be noted here that an injury to Athol Rowan enabled Hugh Tayfield to be given a chance in the Test series. Tayfield, who had left Rhodesia at the end of the previous season for the Transvaal, was one of the few Springboks to emerge from the series with credit and bewildered the Australians in the Third Test with his flighted off-breaks to take 7/23 in eight overs and four balls.

The Salisbury match between the Australians and a South African XI was somewhat one-sided to be a great spectacle with the visitors winning by an innings and 72 runs. Lindwall's bowling (match figures of 16-5-22-7) was a decisive factor and a *Rhodesia Herald* report commented: 'Whenever he came on to bowl the batsmen seemed to be hanging on by a thread.'

Other than the annual match against Northern Rhodesia, cricket supporters had to wait until March the following year before the national side again faced outside opposition. The fixture against Northern Rhodesia at Old Hararians did provide entertaining cricket and the Southerners, set 133 in 75 minutes won by two wickets through Syd Martin hitting a six from the third ball of the last over.

SCORES: versus Northern Rhodesia, 1949-50.

At Salisbury, 28 and 29 January (Not first-class).

Northern Rhodesia — 102 (S. Martin 8/33) and 134 (A.S. Carew 5/37, P.N.F. Mansell 4/41)

Southern Rhodesia — 98-5 dec. (P.N.F. Mansell 45*) and 139-8 wkts. (P.N.F. Mansell 43, R. Ashburner 31)

Southern Rhodesia won by 2 wickets.

A Transvaal side toured towards the end of the 1949-50 season. Captained by Eric Rowan and including the famous Springbok batsman Bruce Mitchell, they were a young team sprinkled generously with up-and-coming stars such as Paul Winslow, Scotch Taylor and Russell Endean. Said the team manager Ken Viljoen: 'Our side is an efficient one and is the youngest ever to have gone on tour.'

They played three fixtures at different venues on their short tour. The first match was a two-day affair against Rhodesia at the Queens ground Bulawayo. Only Syd Martin looked at home against the Transvaal attack and his dismissal in the Rhodesian second innings when he mis-hit a short ball to be caught by Winslow for 38 was the turning-point of the match. Transvaal, left to make 102, coasted home by nine wickets.

The good and the bad in Rhodesian cricket were evident to the full in Rhodesia's three-day match against the Transvaalers in Salisbury. Having dismissed the visitors for 270, rank bad batting saw Rhodesia flatter a sound but never devastating Transvaal attack. All out for 64, the Rhodesians followed on and in an innings of fluctuating fortunes totalled 392 which in the end very nearly brought them a surprise victory.

The Rhodesian second innings was dominated by two century-partnerships with both featuring the Northern Rhodesian batsman, Bernard Carew. A study of caution in an innings of five hours, Carew added 121 for the fifth wicket with Bob Newson and then put on a further 131 runs in 105 minutes for the seventh wicket with "Bebe" Franklin. Franklin was in an aggressive mood and was overhauling Carew

Kevin Curran is stumped by Gil Langley off the bowling of Bill Johnston against the 1949-50 Australians.

rapidly in their association, scoring 94 runs whilst the latter contributed only 27.

With Mitchell demonstrating the technique and judgement that made him South Africa's most prolific run maker in Test history, Transvaal held on to draw the match before moving on to Gatooma for their third tour fixture against a Rhodesia XI. Possibly because the small rural village of Gatooma had not seen a cricket match of any consequence for many years an unpredictable pitch was prepared. It was described as '. . . an Australian substitute wicket, a wet mixture of clay and cut grass rolled out in layers on a brick base; before games a little grass is rolled into the patches on the pitch where needed. The wicket is then wet and rolled and ready for play.'

Play began with the pitch damp and the ball popping in a disconcerting manner. Hence six wickets were down for four runs before Denis Austin, "Bundu" Waller and the tail-enders hit out to take the Rhodesia XI to 113. The wicket certainly appeared to ease out in the course of the game as Transvaal raced to 260 with Paul Winslow slamming his first 50 runs in 25 minutes before being bowled out by Peter Johnson for 70. Further proof of the improvement in the batting conditions came on the second day as the Rhodesians likewise climbed into the bowling with confidence.

Roy Ashburner in an enterprising innings of 151, reached his hundred in two hours despite a couple of lucky escapes and proceeded to add 120 runs in 72 minutes with John Kitcat. The Rhodesian rugby full back and Springbok trialist, Kitcat punished the slow bowlers severely with powerful hooks and attacking shots off the back foot in his 66. But even the gallant efforts of these two were not enough to prevent Transvaal knocking off the 162 runs required by the end of the second day.

SCORES: Transvaal Tour, 1949-50.

At Bulawayo, 11 and 12 March.
Rhodesia — 141 (S. Martin 45)
and 112 (S. Martin 38; R. Furniss 7/38)
Transvaal — 152 (J.M. Leibbrandt 3/33)
and 107-1 wkt.
Transvaal won by 9 wickets.

At Salisbury, 18, 19 and 20 March.
Transvaal — 270 (E.A.B. Rowan 52; E.S. Newson 3/30, A.S. Carew 3/73)
and 135-7 wkts. (B. Mitchell 48*; S. Martin 3/41)
Rhodesia — 64
and 392 (B.J. Carew 107, C.D. Franklin 101*, E.S. Newson 56, R.W. Ashburner 46, S.H. Martin 44)
Match drawn.

At Gatooma, 22 and 23 March (Not first-class).
Rhodesia XI — 113 (D. Austin 49, N. Waller 30; R. Furniss 6/35)
and 305 (R.W. Ashburner 151, J. de W. Kitcat 66; D.A. Clark 8/87)
Transvaal — 260 (E.A.B. Rowan 85, P.L. Winslow 70, O. Grinaker 53; P. Johnson 6/78)
and 162-3 wkts. (O. Grinaker 59, R. Kimber 53*)
Transvaal won by 7 wickets.

After the M.C.C. and Australian tours during the two previous seasons, the Currie Cup competition resumed in 1950-51. "Bebe" Franklin was named as Rhodesia's captain for their opening encounter of the season against North-Eastern Transvaal at the Salisbury Sports Club and the selectors named one new cap, Michael Wakefield, a left-arm medium-pace bowler who had learnt his cricket in England where he played for Oxfordshire. Unfortunately, Wakefield was unavailable, never to get another chance, and was replaced by the former Nuffield star, Howard Montgomery who bowled well in his only Rhodesian appearance.

A great recovery saw Rhodesia snatch a victory over North-Eastern Transvaal, having trailed by 128 runs on the first innings and being set 295 runs to win. Beginning their attempt at the required target ten minutes before lunch on the second day they began badly, losing a wicket almost immediately. But Wallace in a flawless exhibition of controlled batting, stroked a match-winning century, well supported by Franklin, Connie Pretorius and Percy Mansell.

SCORES: versus North-Eastern Transvaal, 1950-51 (Currie Cup).

At Salisbury, 18, 19 and 20 November.

North-Eastern Transvaal — 251 (H.C. Woolley 63, P. Davidson 63; P.N.F Mansell 7/112, A.S. Carew 3/43)
and 166 (H.H. Montgomery 3/13, A.S. Carew 3/26, P.N.F. Mansell 3/57)

Rhodesia — 123 (R.W. Ashburner 32; H.V. Paton 5/34)
and 297-7 wkts. (J.H.A. Wallace 109, P.N.F. Mansell 65*, C.J. Pretorius 49)

Rhodesia won by 3 wickets.

A controversial situation arose prior to the next Currie Cup encounter. Matabeleland thrashed Mashonaland with their galaxy of Rhodesian players by an innings and 58 runs in the Logan Cup final. Yet Mashonaland gained six players in the national side as well as the 12th man who was the dropped skipper, "Bebe" Franklin — *The Rhodesia Herald* commented at the time: 'The team will not meet with unanimous approval.'

Transvaal carried far too many guns for Rhodesia — Eric Rowan led the assault on the attack and hit 176 out of the first 288 runs before Peter Johnson caught him off his own bowling. In a one-sided affair Transvaal rattled up 445 to win easily by an innings as only Percy Mansell held up an end for any length of time during his two visits to the crease. With Michael Melle always hostile and Geoff Chubb immaculate in length and direction, Rhodesia's lack of a pace attack was in contrast patently obvious. Mansell's two knocks of 46 and 59 brought apt comment in an article in *The Rhodesia Herald*: 'There is something correct and almost schoolmasterish in the way Mansell goes about his batting which heightens those occasional brilliant flashes when he seems to revolt against the slow pace of scoring and sends the ball sailing high into the crowd.'

SCORES: versus Transvaal, 1950-51 (Currie Cup).

At Salisbury, 2, 3 and 4 December.

Transvaal — 445 (E.A.B. Rowan 176, A.D. Pinkerton 64, J.H. Ward 61, M.G. Melle 50; P.N.F. Mansell 3/117)

Rhodesia — 153(P.N.F. Mansell 46; G.W.A. Chubb 5/35)
and 151 (P.N.F. Mansell 59; D.A. Clark 5/59)

Transvaal won by an innings and 141 runs.

Prior to the Rhodesian side beginning their Currie Cup tour they had a two-day practice match against the University of Cape Town. Indeed it was a young Rhodesian side that had been selected for the tour, average age 25 with Johnny Leibbrandt the eldest at 30, and their performance against the U.C.T. side provided a good send-off.

SCORES: At Bulawayo, 16 and 17 December, 1950-51.

Rhodesia — 106 (J.H.A. Wallace 41; D. Wills 5/21)
and 213-5 dec. (P.N.F. Mansell 47, C.J. Pretorius 44)

U.C.T. — 62 (J.M. Leibbrandt 6/25, D. Murray 3/32)
and 93-6 wkts. (A.S. Carew 3/20)

Match drawn.

The Rhodesians began their tour in Cape Town where half-centuries from Pretorius and Leibbrandt saw them gain a first innings lead over Western Province. Unfortunately they could only muster 161 in their second innings and Province won by six wickets. Yet it was not through lack of trying — the team was given a good start with an opening partnership of 57 which came in 82 minutes, whilst new cap John Sierra laboured determinedly for 149 minutes for his 29, accompanied by inevitable barracking.

The first day of the match against Eastern Province at Port Elizabeth was washed out but there was still sufficient time for Springbok "Tufty" Mann (5/55 and 7/47) to pave the way for the home team's victory. Only Sierra came to terms with the bowling in Rhodesia's first innings, compiling a workmanlike 62. And in their second effort Dave Rees and Alan Carew prevented a complete fiasco with a rapidly struck ninth wicket partnership of 63 — Rees hit one six clean over the grandstand which necessitated another ball being brought on.

Outplayed in their first two matches the Rhodesians came back with a vengeance in Kimberley against Griqualand West. They hammered 473 with Connie Pretorius left undefeated on 140, made in a little over six hours. But for sheer entertainment value Dave Rees's 84 in eighty minutes made out of a partnership of 112 with Pretorius, was the highlight. The Rhodesians nevertheless had to battle hard to get Griquas out twice, particularly as they missed a number of chances but they did eventually ensure that they returned home with one victory under their belts.

SCORES: Currie Cup Tour, 1950-51.

At Cape Town, 22, 23 and 26 December.

Rhodesia — 235 (C.J. Pretorius 54, J.M. Leibbrandt 50, P.N.F. Mansell 33; R. Delport 7/54)
and 161 (J.M.S. Baldwin 34, J.H.A. Wallace 31; S.A. Thwaits 6/29)

Western Province — 221 (P.N.F. Mansell 7/78)
and 176-4 wkts. (J.E. Cheetham 63)

Western Province won by 6 wickets.

At Port Elizabeth, 30 December, 1 and 2 January.

Rhodesia — 178 (J.P. Sierra 62; N.B.F. Mann 5/55)
and 146 (D. Rees 45; N.B.F. Mann 7/47)

Eastern Province — 289-9 dec. (S.D. du Toit 65, G. Johnstone 52; P. Johnson 3/43, A.S. Carew 3/57)
and 36-1 wkt.

Eastern Province won by 9 wickets.

At Kimberley, 5, 6 and 8 January.

Rhodesia — 473 (C.J. Pretorius 140*, D. Rees 84, P.N.F. Mansell 62, J.M.S. Baldwin 53, J.H.A. Wallace 33, C.M. Harris 32)
and 88-5 wkts. (P.N.F. Mansell 39)

Griqualand West — 273 (C.D. Helfrich 86; P. Johnson 4/44, P.N.F. Mansell 4/86)
and 287 (C. Dickens 105; J.M. Leibbrandt 5/48)

Rhodesia won by 5 wickets.

On their return Rhodesia played against Border without Mansell, Wallace, Pretorius and Harris who were unable to play. In came the promising Marshall Davies, former Transvaaler Johnny Roothman, the 17-year-old Plumtree schoolboy Tony Pithey and Ian Grimmer, rated at the time as the fastest bowler in the country. A year later Pithey was to score a century off the Border attack for the South African Schools XI but on this occasion was caught with his total at 10. Play was affected by rain throughout but Border gained a first innings victory despite Dave Rees's punishing century made in 118 minutes and including seven sixes and eight fours. Rees came in with the score at 65-5 and almost carried the Rhodesians to their target, aided by Johnny Leibbrandt and Peter Johnson.

PERCY MANSELL.

SCORES: versus Border, 1950-51 (Currie Cup).

At Bulawayo, 19, 20 and 21 January.

Border — 259 (C. Kirton 99; P. Johnson 5/70, A.S. Carew 3/72)
and 30-0 wkt.

Rhodesia — 234 (D. Rees 105)

Match drawn.

One last major fixture remained to end off the season which saw Southern Rhodesia just fail to gain an outright victory over their northern counterparts. It did give former Plumtree schoolboys, Marshall Davies and Jeremy Baldwin, an opportunity to display their talents which augured well for the following season.

SCORES: versus Northern Rhodesia, 1950-51.

At Nkana, 25 and 26 March (Not first-class).

Southern Rhodesia — 289 (M.W. Davies 97, J.M.S. Baldwin 61, Griffiths 39*)
and 194 (J. Dell 51, M.W. Davies 37; B.J. Carew 5/63)

Northern Rhodesia — 214 (I. Grimmer 5/62)
and 127-9 (J.M.S. Baldwin 6/43)

Match drawn.

The 1950-51 season had been a triumph for Percy Mansell. Finishing with 345 runs and 27 wickets in five Currie Cup matches, he was invited to the final Springbok trial from 15-19 February. This was a twelve-a-side affair and although Mansell made an unlucky 13 with the bat, his bowling analysis of 5/101 in 29,5 overs was good enough to earn him a place in Dudley Nourse's 1951 Springbok touring side to England.

In terms of results the tour was disappointing as South Africa lost the series 1-3 but the side was beset by many misfortunes and England's victory margin flattered them. On tour, Mansell played in 20 first-class matches, scoring 504 runs at an average of 21,91 with three half-centuries. He also claimed 29 wickets at 36,55 apiece, his best being 5/37 in 26 overs against Glamorgan. But his greatest moment came when he made his Test debut in the Fourth Test at Headingley, Leeds. Coming in at number 7 he attacked the bowling from the start to reach his half-century in 75 minutes. Eventually being dismissed for 90 made in 165 minutes, Mansell hit seventeen fours and came within ten runs of being the first South African to score a century on his Test debut.

The 1951-52 season got off to a flying start in Johannesburg when Len Brown led a Rhodesian Farmers XI against an ex-Springboks side. Unfortunately, the Farmers XI — in batting order Stedall, Bourdillon, Smale, Bentley, McDonald, Brown, Parker, Orford, Guthrie, Staunton and Middleton — started badly and never recovered. First Bob Crisp and then Buster Nupen, both more rotund than in their heyday, grabbed early wickets and the Rhodesians crumbled to be all out for 53. Former Springbok stars, Alan Melville (3) and Syd Curnow (9), went cheaply in reply but Bruce Mitchell (69) and double Springbok, Tony Harris, saw them out of trouble.

Northern Rhodesia visited early in the season to be well beaten by a Southern Rhodesian side that scored 373 in better-than-even time. Dave Rees slammed a characteristic century but like his team-mates had to treat Henry Moll's bowling with respect. In a remarkably sustained performance for a man of 44 years, Moll took 6/137 in 35,7 eight-ball overs on an unresponsive pitch and suffered indignity only when bowling his last overs to batsmen under orders to 'get on or get out'. An interesting selection in the Southern Rhodesian side was that of Springbok spin-bowler, "Fish" Markham who played against England in 1948-49. He scored 26 and bowled a steady line but did not gain selection for the Rhodesian team named after the match.

SCORES: versus Northern Rhodesia, 1951-52.

At Salisbury, 10 and 11 November (Not first-class).

Southern Rhodesia — 373 (D. Rees 133, J.M.S. Baldwin 50, D.J. Lewis 49; H. de V. Moll 6/137)

Northern Rhodesia — 161 (O. Harrison 67; P. Anderson 3/31)
and 98 (C.R.D. Wooler 5/19, D. Walters 4/18)

Southern Rhodesia won by an innings and 114 runs.

Both Charles Wooler and Derek Walters, the two opening bowlers who had run through Northern Rhodesia, were named in the national side for the first Currie Cup encounter against Orange Free State. Wooler, who was selected for the South African Schools XI in 1949, had signed on as a professional for Leicestershire soon afterwards. He had always had an ambition to play county cricket and a Leicestershire player, Vic Jackson, who was watching the Nuffield tournament had recommended Wooler to his county chairman.

In a high-scoring match Rhodesia made a bad start against Free State, losing by 55 runs having led by 15 runs on the first innings. An inexplicable batting collapse in the second innings when they lost the first six wickets for 57 runs led to their defeat despite a brave repair job by Cecil Harris (who hit a maiden first-class century) and Johnny Leibbrandt who helped add 106 for the seventh wicket.

The selectors reacted by dropping skipper Ronnie Hayes and two others, with Dave Rees taking over the captaincy aided by Percy Mansell as his deputy, and David Lewis returning from his university studies to bolster the batting. The Rhodesian performance improved against Griquas, admittedly a far weaker combination than the Free State side. The all-round talents of Mansell saw Rhodesia firmly in the driving seat when rain washed out the last day's play. The groundsman at Salisbury Sports Club was unfortunately on leave during this game and the voluntary ground official who replaced him was busy at his office when a storm caused considerable damage to an uncovered part of the pitch.

CHARLES WOOLER.

Rhodesia made a bad start to their Christmas tour and were well beaten by Border. But they picked up valuable points against North-Eastern Transvaal thanks to a brilliant all-round performance by the bespectacled Percy Mansell. Rhodesia's newly-made Springbok was not out in both his innings — 94 not out and 13 not out — in addition to returning match bowling figures of 10/150. This was the first and remains the only case of a Rhodesian scoring 100 runs and taking 10 wickets in a match. To achieve this feat is in fact a great deal less common than is generally supposed and invariably turns out to be a match-winning performance. During the 1950s, for example, it was achieved a mere eight times in first-class cricket in the entire world — five of these occasions being in county matches. If one studies Percy Mansell's accomplishments during this period it can be seen that his achievements were quite exceptional.

With their tails up the Rhodesians then turned the tables on Free State to win by 34 runs at the Ramblers ground. Most noteworthy in the Rhodesian triumph was a fine second innings of 90 by David Lewis who was involved in a vital last wicket partnership of 40 with "Bucky" Buchanan. The young Oxford Blue shielded Buchanan (3 not out) from the bowling in masterly style.

In their last match of the season Rhodesia also avenged the earlier defeat at the hands of Border by a convincing margin of 238 runs. A 19-year-old opening bowler by the name of Joe Partridge made his debut in this match and finished the first innings with the creditable figures of 10-5-11-2. Partridge also contributed 15 not out in the Rhodesian second innings in an unbroken last wicket partnership of 42 with David Lewis (who only had 74 when Partridge arrived at the crease) which enabled the latter to reach his maiden first-class century. This knock began Partridge's firm conviction over the years that his proficiency with the bat was such that he deserved better than the role of a regular number 11 batsman.

Rhodesia, with a more positive approach to their cricket had therefore ended the season with three consecutive victories. For several players it had been a memorable season. David Lewis topped the batting averages (414 runs — average 51,75) whilst John Wallace was the most prolific run scorer (518 runs — average 43,17). But the side's trump card was undoubtedly Percy Mansell, who scored 485 runs (average 48,50) and took 49 wickets (average 17,51). And in the last first-class match of the season when Mansell captained a B Section XI against Natal, he became the first South African in a domestic season since Ernie Vogler in 1906-07 to score 500 runs and take 50 wickets. Charles Wooler and Johnny Wallace were also selected for this match whilst wicket-keeper Cecil Harris was noted as a surprise omission.

On the local scene there was some closely contested cricket in the Logan Cup matches. Opening bat, Kevin Curran, in a workmanlike 105 not out scored in 5½ hours batted throughout Manicaland's innings of 280 against Mashonaland. But the big shock came when Midlands, under the evergreen Arnold Hyde, won the coveted Logan Cup for the first time ever by beating Mashonaland in the final at Fort Victoria. Gordon Jackson on his home ground scored a match-winning 146 in the Midlands total of 244 to enable his side to edge home by 18 runs.

SCORES: Currie Cup B Section, 1951-52.

At Bulawayo, 24, 25 and 26 November.

Orange Free State — 298 (K. J. Funston 85; P.N.F. Mansell 5/107)
and 314 (J.R. Liddle 77, S.L. Hanson 62, I. Kirby 56; C.R.D. Wooler 4/57, P.H. Anderson 3/100)

Rhodesia — 313 (J.H.A. Wallace 138, P.N.F. Mansell 71, J.M.S. Baldwin 39; J.R. Liddle 7/97)
and 244 (C.M. Harris 114, J.M. Leibbrandt 54; J.R. Liddle 5/115)

Orange Free State won on first innings.

At Salisbury, 1, 2 and 3 December.

Rhodesia — 258 (J.H.A. Wallace 60, J.M.S. Baldwin 50, J.M. Leibbrandt 36, J.B. Roothman 34)
and 248-7 dec. (P.N.F. Mansell 79, J.M.S. Baldwin 36)

Griqualand West — 112 (P.N.F. Mansell 4/33, P.H. Anderson 3/12)
and 42-1 wkt.

Rhodesia won on first innings.

At East London, 24, 26 and 27 December.

Border — 333 (O.C. Dawson 96, K.N. Kirton 53; P.N.F. Mansell 6/91, J.M. Buchanan 3/97)
and 257 (C. Kirton 71; P.N.F. Mansell 7/114)

Rhodesia — 211 (M.W. Davies 61, D. Rees 40; W. Chalmers 5/47)
and 236 (D.J. Lewis 58, P.N.F. Mansell 51, J.B. Roothman 33)

Border won by 143 runs.

At Pretoria, 31 December, 1 and 2 January.

North-Eastern Transvaal — 210 (A. Dennis 76; P.N.F. Mansell 7/71)
and 325 (J. Pickerill 143*, H.V. Paton 67, B. Wiles 62; J.M. Leibbrandt 3/55, P.N.F. Mansell 3/79, C.R.D. Wooler 3/80)

Rhodesia — 328 (J.B. Roothman 99, P.N.F. Mansell 94*, J.M. Leibbrandt 31; B. Wiles 6/90)
and 209-4 wkts. (J.H.A. Wallace 81, D.J. Lewis 50*, D. Rees 31)

Rhodesia won by 6 wickets.

At Bloemfontein, 5, 7 and 8 January.

Rhodesia — 346 (J.B. Roothman 87, P.N.F. Mansell 80, D. Rees 44, M.W. Davies 42, J.H.A. Wallace 30)
and 215 (D.J. Lewis 90; L. Tuckett 6/89)

Orange Free State — 252 (L.B. Koch 95; C.R.D. Wooler 4/70)
and 275 (A.C. Le Sueur 80, K.J. Funston 69, S.L. Hanson 50; P.N.F. Mansell 6/117)

Rhodesia won by 34 runs.

At Bulawayo, 12, 13 and 14 January.

Rhodesia — 255 (D.J. Lewis 59, P.N.F. Mansell 48, J.H.A. Wallace 39, D. Rees 34)
and 291-9 dec. (D.J. Lewis 100*, J.H.A. Wallace 100)

Border — 123 (P. Johnson 3/19, P.N.F. Mansell 3/45)
and 185 (P.N.F. Mansell 5/43, C.R.D. Wooler 4/35)

Rhodesia won by 238 runs.

Mansell was invited to the South African trials at the end of the 1951-52 season and deservedly gained selection for the 1952-53 Springbok tour to Australia and New Zealand. On this terrifically successful visit for South Africa, Mansell played in all five Tests against Australia and two against New Zealand. The statistics perhaps do not fully illustrate Mansell's contribution in the drawn 2-2 series with the powerful Australian combination. The Springboks were a side that based their success on the magnificent value of superb teamwork but commentator Charles Fortune did write of Mansell, after the tour: 'Mansell was always calm and passive to the outward eye. It is not

RHODESIA v. ORANGE FREE STATE, 1951-52.
Back: J. Roothman, C. Wooler, J. Baldwin, J. Leibbrandt, M. Davies, P. Anderson, D. Lewis, J. Buchanan.
Seated: J. Wallace, P. Mansell, A. Bernstein (Manager), D. Rees (Captain), C. Harris.

JIMMY DELL. CECIL HARRIS. MARSHALL DAVIES.

bowling but batsmanship that brings out the power that lies in Mansell's frame. He delights in the desperate hour. My vivid memories of Mansell — slip catches at Brisbane and Perth, battering Miller and baffling Australia's batsmen when alone with Tayfield he held the bowling breach at Melbourne.'

In July and August 1952, the first touring side from Kenya to visit Rhodesia arrived for an eight-match tour. Captained by Denis Dawson, they were known as the Kenyan Kongonis and came up against most of Rhodesia's leading cricketers. They drew their fixtures against Stragglers' teams in Salisbury, Umtali, Fort Victoria and Bulawayo and escaped an outright defeat, having followed on against a strong Country Districts XI. Victories were achieved against Umvukwes, Lomagundi and a Mashonaland Chairman's XI at Ruwa.

Having had such an early start to the season it was certainly a shock to cricket supporters when Southern Rhodesia were beaten in their annual fixture against Northern Rhodesia by two wickets.

SCORES: versus Northern Rhodesia, 1952-53.

At Nkana, 1 and 2 November (Not first-class).

Southern Rhodesia — 142 (C.J. Pretorius 42)
and 205 (B. Fowles 61, T.A. Chapman 44; D.E. Hill 5/35)

Northern Rhodesia — 153 (P. Johnson 6/23)
and 200-8 wkts. (J. van der Merwe 83; J.T. Partridge 5/51)

Northern Rhodesia won by 2 wickets.

Dave Rees continued to captain Rhodesia in 1952-53 and his side again finished second in the B Section of the Currie Cup. The season began well enough with successive victories over Griqualand West and North-Eastern Transvaal — in both encounters Rhodesia came back well having been down on the first innings. But the Rhodesians were humbled badly by Transvaal on the fiery Ellis Park pitch, being all out for 94 and 87 in two miserable totals, to be thrashed by an innings. This was the season in which Neil Adcock first made his appearance on the South African scene. So hostile was his bowling on a lively wicket following two weeks of rain that Tommy Chapman was knocked out and carried off on a stretcher whilst the other batsmen were severely battered and bruised. However, a second triumph over North-Eastern Transvaal and a narrow 18 runs win against Border kept Rhodesia in the running for the Section honours and when Border unexpectedly and convincingly beat Transvaal the B Section title rested on the season's final match.

'If we can dismiss Eric Rowan quickly then we can win' was the slogan in cricket circles once it became clear that Transvaal and Rhodesia would ultimately fight it out for the championship. Ironically Joe Partridge clean bowled Rowan for 9 but it did not matter — Rhodesia's first innings 68 on a wicket suspect owing to water seepage beneath the covers, cost them their chances of succeeding. Admittedly the fact that Rowan won the toss proved decisive but Rhodesia's second innings was equally disappointing save for a 105-run partnership between David Lewis (92), combining aggression with watchful defence, and Bernard Carew.

A report in *The Rhodesia Herald* possibly best summed up the feelings of the cricket fraternity after the 10-wicket thrashing at the hands of Transvaal: 'The overall picture was one of disappointment. Perhaps perspective was put out by the Border defeat of Transvaal and lent a little more optimism to Rhodesia's hopes than the victory justified. At any rate, home supporters hoped for something more.

'There are bound to be changes from this side when the next Currie Cup competition comes around — in two years time — and it may be that with the development of the Colony's younger talent, Rhodesia will field a side which will come nearer achieving the promotion.

'In the meantime Rhodesia were well and truly beaten by a better side and the match suggested that speed bowling assisted by good fielding and generalship is still the best match winner in contemporary cricket.'

However, apart from their dismal showings against Transvaal there were a number of promising aspects about the season with notable individual successes. David Lewis again topped the batting averages whilst Joe Partridge in his first full season of first-class cricket claimed 33 wickets and headed the bowling at 19,06. Against Griqualand West, Partridge's figures read 0 wickets for 50 runs at one stage but brought on for a third spell he eventually finished with 7/85 in 21,2 overs.

The season saw the 6ft 6in Godfrey "Goofy" Lawrence and Partridge team up for the first time in what was to become Rhodesia's most successful opening partnership in history. Lawrence claimed fifteen wickets at 25,00 in his maiden first-class season but was invariably used as a first change bowler whilst Bruce McBride shared the new ball with Partridge. Left-arm spinner Peter Johnson (19 wickets — average 24,63) provided the necessary support and was described in *The South African Cricket Annual* as 'a bowler of real promise'.

Of the other players, Jimmy Dell had the misfortune to miss a maiden first-class century by one run in the course of a record 211-run third-wicket partnership against Border. Bernard Carew hit a record-breaking 179 as an opening bat against North-Eastern Transvaal in Pretoria and former Leicestershire player, Tommy Chapman, scored a century before lunch in his first game for Rhodesia. Hooking, driving and cutting with abandon, Chapman's innings was made particularly creditable by the fact that he batted with a small bone fracture in his left hand.

SCORES: Currie Cup B Section, 1952-53.

At Salisbury, 22, 23 and 24 November.

Griqualand West — 300 (R. G. Draper 145; J.T. Partridge 7/85, P. Johnson 3/71)
and 184 (C. Helfrich 68; P. Johnson 5/41)

Rhodesia — 238 (T.A. Chapman 43, C.M. Harris 38, J.B. Roothman 37, C.J. Pretorius 31; J.E. Waddington 5/73)
and 248-4 wkts. (T.A. Chapman 124*, J.H.A. Wallace 95)

Rhodesia won by 6 wickets.

At Bulawayo, 29, 30 November and 1 December.

North-Eastern Transvaal — 311 (P. Davies 132, B. Spies, 54; G.B. Lawrence 3/45, J.T. Partridge 3/79)
and 50 (J.T. Partridge 4/15)

Rhodesia — 281 (J.H.A. Wallace 90, D. Rees 59, B.J. Carew 45, C.M. Harris 35)
and 85-1 wkt. (T.A. Chapman 46*, J.B. Roothman 31*)

Rhodesia won by 9 wickets.

At Johannesburg, 19, 20 and 22 December.

Rhodesia — 94 (D.J. Lewis 44*; D.E.J. Ironside 6/29)
and 87 (M. Charnas 6/36)

Transvaal — 222-8 dec. (R. Kimber 87; B.J. McBride 4/62)

Transvaal won by an innings and 41 runs.

At Pretoria, 26, 27 and 29 December.

North-Eastern Transvaal — 285 (P. Davies 126, J. Blewitt 84; J.T. Partridge 5/76, B.J. McBride 4/79)
and 261 (B.J. McBride 5/84, G.B. Lawrence 3/55)

Rhodesia — 403 (B.J. Carew 179, D.J. Lewis 88, D. Rees 60, J.B. Roothman 35; B. Wiles 6/135)
and 81-5 wkts. (J. Dell 41*)

Rhodesia won on first innings.

At East London, 1, 2 and 3 January.

Rhodesia — 222 (D.J. Lewis 41, D. Rees 36)
and 302 (D.J. Lewis 114, J. Dell 99, B.J. Carew 32*)

Border — 287 (K. Kirton 122, O.C. Dawson 50; B.J. McBride 3/60, P. Johnson 3/73)
and 219 (R. Phillips 89; J.T. Partridge 4/39, P. Johnson 3/88)

Rhodesia won by 18 runs.

At Salisbury, 7, 8 and 9 March.

Rhodesia — 68 (A. Nickel 7/43)
and 173 (D. J. Lewis 92, B.J. Carew 33)

Transvaal — 222 (A.I. Taylor 98, L. Harris 54*; J.T. Partridge 6/87)
and 23-0 wkts.

Transvaal won by 10 wickets.

CHAPTER FIVE

The David Lewis Influence

BULAWAYO-BORN DAVID LEWIS was selected as Rhodesia's next captain in 1953-54 in succession to Dave Rees. His cricket background was impressive. Commencing his education at Rhodes Estate Preparatory School in the Matopos, he captained both the cricket and rugby teams and later attained a similar distinction at Plumtree School. He went on to captain the first Rhodesian Nuffield XI after the War and at the end of the Week was awarded his South African Schools XI cap and made vice-captain to Clive van Ryneveld for the match against Transvaal in 1946.

Having decided to embark on a legal career his next move was to Cape Town University, where he spent three years and where, apart from being awarded his Cricket Blue in 1948, he gained his B.A.(Jurisprudence). That took him to Oxford to further his legal studies and gave him the opportunity of gaining invaluable experience in top-class sporting circles. With a Double Blue (Rhodesia's first) to his credit he eventually returned to South Africa as a member of the Combined Oxford/Cambridge rugby side, remaining behind at the end of the tour to qualify as an attorney. On representing Rhodesia in 1953-54 against Geoff Rabone's New Zealanders at cricket he became a double sports international because he had earlier been chosen as fly-half for the national rugby side against the 1953 Wallabies at Hartsfield, Bulawayo.

There were a number of other Old Prunitians (ex-Plumtree schoolboys) who were to play key roles in Rhodesia's cricket progress under the leadership of David Lewis. Their numbers included Denis O'Connell-Jones, Jeremy Baldwin, Charles Wooler, Tony Pithey, Guy Barber, Ron Coventry, Marshall Davies, Don Arnott, David Pithey and Dave Napier. And further emphasizing that the Matabeleland schools were the nurseries of Rhodesian cricket at that time was the fact that Milton provided Percy Mansell, Cecil Harris, Kevin Curran, Colin Bland and Eddie Parker whilst Bernard Carew came from the Bulawayo Technical School. From elsewhere in Rhodesia Joe Partridge and Trifon Deftereos had attended the Umtali High School, Chris Duckworth and Rob Ullyett hailed from Chaplin while St. George's contributed "Goofy" Lawrence, Vernon Dickinson and Ray Gripper. Imports from South Africa were conspicuously few although Johnny Wallace, Paul Winslow, Bruce McBride, Harry Birrell, Harold Paton, Lloyd Koch and Jackie Ward all made their mark at different stages and Chris Duckworth benefited from a season playing for Natal.

Lewis initially captained Southern Rhodesia at cricket in their annual fixture against their northern neighbours at the beginning of the 1953-54 season. It was a match the Southerners dominated with Tony Pithey stroking an immaculate 147, new cap Ron Coventry racing to a whirlwind 74 out of an opening stand of 86 with Pithey, and finally Joe Partridge dramatically sending Northern Rhodesian cricket crashing to its lowest ebb. At one stage the Northern Rhodesians were 25-9 wickets in their second innings before a lusty last-wicket partnership enabled them to reach 66. Partridge's figures of 7/7 were amazing particularly when one considers he only bowled five overs.

SCORES: versus Northern Rhodesia, 1953-54

At Salisbury, 14 and 15 November (Not first-class).

Southern Rhodesia — 363-5 dec. (A.J. Pithey 147, P.N.F. Mansell 79, D. J. Lewis 37)

Northern Rhodesia — 115 (J.T. Partridge 4/37, P.N.F. Mansell 3/19)
and 66 (J.T. Partridge 7/7)

Southern Rhodesia won by an innings and 182 runs.

The main feature of the season was the arrival of Geoff Rabone's New Zealanders to play one match against Rhodesia in Bulawayo. It was the first visit by a New Zealand team to southern Africa and the Rhodesians felt with some justification that their chances of succeeding against an international touring side had never been better. The New Zealanders were rated in certain quarters as an inferior team and apart from the world-famous opening bat, Bert Sutcliffe, and a rising young star, John Reid, they were a largely unknown line-up. They were subsequently outclassed in the Test series 4-0, and despite being unbeaten in all other matches of their southern African tour they gained only two victories and drew nine. They were aided somewhat in Bulawayo when the Rhodesians made life difficult for themselves by dropping seven catches which allowed the New Zealanders to scramble to 240. On a lively well-grassed pitch, Partridge alone suffered five lapses in the field. This must have irked Rhodesia's new cricket captain who had always made a fetish of fielding — during his Oxford career one English newspaper wrote: 'He is rated as one of the finest cover points in English cricket and in the same category as old timers of the calibre of Jack Hobbs and Gilbert Jessop.'

Rhodesia started badly in reply, losing three wickets for 18 runs before Mansell and Lewis added 65 but it was a sound 76 from Marshall Davies that ultimately enabled Rhodesia to come within eight runs of the visitors' score in a gallant fight-back. An interesting feature of the innings was that with regular New Zealand wicket-keeper Frank Mooney injured, John Reid kept wicket but as the attack showed signs of flagging after the tea interval, Geoff Rabone decided to use Reid with the new ball and Sutcliffe donned the gloves. Thus for the first time in a first-class match two players batted, bowled and kept wicket — and each captured a wicket whilst 'keeping. The wisdom of Rabone's move was evident when Reid clean bowled Bernard Carew, Joe Partridge and Mike Slaven for 16 runs in 6,1 overs.

New Zealand went for the runs in their second innings, adding 127 before lunch, and eventually left Rhodesia to score 215 runs in 135 minutes. The early dismissals of Tony Pithey and John Wallace subdued their effort and the Rhodesians were never in contention although Ron Coventry, noted as the fastest scorer in the country, hit a grand 63 which included 23 off one over from Reid.

Never before had the burly New Zealander been annihilated in such a manner and years later in his book *Sword of Willow* he wrote a farcical account of the incident no doubt to temper the embarrassment of the blasting he had received, comparing the onslaught to a tennis duel: 'I got the message when . . . a volley-like smash which would have won unstinted applause at Wimbledon rocketed the ball past me — dumbfounded, rooted to the spot — and on to the boundary. Next, I tried to york him and he played a distinguished edge to it, over slips to the fence. He went to 40-love with a forehand drive and took the game with a hook, Chinese in character, between leg stick and pads for another four.

'Then he gave me the delicate treatment — two checked drop shots just over the net . . . Perhaps a little disgruntled by the whole performance I bounced the next one at him. It rose over the peak of his cap and got a top edge to a hopefully waving racquet which projected the ball high over the 'keeper's head — four more.

'For once in my life I didn't know where to bowl.'

John Reid, the great New Zealand batsman, pictured with Ron Coventry when they met again during the 1961-62 tour.

SCORES: versus New Zealand, 1953-54.

At Bulawayo, 27, 28 and 30 November.

New Zealand — 240 (J.E.F. Beck 53, M.E. Chapple 51; M.D. Slaven 4/97, J.T. Partridge 3/56) and 207-8 dec. (J.T. Partridge 3/50)

Rhodesia — 232 (M.W. Davies 76, P.N.F. Mansell 41) and 114-5 wkts. (R.W. Coventry 63)

Match drawn.

Rhodesia's performance against New Zealand had certainly whetted the appetites of all cricket followers but thereafter the 1953-54 season tailed off disappointingly through the cancellation by the R.C.U. of the two-match Transvaal tour due to the unavailability of that province's Springbok players.

The 1954-55 season began with the annual two-day friendly at Nkana against Northern Rhodesia which Southern Rhodesia won comfortably. The game did give Wally Hitzeroth an opportunity to display his talents and he duly gained selection for Rhodesia later in the season in the course of their South African tour. But overall, Northern Rhodesia were again well beaten and press comments after the match argued that this fixture was becoming too one-sided to be viable and urged the cricket administrators to pit a provincial team against Northern Rhodesia in future years. Hence the sudden end of this annual encounter in the form in which it had previously been played.

SCORES: versus Northern Rhodesia, 1954-55.

At Nkana, 16 and 17 October (Not first-class).

N.R. — 159 (W.B. Hitzeroth 40; B.J. McBride 4/35, P.N.F. Mansell 3/68) and 140 (W.B. Hitzeroth 45; J.T. Partridge 3/24)

S.R. — 295 (A.J. Pithey 104, J.H.A. Wallace 53) and 9-0 wkts.

Southern Rhodesia won by 10 wickets.

The following month a two-day match was played against a strong Transvaal combination which provided ideal opposition for Rhodesia's Currie Cup preparations. To all intents and purposes the game was taken as seriously as any Currie Cup clash and was used to gauge Rhodesia's strength at that time. Chris Duckworth's fine 91 undoubtedly caught the attention of the Springbok selectors and must have contributed towards his gaining selection for the 1955 England tour. He and Pithey, both 21-year-olds, defied the full-blooded Springbok pace attack of Neil Adcock and Dave Ironside for 175 minutes to add 122 admirably taken runs.

SCORES: versus Transvaal, 1954-55.

At Bulawayo, 6 and 7 November (Not first-class).

Transvaal — 344 (W.R. Endean 110, C. Tayfield 104; P.N.F. Mansell 4/54)
and 42-1 wkt.

Rhodesia — 247 (C.A.R. Duckworth 91, A.J. Pithey 57; D.E.J. Ironside 5/112)

Match drawn.

Rhodesia made a grand start to their 1954-55 Currie Cup B Section with two outright victories and a first innings win in their three home fixtures. David Lewis set a fine example in the opening match in Salisbury against North-Eastern Transvaal, hitting 170 in 255 minutes with his only blemish at 137. He was well supported by John Wallace (106) in a partnership worth 160, whilst he added 118 with Percy Mansell (72) and then in association with Marshall Davies (56*) put on a hurricane 98 in 35 minutes. Mansell's leg-spinners provided the *coup de grâce* which saw Rhodesia gain a mammoth victory by an innings and 140 runs.

Batting equally confidently in Bulawayo, Rhodesia passed Eastern Province's first innings total of 265 for the loss of four wickets with Tony Pithey (77) impressing in a stylish display whilst Wallace (91) in one of his most aggressive moods, hit three sixes and ten fours. Davies attacking the bowling with gusto registered another half-century but it was Mansell who set up the second Rhodesian victory by scoring 51 and then mesmerising the Province batsmen in 16,2 overs, taking 5/25.

Unfortunately the weather was not so kind to the Rhodesians a week later in Salisbury when two completely blank days followed a rainfall of more than six inches and ruled out hopes of an outright victory over Griqualand West. On the third day Jack Waddington, a little surprisingly, sent Rhodesia in to bat on a sodden wicket. Wallace, Duckworth and Pithey appeared untroubled before Lewis gambled with an early declaration. It was a good move because on a drying pitch Griquas were in trouble from the start and inspired bowling by Dave Napier, making his Currie Cup debut, and Joe Partridge, enabled Rhodesia to take first innings points.

Rhodesia's hopes of winning the B Section were riding high at this stage but a testing three-match tour to South Africa set back their aspirations. The Rhodesians suffered their first blow at the Crusader ground, Port Elizabeth when Eastern Province amassed 422 with only opening bat, Harry Birrell, not reaching double figures. Springbok Anton Murray displayed all the strokes in a polished knock of 121 and then turning his hand to bowling claimed four wickets as Rhodesia slumped to 157. Compelled to follow on the visitors were again only a shadow of the powerful side that had carried all before them in Salisbury and Bulawayo and if it had not been for a valuable 79 from debutant, Denis O'Connell-Jones, who just failed to carry his bat, the Rhodesians would have been completely outclassed.

The Rhodesian bowling suffered further annihilation in East London when Border put together 387 on a plumb wicket and eventually deservedly won a high scoring match by eight runs. This loss cost the Rhodesians their chance of promotion to the A Section but fortunately they shrugged off the blow of two successive defeats to outclass Griqualand West in all departments in their final match of the season. Their arrogant 471 on the opening day assured them of victory. Pithey and O'Connell-Jones put on 98 in 117 minutes for the first wicket but this was merely a prelude to the Mansell/Davies deluge in which 179 runs were scored in just over two hours. Mansell reached his hundred in 127 minutes whilst Davies celebrated his maiden first-class century by keeping pace with the clock. His 100 came in 99 minutes and next to a Roy McLean "ton" was the fastest of the season. The seam-spin attack of Partridge and Mansell did the rest by taking 17 of the wickets to fall — Mansell with a century and 9/99 was undoubtedly "man of the match".

SCORES: Currie Cup B Section, 1954-55.

At Salisbury, 20 and 21 November.

North-Eastern Transvaal — 147 (J.T. Partridge 3/24, P.N.F. Mansell 3/29, B.J. McBride 3/44)
and 155 (P.N.F. Mansell 5/36)

Rhodesia — 442-5 dec. (D.J. Lewis 170*, J.H.A. Wallace 109, P.N.F. Mansell 72, M.W. Davies 56*)

Rhodesia won by an innings and 140 runs.

At Bulawayo, 4, 5 and 6 December.

Eastern Province — 265 (I. Long 66, B. Bradfield 50; B.J. McBride 6/45, J.T. Partridge 3/121)
and 95 (P.N.F. Mansell 5/25, J.T. Partridge 3/30)

Rhodesia — 347 (J.H.A. Wallace 91, A.J. Pithey 77, M.W. Davies 53, P.N.F. Mansell 51)
and 14-1 wkt.

Rhodesia won by 9 wickets.

At Salisbury, 11, 12 and 13 December.

Rhodesia — 138-2 dec. (C.A.R. Duckworth 61, J.H.A. Wallace 35, A.J. Pithey 34*)
and 7-3 wkts.

Griqualand West — 128 (B.A. Goble 73; D.C. Napier 4/39, J.T. Partridge 3/30)

Rhodesia won on first innings.

At Port Elizabeth, 27, 28 and 29 December

Eastern Province — 422 (A.R.A. Murray 126, G.F. Dakin 81; P.N.F. Mansell 4/128)

Rhodesia — 157 (C.M. Harris 39, W. B. Hitzeroth 36, D.J. Lewis 34)
and 148 (D.B. O'Connell-Jones 79)

Eastern Province won by an innings and 117 runs.

At East London, 1, 3 and 4 January

Border — 387 (O.C. Dawson 139, K.N. Kirton 124; J.T. Partridge 8/124)
and 269-6 dec. (O.C. Dawson 72, D. Fenner 57, K.N. Kirton 56*; J.T. Partridge 3/119)

Rhodesia — 316 (P.N.F. Mansell 131, D.J. Lewis 69, M.W. Davies 43)
and 332 (A.J. Pithey 112, P.N.F. Mansell 54, M.W. Davies 45, D.B. O'Connell-Jones 38; O.C. Dawson 5/124)

Border won by 8 runs.

At Kimberley, 7 and 8 January.

Rhodesia — 471 (M.W. Davies 133, P.N.F. Mansell 111, A.J. Pithey 97, D.B. O'Connell-Jones 46, R.W. Coventry 35)

Griqualand West — 95 (P.N.F. Mansell 5/35, J.T. Partridge 4/29)
and 228 (R.L. Gloak 69, D. Lee 67; P.N.F. Mansell 4/64, J.T. Partridge 4/87)

Rhodesia won by an innings and 148 runs.

Two Rhodesians were selected for the 1955 Springbok tour to England. The 35-year-old Mansell was a certainty after a fine all-round season. He had topped the Rhodesian batting in the 1954-55 season with 427 runs (average 61,00) finishing ahead of Wallace (238 runs — average 59,50), Davies (353 runs — average 58,83), Lewis (350 runs — average 58,33) and Pithey (350 runs — average 50,00). He had also captured 27 wickets (average 16,55) and taken the most catches with 10 to his credit.

Rhodesia's other selection, Chris Duckworth, as the reserve wicket-keeper was a surprise and Norman Cutler in his book *Behind the South African Tests* wrote: 'The question that intrigued South Africa was the choice of Chris Duckworth as Waite's deputy. Many fans had not even heard of Duckworth and asked what grounds there were for his inclusion. It was not an unreasonable question for the 21-one-year-old Chris had scored few runs and only kept wicket once for Rhodesia during the pre-tour season.

'The answer was the policy of choosing all-rounders wherever possible . . . the Selectors broke convention by choosing a player with a moderate record because of his excellent fielding and promise as a batsman. It was a long-term policy.'

Duckworth had limited opportunities as Waite's understudy but came to light in the match against Northamptonshire when he made an accomplished 158 in 315 minutes. Mansell played in four Tests with modest figures but overall scored 566 runs (average 35,17) and took 28 wickets (average 22,92) in the fifteen matches he played. His highest first-class score on tour was 99 but he did score 148 in 122 minutes against Durham at Sunderland in a minor fixture. And his 26 catches (9 in Tests) moved the eminent writer, Gordon Ross, to note: 'As a slip fielder he surely has no peer. He took some fantastic catches on this tour.'

The season 1955-56 was a memorable one for Rhodesia. Under the astute leadership of David Lewis they played positive, winning cricket and achieved promotion with six outright victories in the B Section — the first occasion that this had been achieved in the Currie Cup competition.

Percy Mansell (393 runs — average 65,50) and 36 wickets (average 14,38) had a magnificent season and topped the batting and bowling averages for the entire

RHODESIA, 1955-56 — WINNERS B SECTION.
Back: C. Kemp, M. Slaven, D. Arnott, G. Lawrence, V. Dickinson, R. Coventry, J. Partridge.
Seated: M. Davies, C. Duckworth, D. Lewis (Captain), E. Morris (Manager), P. Mansell, J. Baldwin, D. O'Connell-Jones.

B Section. He also hit two fine centuries, both against Griqualand West — 154 in Kimberley and 148 in Bulawayo. David Lewis (468 runs — average 58,50), Denis O'Connell-Jones (461 runs — average 57,62) and Marshall Davies (432 runs — average 51,71) also each scored two centuries during the season. Other useful contributions were made by Don Arnott, Chris Duckworth, Ron Coventry and Jeremy Baldwin.

Three new batting partnership records were set in the course of the season. Pride of place belonged to Mansell and Davies who put on 203 for the fifth wicket whilst flaying the Griqualand West attack in Bulawayo during an entertaining two hours of swashbuckling batting. O'Connell-Jones and Baldwin added 140 together for the first wicket against Griquas in Kimberley and Davies and Arnott put on 77 for the ninth wicket against Border in East London, to establish further records.

Mansell aside, the bowling success of the season was the genial giant, Godfrey Lawrence, who captured 24 wickets at the economical average of 15,08. Joe Partridge (14), Ron Coventry (16) and Mike Slaven (14) were the other leading wicket takers in a well-balanced attack.

The season began in incredible fashion with a two-day friendly against Natal at the Salisbury Sports Club. The two days produced 1119 runs, three brilliant centuries and vintage cricket for 14 000 spectators. For Rhodesia, Duckworth, Lewis, Mansell, Davies and Arnott scored fluently whilst Coventry pasted the Currie Cup champions for an exhilarating 71 in less than an hour. However, the Rhodesian efforts paled into insignificance when McGlew, Watkins and then McLean belaboured the Rhodesian bowlers by reeling off runs at the rate of two a minute. With the match serving as an early season trial for "Goofy" Lawrence, he must have wondered what he had let himself in for as he and Partridge conceded between them 353 runs for their two wickets and Natal ended the day with the highest number of runs scored in a single innings in all classes of cricket in South Africa.

The Rhodesian cricketers pictured here during their 1955-56 Currie Cup tour are (*standing*): J. Baldwin, J. Partridge, R. Coventry and D. Lewis; and (*in front*): D. O'Connell-Jones, M. Davies and E. Morris (Manager).

SCORES: versus Natal, 1955-56.

At Salisbury, 5 and 6 November (Not first-class).

Rhodesia — 405 (C.A.R. Duckworth 80, R.W. Coventry 71, D.J. Lewis 60, P.N.F. Mansell 56, D.B. Arnott 40*, M.W. Davies 37; V.I. Smith 6/103)

Natal — 714-9 wkts. (J.C. Watkins 148, R.A. McLean 146, D.J. McGlew 141, L.A. Upton 89, L.B. Koch 88; R.W. Coventry 3/111)

Natal won by 7 wickets.

The B Section of the Currie Cup was won with ruthless efficiency. At home against Griqualand West, North-Eastern Transvaal and Orange Free State in successive weeks Rhodesia won each match by innings victories. Against Griquas they slammed 570-6 declared, which was the highest score in their history at the rate of 90 per hour and continuing their devastation of B Section bowling attacks amassed 468-7 declared, against North-Eastern Transvaal and 551 against Orange Free State. Everything appeared to be running Rhodesia's way — David Lewis even won all three tosses with a lucky South African crown piece lent to him by national selector, Lance Roberts. And then on tour in early January the Rhodesians were never extended in humbling Border and Griqualand West but were given a fright by North-Eastern Transvaal at Berea Park, Pretoria. North-Easterns, thanks to a fine undefeated 92 by Syd Burke, gained a useful first innings lead but Joe Partridge, having been dropped, returned to replace an unavailable Mansell, and initiated a Rhodesian triumph with second innings figures of 6/13 in 11,4 overs.

SCORES: Currie Cup B Section, 1955-56.

At Bulawayo, 18, 19 and 21 November.

Rhodesia — 570-6 dec. (D.B. O'Connell-Jones 148, P.N.F. Mansell 148, M.W. Davies 100, R.W. Coventry 44*, C.A.R. Duckworth 44, D.J. Lewis 38)

Griqualand West — 109 (R.W. Coventry 3/22, G.B. Larence 3/24)
and 201 (P.N.F. Mansell 4/49, R.W. Coventry 4/50)

Rhodesia won by an innings and 260 runs.

At Bulawayo, 26, 27 and 28 November.

Rhodesia — 468-7 dec. (D.J. Lewis 135, M.W. Davies 85, D.B. O'Connell-Jones 82, J.M.S. Baldwin 59, C.A.R. Duckworth 32)

North-Eastern Transvaal — 310 (T.C. Woolley 116, P. Uren 53; P.N.F. Mansell 4/89, G.B. Lawrence 3/58)
and 139 (C.B. Kemp 3/63)

Rhodesia won by an innings and 19 runs.

At Salisbury, 3, 4 and 5 December.

Rhodesia — 551 (D.B. O'Connell-Jones 121, M.W. Davies 105, D.J. Lewis 103, R.W. Coventry 94, C.A.R. Duckworth 59, J.M.S. Baldwin 30)

Orange Free State — 323 (R. Le Sueur 151; P.N.F. Mansell 4/112)
and 139 (M.D. Slaven 4/52, P.N.F. Mansell 3/23)

Rhodesia won by an innings and 89 runs.

At East London, 31 December, 2 and 3 January.

Rhodesia — 222 (P.N.F. Mansell 55, D.J. Lewis 37, C.B. Kemp 34)
and 230 (M.W. Davies 74, D.J. Lewis 52, D.B. Arnott 45; S. Knott 5/63)

Border — 166 (R. Geach 55; P.N.F. Mansell 5/39, G.B. Lawrence 3/29)
and 106 (P.N.F. Mansell 6/45, M.D. Slaven 4/52)

Rhodesia won by 180 runs.

At Kimberley, 6, 7 and 9 January.

Rhodesia — 483 (P.N.F. Mansell 154, D.B. O'Connell-Jones 71, J.M.S Baldwin 65, D.J. Lewis 63, R.W. Coventry 42, G.B. Lawrence 36, D.B. Arnott 30)

Griqualand West — 205 (G.B. Lawrence 4/29, P.N.F. Mansell 4/68)
and 227 (E. Draper 98; G.B. Lawrence 3/37, R.W. Coventry 3/39)

Rhodesia won by an innings and 51 runs.

At Pretoria, 13, 14 and 16 January.

North-Eastern Transvaal — 222 (S.F. Burke 92*; J.T. Partridge 4/67, R.W. Coventry 3/26)
and 44 (J.T. Partridge 6/13)

Rhodesia — 144 (M.W. Davies 42; B. Wiles 6/58)
and 123-4 wkts. (C.A.R. Duckworth 39*)

Rhodesia won by 6 wickets.

There was a two-year break before Rhodesia could take their place in the A Section of the Currie Cup. This was because of tours by the M.C.C. in 1956-57 and the Australians in 1957-58, when in those days it was not customary also to stage the Currie Cup tournament.

The 1956-57 season was to be a significant one for a number of Rhodesian cricketers despite the lack of Currie Cup competition. The main attraction was obviously the tour of Peter May's M.C.C. side, a particularly strong combination with all the leading English players available. England had just retained the Ashes, beating Australia by three matches to one while the year before Australia had hammered the West Indies in the Caribbean. The Test series with South Africa was heralded therefore as the decider for the world cricket championship.

As a preparation match Rhodesia played a two-day home fixture against the Transvaal in Salisbury. With the prospect of facing the fiery Transvaal pace attack of Neil Adcock and Peter Heine, the Rhodesians were thankful to be able to use for practice an invention devised by Peter Walshe, the former Nuffield player and Oxford Blue. Said *The Rhodesia Herald* in an optimistic article: 'David Lewis and his Rhodesian team have an answer to the cricketing Goliaths labelled Transvaal or M.C.C. — and their secret weapon is almost identical to the one so successfully wielded by the biblical character.' Walshe had in actual fact rigged a mammoth catapult reminiscent of the slings which hurled huge boulders beyond the ramparts of medieval cities. Pulling back the strands of catapult elastic strung between two poles, three metres apart, one could deliver the ball at varying speeds of up to 100 miles per hour over a distance of about 18 yards.

Transvaal batted first and the Rhodesians had to do a fair amount of leather chasing before they could pit their skills against Adcock and Heine, who were almost capable of matching the velocity of the catapult. On an easy-paced pitch Ken Funston, Scotch Taylor, Johnny Waite and Russell Endean, aided by dropped catches, powered their way to a massive 471-7 declared. Limited to four bowlers — Lawrence, Wooler, Coventry and newcomer, left-arm spinner Peter Westray — Lewis had his work cut out in attempting to curb the run rate but Len Brown had this to say of the lanky Lawrence: 'The next fifteen-storey building that goes up in the Federation should be named after Lawrence and made capacious enough to house both his big feet and his big heart.'

Perhaps the many weeks of intensive practice against the catapult paid dividends because Rhodesia put up a good performance when their turn came to bat even though they never looked like challenging the Transvaal total. Jeremy Baldwin and Denis O'Connell-Jones withstood a sustained pace attack from the Transvaal pair for an hour in which time they put together a mere 16 runs. But they did their job well and blunted the attack to such an extent that Heine and Adcock claimed only one wicket between them for 62 runs.

Chris Duckworth and David Lewis added 111 for the third wicket in 140 minutes but for Len Brown the highlight was Paul Winslow's lightning 47 which included three huge sixes, one of which landed in North Avenue. He wrote: 'For 99 per cent of the people present the light went out of the game when Ron Kimber, standing a foot inside the boundary, coolly hugged another six to his chest to dismiss

Winslow... To the average spectator those 25 minutes of "Pop" Winslow made their day.'

Paul Winslow, who was acknowledged as one of the most forceful batsmen in South African cricket had arrived in Rhodesia at the beginning of the season. He came with an exciting reputation — his feats at Old Trafford during the 1955 Springbok tour had rocketed him into the cricket headlines. Against Lancashire he had struck 40 off eight consecutive balls and then in the Third Test had scored a century that will long be remembered by the older cricket fraternity. In a superb exhibition of driving Winslow hit thirteen fours and three sixes, reaching his hundred in grand style by hitting a ball from Tony Lock straight over the sight screen. His captain during that Test, Jackie McGlew, wrote in his book *Cricket for South Africa*: 'Winslow was well worthy of the demonstration which greeted his century. I doubt that I have ever seen a more calculated assault in Test match cricket.'

at times painfully slowly but for the most part did an admirable job. Whilst Mansell made the first 50 to be scored against the tourists, O'Connell-Jones was a model of determination in providing a solid foundation to the innings. He was floored by a "Typhoon" Tyson bumper when 41, taking the full force of the ball on the left temple. In several anxious moments he swayed, gently dropped his bat and collapsed backwards to the turf. Fortunately he was soon up and in the next over drove a no-ball for four but then apparently still muzzy stuck out his bat vaguely to be easily caught.

On the second day, a Sunday, the biggest crowd to attend a match in Bulawayo — officially estimated at 9 000 — had the privilege of watching Peter May make 124 not out. His chanceless innings was a classic, containing two sixes and thirteen fours with the second fifty coming in 48 minutes. Rhodesia's total of 192 was easily overtaken but local cricket followers

Paul Winslow hitting out in the course of his 108 for South Africa against England at Old Trafford in 1955.

SCORES: versus Transvaal, 1956-57.

At Salisbury, 20 and 21 October (Not first-class).

Transvaal — 471-7 dec. (K.J. Funston 114, A.I. Taylor 93, J.H.B. Waite 93, W.R. Endean 72; G.B. Lawrence 4/142)

Rhodesia — 298 (C.A.R. Duckworth 65, P.L. Winslow 47, D.J. Lewis 42, C.R.D. Wooler 39, R.W. Coventry 30; K. Gibbs 6/52)

Transvaal won on first innings.

The M.C.C. arrived in Bulawayo by air having already blazed a trail of three successive innings victories in South Africa in the course of their three opening fixtures. They were not taking any chances either against an unknown quantity and named a strong side for their first match at the Queens ground, Bulawayo.

The Rhodesians batted grimly on the opening day,

had much to enthuse over in the talents of a teenage fielding prodigy. Prior to the match an 18-year-old Milton schoolboy, Colin Bland, had been named 12th man but with O'Connell-Jones still feeling the effects of the Tyson bumper Bland fielded throughout the day and *The Chronicle* reported: 'The crowd gave young Colin Bland a great ovation for his fielding... some of his stops were magnificent and his efforts were crowned with a catch at the end of the day.'

The M.C.C. declared 215 runs ahead but with Rhodesia going into lunch at 85-2 on the final day a draw was confidently anticipated. However, it was not to be because one over after lunch the rain poured down and 95 minutes were lost which ironically led to Rhodesia's downfall. With the wicket giving considerable assistance, the last seven wickets — three of them "gifts" — tumbled for a mere 27 runs. The M.C.C. had won convincingly by an innings and 86 runs.

Ron Coventry catches Colin Cowdrey for 20 off the bowling of Guy Barber during the match against the M.C.C. in 1956-57 at Salisbury.

Winslow, Baldwin and Wooler forfeited their places for the match in Salisbury (where an all-time record of 26 500 people watched the 2½-day match) and the selectors brought in Marshall Davies, Guy Barber and Colin Bland. The last-named was a bold step although his brilliant fielding had obviously weighed heavily in his favour. However, Rhodesia stood little hope of halting the tourists' spectacular run of success and Louis Duffus began his opening remarks on the Salisbury encounter: 'Peter May strode like a monarch into a tottering kingdom at the Sports Club ground yesterday and raised the M.C.C. to a match-winning position with the batting more majestic than any he has devised this season. The 15 000 spectators saw one of the gems of the tour.' May raised his aggregate in four innings to 542 and became the first batsman to score four successive centuries in southern Africa.

At the same time, catches were dropped and Lawrence's figures of 6/104 could have been even better. But to the Rhodesians' credit their ground fielding in which Duckworth, Bland and Lewis excelled, was often superb and never let up well into the second day. It should also be mentioned that the match had continued through a persistent drizzle during the morning session of the second day despite an appeal by Lewis to stop play and get the pitch covered. The effects of this were immediately apparent after lunch. The hitherto batting paradise suddenly favoured the bowlers and Lawrence claimed three wickets in one over as the M.C.C. lost five wickets for 36 runs and were all out for 501. Unfortunately the Rhodesians were even more seriously affected and were completely at sea against the speed and skill of Peter Loader.

Six wickets fell for 11 runs before a stout-hearted innings of 19 by Bland and a painstaking 9 by Don Arnott in 88 minutes saved Rhodesia from a complete rout. Early that morning Bland had sat his science paper for the Cambridge Certificate with an invigilator all to himself. Later in the day he became a hero to the large crowd which cheered enthusiastically as he scored the first boundary of the ill-fated innings. From a background in which his sum batting experience had been gained in inter-school matches and a few club league games, he was suddenly defying the world's greatest fast bowler, Frank Tyson, and Peter Loader at his most devastating.

On the Sunday, Rhodesia, embarrassingly before a crowd of 11 500, were all out for 57 and followed on. Again it was Bland and Arnott who showed in the second innings their quality by putting on 50 after six wickets had fallen for 48. Bland (38) made top score for the second time while Arnott occupied the crease for two hours for his 22. Harold Paton smashed 21 in ten minutes and Rhodesia were all out for 152 to give the M.C.C. their biggest victory so far — by an innings and 292 runs.

SCORES: M.C.C. Tour, 1956-57.

At Bulawayo, 17, 18 and 19 November.

Rhodesia — 192 (D.B. O'Connell-Jones 45, P.N.F. Mansell 50, D.J. Lewis 37; T.E. Bailey 4/22)
and 129 (C.A.R. Duckworth 40, D.J. Lewis 30; G.A.R. Lock 5/12)

M.C.C. — 407-7 wkts. (P.B.H. May 124*, D.J. Insole 67, D.C.S. Compton 49; H.V. Paton 3/59)

M.C.C. won by an innings and 86 runs.

At Salisbury, 23, 24 and 25 November.

M.C.C. — 510 (P.B.H. May 206, T.E. Bailey 110, T.G. Evans 50; G.B. Lawrence 6/104, G.M.H. Barber 3/108)

Rhodesia — 57 (P.J. Loader 7/28)
and 152 (K.C. Bland 38)

M.C.C. won by an innings and 292 runs.

"Goofy" Lawrence's tireless bowling, one of the few redeeming features of the cricket from a Rhodesian point of view, was rewarded when he was included in a

South African XI to play against the M.C.C. at Pretoria. In an exciting encounter the home side inflicted the first defeat on an English touring team in South Africa in a match other than a Test since 1913-14. In the 38-run victory Lawrence's highly economical figures were 13-4-26-2 and 24-9-24-1.

Two other Rhodesians had a further crack at the M.C.C. tourists after being selected for the South African Country Districts XI. They were Guy Barber and Dick Faasen with the former having the distinction of bowling Peter May. The Districts side were outclassed and beaten by an innings and 110 runs but Faasen did make a useful 21 in his second visit to the crease.

Rhodesia had one further first-class fixture — a return match against the Transvaal in Johannesburg. Whilst several key players were unavailable, the Rhodesians were pleased to welcome back the Pithey brothers on holiday from the University of Cape Town. With both having represented the South African Universities XI in the course of the season they were immediately drafted into the Rhodesian side.

Twenty-three-year-old Tony Pithey took full advantage of the opportunity and played himself into the South African side for the Third Test against the M.C.C. with two fine innings. In addition Don Arnott was asked to stand by at the Test in case John Waite proved unfit to keep wicket for the Springboks. It was also reported in the Press that if Chris Duckworth had made his 105 against Transvaal in the first innings he would also have secured a place in the side — this appeared to ring true as he was to gain selection later in the series.

SCORES: versus Transvaal, 1956-57.

At Johannesburg, 18, 19 and 21 January.

Transvaal — 417 (W.R. Endean 171, K.J. Funston 89, A. Tayfield 69; G.B. Lawrence 5/95, P.N.F. Mansell 4/131)

Rhodesia — 212 (A.J. Pithey 90, D.J. Lewis 47) and 252-6 wkts. (C.A.R. Duckworth 105, A.J. Pithey 69)

Match drawn.

M.C.C. v. RHODESIA, 1956-57.
Back: H. Fox (Umpire), P. Richardson, J. Wardle, R. Coventry, A. Lock, B. Taylor, P. Loader, J. Baldwin, F. Tyson, M. Pengelly (Umpire).
Middle: D. O'Connell-Jones, D. Compton, C. Duckworth, P. May (M.C.C. Captain), D. Lewis (Rhodesia Captain), D. Insole, P. Mansell, T. Bailey.
Front: H. Paton, C. Bland, C. Wooler, G. Lawrence, A. Oakman, P. Winslow, D. Arnott.
Insets: G. Barber, M. Davies, A. Maddocks (Manager), D. Leather.

TONY PITHEY.

It was an absorbing Test series — the M.C.C. had won the first two Tests but the third was drawn with South Africa requiring 48 runs for victory with four wickets in hand. This Test, staged at Kingsmead, Durban, was to prove the turning-point of the series — Rhodesia's Tony Pithey played his part in the recovery by staying an invaluable 126 minutes at the crease during which he helped Trevor Goddard tire the rampant pace attack. Pithey twice hooked Loader to the boundary with perfect timing, drove Wardle straight to the pickets with well-judged footwork and hit Laker to the long-off fence in the course of his 25.

Chris Duckworth joined Pithey in the side for the Fourth Test which the Springboks won dramatically with Hugh Tayfield the architect of destruction by taking 9/113 in the second innings. Both Rhodesians were retained for the Fifth Test — a thrilling encounter in which Tayfield again bowled his side to victory by taking 6/78 in the English second innings. The Rhodesian contribution to the last two Tests was small but for both players it had been a great experience participating in South Africa's miraculous recovery to square the rubber after being two down with two to play.

As a prelude to the 1957-58 season Transvaal again visited for a week-end match against Rhodesia. It was intended to provide the necessary big-match practice so vital for the scheduled tour by Ian Craig's Australians one month later. Played at the Raylton ground, Bulawayo, it was throughout a thoroughly interesting duel until prematurely ended when a murky gloom descended followed by a freak hail-storm. At that stage Transvaal needed only 60 runs in 40 minutes with five wickets remaining and as they had just rattled up 119 runs in 55 minutes the task was presumably within their capabilities. The severest critics might have asked why David Lewis had not enforced the follow-on and given Transvaal no chance of victory. The answer would simply have been that such a decision would have been to the detriment of the game apart from preventing the Rhodesians having the benefit of second innings batting practice.

SCORES: versus Transvaal, 1957-58.

At Bulawayo, 28 and 29 September (Not first-class).

Rhodesia — 307 (H.B. Birrell 77, R. Coventry 77, D.B. O'Connell-Jones 43, V.E.J. Dickinson 30, D.J. Lewis 30)
and 64-5 dec. (H.B. Birrell 43*)

Transvaal — 194 (J.H.B. Waite 85; P.N.F. Mansell 4/41, G.B. Lawrence 3/38)
and 119-5 wkts. (K.J. Funston 54)

Match drawn.

In contrast to the traditional cool baptism of the Cape vineyards the 1957-58 Australians began their tour amid the scorching heat of the copper mines, a two-day game against a Northern Rhodesian Invitation XI at the attractive Ek Park ground, Kitwe. The home side, captained by the former Transvaal player Jack Ward, gave a large Saturday crowd a treat by inviting the Aussies to take first knock. Initially they did well to have Les Favell and "Slasher" Mackay back in the pavilion for 44 on the board but thereafter Jim Burke, Ian Craig, Peter Burge and Bobby Simpson piled on the score to register a total that ultimately proved well beyond Northern Rhodesia's reach.

In Salisbury the Rhodesians played their first four-day fixture against a touring side and fielded a well-balanced team. David Lewis had three Springboks in his side, Mansell, Winslow and Duckworth plus another Oxford Blue and former Eastern Province captain, Harry Birrell. In addition there was Don Arnott, who the previous year had been considered next in quality as a 'keeper to John Waite. The Australians were therefore expected to have their work cut out controlling such powerful opposition so early on in the tour.

The visitors made a good start in fact and offset the losing of the toss by having both Rhodesian openers out for only four runs. Duckworth then partially retrieved the position prior to Paul Winslow arriving at the crease. Reminiscent of his Old Trafford Test century in 1955 Winslow hit his second ball to the

David Lewis welcomes Ian Craig, captain of the 1957-58 Australians, to Rhodesia.

boundary and hammered his way to 50 in 47 minutes. Said a *Herald* report: 'He played an innings that must have included everything from the rankest bad shot to one of the best on-driven sixes seen for a long time.' In all he batted 95 minutes for his 81 (one six and eleven fours) and enabled Rhodesia to pass the 200 mark.

The Rhodesian score, however, was dwarfed into insignificance as the Australians coasted to a formidable lead. Skipper Ian Craig, at age 22 the youngest Test captain on record at that time, Richie Benaud and Alan Davidson all scored centuries as the visitors established a lead of 310. Benaud and Davidson's unbeaten partnership was worth 177 before Craig declared to give his bowlers sufficient time to give the tired Rhodesians a work-out before the end of play on the third day.

O'Connell-Jones and Birrell provided Rhodesia with a better start to their second innings and added 51 before being separated. Duckworth, like the openers, also appeared to be getting into his stride when he lost his wicket. Lewis batted cautiously for his 35 but circumstances dictated that he should keep one end intact whilst Winslow climbed into the bowling during their partnership of 109 runs. When the Rhodesian captain was out, Winslow, with his cap cocked over one eye to keep out the sun, was left to fight the Australian attack in a lone stand. By farming the bowling skilfully and being more discerning in his selection of the ball to punish, he entertained the crowd to a powerfully struck but responsible 139 which included one six and eighteen fours. But even though he managed to score 57 of the last 73 runs his admirable effort could not prevent the tourists winning their opening first-class fixture by an innings.

Percy Beames, the Australian journalist travelling with the team, wrote of Winslow: 'In two innings he has left his mark so deeply imprinted that it will take more than a few failures to erase. He is the type of batsman who is capable of thrashing and humbling practically any type of bowling. No bowler relishes being lifted over the top and the Australian bowlers are no exceptions in their dislike for this enterprising treatment.'

In Bulawayo Ian Craig scored his second successive century and put on 188 for the third wicket with Jim Burke, but a grand final spell by "Goofy" Lawrence, who dismissed both Craig and Burke, resulted in him taking 4 for 12 to reduce the total to one of reasonable proportions. The "Wild man from Mufulira", Mike Lee, a 22-year-old medium pace bowler, gave Lawrence good support and took the other four wickets to fall. Lee had earlier taken 3/66 at Ek Park and 3/90 at the Police ground, Salisbury, and appeared a most promising prospect.

Rhodesia's two batting displays were terribly disappointing and had it not been for a spate of seven dropped catches between first slip and gully in their second innings they would have been easily beaten by an innings. They were persistently vulnerable outside the off-stump and lost wickets at regular intervals accompanied by the vociferous appeals and the hurling of arms into the air amid other strange postures which typified the Australians registering their overwhelming triumph. Only Winslow, despite suffering from acute gastritis, made a determined stand in the first innings whilst Mansell and Lawrence added a valiant 61 for the ninth wicket during their second visit to the crease.

SCORES: Australian Tour, 1957-58.

At Salisbury, 25, 26, 28 and 29 October.

Rhodesia — 210 (P.L. Winslow 81, C.A.R. Duckworth 52; J. Drennan 5/53)
and 296 (P.L. Winslow 139, D.J. Lewis 35, D.B. O'Connell-Jones 32, C.A.R. Duckworth 30; R. Benaud 6/93)

Australia — 520-6 dec.(R. Benaud 117*, I.D. Craig 113, A.K. Davidson 100*, K.D. Mackay 54; J.M. Lee 3/90)

Australia won by an innings and 14 runs.

At Bulawayo, 1, 2 and 4 November.

Australia — 292 (J.W. Burke 106, I.D. Craig 100; G.B. Lawrence 6/83, J.M. Lee 4/84)
and 1-0 wkt.

Rhodesia — 126 (P.L. Winslow 40; A.K. Davidson 5/36)
and 166 (P.N.F. Mansell 50*, J.H. Ward 31)

Australia won by 10 wickets.

Rhodesia had one further home fixture during the season before they embarked on a three-match tour to South Africa. Jackie McGlew's Natal side arrived in Salisbury for a three-day friendly that was unfortunately ruined by rain. Despite being all out for a relatively low total of 182, Rhodesia did well, thanks to the perennial Percy Mansell, to all but dismiss a side containing six Springboks for a narrow 15-run lead. And when play was eventually stopped Jackie Ward and Paul Winslow in an unbroken second innings stand of 88 were well on top of the bowling attack.

SCORES: versus Natal, 1957-58.

At Salisbury, 7, 8 and 9 December.

Rhodesia — 182 (J.H. Ward 49, P.N.F. Mansell 30, R.B. Ullyett 30; J.C. Watkins 5/37)
and 117-2 wkts. (J.H. Ward 69*, P.L. Winslow 43*)

Natal 197-9 dec. (D.J. McGlew 61; P.N.F. Mansell 5/49, G.B. Lawrence 3/42)

Match drawn.

A number of senior players were unavailable for the South African tour including Harry Birrell who had had to withdraw from the Natal match because of housemaster duties at Milton School. In addition the in-form Jackie Ward, Denis O'Connell-Jones, Vernon Dickinson and the greatest blow, Percy Mansell, all informed the selectors of their inability to tour. However Mike Lee, who was emigrating to Cape Town, broke his journey on hearing of his selection and joined the tour party in Bulawayo. Rob Ullyett who had made a satisfactory debut against Natal, Trifon Deftereos a talented all-round sportsman from Umtali, the Pithey brothers on university vacation and former Nuffield star, Ray Gripper, gave the side a youthful but balanced appearance.

The tour was in fact a great success. A fine performance by David Pithey resulted in a 96-run win over Eastern Province in a low scoring match when the game had remained in the balance until Pithey and Lawrence had put together a match-saving 74 for the ninth wicket in the Rhodesian second innings. Despite losing the opening day because of rain against the Orange Free State, Rhodesia achieved a second dramatic victory when Deftereos hit the winning runs (a six) in the last over of the match.

Finally on the way home Rhodesia overpowered North-Eastern Transvaal in a match which belonged to two youngsters, David Pithey and Rob Ullyett. Pithey, incredibly unlucky to be left stranded on 99 not out, and Ullyett, had put on 144 when Rhodesia were floundering at 103-6 wickets, and then in a controlled second innings bowling spell Ullyett paved the way to an innings victory.

The younger Pithey who had been the tour "discovery" with 230 runs (average 76,66) and 19 wickets (average 13,68) joined his brother Tony in the Western Province side to play against the Australians towards the end of the season. In fact there was another "Rhodesian" in the side — Mike Lee, who had collected his car in Bulawayo on the Rhodesian tour side's return, had motored south, made an immediate impression and was drafted into the Western Province team.

SCORES: South African Tour, 1957-58.

At Port Elizabeth, 26, 27 and 28 December.

Rhodesia — 186 (C.A.R. Duckworth 71*, D.J. Lewis 43)
and 183-9 dec. (D.B. Pithey 77, A.J. Pithey 34; J. Ferrant 6/45)

Eastern Province — 117 (D.B. Pithey 4/16)
and 156 (R.B. Ullyett 3/18, D.B. Pithey 3/65)

Rhodesia won by 96 runs.

At Bloemfontein, 1, 2 and 3 January.

Orange Free State — 159 (D.B. Pithey 6/58, R.B. Ullyett 3/44)
and 167 (S. Hanson 56; D.B. Pithey 4/76, G.B. Lawrence 3/32)

Rhodesia — 239-6 dec. (A.J. Pithey 59, C.A.R. Duckworth 41, D.B. Pithey 40*, R.B. Ullyett 40, P.L. Winslow 36)
and 91-7 wkts.

Rhodesia won by 3 wickets.

At Benoni, 4, 6 and 7 January.

North-Eastern Transvaal — 95 (R. Coventry 4/21, G.B. Lawrence 4/45)
and 137 (R.B. Ullyett 7/42)

Rhodesia — 255 (D.B. Pithey 99*, R.B. Ullyett 50, R.A. Gripper 37; J.T. Botten 5/97)

Rhodesia won by an innings and 23 runs.

In 1958-59 Rhodesia made their entry into the A Section of the Currie Cup and did well to finish joint second in the final points table. To their credit they did not lose one of their six fixtures outright although they were down on four occasions on the first innings. Of their other two matches they beat Transvaal on first innings in the opening match of the season and won outright against Western Province in their final game. It may also be pointed out that despite going down to Western Province on the first innings in Cape Town, Rhodesia could count themselves unlucky with good performances from Tony and David Pithey, Colin Bland, Lloyd Koch and Percy Mansell not to have won outright. But by the same measure they escaped an innings defeat by the skin of their teeth against Natal at the Queens Club, Bulawayo, when bad light saved them after the last pair, Rob Ullyett and "Goofy" Lawrence had added 14 runs in 35 exciting minutes.

The season's outstanding performers were Tony Pithey and Godfrey Lawrence. The former made 497 runs (average 55,22), away ahead of the next leading run scorer who was Chris Duckworth (283 runs). Pithey also compiled two centuries with his best effort being a determined 161 not out in the 440 minutes at the Wanderers during which he defied every move the Transvaal captain, Johnny Waite, essayed in order to remove him.

Lawrence was the leading wicket-taker with 24 at the economical average of 17,16. At no stage of the season was he ever collared and even when McGlew, Goddard, McLean and Burger were in full cry as Natal hammered 552 in better than even time, Lawrence returned figures of 38-11-75-3. The next leading wicket-taker was Rob Ullyett with 15 which included an outstanding first innings analysis of 7/59 against Transvaal in the season's opening match when David Lewis sent his opponents in to bat on a damp wicket. Harold Paton, the Springbok soccer international, actually topped the bowling averages and played an important part in the end of season triumph over Western Province. After the pacemen, Lawrence and Partridge had struck the initial blow by dismissing four batsmen for 25 runs, Paton assumed the mantle of destructor-in-chief and helped himself to five wickets for a mere 13 runs in 14,4 overs. Western Province, all out for 69, were ultimately defeated by six wickets.

SCORES: Currie Cup A Section, 1958-59.

At Salisbury, 25, 26 and 27 October.

Transvaal — 187 (W.R. Endean 53; R.B. Ullyett 7/59)
and 169-5 dec. (K.J. Funston 59*; G.B. Lawrence 3/28)

Rhodesia — 248 (C.A.R. Duckworth 56, P.L. Winslow 46, K.C. Bland 41)
and 22-0 wkts.

Rhodesia won on first innings.

At Bulawayo, 1, 2 and 3 November.

Natal — 552 (D.J. McGlew 167, T.L. Goddard 100, R.A. McLean 91, C.G. Burger 70*; G.B. Lawrence 3/75, E.F. Parker 3/106)

Rhodesia — 279 (P.N.F. Mansell 68, A.J. Pithey 56, D.B. Arnott 39*, E.F. Parker 30; T.L. Goddard 5/41)
and 162-9 wkts. (C.A.R. Duckworth 51, A.J. Pithey 45)

Natal won on first innings.

At Johannesburg, 19, 20 and 22 December.

Rhodesia — 202 (D.J. Lewis 46, R.B. Ullyett 43)
and 312-7 wkts. (A.J. Pithey 161*, H.V. Paton 34)

Transvaal — 337-9 dec. (A.I. Taylor 82, W.R. Endean 56, K.J. Funston 55; G.B. Lawrence 4/76)

Transvaal won on first innings.

At Cape Town, 24, 26 and 27 December.

Rhodesia — 217 (K.C. Bland 62, R.B. Ullyett 35, L.B. Koch 32)
and 349-8 dec. (A.J. Pithey 138, L.B. Koch 63, K.C. Bland 38, P.N.F. Mansell 37, D.B. Pithey 30)

Western Province — 313 (M. Richardson 132, J. Maile 92; H.V. Paton 3/17)
and 151-7 wkts. (G.A.S. Innes 50; D.B. Pithey 4/45)

Western Province won on first innings.

At Durban, 1, 2 and 3 January.

Natal — 285 (D.J. McGlew 68, L. Morby-Smith 60, K. Elgie 59, C. Wesley 50; G.B. Lawrence 4/57, J.T. Partridge 4/102)
and 126-8 wkts. (D.B. Pithey 3/52)

Rhodesia — 261 (P.N.F. Mansell 52, C.A.R. Duckworth 43, A.J. Pithey 41, R.B. Ullyett 41, L.B. Koch 33; G.M. Griffin 5/58)

Natal won on first innings.

At Salisbury, 21, 22 and 23 February.

Western Province — 69 (H.V. Paton 5/13, G.B. Lawrence 3/9)
and 158 (J.T. Partridge 6/40)

Rhodesia — 133 (R.B. Ullyett 35)
and 95-4 wkts.

Rhodesia won by 6 wickets.

In March 1959, the annual South African Country Districts Festival was held in Salisbury and Rhodesia fielded two sides. The tournament began in an exciting fashion because Gerald Ziehl (Rhodesia B), who had developed an uncanny knack for the unexpected, claimed a hat-trick on the opening day against North-Eastern Transvaal. It brought back memories of Ziehl's superb bowling against Natal in the 1948 Nuffield tournament and his phenomenal six wickets in one eight-ball over in an Umtali league match in the early 1950s. The latter performance created quite a stir at the time and reports of the feat were published in London and South African newspapers.

To round off the tournament a two-day match was played between the Rhodesian Currie Cup side and the South African Country Districts. Nine provincial teams were represented in the Country Districts Festival and Rhodesia did well to have three players selected for the final side — Guy Barber, Raymond Lees and Pat Fallon. Lees had a particularly outstanding second innings knock when he carried his bat for an undefeated 49 in a vain attempt to stave off defeat. The Lawrence-Partridge combination ultimately proved too much for the Country Districts XI and Rhodesia gained an easy nine-wicket victory.

SCORES: versus South African Country Districts XI, 1958-59.

At Salisbury, 21 and 22 March (Not first-class).

S.A.C.D. — 165 (E. Eaglestone 65, G.M.H. Barber 38*; J.T. Partridge 6/47)
and 90 (R. Lees 49*; G.B. Lawrence 3/28, J.T. Partridge 3/32)

Rhodesia — 208 (C.A.R. Duckworth 57, H.V. Paton 34; L.W. Payn 5/84)
and 50-1 wkt.

Rhodesia won by 9 wickets.

The 1959-60 season began on a tremendous note with the short tour of Rhodesia by Stuart Surridge's

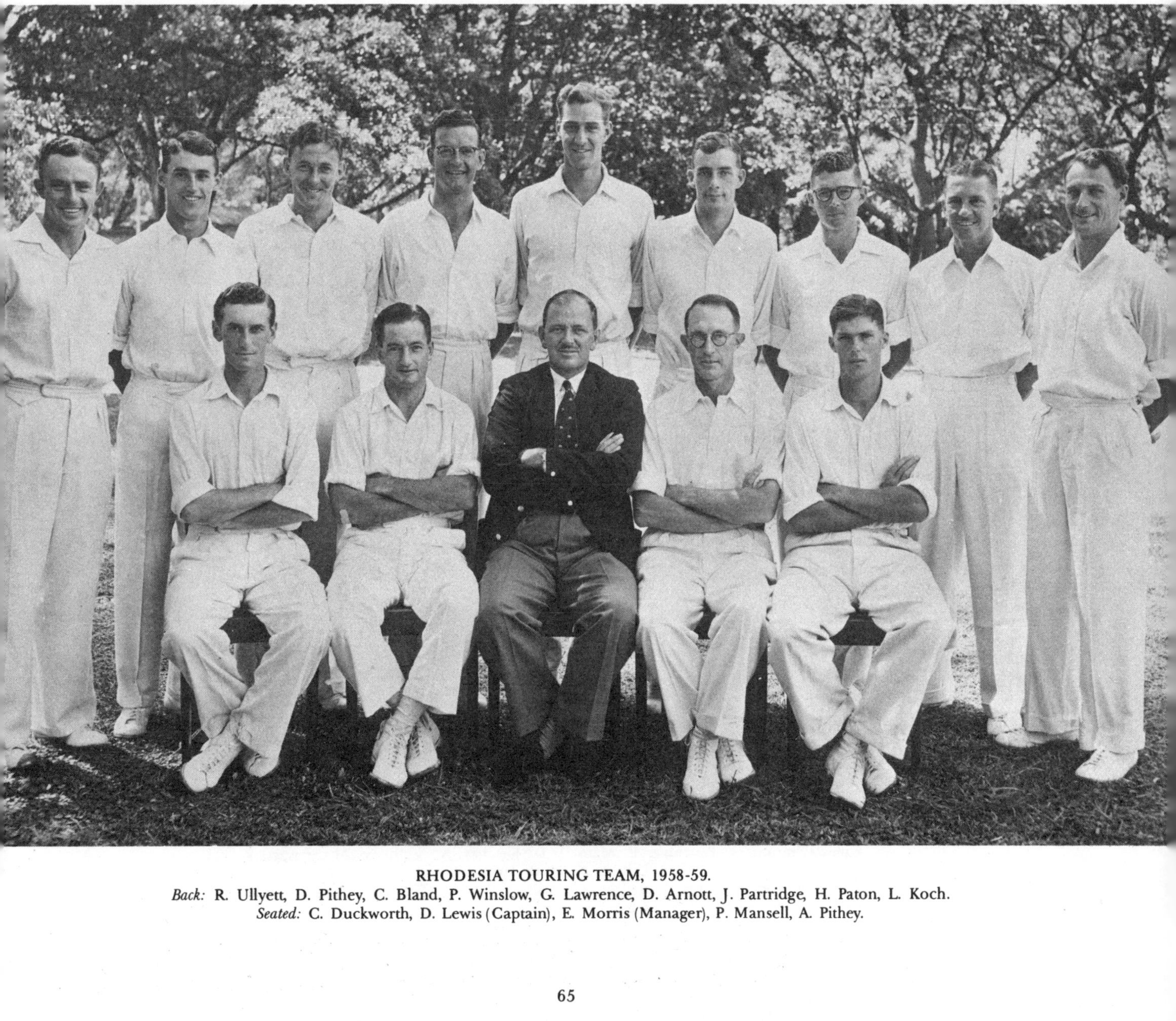

RHODESIA TOURING TEAM, 1958-59.
Back: R. Ullyett, D. Pithey, C. Bland, P. Winslow, G. Lawrence, D. Arnott, J. Partridge, H. Paton, L. Koch.
Seated: C. Duckworth, D. Lewis (Captain), E. Morris (Manager), P. Mansell, A. Pithey.

Surrey side, the English county champions for seven successive years between 1952-58. The touring squad included six English Test players plus the promising John Edrich and Mickey Stewart who were to make their England debuts at a later stage.

The opening match at the Police ground, Salisbury, was one of the most enthralling games ever seen in the capital. And for the 39-year-old maestro of Rhodesian cricket, Percy Mansell, it was a personal triumph in his last year of first-class cricket.

Batting first, Rhodesia struggled against Tony Lock the England veteran of 31 Tests, with Ray Gripper (73) holding the batting together in the early stages, and Mansell (66*) for the remainder of the innings. The Rhodesian total of 246 was comfortably passed as Surrey established a first innings lead of 51. Unfortunately only Gripper came to terms with the bowling the second time round and Surrey were left with what appeared to be the comparatively simple task of obtaining 109 runs for victory in 265 minutes.

Admittedly the pitch was powdery and dry but batting cautiously the tourists reached 50 for the loss of two wickets in the first hour and a half. At 71 their third wicket fell when Barrington was caught by Duckworth at slip off Mansell. This began the Surrey slide because at 82 Stewart tried to hook Mansell, miscued and Duckworth ran from slip to take the catch at backward short leg. Then Tom Clark lifted a ball to John McPhun at wide mid-on — the latter fielding as a substitute for Joe Partridge who had stopped bowling in his thirteenth over due to cramp in his groin. The sixth wicket fell at 90 but in the meantime the perky Roy Swetman was taking runs whenever he could and Surrey appeared destined to win as the hundred was hoisted.

The last part of the game was an excruciatingly tense battle for ascendancy. Rob Ullyett had Lock caught at forward short leg at 101 before skipper Surridge and Swetman scraped together five more runs. At this stage Surridge, who was facing Mansell, gambled on winning the match through one hefty blow, swung wildly, mistimed the ball and was caught by Gripper at mid-on. This brought last man Alec Bedser to the wicket — Peter Loader was confined ill to his hotel bed and unable to bat. Having crossed in the course of the previous catch, Swetman faced Mansell. Surrey scampered a single and Mansell was given the opportunity of bowling at Bedser. The famed Surrey bowler was no mean batsman — having a first-class century to his credit — but he played and missed and was bowled. Percy Mansell with a match analysis of 13/120 had inspired a magnificent victory over the pride of English cricket.

There was more excitement in Bulawayo. Devastating bowling by Joe Partridge well supported by Lawrence and Ullyett, saw Surrey humbled and back in the pavilion for 75. To prove that there was nothing ominous in the pitch the Rhodesians proceeded merrily to 321 in reply. Gripper again scored runs whilst David Lewis made a welcome return to form after a lean period during 1958-59, registering his century in 273 minutes of copybook batting.

It was a very determined Surrey side that came in a second time to wipe off the arrears and avoid defeat. With John Edrich providing the backbone to the innings, the Rhodesian attack was kept at bay during a fascinating fight-back culminating in Alec Bedser, captain for the match, stroking an unbeaten 42, to put the match beyond the home side's reach.

RHODESIA v. SURREY, 1959-60.

Back: R. Swetman, T. Clark, C. Duckworth, J. McPhun, D. Arnott, J. Edrich, B. Constable, D. Napier, J. Buckley (Manager).

Middle: W. Bailey (Umpire), J. Partridge, P. Mansell, D. Fletcher, A. McIntyre, M. Stewart, R. Gripper, R. Ullyett, W. Smith (Umpire).

Front: V. Dickinson, A. Lock, A. Pithey, E. Bedser, A. Bedser, S. Surridge (Surrey Captain), D. Lewis (Rhodesia Captain), K. Barrington.

The Rhodesians celebrate their victory over Surrey in the old communal bath at the Police ground, Salisbury. Clockwise from the front: Harry Birrell, Ray Gripper, John McPhun (wearing Napier's glasses), Vernon Dickinson, Chris Duckworth, Rob Ullyett, Tony Pithey, Dave Napier and Don Arnott.

SCORES: Surrey Tour, 1959-60.

At Salisbury, 10, 11 and 12 October.
Rhodesia — 246 (R.A. Gripper 73, P.N.F. Mansell 66*; G.A.R. Lock 6/76)
and 160 (R.A. Gripper 46; G.A.R. Lock 5/44)
Surrey — 297 (K.F. Barrington 111; P.N.F. Mansell 6/77, J.T. Partridge 3/35)
and 107 (P.N.F. Mansell 7/43)
Rhodesia won by 2 runs.

At Bulawayo, 17, 18 and 19 October.
Surrey — 75 (J.T. Partridge 6/27)
and 380 (J.H. Edrich 151, D.G.W. Fletcher 91; P.N.F. Mansell 6/158, G.B. Lawrence 4/81)
Rhodesia — 321 (D.J. Lewis 118, R.A. Gripper 46, P.N.F. Mansell 33)
and 53-3 wkts.
Match drawn.

Rhodesia's achievements in the A Section of the Currie Cup during 1959-60 were decidedly disappointing. There had been great hopes after the Surrey visit that the Currie Cup might even have wended its way back across the Limpopo by the end of the season. During the aftermath of the Surrey tour Len Brown wrote: 'Without any doubt, this is the best balanced and most powerful Rhodesian side I have known in fifteen years . . . and I doubt whether many will dispute its being labelled best ever.' Sadly this potential never came to fruition in the course of the season and Rhodesia's only successes were in the two matches against an overawed Border side.

In the opening Currie Cup encounter of the season Border just could not cope with the Rhodesian attack in a low-scoring match and were shot out for 116 and 69 within two days. The South African selectors, Alan Melville and Bob Wooller, were present and must have been impressed with Joe Partridge's amazing second innings figures of 12,1-8-9-7 which found a place in the *Wisden Cricketers' Almanack*. Victory over a demoralized Border came in a mere 9 hours 37 minutes playing time and on the second day 29 wickets fell in 7½ hours of play.

The arrival of Natal was seen as a better indication of Rhodesia's strength. On a slow, damp wicket Jackie McGlew sent the Rhodesians in to bat, a decision that paid dividends when only Winslow, in a Jessopian-styled knock, and Duckworth made runs. All out for 167, the Rhodesians struck back. Goddard and McGlew were dismissed with only 17 runs on the board and it was left to Roy McLean in a truly characteristic innings to register top score. The last five Natal batsmen scratched together 29 runs to give Rhodesia a 13-run lead.

Unfortunately the Rhodesian batting fared even worse in their second innings — eight batsmen mustered a meagre ten runs between them. Tony Pithey, in the finest innings of the match, and Paul Winslow recorded half-centuries but Natal, with Jackie McGlew leading the way, hit off the required total with four wickets in hand.

Rhodesia's batting failed again in their next match at home when the side was well beaten by Transvaal. But matters did not improve and in all three matches on tour the Rhodesian top order batting let the team down badly. Against Natal a fighting century by Harry Birrell dissipated any hopes the home side had of an outright victory but two shocking batting displays resulted in an outright defeat at the hands of Western Province. A second win over Border came in two days through the efforts of "Goofy" Lawrence and Joe Partridge despite the fact that once again Rhodesia had lost six wickets before the hundred was up in both innings.

There was cause for alarm when "Goofy" Lawrence

arrived in East London because his kitbag had been lost on the way. The main problem presented by this occurrence was that he had size 13 cricket boots and despite every endeavour in East London, Queenstown and King William's Town no new or second-hand pair could be located. He had no alternative but to use his going-out shoes to bowl in, having first had them painted white. Fortunately this had no great affect upon his performance — the only losers were the Border side of whose wickets he took 9 for 90. Bowling at a slightly slower pace and using the considerable wind to good effect seemed to improve his performance. It is not known what became of those shoes or whether they were ever again used for their intended purpose.

Rhodesia's regular top order batsmen — Gripper, Pithey, Duckworth, Lewis, Winslow, Mansell, Birrell

"Goofy" Lawrence headed the bowling (37 wickets at 16,62) followed by Mansell (26 wickets at 17,84) and Joe Partridge (32 wickets at 19,87). Mansell was not available for the tour and he quietly retired at the end of the season from first-class cricket. Lawrence and Partridge with their figures were obviously in contention for places in the Springbok side to tour England in 1960. But in a momentous piece of ingratitude the Rhodesian selectors dropped Partridge for the last game against Western Province at Newlands. This virtually ruled out his chances and Jimmy Pothecary grasped the opportunity for a place in the Springbok side with both hands in front of selector, Lindsay Tuckett. He captured eight Rhodesian scalps during the match for 59 runs in 45 overs as the visiting batsmen surrendered their wickets with little aggression.

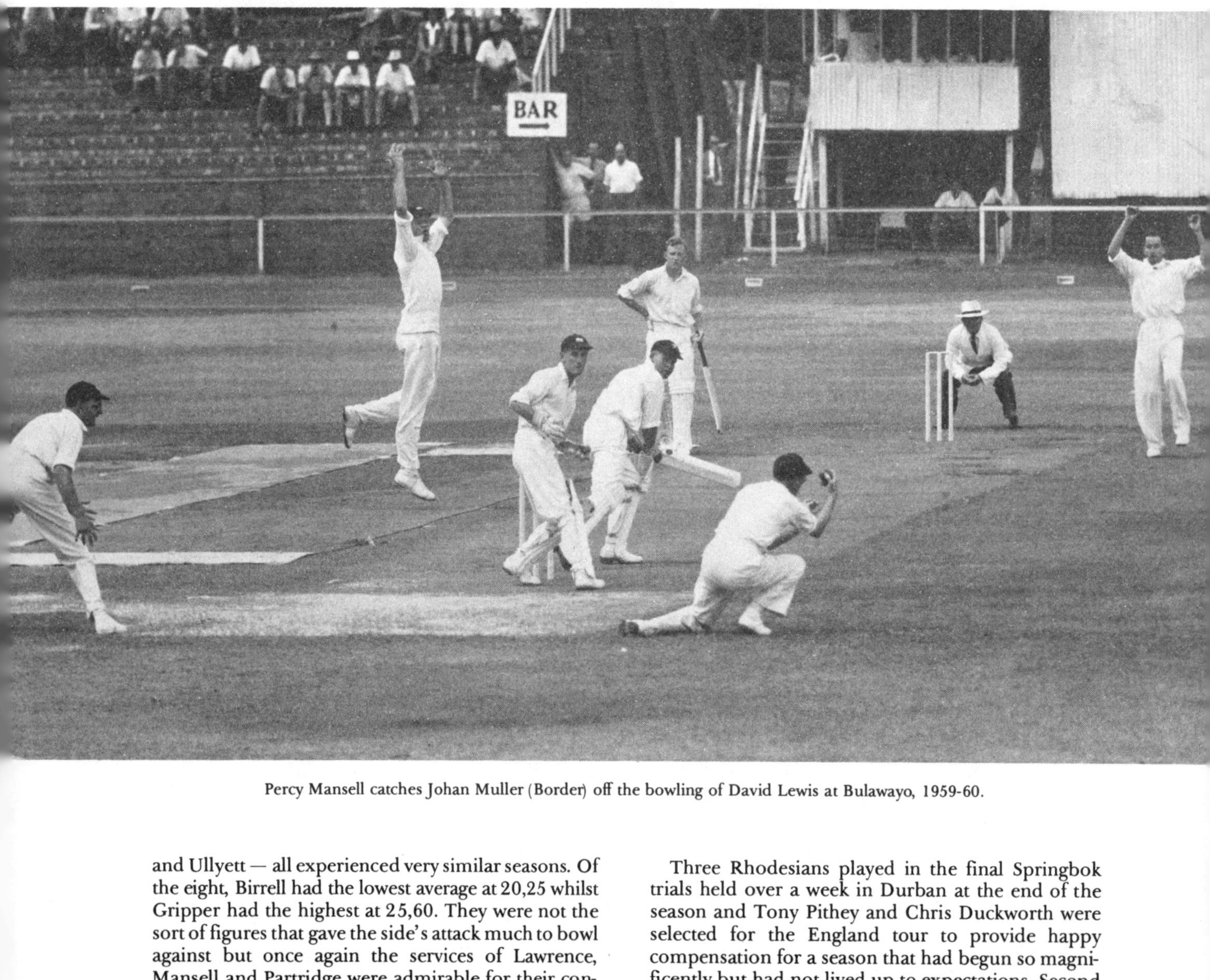

Percy Mansell catches Johan Muller (Border) off the bowling of David Lewis at Bulawayo, 1959-60.

and Ullyett — all experienced very similar seasons. Of the eight, Birrell had the lowest average at 20,25 whilst Gripper had the highest at 25,60. They were not the sort of figures that gave the side's attack much to bowl against but once again the services of Lawrence, Mansell and Partridge were admirable for their consistency and effectiveness. Praise must also be given to Peter Oldham who was recalled to the Rhodesian side after a break of nine years and performed creditably at Newlands to score 28 and take 3/93 in 26 overs.

Three Rhodesians played in the final Springbok trials held over a week in Durban at the end of the season and Tony Pithey and Chris Duckworth were selected for the England tour to provide happy compensation for a season that had begun so magnificently but had not lived up to expectations. Second last place in the A Section hardly reflected the abundant cricket talent that had seeped into the Rhodesian ranks. In fact it was an undeserving conclusion to a decade that had seen so many promising and essentially Rhodesian-bred cricketers make their mark in first-class cricket. The period had been an active one in the construction of the national side and the building up of the necessary depth for the team to become a cricket force. Much of the groundwork must be attributed to the captain, David Lewis, whose deep knowledge, disciplined approach and encouragement played such an influential role in the development of the Rhodesian team during this phase of its history. Indicative of his efforts were the remarks "Goofy" Lawrence had to make at the end of the season. He said of David Lewis: 'I've played almost every first-class match of my career under him and I'm the only one who realises just how much he has helped me in that time.

'All I knew about bowling when I first started under him was that I just wanted the ball so I could get at the batsmen at the other end as quickly as I could.

'Lewis taught me there was more to it than that. How to study batsmen for their weaknesses, how to alter my field for different batsmen. But he helped me most when things were not going too well for me; when the batsmen were set, the day was hot, the pitch was plumb, I hadn't got a wicket and the catches were not sticking. David Lewis taught me that that was the time to roll my sleeves up and start battling.'

It might be appropriate to conclude this chapter with Stuart Surridge's remarks about David Lewis after the Surrey tour: 'What a little fighter he is and what a grand skipper . . . his handling of his attack, his field placings, and his general example in the field were absolutely first-class.'

SCORES: Currie Cup A Section, 1959-60.

At Bulawayo, 14, 15 and 16 November.

Border — 116 (G.B. Lawrence 4/29, P.N.F. Mansell 3/11)
and 69 (J.T. Partridge 7/9, P.N.F. Mansell 3/41)

Rhodesia — 138 (D.J. Lewis 46; R. Thorne 7/40)
and 49-4 wkts.

Rhodesia won by 6 wickets.

At Salisbury, 21, 22 and 23 November.

Rhodesia — 167 (C.A.R. Duckworth 48, P.L. Winslow 47)
and 164 (A.J. Pithey 68, P.L. Winslow 54; T.L. Goddard 5/67)

Natal — 154 (R.A. McLean 57; J.T. Partridge 4/48, G.B. Lawrence 4/53)
and 180-6 wkts. (D.J. McGlew 63)

Natal won by 4 wickets.

At Bulawayo, 28, 29 and 30 November.

Transvaal — 245 (S. O'Linn 89*, A.I. Taylor 59; G.B. Lawrence 7/43)
and 227-4 dec. (W.R. Endean 117*)

"Goofy" Lawrence catches Peter Fenix (Border) off the bowling of Percy Mansell at Bulawayo, 1959-60.

Percy Mansell batting in the twilight of his illustrious career for Matabeleland against Midlands.

Rhodesia — 184 (A.J. Pithey 56, P.L. Winslow 42; G.S. Bunyard 5/35)
and 205 (K.C. Bland 54, C.A.R. Duckworth 40, P.N.F. Mansell 30; J.P. Fellows-Smith 5/57)

Transvaal won by 83 runs.

At Durban, 1, 2 and 4 January.

Natal — 500-7 dec. (T.L. Goddard 200, B.P. Armitage 79, R.A. McLean 73)

Rhodesia — 273 (H.B. Birrell 116, A.J. Pithey 45, D.J. Lewis 38; G.M. Griffin 5/45)
and 82-1 wkt. (C.A.R. Duckworth 37*)

Natal won on first innings.

At East London, 8 and 9 January.

Rhodesia — 201 (R.B. Ullyett 49, J.D. McPhun 39, P.L. Winslow 34)
and 121 (R.B. Ullyett 44)

Border — 95-9 dec. (J.T. Partridge 5/51, G.B. Lawrence 3/42)
and 180 (P.J. Muzzell 50; G.B. Lawrence 6/48)

Rhodesia won by 47 runs.

At Cape Town, 15, 16 and 18 January.

Rhodesia — 189 (D.J. Lewis 33, R.B. Ullyett 31, R.A. Gripper 30; H.D. Bromfield 5/52)
and 170 (C.A.R. Duckworth 67, R.B. Ullyett 31; J.E. Pothecary 5/29)

Western Province — 378 (G.A.S. Innes 99, P.L. van der Merwe 95, R.J. Westcott 56; D.C. Napier 3/78, G.B. Lawrence 3/84, P. Oldham 3/93)

Western Province won by an innings and 19 runs.

JOE PARTRIDGE.

GODFREY LAWRENCE.

CHRIS DUCKWORTH.

CHAPTER SIX

The Golden Years

THE YEARS 1960-65 saw a number of Rhodesians recognized at international level and perform outstandingly well. Those selected for Test matches against England, Australia and New Zealand played their part in the transition of South African cricket into a major force amongst cricket-playing nations during the 1960s.

Tony Pithey and Chris Duckworth, both of whom had already been capped for South Africa, were selected for the 1960 tour to England. This was an ill-fated expedition marred by unforeseeable incidents that undoubtedly affected the morale and form of a talented Springbok squad. Excuses are never palatable fare but the anti-apartheid demonstrations, a particularly wet summer, the Geoff Griffin 'throwing' saga and the loss of the toss in all five Tests each contributed to the difficulties encountered.

Neither Pithey nor Duckworth set the cricket world alight but the tour captain, Jackie McGlew, wrote of the former: 'Pithey looked like developing into the number three batsman whom we sought. Regardless of conditions which were entirely strange to him, he was hitting the ball harder than I had ever seen him do. His South African reputation for stolidity looked like being belied when he straight-drove two sixes in successive matches of astonishing power . . . and then came the onset of back trouble and a run down condition which kept him out of action and then continued to handicap his batting.' And of Duckworth the *Wisden Cricketers' Almanack* remarked: 'Duckworth disappointed as a batsman but was a fine deputy wicket-keeper.'

Many critics thought either of Rhodesia's opening bowlers, Lawrence and Partridge, should have gone on the tour. Peter Pollock supported this view in his book *The Thirty Tests*: 'I do believe that when the 1960 team was chosen to tour England "Goofy" should have made the trip for I have seldom taken the field with a swing and seam bowler of such extraordinary talent. And the same can be said of his compatriot Joe Partridge.'

Lawrence gained selection against New Zealand in 1961-62 during a season of rebuilding after the traumatic tour. He had a 'dream' series, taking 28 wickets with a best innings performance of 8/53 in the drawn Second Test at the Wanderers — both records for Tests between South Africa and New Zealand. And when Springbok captain, Jackie McGlew, through injury was unable to open the batting in the Fifth Test, Lawrence was drafted into going out first with Eddie Barlow. The lanky fast bowler more than justified his elevation when he top-scored with 43.

The New Zealand captain, John Reid, wrote in his book *Sword of Willow* of Lawrence '. . . here was a really good bowler . . . His movement away from the bat is, of course, the best ball that can be bowled in cricket and his ability to mix it with a ball screaming back from outside the off-stump has a batsman constantly watching him. His delivery from two or three feet above his own 6 foot 6 inches enables him to get an unusual amount of lift. I believe he must be the best of his type in the world. What an asset he'd have been to South Africa in England, in 1960.'

Colin Bland, who was Rhodesia's other Test representative during the 1961-62 series had a relatively quiet series with the bat scoring 205 runs with a top score of 42. But he was soon adding a new dimension to the art of fielding that in time he was to develop to a standard such that not even the finest exponents of the craft could quite attain. And it was in his first Test series that he brought off 'one of the greatest catches of all time' to dismiss John Reid off the bowling of "Goofy" Lawrence.

Brian Crowley in his book *The Currie Cup Story* described the scene: 'Determined to dominate the six-foot-six Lawrence, the Kiwi captain slammed into a sizzling cover drive. The ball sped not more than eighteen inches from the ground and looked a certain four, but, diving like an international scrum-half, Bland held the catch with both hands to his right at full stretch.' In fact so brilliant was the effort that even Reid stood his ground for a few seconds to applaud whilst Lawrence shook his head in disbelief — it is most fortunate that this dazzling effort has been recorded on film for posterity.

When the Springboks toured Australia and New Zealand in 1963-64, a record four Rhodesians were included in the party of fifteen. Joe Partridge deservedly gained a belated selection, having been on the fringe of international honours for so many years. He performed exceptionally well in his first series against Australia (25 Test wickets at 33,32 and 62 tour wickets at 25,91) and according to Louis Duffus in his book *Play Abandoned* was 'the bowling discovery of the tour'.

Rhodesia's Springbok representatives in Australasia, 1963-64.

Partridge's favourite ground was Sydney, highlighted by the fact that he claimed 7/91 in Australia's first innings of the Fifth Test. In the three matches he played there on tour — two Tests and against New South Wales — he claimed 27 wickets, nine on each outing. This success caused a wag to comment as the police circled the field at the close of play on one of those days: 'Copper, you don't have to watch us. Watch Joe. He is going to steal the pitch, put it in his bag and take it around the world with him.'

On the tour the Pithey brothers both emerged as players of Test calibre. Tony established himself as South Africa's number 3 batsman and his captain, Trevor Goddard, wrote of him: 'He is one of the most

"Goofy" Lawrence roars an impassioned appeal during the 1961-62 Test series against New Zealand.

correct batsmen I have ever seen.' Brother David played three Tests in Australia and then all three in New Zealand — his figures of 6/58 in 35 overs at Dunedin all but brought South Africa victory before time ran out.

Colin Bland became the most improved player in the side. Peter Pollock maintained 'his fielding alone . . . was worth 20 to 30 runs an innings,' and largely because of this he gained selection for the Second Test against the Aussies. He never looked back with Test scores in Australia of 50, 22, 51, 85, 33, a masterful 126 at Sydney in the Fifth Test, and in New Zealand 40, 46*, 1, 16*, 83 and 23*.

Bland's batting continued to blossom at home against the M.C.C. in 1964-65. His 144 not out in the Second Test not only saved South Africa but, punctuated by two sixes and seventeen fours, it was a vital innings in that it broke the spell that the English spinners had cast up to that stage. Well-known sportswriter, Eric Litchfield, commented afterwards: 'I have waited 34 years to see such a coldly analytical innings . . . since 1930 when Don Bradman scored a superlative 254 out of 423 in five and a half hours.'

David Pithey bowling against New South Wales at Sydney during the 1963-64 Australasian tour.

Of the 1964-65 series the former South African skipper, Jackie McGlew, wrote: 'There is no doubt that the real Personality Man of the series was in the Springbok team. I refer to Colin Bland. He is recognised as the best fieldsman in the world today . . . The tall, lithe Rhodesian simply eats up the yards with his long, loping strides and it says much for his throwing arm that the English batsmen would not risk taking an extra single once the ball was in his possession, whatever his position on the field.'

Joe Partridge, with limited success due to the after-effects of an attack of bilharzia, and Tony Pithey also took part in the series against Mike Smith's M.C.C. side. Pithey compiled his highest-ever Test score of 154 in the Third Test at Newlands and followed this with 95 at the Wanderers. It was a pity that he chose not to tour England in 1965 and slip quietly out of the international scene.

Colin Bland toured again and continued to take the cricket world by storm, thrilling the English crowds with his incredible fielding and being hailed as the finest outfielder in history. In his book *The Thirty Tests* Peter Pollock commented on Bland's fielding in the First Test at Lords: 'The England total would no doubt have been much higher but for the "Golden Eagle" — Colin Bland. A fielder has never been given such publicity before and the national British Sunday papers blazoned Bland's name in banner headlines across their sports pages the next morning. He deserved the credit. His two run-outs (Ken Barrington and Jim Parks were the victims of direct hits on the stumps) were probably more vital to the Springbok cause than we cared to acknowledge at that stage. Colin had made the vital break-through at a stage when none of our bowlers seemed capable of doing so.

'Barrington's run-out saw Colin run in from mid-wicket to mid-on to gather the ball and to throw without hesitation. A single stump was all he had to aim at and he smashed it with Barrington yards out of his crease.

'Jim Parks realising he was in trouble with the ball already in Bland's giant palm, tried to interpose his body in the way of the throw. Dangerous, I would have thought, because I would rather head back to the pavilion than to have a cricket ball thrown by Colin Bland, blast into my kidneys. Such was Bland's accuracy that Jim's best efforts at blocking did not succeed, fortunately for him.

'Colin Bland became a national hero and he firmly established a new respect for the art of fielding. His mere presence on the field, patrolling the covers like a hungry lion saved us runs, for the batsmen refused to take the slightest risk.'

At Canterbury he gave (at Colin Cowdrey's insistent request because the modest Bland would never have so thrust himself forward) a most amazing display of fielding for the spectators, photographers and television cameras. John Parker in his book *Cricket Styles and Stylists* wrote: 'Three stumps were set up in front of a net and then someone got a box of six balls and rolled them out one by one, to Bland, about ten yards to his right and then ten yards to his left, at cover point distance, about 25 yards away. Bland never stopped moving. He swooped on them in turn and with one

Tony Pithey square cuts against the 1964-65 M.C.C. whilst Jim Parks looks on.

flowing movement threw them on the run. With his first throw he knocked the stumps sideways; with the next two he missed, by a whisker; with his fourth he knocked two stumps out of the ground and with his fifth he laid the remaining one flat. He was cheered to the echo by about 200 lucky spectators, just as he had been when he ran out Parks by throwing the ball through the batsman's legs, under his body as he raced for home. Bland is the only man who could add thousands to any gate at a cricket match by his fielding alone.'

As a batsman Bland was at his majestic best in the Third Test at The Oval when he led an assault on the English bowlers to hammer a handsome 127. And at the end of the tour he was invited to play for the World XI against England — in a match at Scarborough alongside Hunte, Barlow, Mohammad, Sobers, Kanhai and Reid he easily made top score of 62 in a rain-ruined encounter. After that season he was to become a regular in the World XI — scoring 132 in a preliminary match against Sussex in 1967 — until he was prevented from entering Britain in 1968 because of his Rhodesian passport.

On the home front, the 1960-61 season got under way with a short two-match visit by a star-studded Cavaliers side. With an array of big names, Richie Benaud's team attracted capacity crowds to the Police ground, Salisbury, for their opening game. Indeed the public could not have asked for better than the famous English pair, Trueman and Statham, opening the bowling backed up by a four-pronged leg spin attack of Benaud, Simpson, Barrington and O'Neill.

Drama occurred in the first overs with Rhodesia's newly appointed captain, Tony Pithey, breaking a finger after facing only two balls. Effectively a wicket down already they lost Lloyd Koch at 13 before Ray Gripper and David Lewis dug themselves in. The latter, who provided the backbone of the innings in a series of partnerships with Ullyett, McPhun, Lawrence and Napier, went on to a brave century.

Freddie Trueman wrote in his book *Fast Fury*: 'In my very first over I realized that the wicket was a dangerous one for really fast bowling. My first delivery shot up off a length, the second went over the batsman's shoulder and the third hit Pithey on the hand, causing him a great deal of pain. His finger was like a corkscrew, and an X-ray revealed a fracture, which was most unfortunate . . . A fellow called David Lewis took a hundred off us . . . his was a most courageous knock. Lewis's hand was hit, too, and I could actually see the blood coming through his glove.'

With a creditable total behind them, the Rhodesian pace attack of Lawrence, Partridge and Napier bowled their hearts out. The 11 000-strong crowd was given plenty of excitement as the international batsmen floundered against the local heroes. Simpson went cheaply to Partridge but the rot really began to set in when Lawrence had Geoff Pullar trapped leg before at 41. Barrington, O'Neill, Graveney, Mike Smith and Benaud followed. Illingworth and Trueman temporarily held up the proceedings with the latter, amid his clowning, making a mess of Partridge's good bowling analysis by carting him for two sixes, a four and a two in one over.

All out for 155 — 86 runs behind — the Cavaliers were stung and Trueman, Statham and Benaud proceeded to mow down the Rhodesian batsmen. Wickets tumbled — new cap Dalton Cornwall made top score of 12 whilst John McPhun clung to his wicket for 61 minutes before being stumped for 4. Rhodesia collapsed to be 52 all out leaving the Cavaliers to make 139 which they achieved with the best part of a day to spare.

Bulawayo were then entertained to a two-day fixture and *The Chronicle* commented on the Cavaliers' first day's performance: '. . . here was the game at its highest level, alternately graceful and careful, then spontaneous and carefree. And how we loved every marvellous minute of it.'

David Lewis put the Cavaliers in to bat and after twenty minutes the left-handed Pullar was brilliantly snapped up in the gully by John McPhun off "Goofy" Lawrence. But the Rhodesians had to wait a further 110 playing minutes before their next success whilst Bobby Simpson and Mike Smith added 158 glorious runs. Both went out within 4 runs of each other, the highly rated Norman O'Neill was out without scoring, Tom Graveney was caught by the neat Trifon Deftereos soon afterwards and from 167-1 the Cavaliers slumped to 193-5. Benaud and Illingworth hit out handsomely but nevertheless Rhodesia did well to dismiss the tourists for 291.

With Alan Moss brought in to support Trueman bowling virtually at his fieriest and fastest, and Statham, the Rhodesians began badly in reply. The day, however, belonged to new cap Ian Haig who faced the onslaught for 125 resounding minutes before running out of partners with his score at 64. Only John McPhun in a steadfast innings stayed for any length of time with him, taking the total from 70-5 to 140-6 before Trueman and Moss polished off the tail to end a heroic fight-back at 185.

The cavaliers batted out the rest of the day —

Colin Bland thrilled English crowds in 1965 with his incredible fielding and is shown here during his Canterbury exhibition and (*below*) running out Jim Parks at Lord's. Richard Dumbrill and Jackie Botten are the fielders appealing.

Norman O'Neill returning to form to provide the fireworks with a sparkling century in 99 minutes.

SCORES: Cavaliers Tour, 1960-61.

At Salisbury, 17, 18 and 19 September.

Rhodesia — 241 (D.J. Lewis 107, R.A. Gripper 40; J.B. Statham 5/41)
and 52

Cavaliers — 155 (G.B. Lawrence 4/45, J.T. Partridge 4/67)
and 139-4 wkts. (K.F. Barrington 66, R.B. Simpson 53*)

Cavaliers won by 6 wickets.

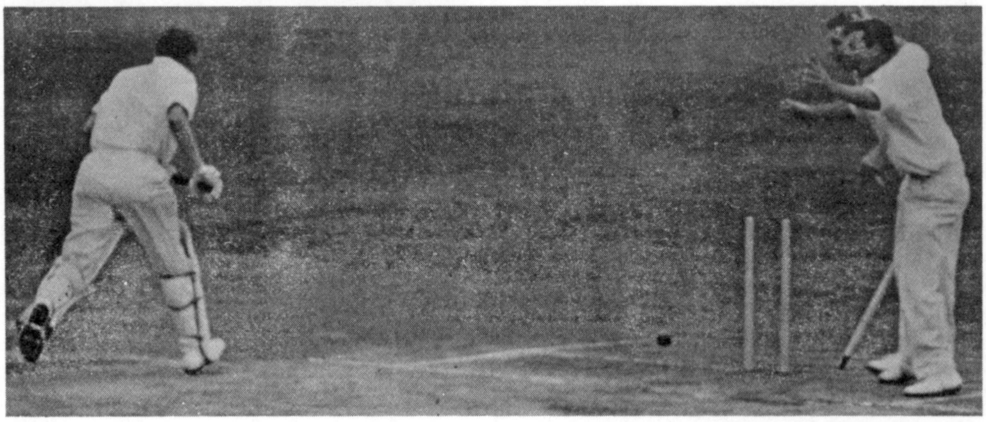

At Bulawayo, 21 and 22 September, (Not first-class).
Cavaliers — 291 (M.J.K. Smith 93, R.B. Simpson 71; D.C. Napier 4/69, G.B. Lawrence 3/37)
and 257-2 wkts. (N.C. O'Neill 104*, G. Pullar 81)
Rhodesia — 185 (I.E. Haig 64*, J.D. McPhun 41; F.S. Trueman 5/41)
Match drawn.

Rhodesia made a bad start in the Currie Cup by losing in successive weeks on the first innings to North-Eastern Transvaal and Transvaal B. The competition had reverted back to the old system with the teams not being divided into sections and Rhodesia's opposition on their Christmas tour varied considerably in strength. They were beaten by five wickets by Transvaal A on account of their poor batting but came from behind to beat Eastern Province by seven wickets. The Rhodesians followed this up with an overwhelming 217-run win over Griqualand West in Kimberley and in the last match of the season lost an exciting encounter to Natal at the Police ground, Salisbury.

The Natal match was a low scoring affair with Rhodesia taking a 33-run first innings lead largely through a brilliant 72 not out by David Lewis which was described in *The South African Cricket Annual* as being 'the former Oxford Blue's finest innings in this country and bore the hallmark of many a fine century'. Through a half-century by Ian Haig with Rodney Keast and "Goofy" Lawrence giving invaluable support, Natal were set 187 to win — a target they achieved for the loss of eight wickets due almost entirely to Chris Burger's 87.

IAN HAIG.

The batting was invariably weak throughout the season and only against Griqualand West, with Colin Bland and Tony Pithey hammering centuries, did the Rhodesians ever look masters of the attack. Pithey and Ray Gripper developed into a reliable opening pair, whilst Bland added punch and power to the batting on the tour during his university vacation. The most encouraging strides were made by Ian Haig as a dependable middle-order batsman and after his 70 against Eastern Province, Len Brown wrote: 'It was a great effort and showed once again how temperament-

THE 1960-61 RHODESIAN TOURING TEAM.

(*Above*): Geoff Griffin bowling for Rhodesia against the 1961-62 New Zealanders at Bulawayo and (*below*) he is closely watched by English umpire, Syd Buller, during the 1960 Lord's Test.

ally suited he is to the demands of first-class cricket.'

The bowling painted a far brighter picture. It was spearheaded by "Goofy" Lawrence who took 26 wickets in the six Currie Cup matches and many scratched their heads in amazement that South Africa could have left him behind on their 1960 England tour. He was given good support by Joe Partridge and when the bespectacled seamer was unavailable for the Christmas tour, 19-year-old "Tinker" Beets burst on to the scene. In dramatic fashion Beets returned figures of 4/34 and 6/25 against Griqualand West. Left-arm spinner Vernon Dickinson also had his moments and against North-Eastern Transvaal (6/61) and Eastern Province (3/63 and 7/22) he was devastating. Add Rob Ullyett (who took 6/42 against North-Eastern Transvaal) and Dave Napier to the attack and it could be seen that Rhodesia had plenty of bowling talent to offer.

On top of this the exciting news of the season was the arrival in Rhodesia of Geoff Griffin, South Africa's controversial fast bowler. The storm that arose over his bowling action had overshadowed everything else on the 1960 tour to England and he had become the most discussed name in world cricket. It was in the Second Test at Lord's that the likeable South African experienced both tragedy and triumph in a match of bizarre happenings. He was no-balled eleven times for throwing — the first bowler to be called in a Test in England — and then he sensationally achieved a hat-trick in the same innings. To add to the drama, in an exhibition match staged for the benefit of the Queen and the Duke of Edinburgh, Griffin was no-balled four times out of five balls, changed to underarm and was promptly no-balled again for forgetting to notify the batsman of his change of action.

Griffin's hat-trick might not have had that much influence on the course of the game but after the ordeal he had been through it could not have come at a more opportune time. Mike Smith, sweating on the vital single required for his hundred, was the first victim, caught by a diving Johnny Waite off the last ball of an over. Peter Walker pulled two sixes off Goddard's over in between and then Griffin beat him comprehensively to shatter the wickets. It was at this stage that Jackie McGlew, South Africa's captain at the time, wrote vividly of the scene in his book *Cricket for South Africa*: 'Of all the cricketers who might be called upon to face a situation such as this, the colourful Trueman, I imagine, could be calculated to be the least perturbed. Again I pushed the fielders nearer to the bat. For all I knew, Trueman gave no thought to the fact that Griffin was waiting now for a hat-trick, since Smith's wicket had fallen in the previous over. If he did, there was no evidence that he was bothered by it. Down came Griffin, swinging in a shade on to the line of the leg stump and Trueman swung lustily . . . and as that leg stump vanished from his "castle" Lord's rose to acclaim the first hat-trick ever performed in a Test match at the hallowed home of cricket, and the first by a South African in any Test.'

Griffin was an extremely popular figure and many sympathized wholeheartedly with his predicament. As a youngster he had had a fall and the fracture was set in a manner which was unnatural — it was physically impossible thereafter for him to straighten his right arm in the normal manner. Denis Compton wrote in the *Sunday Express*: 'I feel the umpires have been too severe on this boy. Certainly he has a bent arm, but he cannot straighten it because of a physical disability. I have seen bowlers with more suspect actions get away with it. And I will say definitely that Griffin does not throw.'

One wonders if news of Griffin's intended arrival did not spread alarm amongst local umpires because rumours began to spread after a headline in *The Rhodesia Herald* read: 'Now chucking hits Rhodesian cricket.' The headline referred to a former Manicaland cricket captain being called four times in one over for throwing whilst playing for Old Boys against Makoni. Fortunately the outcry blew over and the controversy took a back seat for a while as it became a tremendously interesting argument as to whether Griffin would force his way into the Rhodesian side at the end of the season. Would he get in ahead of Lawrence, Partridge, Napier or Beets? There was also a fine seam bowler waiting in the wings prior to leaving for overseas. Tony Nicholson, who was playing for Salisbury Police, was to become Yorkshire's opening bowler and was selected for the 1964-65 M.C.C. tour to South Africa before a troublesome back forced him to withdraw.

Perhaps the question was partially solved when the throwing problem raised its ugly head again in Geoff Griffin's debut in Salisbury league cricket. He was 'called' four times by the experienced local umpire, Bill Bailey, although on changing ends Currie Cup umpire, W.K. Smith, seemed satisfied in the course of the 21 overs Griffin bowled. The blond Springbok nevertheless had to wait until the following season for his Rhodesian debut.

SCORES: Currie Cup, 1960-61.

At Salisbury, 19, 20 and 21 November.

North-Eastern Transvaal — 245 (P.L. Corbett 83; V.E.J. Dickinson 6/61, J.T. Partridge 3/43)
and 203 (H.R. Lance 93; R.B. Ullyett 6/42, G.B. Lawrence 3/52)

DAVE NAPIER.

Rhodesia — 170 (R.A. Gripper 45, I.E. Haig 39; G. Steyn 5/47)
and 62-2 wkts.

North-Eastern Transvaal won on first innings.

At Bulawayo, 26, 27 and 28 November.

Transvaal B — 315-9 dec. (A. Bacher 101, G. Stein 62, L. Harris 51; G.B. Lawrence 5/94)
and 178-9 dec. (V.E.J. Dickinson 4/48)

Rhodesia — 212 (A.J. Pithey 50, R.B. Ullyett 46, I.E. Haig 44; B.D. Thorp 5/51)
and 176-7 wkts. (R.A. Gripper 59, A.J. Pithey 36; G. Fairon 5/45)

Transvaal B won on first innings.

At Johannesburg, 24, 26 and 27 December.

Rhodesia — 226 (K.C. Bland 42, D.J. Lewis 38)
and 196 (I.E. Haig 62, A.J. Pithey 60, V.E.J. Dickinson 30; K.A. Walter 6/45)

Transvaal A — 366-6 dec. (W.R. Endean 122, A. Bacher 86, D. Varnals 57, S. O'Linn 54; G.B. Lawrence 4/64)
and 57-5 wkts. (G.B. Lawrence 4/26)

Transvaal A won by 5 wickets.

At Port Elizabeth, 31 December, 2 and 3 January.

Eastern Province — 239 (R.G. Pollock 60, P.H. Copeland 50; G.B. Lawrence 3/32, V.E.J. Dickinson 3/63)
and 92 (V.E.J. Dickinson 7/22, G.B. Lawrence 3/24)

Rhodesia — 160 (I.E. Haig 70, A.J. Pithey 38; J. Ferrant 6/67)
and 172-3 wkts. (A.J. Pithey 49, D.B. Arnott 41*, D.J. Lewis 39)

Rhodesia won by 7 wickets.

At Kimberley, 6, 7 and 9 January.

Rhodesia — 152 (G.B. Lawrence 40, D.J. Lewis 39; B.W. Burrow 5/56)
and 317-4 dec. (K.C. Bland 130*, A.J. Pithey 111, R.A. Gripper 45)

Griqualand West — 155 (D.J. Beets 4/34, G.B. Lawrence 3/49) and 97 (D.J. Beets 6/25)

Rhodesia won by 217 runs.

At Salisbury, 4, 5 and 6 March.

Rhodesia — 155 (D.J. Lewis 72*) and 153 (I.E. Haig 54)

Natal — 122 (J.T. Partridge 3/32, G.B. Lawrence 3/32) and 187-8 wkts. (C.G. Burger 87; G.B. Lawrence 3/43)

Natal won by 2 wickets.

In the off-season two Rhodesians, Ray Gripper and Colin Bland, took part in a 21-match tour of England sponsored by Stanley Murphy, a retired sugar planter and a sports enthusiast. Known as the Fezelas, the team was comprised of the cream of southern Africa's young players under the experienced leadership of Springbok Roy McLean. The value of Mr. Murphy's far-sighted generosity became apparent in the year which followed because Bland, Barlow, Peter Pollock, Lindsay, Van der Merwe, Elgie and Botten all went on to become Springboks.

New Zealand team that went on to achieve what no previous side from that country had, by winning a Test on foreign soil. They went even better by gaining a second victory to halve the rubber with South Africa — the only time a New Zealand team had won more than a single Test in a series.

The opening tour match attracted 5 000 spectators and a flawless 91 by Bland, coupled with Don Arnott's career-best 58 and Ian Haig's hard-hit 54, enabled Pithey to declare at 311-8 at the end of the first day. Partridge and Griffin then put Rhodesia firmly on top by having three wickets down for 46 before John Reid and John Guy proceeded to repair the damage. The rambunctious Reid gave an opening warning to South Africa by thrashing the attack for a six and seventeen fours in his 97. New Zealand were all out for 262.

Another entertaining display by the Rhodesian batsmen with Gripper, Bland and Pithey to the fore, saw a nicely-timed declaration leaving New Zealand 247 to get in 192 minutes. The visitors made a bold bid to go for the runs but the match ended with the entire Rhodesian team clustered around New Zealand's fair-haired pace bowler and number 11 batsman Frank

David Lewis is caught by the New Zealand wicket-keeper, John Ward, off the bowling of John Reid at the Queens ground, Bulawayo in 1961-62.

The Fezelas did outstandingly well and were unbeaten on tour which included winning convincingly the three first-class matches they played. They produced magnificently positive cricket and scored 6 000 runs of which 4 000 came in fours in addition to eighty sixes. Highlighting their vigorous scoring talents was the first-class match against Essex when Denis Lindsay completed proceedings with five successive sixes off an over from Greensmith. Ray Gripper was one of the leading run scorers on tour and compiled a century against Winchester College whilst Colin Bland powered his way to 152 not out (110 minutes — ten sixes) against a Surrey XI.

Incredible as it may seem, "Goofy" Lawrence was dropped from the Rhodesian side for their opening game of the 1961-62 season against the touring New Zealanders. There were three new caps in the Rhodesian team — Robbie Robertson, Jack du Preez and Geoff Griffin. And how well the local side did against a

Cameron. Rhodesia just failed to gain their first outright victory against an international touring side.

The New Zealanders then played a two-day fixture against the Rhodesian Country Districts XI in Que Que which saw a welter of run-making produce 918 runs in twelve hours. The visitors probably felt that 326-5 declared was an amply sufficient total and could never have visualized that the next day's headline 'Tornado Taberer cuts New Zealand attack to ribbons' would ever occur. Louis Duffus wrote: 'Taberer's good eye and placing were a revelation. He hit one six off Alabaster and two off Yuile — all to the onside with robust servings of the bat.' A relative of the 1902-03 Springbok captain, Taberer hit 101 in 146 minutes and was joined in his spectacular hitting by Don Bailey who scored 84 in just over two hours with sixteen boundaries. "Bundu" Waller and D.M. Bentley (father of the future Rhodesian and Natal cricketer) also joined in the run feast that saw the Districts XI pass

New Zealand's tally before declaring at 347-8.

In their last match on Rhodesian soil in Salisbury, the New Zealanders for the first time came up against their tormentor of 1961-62, the re-called "Goofy" Lawrence. In a game that rain prematurely ended with New Zealand chasing 259 in 237 minutes, two Rhodesians made a great impression on Jack Cheetham the Springbok selector who was watching. Lawrence wrecked the New Zealand middle-order with figures of 5/32 in 18,1 overs whilst Bland took his run total against the tourists to 261 via two further half-centuries. Both were rewarded with Springbok selection.

SCORES: New Zealand Tour, 1961-62.

At Bulawayo, 21, 22 and 23 October.

Rhodesia — 311-8 dec. (K.C. Bland 91, D.B. Arnott 58, I.E. Haig 54, G.M. Griffin 35*)
and 197-5 dec. (R.A. Gripper 52, A.J. Pithey 47, K.C. Bland 45; R.C. Motz 5/65)

New Zealand — 262 (J.R. Reid 97, J.W. Guy 63, P.G.Z. Harris 56*; G.M. Griffin 4/74, J.T. Partridge 4/80)
and 162-9 wkts. (J.T. Partridge 5/52)

Match drawn.

At Que Que, 25 and 26 October (Not first-class).

New Zealand — 326-5 dec. (P.G.Z. Harris 86, S.N. McGregor 66, J.W. Guy 60, M.E. Chapple 50*, P. Elgin 3/96)
and 245-3 wkts. (J.W. Guy 83, J.T. Sparling 57, P.T. Barton 56*)

Rhodesian Country Districts — 347-8 dec. (A. Taberer 101, D.C. Bailey 84, N. Waller 40)

Match drawn.

At Salisbury, 28, 29 and 30 October.

Rhodesia — 189 (K.C. Bland 67, I.E. Haig 37)
and 255-8 dec. (A.J. Pithey 66, K.C. Bland 58, R.A. Gripper 54, D.J. Lewis 40*)

New Zealand — 186 (J.W. Guy 54; G.B. Lawrence 5/32)
and 27-0 wkts.

Match drawn.

Two friendly matches against South African provincial sides were staged during the 1961-62 season. The first was an historic match in that it was Rhodesia's first ever victory over Natal. It was also a memorable occasion for Joe Partridge who bowled magnificently to record match figures of 14/101 — the best bowling performance by a Rhodesian in first-class cricket. The villain of the piece had to a great extent been a whirlwind that whipped the covers from the pitch and allowed the rain to turn an expected easy-paced pitch into a seam-bowler's paradise. Nevertheless, the Rhodesian trio of Partridge, Griffin and Lawrence had the edge over the Natal attack of Adcock, Trimborn and Cole. The superb, controlled swing bowling of Partridge and Lawrence which wrecked the Natal second innings ultimately swung a low-scoring match in Rhodesia's favour.

In the other "friendly" fixture Rhodesia's disappointing batting let them down badly against Transvaal after Partridge and Lawrence had again placed them in an advantageous position. Only Rob Ullyett made runs in Rhodesia's miserable first innings total of 134. But Partridge struck back when he bowled Eddie Barlow and Ali Bacher with only seven runs on the board whilst Johnny Waite departed for an X-ray on a swollen thumb. He also had Carlstein leg before at 35 before "Goofy" Lawrence took over. In a spell of 35 balls the giant seam bowler took 6/10 to create a sensational collapse and dismiss Transvaal for 79. Unfortunately a second Rhodesian batting failure allowed Transvaal to canter home to a five-wicket victory.

SCORES: Friendly Inter-provincial matches, 1961-62.

At Salisbury, 25, 26 and 27 November.

Natal — 158 (M.K. Elgie 66, B. Versfeld 53; J.T. Partridge 8/69)
and 85 (J.T. Partridge 6/32, G.B. Lawrence 4/38)

Rhodesia — 133 (G.M. Griffin 40)
and 113-2 wkts. (A.J. Pithey 34*)

Rhodesia won by 8 wickets.

Following his record-breaking match analysis of 14/101 against Natal at Salisbury in 1961-62, a trophy presentation was made to Joe Partridge.

At Bulawayo, 2, 3 and 4 December.

Rhodesia — 134 (R.B. Ullyett 46; H.J. Tayfield 5/39)
and 125 (K.C. Bland 44, D.J. Lewis 30)

Transvaal — 79 (G.B. Lawrence 6/19, J.T. Partridge 4/46)
and 182-5 wkts. (I. R. Fullerton 71)

Transvaal won by 5 wickets.

To round off the season a Commonwealth XI made a five-match visit to Rhodesia as part of their eight-week world tour. Captained by Ray Lindwall, the side included three famous West Indians, Everton Weekes, Roy Marshall and Sonny Ramadhin, the Indian spinner, Subhash Gupte, the great Australian opening bat, Colin McDonald, Englishmen Tom Graveney, Norman Gifford, Harold Rhodes, Dave Larter and Harold Stephenson, the South African Basil d'Oliveira and two Pakistani stars, Hanif Mohammad and Saeed Ahmed. The diminutive Mohammad is of course the holder of the highest individual first-class score of 499 and the longest innings on record with a 16 hours 39 minutes marathon Test knock of 337 against the West Indies in 1957-58.

The tour began at the Harrison Oval, Nkana against a Rhodesian XI in a match spoilt by rain. Compensating features were two superb centuries — Graveney in 211 minutes and Tony Pithey in 158 minutes — and an impressive sustained spell of seam bowling by Joe Partridge.

From there the tourists moved to the tiny rural village of Ruwa where they played the Rhodesian Country Districts. The Commonwealth XI surprisingly collapsed to be 145 all out but at the same time not one iota of credit should be taken from a steady performance by Pat Elgin, Ken Ziehl and their support bowlers. Unfortunately, their sterling efforts in the field were tossed away by the batsmen who had difficulty trying to fathom out the spinners. Tony Taberer lived dangerously and succeeded for a while but in the end the experience of the visitors told after two days of attractive cricket.

In the second three-day encounter in Bulawayo Joe Partridge again stole the bowling honours, Colin Bland entertained the crowd with a hurricane first innings 60 in 54 minutes whilst Ian Haig made runs on both his visits to the crease. But the Commonwealth XI were always in control with the compact Pakistan captain, Hanif Mohammad providing the final ingredient to a comprehensive six-wicket victory by stroking a masterly 86 in 102 minutes.

A crowd of 850 in Que Que watched Mohammad, Saeed Ahmed, Graveney, Weekes and local 'guest' Mike Laws hammer swashbuckling half-centuries against the Rhodesian Colts XI. They also saw Ray Lindwall, following an injury, return to send down a dozen overs in the Colts' first innings and give the young players an object lesson in how to use the ball and out-think the batsmen. However it was not all one-way traffic as Ken Tonkin and Ross Fuller bowled well whilst John McPhun scored a highly promising second innings century and added 139 for the third wicket with Nick Frangos.

For their final match the Rhodesian selectors invited Springbok Jackie McGlew to captain the side and the promising Denis Lindsay to keep wicket whilst Springboks, Paul Winslow and Percy Mansell, were recalled for their final appearances in first-class cricket. Mansell had two months earlier been awarded the M.B.E. in the New Year's Honours list — a fitting award to a man who had performed so creditably for Rhodesia on the cricket field in a career that had spanned twenty-four years.

In a highly entertaining encounter Ray Gripper, Denis Lindsay and Colin Bland demonstrated the Fezela approach to good effect and helped to set up the Rhodesian Invitation XI's five-wicket victory. Lindsay's two innings were gems and amid such august company he stamped his personality firmly on the game. The crowd marvelled at the neat and technically perfect way he paraded his array of shots and local hero, Colin Bland, could do no more than play the 'junior partner' in the second innings in a stand which massacred the bowling and realised 105 runs.

On his return to first-class cricket Mansell bowled as tightly as ever and in the visitors' second innings claimed the vital wickets of Hanif Mohammad and Tom Graveney when both were into their stride. But it was Joe Partridge who created the greatest problems for the international line-up and increased his bag of wickets to 22 in three matches. For the most part he had all the batsmen in difficulties and took his fiftieth first-class wicket of the season when he had Stephenson leg before — a feat "Goofy" Lawrence had accomplished the previous afternoon when he yorked Everton Weekes.

To crown a great season for Colin Bland, he was invited to accompany the Commonwealth XI for two matches in Nairobi and Pakistan. Tom Graveney's quip at the time was: 'That's just dandy. We can put him in the covers to look after the off side, while the rest of us gather round on the leg side and bamboozle the opposition out.'

The Commonwealth XI travelled some 40 000 miles and visited a number of far-flung territories in order to complete their tour. Bland actually played in a first-class match at Dacca against the East Pakistan Governor's XI and made top score of 89 out of a total of 266 for the Commonwealth XI.

SCORES: Commonwealth XI Tour, 1961-62.

At Nkana, 17, 18 and 19 February.

Commonwealth XI — 234 (T.W. Graveney 112*, B.L. d'Oliveira 51; J.T. Partridge 5/52)
and 123-3 wkts. (T.W. Graveney 52*)

Rhodesia XI — 247-7 dec. (A.J. Pithey 115, I.E. Haig 43)

Match drawn.

At Ruwa, 21 and 22 February (Not first-class).

Commonwealth XI — 145 (P. Elgin 5/45)
and 158-2 dec. (Hanif Mohammad 77, C.C. McDonald 69)

Rhodesian Country Districts — 102 (A. Taberer 38, G.M.H. Barber 22; S.P. Gupte 4/22, S. Ramadhin 4/26)
and 99 (A. Taberer 34, D.B. Arnott 25; N. Gifford 5/31)

Commonwealth XI won by 102 runs.

At Bulawayo, 24, 25 and 26 February

Rhodesia — 287 (K.C. Bland 60, R.B. Ullyett 59, I.E. Haig 47, A.J. Pithey 31, R.A. Gripper 30)
and 210-8 dec. (I.E. Haig 44, K.C. Bland 34, G.B. Lawrence 32, A. de Caila 31*)

Commonwealth XI — 305 (C.C. McDonald 70, R.E. Marshall 59, T.W. Graveney 52, Hanif Mohammad 50; J.T. Partridge 4/54, J.H. du Preez 4/97)
and 196-4 wkts. (Hanif Mohammad 86; J.T. Partridge 3/69)

Commonwealth XI won by 6 wickets.

At Que Que, 28 February, 1 March (Not first-class).

Commonwealth XI — 383-9 dec. (Hanif Mohammad 71, Saeed Ahmed 68, T.W. Graveney 62, E.D. Weekes 56, M. Laws 52*; K.J. Tonkin 3/60, E.D.R. Fuller 3/94)

Rhodesian Colts XI — 168 (J.D. McPhun 39, W.H. Hodnett 34, N.J. Frangos 30)
and 255-3 wkts. (J.D. McPhun 107, N.J. Frangos 74, S.D. Barbour 45*)

Match drawn.

At Salisbury, 3, 4 and 5 March.

Commonwealth XI — 294 (C.C. McDonald 82; J.T. Partridge 3/71)
and 154 (T.W. Graveney 70; J.T. Partridge 5/42, P.N.F. Mansell 3/41)

Rhodesian Invitation XI — 232 (R.A. Gripper 67, D.T. Lindsay 48; Saeed Ahmed 6/32)
and 217-5 wkts. (D.T. Lindsay 84, K.C. Bland 41*, R.A. Gripper 35)

Rhodesian Invitation XI won by 5 wickets.

The 1962-63 season was to prove an exciting one for Rhodesia on a number of counts. One cannot deny that there was obvious disappointment in the side being pipped for first place in the B Section by Transvaal B but for once cricket tables took a back seat to the game because the type of cricket played captured a wider audience than before and dominated the various media in an unprecedented manner throughout the season. Once again that great friend of Rhodesian cricket, Ron Roberts, brought out Commonwealth sides to set the scene and start the season off in grand fashion before returning to conclude it on a high note. And in addition for the national side there was the incentive of a place in the Springbok tour squad to Australasia in the following 1963-64 season. Whilst names were constantly being bandied about by armchair selectors and the Press throughout the season, as many as seven Rhodesians were seemingly in the running at various stages. With the tour selection barometer featuring weekly in the Press, rarely has a cricket tour ensnared the public's interest to such an extent as did the 1963-64 Australian adventure and Rhodesia's eventual reward of four places was a wonderful achievement and was greeted enthusiastically.

The first Commonwealth side which toured in September 1962, was led by joint captains, Colin Ingleby-Mackenzie and England's double international at soccer and cricket, Willie Watson. Of particular interest were the West Indian Test players — the dynamic and highly rated right-hand batsman Rohan Kanhai, the well-known Hampshire professional Roy Marshall, pace bowler Chester Watson, and the acknowledged fastest bowler in the world, Wes Hall. The South African Trevor Goddard joined the side after his lengthy stay in England, Basil d'Oliveira was again a welcome visitor and to make it a multi-representative side, Ron Roberts had acquired the services of Indians, Chandrakant Borde and Ali Baig.

The first match was a three-day fixture at the Ek Park ground, Kitwe, where Rhodesia batting first, made a poor start. Their total of 169 was quickly overhauled by the visitors through the efforts of Willie Watson (100) and Rohan Kanhai (76) who both captivated the Sunday crowd of 2 200 with their assured stroke play. The Commonwealth side were all out for 308 which gave them a lead of 139.

Rhodesia's second innings was a vast improvement. Tony Pithey scored his third century at Ek Park and steered Rhodesia to safety before declaring. He left the visitors 130 minutes to score 202 runs which was by no means an impossible task on a wicket that seldom gave the bowlers much joy. Surprisingly the experienced Commonwealth batsmen set off at a rash pace, wickets tumbled, and at the finish Rhodesia only needed two wickets with 62 runs to spare.

Wes Hall, who took no part in the Northern Rhodesian match, came into the side for a two-day encounter in Bulawayo. The Commonwealth XI batted first and were immediately in trouble as the keyed-up Rhodesians created havoc among their more illustrious opposite numbers. Roy Marshall was bowled by "Goofy" Lawrence for 4 and Ali Baig suffered the same fate with the very next ball. Rohan Kanhai went to a skied catch at 20, D'Oliveira was bowled by an inswinging beauty from Partridge at 48 and at 56 Goddard touched a ball to Eddie Parker at third slip. In an unusual dismissal the Bulawayo all-rounder dived foward and scooped the ball back to Tony de Caila but it required a consultation of umpires before the judicial finger went up. Half the side were out and the visitors were in dire trouble until Martin Young hauled them to a respectable 257, carrying his bat for 138.

The all-West Indian pace attack of Wes Hall and Chester Watson in retaliation decided to warm matters up. Working towards maximum pace they had the crowd on the edge of their seats but the fact that they only bowled six overs in the first half-hour caused Bulawayo correspondent Martin Lee to write: 'It was frustrating in the extreme, especially as an alarmingly high proportion of Hall's deliveries were balls which the batsmen decided to duck.'

The Rhodesians squared up admirably to the task that confronted them and the young opening pair of Ray Gripper and John McPhun put on 80 runs. By the time Lewis declared with Rhodesia comfortably placed at 211-2 the Rhodesian captain and Bland were in fact going great guns. Lewis's declaration, 46 runs behind, was an attempt to force an outright in this two-day fixture. But when the Commonwealth XI in turn declared their second innings closed and left Rhodesia 192 to make at a cracking pace the home side were not up to it. Eddie Parker, who hit 60 in 100 minutes, and Ray Gripper, gave rise to some hope but when three wickets fell for one run Rhodesia put the shutters up.

The final match in Salisbury was a magnificent game of cricket. The Rhodesian Invitation XI batting first were in top form with the Pithey brothers, Colin Bland, Ian Haig and guest star, Buster Farrer, all notching half-centuries. Their carefree batting, particularly towards the end when Farrer and Haig took advantage of an attack feeling the strain of a long day, certainly overshadowed the subsequent batting display of the Commonwealth XI.

Six of the visiting batsmen were clean bowled, Geoff Griffin bowling impressively had Goddard leg before, there were two run outs, and Colin Bland, recovering after slipping, held a sizzling catch on the long-on fence off a Wes Hall 'hoick' to wrap up the innings. Yet Len Brown felt that 'if ever one ball could be said to have wrecked an innings, Joe Partridge produced it when he dipped right down into the bottom of the bag and came up with a vicious late inswinger which bowled Rohan Kanhai. The little West Indian had played a glorious knock of 42 in 48 minutes which included seven fours and a juicy six off Partridge.'

Rohan Kanhai was in fact full of admiration for Partridge's bowling and admitted: 'I went after Partridge quite deliberately. He was bowling well enough to run through our innings and I thought if I made a dead set at him, I'd knock him out of the firing line. Well I didn't . . . but I've known a lot of bowlers

Wesley Hall, the West Indian opening bowler who was regarded as the fastest in the world in 1962, delivers his thunderbolts to Rhodesia's opening batsmen, John McPhun and Ray Gripper, at Bulawayo in September of that year.

who would have been quite pleased to take their sweaters and rest up, after what I did to Partridge.

'But not Joe. He kept after me and eventually bowled me with one of the best balls I've had in a long time . . . an inswinger that ripped away off the pitch and hit my off stump.'

The Commonwealth XI were all out for 239 — 99 runs behind — and the Rhodesians set about increasing their lead. The final day's play produced some marvellous cricket. Grand attacking strokes from Ray Gripper, particularly on the on-side supported by a second half-century by Tony Pithey

"Goofy" Lawrence uproots Bill Alley's middle stump as the veteran Australian swings mightily during the 1962-63 Commonwealth tour.

enabled the latter to set the visitors 306 runs to chase in 275 minutes with a well-timed declaration. Showing a sense of urgency, the Commonwealth XI batsmen set about the task. They lost wickets initially and gloomily placed at 48-4 appeared to be out of the running as Goddard, Young, Watson and Alley had fallen to the old firm, Partridge and Lawrence. But then came an innings rated by many at that time to be the finest ever seen in the country. In a flawless display of tremendous power Rohan Kanhai enlivened proceedings by smiting 110 in 113 minutes out of a partnership of 144 with Basil d'Oliveira. There was little any of the Rhodesian bowlers could do to curb the controlled hitting of Kanhai and it seemed until his dismissal at 192-5 that he might swing the game his team's way.

For Rhodesia, their 74-run victory was a great achievement and Ron Roberts spoke highly of the batting talents of Tony Pithey and Ray Gripper whilst adding '... that attack of yours backed up by one of the finest fielding sides I've seen in a long time would have given England far more trouble last summer than did the Pakistan bowlers. Yes, your cricket has improved immeasurably.'

SCORES: Commonwealth Tour, 1962-63.

At Kitwe, 15, 16 and 17 September.

Rhodesia — 169 (D.B. Pithey 46, A.J. Pithey 41; C.G. Borde 8/52)
and 340-9 dec. (A.J. Pithey 120, I.E. Haig 52, K.C. Bland 47)

Commonwealth XI — 308-6 dec. (W. Watson 100, R. Kanhai 76)
and 137-8 wkts. (W.E. Alley 54; G.M. Griffin 4/32)

Match drawn.

At Bulawayo, 19 and 20 September (Not first-class).

Commonwealth XI — 257 (D.M. Young 138*; G.B. Lawrence 5/57, J.T. Partridge 5/76)
and 145-6 dec.

Rhodesia — 211-2 dec. (R.A. Gripper 68, D.J. Lewis 49*, K.C. Bland 48*, J.D. McPhun 36)
and 132-6 wkts. (E.F. Parker 60, R.A. Gripper 39)

Match drawn.

At Salisbury, 22, 23 and 24 September.

Rhodesian Invitation XI — 338-5 dec. (W.S. Farrer 96, I.E. Haig 65*, D.B. Pithey 54, A.J. Pithey 52, K.C. Bland 50)
and 206-5 dec. (R.A. Gripper 61, A.J. Pithey 55)

Commonwealth XI — 239 (T.L. Goddard 72; G.M. Griffin 4/48)
and 231 (R. Kanhai 110; J.T. Partridge 5/56, G.B. Lawrence 3/56)

Rhodesian Invitation XI won by 74 runs.

Rhodesia then embarked on their Currie Cup programme playing against North-Eastern Transvaal at home. A big welcome was reserved for their young wicket-keeper/batsman Denis Lindsay who had made such an impression for the Rhodesian Invitation XI against Ray Lindwall's XI the previous season. But like chalk and cheese he pottered around defensively for four miserable runs and it came as a relief when he was run out by a brilliant Bland pick-up and throw which hit the stumps direct. There was little for the crowd to enthuse over as an inept batting display by Rhodesia saw the visitors chalk up a comfortable first innings victory. In fact, if it was not for a responsible maiden first-class century by Ray Gripper in the second

1962-63 Commonwealth XI players, Wes Hall, Rohan Kanhai and Chandrakant Borde relaxing in a local hotel with Rhodesian cricket officials, Denis Hayter and "Jock" Holden.

innings Rhodesia might well have suffered the ignominy of an outright defeat.

Tragically the match also saw Geoff Griffin's final appearance in first-class cricket as he was no-balled out of the game in the course of eight drama-filled overs. The calling of Griffin sent a wave of emotion around the ground and the state of the game itself was forgotten as the two-year-old controversy flared anew. But despite the crowd's obvious sympathy for his predicament, the despondent fast bowler resigned himself to the fact that he could no longer pursue his present style, when he wrote in an article for *The Rhodesia Herald*: 'I can honestly say that I have always thought my action fair, and I still do. Tests have proved that the pace which I attain off the wicket is mainly from a wrist flick action. I will not deny my action is unusual and attention has been brought to it . . . but one thing I have realised is that if I intend to play for Rhodesia again I will have to make a change no matter what I think.'

An easy victory over the Orange Free State in Bulawayo followed, and then a valiant fight-back after a first innings loss saw Rhodesia defeat Transvaal B outright in Salisbury. The latter match was a thriller because Transvaal B began the third day 100 runs ahead with nine second innings wickets in hand. Great bowling and a majestic 74 by Tony Pithey enabled Rhodesia to race to within striking distance of winning as the rain pelted down less than half a mile away. Unruffled with nine runs required, Eddie Parker, facing Hector, thumped a four over cover point and the next ball sealed the victory as a massive six soared high over the boundary fence.

To complete the Currie Cup programme the Rhodesians, under manager Jock Holden, set off on a three-match tour of South Africa. A first innings win was achieved over North-Eastern Transvaal, whilst full points were taken off Border and Griqualand West. Yet it could so easily have been three outright victories because the Rhodesians threw away a golden opportunity against North-Easterns even though five hours were lost to rain. Batting first, Rhodesia had amassed 560 for 8 declared — David Pithey scoring a classic 166, and Colin Bland a scorching back-to-form 162. North-Easterns were dismissed cheaply, followed on, and had lost eight wickets when play ended, escaping defeat through eight dropped catches on the last day and two vital ones in the final fifteen minutes.

The two tour victories were matches won convincingly although Rhodesia might well have been in trouble against Border if it had not been for a doughty 106 in 276 minutes by David Lewis. Griqualand West, however, provided less of a problem and the match was over in two days. Both Joe Partridge and David Pithey took advantage of the fact that the South African national selector, Dennis Dyer, was watching the game and returned excellent figures whilst Tony Pithey's half-century enhanced his chances of tour selection.

SCORES: Currie Cup B Section, 1962-63.

At Salisbury, 17, 18 and 19 November.

Rhodesia — 157 (R.A. Gripper 50)
and 256 (R.A. Gripper 106, G.M. Griffin 51, D.J. Lewis 35)

North-Eastern Transvaal — 254 (P.L. Corbett 60, S.B. Spies 50; J.T. Partridge 4/60, J.H. du Preez 3/37)

North-Eastern Transvaal won on first innings.

At Bulawayo, 24, 25 and 26 November.

Orange Free State — 83 (J.T. Partridge 4/22, G.B. Lawrence 3/33)
and 174 (S. Strydom 67; J.T. Partridge 4/38, J.H. du Preez 3/21)

Rhodesia — 201 (D.B. Pithey 53, I.E. Haig 53)
and 60-4 wkts.

Rhodesia won by 6 wickets.

RHODESIAN TOURING TEAM, 1962-63.
Back: J. du Preez, I. Haig, D. Pithey, E. Parker, A. de Caila, C. Hepker.
Seated: G. Lawrence, R. Gripper, D. Lewis, A. Pithey (Captain), A. Holden (Manager), J. Partridge, C. Bland.

At Salisbury, 8, 9 and 10 December.

Transvaal B — 224 (T. Rex 81, G.G. Ritchie 50; J.T. Partridge 7/69)
and 164 (G.B. Lawrence 4/37, D.B. Pithey 3/30)
Rhodesia — 165 (A.J. Pithey 74)
and 225-5 wkts. (A.J. Pithey 74, R.A. Gripper 58, K.C. Bland 38)

Rhodesia won by 5 wickets.

At Pretoria, 26, 27 and 28 December.

Rhodesia — 560-6 dec. (D.B. Pithey 166, K.C. Bland 162, I.E. Haig 72, R.A. Gripper 50)

North-Eastern Transvaal — 176 (J.A. Corbett 57; J.T. Partridge 5/81, J.H. du Preez 3/17)
and 186-8 wkts. (D.B. Pithey 3/62)

Rhodesia won on first innings.

At East London, 31 December, 1 and 2 January.

Border — 154 (J.T. Partridge 4/26, J.H. du Preez 3/31)
and 176 (W.S. Farrer 61; D.B. Pithey 4/22, J.T. Partridge 3/49)

Rhodesia — 245 (D.J. Lewis 106)
and 87-2 wkts. (D.B. Pithey 53)

Rhodesia won by 8 wickets.

At Kimberley, 5, 7 and 8 January.

Griqualand West — 90 (J.T. Partridge 5/36, G.B. Lawrence 3/22)
and 127 (D.B. Pithey 5/30, G.B. Lawrence 3/19)

Rhodesia — 207 (A.J. Pithey 55, R.A. Gripper 43, K.C. Bland 33; M. Glover 5/72)
and 12-0 wkts.

Rhodesia won by 10 wickets.

The season's bumper cricket feast continued with the arrival for one match of Richie Benaud's Cavaliers and Salisbury witnessed perhaps the most exciting of all the matches against Ron Roberts's invitation sides. Three current Test captains were included in the formidable visiting line-up — Benaud (Australia), Ted Dexter (England) and John Reid (New Zealand). They were backed up by English Test stars John Edrich, Roy Swetman and Phil Sharpe, the Australians Norman O'Neill, Barry Shepherd, Graham McKenzie and Johnny Martin, and the experienced Somerset professional, Bill Alley.

Few people in the crowd would have given Rhodesia any hope of winning the game after their attack had been annihilated and the Cavaliers had declared with 379 runs on the board, especially as Rhodesia began badly, losing David Pithey and Rob Ullyett early in the innings whilst Ray Gripper battled to keep his wicket intact in the course of a tense start. It was only when Pithey joined Gripper that the Rhodesians managed to climb back into the game. With Gripper favouring the square cut, Pithey driving superbly and both using their feet well to the spinners the runs came effortlessly. Throughout, judicious short singles kept the scoreboard operators busy in a third wicket partnership realizing 173 before Gripper (111) eventually skied a lofted pull shot to wide mid-on. Tony Pithey, playing one of the grandest innings of his career, became involved in another three-figure stand with David Lewis, adding 103. This took Rhodesia past the 300 mark — Pithey was stumped by Swetman for 141 made in 203 minutes — and the side was all out for 360.

The match changed fortunes dramatically as Partridge, Lawrence and David Pithey bowled magnificently to place Rhodesia in a winning position by the last afternoon. Yet such is cricket that the match was left undecided even though *The Rhodesia Herald* headline which referred to the last day, read appropriately: 'Tony Pithey the Toast of the Town.' How well he deserved such an accolade! Set to get 156 in 145 minutes, Rhodesia had fallen behind the clock when Pithey came to the wicket. Three wickets were down with 52 on the board — 104 required in about 75 minutes. Pithey's batting had the record Monday afternoon crowd in frenzied excitement as he raced to his 50 in just over an hour and struck three glorious sixes. Said Len Brown: 'There were times when his aesthetic batting soul must have shuddered as he swung lustily across the line of flight.'

In a wonderful finish five runs were needed off the last over from Graham McKenzie. Pithey square cut the first ball for two — it finished agonizingly close to the boundary boards — and took a single off the fourth. Graham Bunyard was unable to do anything with the fifth and off the last ball which rebounded off his thigh to roll a few feet from the stumps the Rhodesians dashed through for a single. In the tightest of finishes the scores were tied but officially the match had been drawn. Richie Benaud fittingly wrote: 'Lucky, lucky Rhodesia... to have seen such a fine game of cricket . . . possessing all the mixed ingredients that finally blended into an exciting drawn climax.'

Although the Cavaliers only played one match in Rhodesia, several Rhodesians gained the opportunity of additional representative matches. Partridge and Bland had earlier been selected for the Western Province Invitation XI with the former returning figures of 4/78 and 4/46 against the Cavaliers. Partridge's performance inspired Richie Benaud to write a special article for his Sydney paper, *The Sun*: 'It was one of the most impressive seam-bowling performances I have seen for a long time, and produced before two of the national selectors should have enabled "Jo-Jo" to at least put a pair of socks and shirts into his touring kitbag.'

Partridge, along with Du Preez and David Pithey, was also selected for a Transvaal Invitation XI against the Cavaliers before the long-awaited announcement of the Springbok touring team was made. If ever a player deserved Springbok selection it was Joseph Titus Partridge. After being on the verge of Test cricket for a number of years his new South African domestic record of 64 wickets (average 16,68) in eleven matches made it impossible for the selectors to overlook him. His great bowling partner, "Goofy" Lawrence, was unlucky not to make the trip but Rhodesia was well represented with the Pithey brothers and Colin Bland gaining places in the side.

SCORES: versus Cavaliers, 1962-63.

At Salisbury, 23, 24 and 25 March.

Cavaliers — 379-6 dec. (N.C. O'Neill 96, B. Shepherd 75*, P.J. Sharpe 73; G.S. Bunyard 3/82)
and 136 (J.T. Partridge 4/51, G.B. Lawrence 3/45)

Rhodesia — 360 (A.J. Pithey 141, R.A. Gripper 111, D.J. Lewis 32)
and 155-8 wkts. (A.J. Pithey 67*)

Match drawn with the scores level when stumps were pulled up.

With four of their players away during the 1963-64 season on tour to Australasia the Rhodesians nevertheless won the B Section of the Currie Cup. David Lewis returned to captain the side in its endeavour to regain its A Section status and as a result of a specific campaign by their seasoned skipper the players exuded the confidence so necessary in their aspirations. Their only lapse in the course of the season was a first innings loss to the Orange Free State — a match they might well have won if time had not run out on them.

THERE will be some of you who can recall times when Tony Pithey wasn't mounted on that pedestal, garlanded, and receiving the plaudits of the crowd . . . but I doubt that last weekend's match will ever be mentioned by any other name than . . . "Pithey's match."

Tony Pithey receiving the plaudits of the crowd.

Victories were achieved against Border and Griqualand West at home and over North-Eastern Transvaal B away.

It was in Pretoria against North-Eastern Transvaal that Rhodesia were all out for 47 (Gripper 25) to record their lowest ever first-class total. Jackie Botten literally carved his way through the batting line-up for figures of 9/29 and North-Easterns faced the apparently easiest of assignments in their second innings — 98 runs with no time restrictions. However, they did not reckon with the determination and indeed, the preparation that had gone into the challenge to become again an A Section side. According to David Lewis even when the score had reached the total of 42-1, 'not one of the Rhodesians had any doubt that they would win through'.

At tea-time on the Saturday afternoon Syd Burke, the North-Easterns' captain, informed Lewis at 5.55 p.m. of his intention to claim the extra half-hour if they had not won by then. The visiting captain, infuriated by the impertinence, retorted confidently that if there was to be any such claim made it would be for the reason that Rhodesia would need it to clinch victory and have a free day on the Monday. In a fascinating contest and in a fantastic finish Rhodesia won through by 18 runs after taking the extra half-hour. This most satisfying of victories was attained by a combination of team skills; of good bowling (particularly Lawrence and Dickinson), superb catching and fielding, brilliant captaincy and the application of pressure from the whole team. Said David Lewis: 'For those who took part in the game it will be remembered as a unique experience and a turning point in the side's predetermined quest for higher status.'

The season presented opportunities in particular for some of the younger players and for several of them the experience was a memorable one. John McPhun, despite a mid-season injury, was in outstanding form with the bat, scoring 318 runs (average 106,00) in the three matches he played. He and Rob Ullyett (455 runs — average 50,55) both registered their maiden first-class centuries in a record partnership for the second wicket of 226 against Border at the Police ground, Salisbury. Ullyett went on to score a second hundred against Griqualand West and on this occasion was involved in a partnership of 129 with McPhun.

Nick Frangos, who had succeeded John McPhun as captain of the South African Schools XI in 1960, was called down to Johannesburg to join the team and was given the opportunity of opening the Rhodesian batting when McPhun was injured. He immediately made his mark and retained the role when McPhun returned. One of the reasons for the season's success was the number of good starts given to the innings and both McPhun and Frangos received solid support from the regular opening bat Ray Gripper (317 runs — average 34,62) who enjoyed a relatively successful season. *The South African Cricket Annual* also records that Gripper, thanks to a rare bowling appearance against Griqualand West, topped the Rhodesians' averages with figures of 2-0-9-1.

Godfrey Lawrence was again the power in the Rhodesian attack capturing 27 wickets in the five matches at the comparatively low cost of 11,07. He did not have a regular opening partner, with Gordon Den, Eddie Parker, and Rodney Keast filling this berth at different stages. Den, a left-arm medium pace bowler returned a match-aggregate of 9/94 in his debut against Border.

The spinners, Vernon Dickinson and Jackie du Preez captured 36 wickets between them with Dickinson's effort (6/61 and 3/34) against North-Eastern Transvaal being the most impressive contribution during the season. Like the fast bowlers, they were ably backed up by the competent wicket-keeping of Tony de Caila who was responsible for 17 dismissals (13 catches and 4 stumpings). His captain, David Lewis, said: 'Tony de Caila was one of the best of a long line of outstanding Rhodesian wicket-keepers. As he was slightly unorthodox he seldom received full credit but he equally very seldom missed an opportunity — his real value was well known to the bowlers.'

SCORES: Currie Cup B Section, 1963-64.

At Salisbury, 30 November, 1 and 2 December.

Border — 238 (R.K. Thorne 58; G.M. Den 6/75, G.B. Lawrence 3/50)
amd 101 (G.B. Lawrence 5/23, G.M. Den 3/19)

Rhodesia — 413-8 dec. (J.D. McPhun 131, R.B. Ullyett 115, I.E. Haig 51, R.A. Gripper 35, G.B. Lawrence 33)

Rhodesia won by an innings and 74 runs.

At Pretoria, 27, 28 and 30 December.

Rhodesia — 204 (J.D. McPhun 93)
and 47 (J.T. Botten 9/29)

RHODESIAN TOURING TEAM, 1963-64.
Back: J. du Preez, I. Haig, A. de Caila, E. Parker, N. Frangos, V. Dickinson, R. Keast, D. Leather.
Seated: G. Lawrence, D. Lewis (Captain), A. Holden (Manager), R. Gripper, R. Ullyett.

Rob Ullyett batting during his highly successful 1963-64 season — Ali Bacher is keeping wicket.

"Goofy" Lawrence bowls Robin Thorne (Border) in spectacular fashion at the Police ground, Salisbury, in 1963-64.

North-Eastern Transvaal — 154 (L. Liebenberg 63; V.E.J. Dickinson 6/61, G.B. Lawrence 3/30)
and 79 (G.B. Lawrence 5/14, V.E.J. Dickinson 3/34)

Rhodesia won by 18 runs.

At Johannesburg, 31 December, 1 and 2 January.

Rhodesia — 324 (I.E. Haig 72, E.F. Parker 43, A. de Caila 42, J.H. du Preez 36, D.J. Lewis 31; A.J. Motley 5/75)
and 289-7 dec. (R.A. Gripper 113, R.B. Ullyett 70, N.J. Frangos 45)

Transvaal B — 212 (J.H. du Preez 4/41, G.B. Lawrence 3/25)
and 292 (N. Holmes 67, T. Vorster 59; E.F. Parker 4/54, G.B. Lawrence 3/51)

Rhodesia won by 109 runs.

At Bloemfontein, 4, 6 and 7 January.

Rhodesia — 220 (N.J. Frangos 87, R.A. Gripper 43; M. Macaulay 7/49)
and 253 (R.B. Ullyett 64, N.J. Frangos 50, J.H. du Preez 42)

Orange Free State — 246 (R. de Bruin 83*; E.F. Parker 3/46, V.E.J. Dickinson 3/62)
and 153-7 wkts.

Orange Free State won on first innings.

At Salisbury, 7, 8 and 9 March.

Griqualand West — 139 (J.H. du Preez 4/42, N.R. Williams 3/38)
and 215

Rhodesia — 269-4 dec. (R.B. Ullyett 121, J.D. McPhun 69*, E.F. Parker 38)
and 89-2 wkts. (R.A. Gripper 49*)

Rhodesia won by 8 wickets.

During August and September 1964, the Mashonaland Country Districts under the outstanding captaincy of Don Bailey, became the first senior side from Rhodesia to tour England and enjoyed a most successful, though exacting visit. John Reason summed up the tour in the October 1964 issue of *The Cricketer*:

'Any self-respecting expert in logistics would have been horrified by the tour of this country which has just been completed by a team of Rhodesian tobacco farmers who play cricket for fun in the African winter.

'First they raised £7 000 to pay for the tour. That took two years. Then they selected 14 players from the 30 clubs in the country districts of Mashonaland where they live. Then they flew to this country and calmly set off to play 31 full days of cricket out of a possible 36 on a 27-match whistle-stop tour of the South of England. This with only 14 players, and none of these were professional athletes, or anything like it.

' "Everybody said we were mad," said their manager, Peter Carr. "But despite the gloomy predictions about injuries and fatigue, I had to turn out in only one match out of the whole 27. Hospitality was wonderful. The sun shone day after day. We even gave up looking out of the window in the mornings."

'Mashonaland also built up a formidable playing record. They won 15 of their matches, drew 10 and lost only 2. All nine of their batsmen scored more than 400 runs, three of them hit centuries and they all averaged more than 26 runs each.

'All their bowlers took more than 35 wickets, too. Colin Bray easily topped the list with 64 at the splendid average of 12,58 each.

'Peter Carr is sure that the playing success of the tour stemmed from the decision to choose each day's team and twelfth man in strict rotation, absolutely irrespective of form or the competition. "That way we had no lesser brethren. Everybody was equal. And sooner or later, everyone either made runs or took wickets."

'Mashonaland were particularly pleased to beat the 2nd XIs of Sussex and Hampshire, both in two-day matches though they felt that teams like the Bristol and District Cricket Association were every bit as strong.

'Against Hampshire, John Kitcat hit a six clean over the pavilion at Southampton, one of the biggest hits seen on the ground.

The Mashonaland Country Districts team at London Airport: C. Heurtley, E. Campbell (Rhodesian High Commissioner), C. Postlethwayt, C. Bray, E. Harben, J. Kitcat, P. Carr, T. Bridges, R. Bucquet, D. Bailey, D. Arnott, T. Wilson, H. Duncan, R. Mundy, N. Waller, G. Deary, K. Curran, P. Densem, R. Lees, W. Hammond, N. Williams, B. Hodnett, Mrs. P. Carr, T. Visagie, A. Hoskins, and E. Harrison.

JOHN KITCAT.

'In the match against R.P. Chester's XI, Rex Chester Senior offered Mashonaland £5 for every six they hit. Kitcat started as if he was going to bankrupt the Chester family in about 10 minutes. He hit three successive sixes and the cash register was fairly ringing. He managed one more before he was out, and the tourists' funds benefited by £20.

'Of course the big day of the tour came when they played at Lord's against the Cross Arrows. This was one occasion when Carr thanked his rota system of selection. "Everyone naturally wanted to play," he said, "but the two men who were due to stand down did so, and no one complained."

'Again Kitcat was in terrific form. He was another one who had cause to thank the selection system, because he started the tour badly. It was the knowledge that he was always going to get his quota of games, however badly he played, that helped him to regain his touch. He hit three sixes and twelve fours in his 89 not out, though for sheer ferocity, even this was overshadowed by the performance of Don Bailey. He scored 34 off seven balls.

'What with that, and the Rhodesians' charming habit of carrying presentation cigars in their breast pockets, Lord's certainly relished their visit.

'Mashonaland ended their last match and their tour with the most dramatic flourish possible. The Standard Bank of South Africa were 208 for 3 in reply to Mashonaland's 222 for 3 declared. Three balls of the last over remained. Charles Postlethwayt then took a hat trick.'

AVERAGES

Batting	Innings	Not outs	Runs	Highest inns.	Average
D. Bailey	20	4	558	77	34,87
K. Curran	19	4	520	68	34,66
W. Hodnett	22	4	611	83*	33,94
R. Lees	16	3	429	110	33,00
H. Duncan	23	2	670	101*	31,90
D. Arnott	21	4	491	67*	28,88
P. Densem	24	3	597	107	28,42
J. Kitcat	19	4	407	89*	27,13
G. Deary	18	2	428	74	26,75
N. Waller	16	3	207	41	15,92
C. Bray	13	2	147	38	13,36
N. Williams	14	5	116	35*	12,88
A. Wilson	7	3	44	14*	11,00
C. Postlethwayt	7	2	16	6*	3,20

** Signifies not out.*

Bowling	Overs	Maidens	Runs	Wickets	Average
C. Bray	369,2	113	805	64	12,57
C. Postlethwayt	235,3	64	612	39	15,69
A. Wilson	266,4	74	686	36	19,05
N. Williams	382,4	16	956	50	19,12
N. Waller	237,3	38	799	35	22,82
G. Deary	181,1	44	523	21	24,90

At a reception for the Mashonaland Country Districts cricketers at Rhodesia House, London, were: The Rhodesian High Commissioner, Mr. Evan Campbell, Peter Carr, Alec Bedser, G.O. Allen (President of M.C.C.) and Don Bailey.

Padding up for practice at Lord's: Peter Densem, Don Bailey and Billy Hodnett chat to Peter Carr whilst Raymond Lees makes his way to the nets.

In what Trevor Goddard described as "a pointless duel" the 1964-65 season opened with the Springboks touring side that had visited Australasia playing against the Rest of South Africa at the Wanderers, Johannesburg. It was with relentless efficiency that the six Springbok batsmen who went to the crease that day established a new record of the greatest number of runs scored in a day's play. Of the four centuries, Tony Pithey's (110 — 223 minutes) was a classic, Graeme Pollock's (123 — 105 minutes — 23 fours) was majestically effortless, but the fantastic run-rate really exploded when Colin Bland (151 not out) and Denis Lindsay (107 not out) flayed the attack unmercifully for 267 in the final 99 minutes of the innings. *The South African Cricket Annual* recorded: 'One was left speechless at the sheer audacity of the batting.'

For Bland and Pithey the season was to be a memorable one. Bland became the first batsman in South African cricket to score 1 000 runs in a domestic first-class season whilst Pithey on 957 was not far behind. They were in tremendous form, both in the Test matches against Mike Smith's M.C.C. tourists, and for Rhodesia in the latter's limited match programme.

As the Currie Cup again fell away because of an international tour, Rhodesian cricket was confined to tours by the M.C.C. and Worcestershire and to a friendly match against Natal. In the course of these

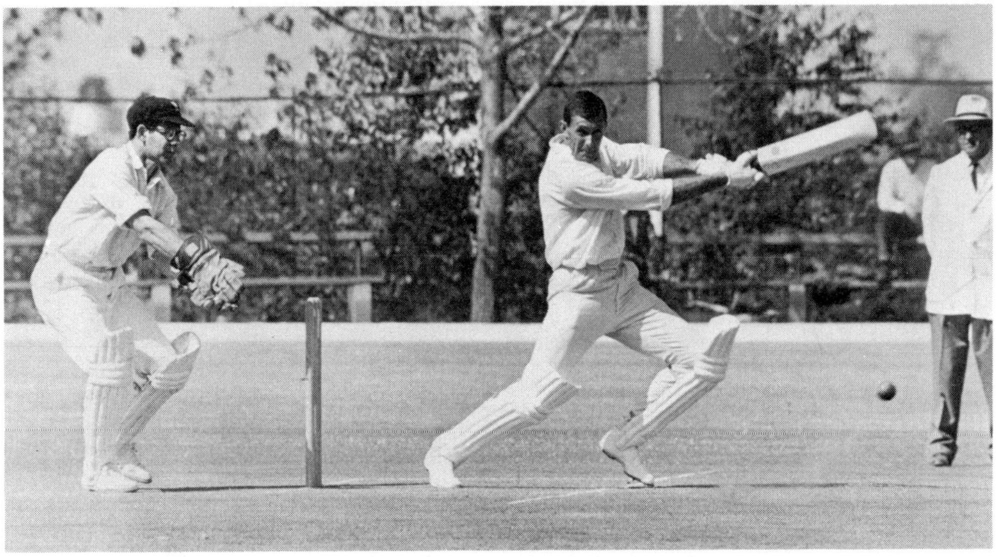

Colin Bland in command at the wicket for the Wilf Isaacs' XI in a festival match at the Wanderers with Denis Gamsy keeping wicket (1964-65).

Mike Brearley is dramatically run out by Colin Bland during M.C.C. versus Rhodesia match at Salisbury in 1964-65.

matches the promise of the previous season was further realised and Rhodesia's performances, climaxed by a great victory over the English County Champions, Worcestershire, were encouraging.

The M.C.C. tourists played two matches in Rhodesia on their way to South Africa where they were destined to win the series 1-0. The first encounter was a pipe-opener against a Matabeleland Invitation XI in Bulawayo. The opposition were intended to provide the M.C.C. with a light warm-up and consequently Eddie Parker led a young side with most of the players tasting cricket for the first time at this level. As expected, the Invitation XI were well beaten by the more experienced tourists but they did not disgrace themselves. Seam bowler, Ted Turner, who made the ball move away effectively, claimed four wickets in an impressive big-time baptism, and of the others, M.C.C. manager Donald Carr commented: 'Russell McTavish, Alistair Carlisle and Brian Davison showed a tremendous amount of promise and all looked good players whom any English county would be pleased to have around at their age.'

Travelling to Salisbury for their second match, the M.C.C. found the full Rhodesian side to be stronger opposition. With Springboks Tony Pithey and Colin Bland setting the pace, the Rhodesians did well to tally 281. The M.C.C. attack, although lacking in penetration, was difficult to score off because of the tight field placing and the accurate, on-the-spot bowling of Ian Thomson, David Brown and Tom Cartwright. However, southern African cricket followers must have been heartened by the performance of Pithey and Bland who put on a confident 99 in 64 minutes. Colin Bland hit two huge sixes off Bob Barber and Charles Fortune wrote: 'The second six was driven at about fifteen degrees to the off-side of the straight hit. Never have I seen an off-drive carry further than this shot. We estimated its carry to be about 95 yards and it landed on a bank some 15 feet above field level.'

In reply the M.C.C. looked in trouble at 98-3 but a workmanlike partnership of 146 by Ken Barrington and Peter Parfitt helped to set the visitors firmly on their way to overhauling the Rhodesian total. An unspectacular side, the M.C.C. were nevertheless ultra-professional in everything they did. Their runs were accrued in a business-like manner with no frills attached and the one moment of excitement in their innings that will forever remain in the memories of all who were in the ground at the time was created by a Rhodesian. Len Brown described the action in an introduction to Colin Bland's book, *Dynamic Cricket*: 'Bland was in the covers with his club colleague, left-arm spinner Vernon Dickinson, at mid-off. Brearley would push the ball towards mid-off, Bland would come cantering in, stoop as though to pick up the ball then let it go through to Dickinson while the batsmen went through for an easy single. This went on for several overs with the procedure being repeated, and Brearley obviously happy at this simple way of getting runs.

'But I've seen this man Bland up to his tricks too often, and when I noticed at the beginning of the next over that Dickinson was standing a good 20 yards deeper, with Brearley facing the bowling, I sat up, caught the late Ron Roberts's eye further down the Press Box, and indicated by sign language that the hunt was on.

'Sure enough, Brearley played the ball to mid-off, saw Dickinson was a lot deeper, and set off at a gentle canter for an easy run on offer. But this time Bland didn't amble in . . . he came storming at the full gallop, scooped up the ball and let fly one of his bullet-like throws. Although he was running away from us in the Press Box, one could almost sense the alarm of Brearley as he realised he was yards from the safety of the opposite crease when the middle stump took off as Bland's throw shattered the stumps.'

Batting a second time, Tony Pithey and Nick Frangos put on 102 in 142 minutes for the second wicket and Rhodesia seemed to have made the match safe. But all credit to Brown and Cartwright who toiled admirably in the oppressive heat to whittle away the lower order batsmen despite some stubborn resistance from David Pithey and Jackie du Preez. Bowling defensively at the leg stump with a ring of fielders on the on side, the M.C.C. were difficult to score runs off. All out for 225 the Rhodesians left the M.C.C. nearly five hours to make 209 — a task they accomplished comfortably thanks to a fluent 108 by opening bat, Bob Barber.

An interesting occurrence in the course of the match was that of former national captain, David Lewis, substituting in the field. The Rhodesians had been handicapped by injuries to their promising seam bowler, Brian Bennett, and to Nick Frangos, and with twelfth man, Russell McTavish therefore already occupied, David Lewis obliged as "thirteenth man". It was indeed a strange coincidence that Lewis should end his career at first-class level in the manner in which he began it — as a substitute. Len Brown, who was reporting on the M.C.C. match, remembered playing for Transvaal against Rhodesia in 1945-46 when Lewis, then a schoolboy, had substituted as a fielder. Recalling his innings for Transvaal in that fixture and swinging a ball lustily in the direction of long-on, Len Brown wrote of his first encounter with David Lewis: 'Lewis was just behind the bowler, right on the fence. He careered round the boundary and more or less plucked the ball off a spectator's hat . . . never looked like dropping it.'

SCORES: M.C.C. Tour, 1964-65.

At Bulawayo, 21 and 22 October (Not first-class).
Matabeleland Invitation XI — 133 (A. Carlisle 23, D. Townshend 22)
and 144 (C.R. McTavish 48; F. Titmus 7/58)
M.C.C. — 253-9 dec. (M.J.K. Smith 60, P.H. Parfitt 55; E. Turner 4/72)
and 28-0 wkts.
M.C.C. won by 10 wickets.

At Salisbury, 24, 25 26 and 27 October.
Rhodesia — 281 (K.C. Bland 66, A.J. Pithey 65, A. de Caila 40)
and 225 (N.J. Frangos 82, A.J. Pithey 49, J.H. du Preez 34)
M.C.C. — 298 (P.H. Parfitt 82, K.F. Barrington 74; J.T. Partridge 4/66, G.B. Lawrence 3/58)
and 209-5 wkts. (R. Barber 108)
M.C.C. won by 5 wickets.

Natal arrived with a powerful batting line-up that saw the young Barry Richards come in to bat at number 8. Dennis Gamsy and Derek Varnals both made centuries whilst every other player made double figures in Natal's huge score of 537. After their bowling attack had been carted to all corners of the Police ground, the Rhodesian batsmen also fared poorly and they were all out for 174. But any hopes that Natal might have had of forcing an outright win were dashed by an undefeated third wicket partnership of 165 in Rhodesia's second innings by Ray Gripper and Tony Pithey. In an innings lasting 5½ hours Gripper hit eighteen fours and established a new record highest score for a Rhodesian against Natal.

SCORES: versus Natal, 1964-65.

At Salisbury, 28, 29 and 30 November.
Natal — 537 (D. Gamsy 129, G.D. Varnals 105, N.S. Crookes 68, P.R. Carlstein 61; J.H. du Preez 4/129)
Rhodesia — 174 (J.H. du Preez 53, R.B. Ullyett 46, A.J. Pithey 30; J.McG. Cole 5/48)
and 311-2 wkts. (R.A. Gripper 153*, A.J. Pithey 75*, J.D. McPhun 43, R.B. Ullyett 34)
Match drawn.

Worcestershire's tour towards the end of the 1964-65 season was a great success. They played three matches, winning the first easily by 196 runs against a Rhodesian side in Bulawayo without Bland or Pithey. "Goofy" Lawrence and Joe Partridge were the two local heroes in a contest in which the Rhodesian batting failed dismally. Between them the two great-hearted bowlers took 14 of the 15 wickets to fall and then they added 69 for the tenth wicket in the Rhodesian second innings to show up the failings of their colleagues.

Que Que saw some fine cricket in a two-day match played against the Rhodesian Country Districts XI. The West Indian, Ron Headley, scored a brilliant 178 in 190 minutes (five sixes and twenty-one fours) to enable the tourists to declare their first innings at 348-6. In reply the Districts XI declared 179 runs behind with Evan Butcher, Kev Curran and Don Bailey making runs which meant the game was kept open. A further well-timed declaration by visiting skipper Don Kenyon, ultimately brought his team an exciting 85-run victory with 25 minutes to spare.

Pithey and Bland were included in the Rhodesian side for the return game in Salisbury and made a tremendous difference in an absorbing match. There appeared little chance of Rhodesia winning after Kenyon had declared 73 runs ahead on the first innings largely due to an attractive, undefeated 136 by Tom Graveney. However, the Rhodesian second innings witnessed the unleashing of a barrage of attacking strokes as Ray Gripper in his fifth career century, McPhun, Pithey and Bland mastered an attack that contained three England Test bowlers — openers Flavell and Coldwell and left-arm spinner Gifford — plus future star, Basil d'Oliveira. Amid terrific excitement Rhodesia, having set Worcestershire a target of 272 in 210 minutes, proceeded to bowl the County Champions out for 115, thanks to the sustained accuracy of spinners Jackie du Preez and Vernon Dickinson.

SCORES: Worcestershire Tour, 1964-65.

At Bulawayo, 20, 21 and 22 February.

Worcestershire — 277 (B.L. d'Oliveira 73, D.N.F. Slade 64*; G.B. Lawrence 6/61, J.T. Partridge 3/74)
and 161-5 wkts. (D. Kenyon 63; J.T. Partridge 4/53)

Rhodesia — 82 (L.J. Coldwell 5/18)
and 160 (G.B. Lawrence 60*; L.J. Coldwell 5/26)

Worcestershire won by 196 runs.

At Que Que, 24 and 25 February (Not first-class).

Worcestershire — 348-6 dec. (R.G.A. Headley 178, B.L. d'Oliveira 51)
and 56-3 dec.

Rhodesia Country Districts XI — 169-6 dec. (E. Butcher 51, D.C. Bailey 37, K.P. Curran 35)
and 150 (G.R. Deary 37; N. Gifford 5/54)

Worcestershire won by 85 runs.

At Salisbury, 27 February, 1 and 2 March.

Rhodesia — 235 (A.J. Pithey 98, E.F. Parker 45)
and 344-4 dec. (R.A. Gripper 116, A.J. Pithey 68*, K.C. Bland 62, J.D. McPhun 61)

Worcestershire — 308-6 dec. (T.W. Graveney 136*, D.N.F. Slade 58; G.B. Lawrence 3/44)
and 115 (J.H. du Preez 5/36, V.E.T. Dickinson 5/44)

Rhodesia won by 156 runs.

CHAPTER SEVEN
Difficult Days

THE 1965-66 SEASON began quietly with no planned visits from overseas sides but there was nevertheless, both incentive for the players and interest for the spectators. Rhodesia's return to the A Section was keenly awaited and there were high hopes for the side to do well. Rhodesia had never managed to maintain a permanent place in the higher sphere of the Currie Cup, inevitably finding it difficult to adjust immediately on the occasions when they won promotion. This problem was not confined to the Rhodesians and consequently the sixties saw heated criticism of the structure of the sections as well as the system of promotion and relegation. The Rhodesian cricket administrators argued that a side placed in the A Section should be given at least a couple of years to adjust to the better standard of cricket. It was certainly detrimental to the players' progress to be continually moved to and fro from one grade of cricket to the other without allowing sufficient time to adapt to a higher league. Unfortunately this trend continued throughout a difficult period for Rhodesian cricket when major changes were enforced in the side because of retirements and emigration. It was with a trace of humour that Len Brown commented on the 1965-66 Rhodesian side: 'There's a lot of experience in this Rhodesian cricket side. As the "yo-yo" of South African cricket — A Zone one year, B Zone the next — they have played in more centres than any other side in the competition, met more players round the country and done more travelling.'

The deeds of Colin Bland on the 1965 South African tour to England and the Press coverage he received also generated eager anticipation for the new season in local circles. Rhodesians were certainly proud of their talented cricket ambassador and it would be appropriate in this regard to quote the editorial comment in the renowned English magazine *The Cricketer*: 'Like a breath of fresh air wafted into a dark cell in which the main topics have been the unsavoury ones of throwers and the weather, one man arrived in mid-season to stimulate new thinking, and capture the cricket public's imagination in a new, strange way.

'There have been great fielders in the past. The names of Hobbs, Jessop, Constantine and Harvey leap to mind, from different generations. But none has exploited the possibilities in fielding to such an extent as Colin Bland . . . none has made fielding at cover-point or mid-wicket a spectacle to set the cricket world talking and the crowds flocking to see him.

'That a fielder should become an outstanding attraction by virtue of his athleticism and his ability to throw down the wicket with a regularity of which Miss Annie Oakley herself would have been proud is something entirely new.

'The impact of Bland's fielding is an entirely admirable event for two reasons . . . as a spectacle, and because it is a simple and compelling model for all young cricketers.

'In a few weeks Colin Bland has made a contribution to the game in England such as few individuals are able to make. It is all the worthier because it is not just a fortuitous accident, as it might be in the case of a batsman who had hit on a rich streak of runs. It is the prowess of a skilled craftsman who has developed his skill over a number of years by sheer hard work and enthusiasm . . .

'Dedication is an overworked word, but peculiarly apt in this remarkable story, of a remarkable young man.'

Soon after his return Bland married the former Rhodesian hockey captain, Dot Cornwall, and because of his honeymoon was unavailable for Rhodesia's opening Currie Cup match against Transvaal at the Queens ground, Bulawayo.

This match was poised for an exciting conclusion when the rain came down and denied Rhodesia the possibility of their first Currie Cup victory over Transvaal. Play stopped forty minutes from the scheduled close when Ali Bacher's team had their last man in to bat and still required 20 runs to win. However, Transvaal could equally claim that they would have won because in their first innings the same last wicket pair, Don Mackay-Coghill and Atholl McKinnon, had taken their side's score from 193-9 to 219 to earn the visitors vital points.

Rhodesia's second match was an historic occasion in that it was Eastern Province's first visit to Salisbury — the last match between these sides had been staged in Bulawayo during the 1954-55 season. Rhodesia had won by nine wickets on that occasion with four minutes to spare when Marshall Davies had hooked a ball from Anton Murray over the square leg fence for six to end the match on a high note. In 1965-66 the fixture was played on a plumb pitch which gave the bowlers little assistance and both sides took advantage of the fact. Rhodesia amassed 450 — David Pithey 143 and Rob Ullyett 135 — but Eastern Province in reply

Peter Swart represented Rhodesia before departing for Cape Town where he became a key member of the Western Province side and enjoyed many successes against his former province. However, on this occasion (*below*) he had his stumps spreadeagled by Mike Procter at the Police ground, Salisbury, in 1972-73.

took first innings points by scoring 487 with Lorrie Wilmot recording an undefeated 222. For the Rhodesians the Province innings was one of 'alarms and excursions' and injuries to Tony Pithey, Partridge, Lawrence and Parker, who were off the field at different stages. For the most part Lawrence and Parker were forced to bowl off shortened run-ups at half-pace but in retrospect did a brave job.

Rhodesia then embarked on a three-match visit to South Africa. Joe Partridge's groin injury prevented him from leaving with the tour party for the opening fixture and Peter Swart from Gatooma was drafted into the side. Less than a year out of Jameson High School, Swart was to play once for Rhodesia before leaving for the Western Province where he was to make a great impression and prove a thorn in the side of his old province during many future clashes.

Jackie McGlew (*extreme left*), former captain of the South African cricket team with Rhodesian cricket officials, Jock Holden, Arthur Maddocks, Tim Francis and Charles Martin.

Unfortunately, a place could not be found on tour for the lanky wicket-keeper, Howie Gardiner, who had been whisked into the Rhodesian team at very short notice for the Eastern Province match when Tony de Caila fell ill. Gardiner had scored a powerful 42 not out and kept wicket well but first choice 'keeper, De Caila, returned for the tour.

Rhodesia came out of their opening tour match against Natal at Pietermaritzburg with first innings points but were severely criticized for an unenterprising approach. In his team's defence, Rhodesian manager, Jock Holden replied: 'You can put it down to the rule of promotion and relegation. We have had to fight to get into the A Section and we mean to stay there.' And on the question of why Rhodesia did not speed up their play having overtaken Natal's first innings score, Mr. Holden pointed out: 'It is a rule that a team leading on the first innings loses its three points if it is beaten outright. Consequently teams do not risk losing what they have gained.'

Admittedly the game played at Pietermaritzburg was not conducive to good cricket but it drew attention to the problems that were so blatantly prevalent at the time and the secretary of the South African Cricket Association, Algy Frames, remarked: 'Rhodesia have a pretty good side but because of the fear of relegation they are not playing the cricket they are capable of producing.'

Those two old bowling "war horses" of Rhodesian cricket, Lawrence and Partridge, took it upon themselves to demonstrate the fighting qualities of Rhodesian cricket in the very next match against Western Province at Newlands. On the opening day they bowled Rhodesia into a strong position, taking eight of the wickets to fall, as Western Province were all out for 194. And then with Rhodesia batting timidly in their innings, Partridge joined Lawrence at 119-9. Jock Holden wrote: 'Before taking guard, Joe, although the junior partner, called a tactical discussion. The fight was on — it appeared that any balls offering runs were to be dealt with appropriately, but with no stupid risks. Everything went to plan for a few runs — "Goofy" took a swish — Joe shook his head — "Goofy" took another swish — Joe called another conference. More runs came — Joe, feeling more satisfied, hit a six. A bit of smart running, some good shots — some not so good — aggression interspersed with defence — a couple of dropped catches — conferences called, adjourned and resumed were having their effect. Much laughter, some bordering on the hysterical, in the Rhodesian camp helped to relieve the tension.

'Unfortunately, this summit meeting-cum-batting-partnership broke down before the Western Province score was reached. However, 53 runs had been added in 44 minutes — only 22 behind — and it went a long way towards the subsequent winning of the match, together with magnificent bowling by "Goofy", ably backed by Joe in Province's second innings.

'Joe and "Goofy", on occasion, have passed some amusing comments on the frailties of Rhodesian batsmen. On this occasion their poker-faced expressions on returning to the pavilion seemed to convey the message.'

Lawrence's bowling was indeed magnificent in the Western Province second innings. The close of the second day (78-4) quickly became 99 all out early the following morning. In a devastating spell of 5,1 overs, Lawrence claimed 5/13 to finish with innings figures of 8/42 and prompted Herby Taylor, South Africa's pre-War batsman, to comment: 'I've never seen pace bowling like this at Newlands. What a grand pair they make.'

The third tour match was a little disappointing in that Eastern Province clinched victory with the third ball off what might have been the last over of the match. Missed chances in the field allied to a varied Eastern Province attack used shrewdly by Eddie Barlow, cost the Rhodesians this match.

With one first innings win and an outright victory on the credit side, Rhodesia stood an outside chance of winning the Currie Cup when Western Province arrived in Salisbury during the last week of February.

The day before the match was due to commence, Louis Duffus wrote: 'Rain on 18 days out of 20 . . . no practice yet for Western Province . . . gum boots needed to walk on the Police ground — this is the preliminary setting for the final Currie Cup match of the season due to start tomorrow.' That is how the situation remained with both sides kicking their heels for three days before the match was eventually abandoned without a ball being bowled.

SCORES: Currie Cup A Section, 1965-66.

At Bulawayo, 20, 21 and 22 November.

Rhodesia — 195 (N.J. Frangos 53, E.F. Parker 39; A.H. McKinnon 5/59)
and 202 (E.F. Parker 45, N.J. Frangos 40, R.A. Gripper 31, R.B. Ullyett 31)

Transvaal — 219 (R.C. White 58; E.F. Parker 3/65, J.T. Partridge 3/84)
and 159-9 wkts. (G.B. Lawrence 3/28, D.B. Pithey 3/47)

Transvaal won on first innings.

At Salisbury, 4, 5 and 6 December.

Rhodesia — 450 (D.B. Pithey 143, R.B. Ullyett 135, J.H. du Preez 49, H.A.B. Gardiner 42*; A.C. Hector 5/121)
and 38-3 wkts.

Eastern Province — 487 (A.L. Wilmot 222*, E.J. Barlow 142, R.G. Pollock 53; E.F. Parker 5/76, J.T. Partridge 3/78)

Eastern Province won on first innings.

At Pietermaritzburg, 18, 20 and 21 December.

Rhodesia — 359 (N.J. Frangos 85, A.J. Pithey 57, D.B. Pithey 57, K.C. Bland 51, R.A. Gripper 41)
and 162-5 dec. (A.J. Pithey 59*, R.A. Gripper 35)

Natal — 299 (B.A. Richards 68, M.J. Procter 56; D.B. Pithey 5/67)
and 21-0 wkts.

Rhodesia won on first innings.

At Cape Town, 27, 28 and 29 December.

Western Province — 194 (P.L. van der Merwe 61; J.T. Partridge 5/85, G.B. Lawrence 3/56)
and 99 (G.B. Lawrence 8/42)

Rhodesia — 172 (A.J. Pithey 38, J.H. du Preez 38, G.B. Lawrence 32*; J. McG. Cole 5/45)
and 122-4 wkts. (R.A. Gripper 51)

Rhodesia won by 6 wickets.

At Port Elizabeth, 1, 3 and 4 January.

Eastern Province — 272 (E.J. Barlow 111, D. Gradwell 69; E.F. Parker 4/59, G.B. Lawrence 4/87)
and 159 (R.G. Pollock 61; G.B. Lawrence 5/46)

Rhodesia — 236 (E.F. Parker 44, D.B. Pithey 40, R.A. Gripper 30, K.C. Bland 30; P. MacL. Pollock 5/45)
and 129 (D.B. Pithey 37)

Eastern Province won by 66 runs.

At Salisbury, 26, 27 and 28 February.

Versus Western Province — match abandoned without a ball being bowled.

A performance at club level worthy of note during the 1965-66 season was Charles Postlethwayt's bowling analysis during Karoi's tour of the North-Eastern Cape. Playing against the Popular Grove XI, a country club near Queenstown which included four Border players in their line-up, Postlethwayt took all 10 wickets in an innings for 16 runs in 11,5 overs.

At the end of the 1965-66 season "Goofy" Lawrence and David Pithey left Rhodesia to take up posts in Durban. In 1966-67 Lawrence, who had been the Currie Cup competition's outstanding bowler of the previous year, turned out for Natal B whilst Pithey was selected for South Africa in the Test series against Bobby Simpson's Australians. Their departures left big holes in the Rhodesian line-up which were never adequately filled during the ensuing years.

Louis Duffus summed up Rhodesia's cricket predicament early on in the 1966-67 season when he wrote: 'These are fateful days for Rhodesian cricket. Three years ago they had four players — the Pithey brothers, Colin Bland and Joe Partridge — in a South African touring team.

'This season they face a threat of lean times ahead. It is not only because they have lost Godfrey Lawrence and David Pithey or because Partridge after fifteen years of priceless service is nearing his end.

'The prospect of a possible decline stems from a lack of young players competing to fill the gaps which will increase in the next few summers.

'Whereas South Africa developed a string of provincial players and several potential Test candidates from the schoolboys' tour of England in 1963, the highly successful visit of the Fawns overseas in 1962 has paid no dividend.

'What has happened to them? Stan Barbour switched to tennis. Giles Ridley is Oxford's next captain, Mike Burton is playing for Eastern Province and Alistair Carlisle for Balfour Park.

'Others have drifted away from the game. Rhodesia's one-time fervent public interest in cricket has fallen away.'

To commemorate Salisbury Sports Club's 75th anniversary a three-day cricket match was staged during a long week-end in September 1966, between Jackie McGlew's XI and Tony Pithey's XI. It featured a number of past, present and future Springboks — the hero of the first day was the young Barry Richards (Pithey's XI) who stroked a fluent 126. In reply Nick Frangos made a century for McGlew's XI and Eddie Parker (97) narrowly missed the three-figure mark which would have been most deserved because in a match that saw some big hitting, Parker accounted for ten of the seventeen sixes that were struck.

As a result of the scheduled Australian tour Rhodesia's Currie Cup programme was restricted to four fixtures, beginning with a ten-wicket defeat at the hands of Transvaal. This was the first visit by the Transvaal senior team in eight years and they steamrolled the Rhodesian side in an impressive manner. Said Ali Bacher after the match: 'Since I've been playing for Transvaal — about six years now — this is possibly the most efficient, workmanlike performance I've seen from the side.'

SCORES: versus Transvaal (Currie Cup), 1966-67.

At Salisbury, 22, 23 and 24 October.

Rhodesia — 227 (K.C. Bland 48, R.B. Ullyett 42, E.F. Parker 37; A.H. McKinnon 5/76)
and 129 (N.J. Frangos 37; A.H. McKinnon 6/25)

Transvaal — 334 (R.C. White 103, E.J. Barlow 79, A. Bacher 52; E.F. Parker 5/84, J.H. du Preez 3/112)
and 23-0 wkts.

Transvaal won by 10 wickets.

The Transvaal débâcle was hardly an ideal prepara-

Howie Gardiner, whose batting delighted Rhodesian crowds for many years, hits out *(above)* against the 1966-67 Australians whilst the wicket-keeper, Brian Taber, looks on in awe and *(below)* displays lightning reflexes behind the stumps at the Police ground, Salisbury.

tion for matches against a fully-fledged international touring side. The Australian tourists under Bobby Simpson visited Rhodesia on a similar basis to the 1964-65 M.C.C. side, playing against a Matabeleland Invitation XI in Bulawayo and then against the national side in Salisbury. A tremendous pre-tour build-up had been given to the tour largely because it appeared that the prospect of a first-ever victory over an Australian touring side on South African soil was more than merely a pipe dream. In Rhodesia, Simpson's team won its first-class match without difficulty but it was at this early stage of the tour that the aggression of Howie Gardiner and the experience of Bland, Ullyett and Pithey laid bare certain limitations in the visiting attack that were later exploited.

The Matabeleland Invitation XI was a happy blend of experienced players and promising youngsters. When the 1964-65 M.C.C. side had toured, they had asked that no one who had represented Rhodesia should play in the first match but the Australians made no such stipulation.

The game began poorly for the home side, who were all out for 107, but they struck back well to dismiss the Aussies for 211. Huntsman Williams, who had the famous Australian captain, Bobby Simpson, leg before for a duck, bowled well to take 4/81 in grilling Bulawayo temperatures. Wrote Louis Duffus: 'Well might Huntsman Williams leap like an impala as he dismissed Simpson. He had three more joyful leaps from excellent bowling. He will be the pride of his Inyati farming neighbours.'

The match was really set alight when the Invitation XI batted a second time and Louis Duffus continued: 'Colin Bland (94) swept away magnificently thoughts about his waning capabilities, Rob Ullyett (87) played an innings of outstanding competence and "Hurricane Howie" Gardiner challenged the whirlwinds of Winslow when the Aussies today suffered the biggest pasting meted out to any visiting team in their opening match . . . As a two-day match it did not call for all-out endeavour. It was not their best XI but Australians are jealous of prestige. They would not cast away a chance to gain a demoralizing ascendancy.'

Richie Benaud, too, heaped praise upon the Rhodesians: 'Once Bland and Ullyett really cut loose, no Australian bowler except McKenzie, had any real answer to them and the latter only because of his extra pace and vast experience of bowling against attacking batsmen.

'In the end he removed both in the space of a couple

of overs and then lightning really struck in the person of Howie Gardiner who, in 58 minutes of savagery, hit 86 runs.

'I was most impressed — he is not just a hitter but a powerful stroke player with a sound defence allied to his magnificent driving and hooking.'

In Salisbury the pitch was tailor-made for spin and consequently McKenzie, whose bowling had borne the hallmark of class in Bulawayo, was rested. After Tony Pithey had won the toss and had elected to bat it was the diminutive Johnny Martin who created problems for the Rhodesians in their first innings — Ullyett alone batted impressively as the Rhodesian lower order collapsed from 97-2 to 149 all out.

The Australian innings of 307 was held together by opening bat Ian Redpath, who carried his bat after a chanceless 322 minutes at the crease. His knock was a mixture of caution and aggression and was most invaluable to the visitors' cause after Jackie du Preez had gouged the middle out of their batting line-up. Du Preez claimed the wickets of Ian Chappell (0), Keith Stackpole (4), Graeme Watson (5) and Tom Veivers (9) cheaply and at one stage had captured 6 wickets for 33. Said Louis Duffus of Jackie du Preez: 'After six years in representative play he has suddenly burst into bloom like a desert cactus that long lies dormant before it flowers.'

There was little hope of the home side avoiding an outright defeat but the Rhodesian second innings was an improvement despite some fine leg-spin bowling by Ian Chappell who took five wickets in 34 overs. Nick Frangos made runs in the early stages and Tony Pithey batted superbly for his 67, using his feet well to smother the spinners and playing his shots with admirable judgement. But it was Howie Gardiner who again brought the spectators to their feet in an innings of 81. He made his runs out of a sixth wicket stand of 107 with Pithey and on this occasion lashed six mighty sixes and seven fours.

SCORES: Australian Tour, 1966-67.

At Bulawayo, 2 and 3 November.

Matabeleland Invitation XI — 107
and 298-6 dec. (K.C. Bland 94, R.B. Ullyett, 87, H.A.B. Gardiner 86)

Australia — 211 (R.M. Cowper 65, W.M. Lawry 62; B.H. Williams 4/81, J.H. du Preez 3/22)
and 62-3 wkts.

Match drawn.

At Salisbury, 5, 6 and 7 November.

Rhodesia — 149 (R.B. Ullyett 60; J.W. Martin 5/26)
and 265 (H.A.B. Gardiner 81, A.J. Pithey 67, N.J. Frangos 49; I.M. Chappell 5/53)

RHODESIA, 1966-67.
Back: J. du Preez, N. Williams, A. de Caila, E. Parker, N. Frangos, M. Huckle, J. Wallace.
Seated: J. Partridge, R. Gripper, A. Pithey (Captain), A. Pichanick (Manager), R. Ullyett, C. Bland.

JACKIE DU PREEZ.

Doug Neilson is shown backing up to Du Preez bowling.

> Australia — 307 (I.R. Redpath 139*; J.H. du Preez 6/95)
> and 111-2 wkts.
>
> Australia won by 8 wickets.

Rhodesia's remaining Currie Cup matches were all lost outright. Humiliating defeats were suffered against Natal and Transvaal before being pipped by one wicket in the final match against Eastern Province.

Against Natal, overnight rain which had seeped through the covers triggered off Rhodesia's dramatic first innings collapse. On a wicket full of uncertainty the new pace sensation, Mike Procter, bowled brilliantly, moving the ball appreciably in the air with some movement off the pitch. Jackie du Preez batted courageously to register top score of 28 in a total of 112 and then in the second innings withstood the Natal attack for just over three hours to make an unbeaten 76. The Natal side which included Anton Procter, who was Rhodesia's twelfth man on one occasion the previous season, and David Pithey, won by an innings and six runs.

Transvaal also thumped the Rhodesians by an innings with Eddie Barlow scoring a typically pugnacious 212. Jackie du Preez again made his mark with a second innings half-century and less than a week later compiled his maiden first-class hundred at St. George's Park, Port Elizabeth.

Against Eastern Province, Du Preez added 210 in partnership with Tony Pithey and reached his century (one six and sixteen fours) with Pithey on 75, having given his captain an hour's start. Du Preez also fought a lone battle in scoring 70 in the second innings which enabled Rhodesia to set Eastern Province a reasonable target of 195 to win. And in a tense finish Eastern Province managed to scamper home with their last pair at the wicket. Joe Partridge, in his "final fling" for Rhodesia had taken three wickets whilst Eastern Province's score stood at 10, including Graeme Pollock first ball, and he finished with a meritorous 6/20. But it was Du Preez who bowled the last over — Eastern Province needed one run to tie and 2 to win. Ronnie Colling and former Rhodesian, Gordon Den, dashed through for a risky single after the former had placed a shot somewhere in the region where Colin Bland was fielding. Den then thrashed out at Du Preez's next ball and Neville Deudney fielding at square leg jumped high in the air to get a hand to the ball but in a grand effort could not hold it. Eastern Province ran two runs to win the match.

The season's record was a gloomy one but for Jackie du Preez it was to contain the most momentous occasions of his career. He topped the Rhodesian batting averages (394 runs — average 43,78) as well as picking up 21 wickets. But his greatest achievement was making his Test debut for the Springboks against the touring Australians. He had been twelfth man in the Third Test at Kingsmead, Durban, when the moment that he remembers most off the field occurred on his plane trip back to Salisbury: 'I didn't expect to make the Springbok final team and was quite ready to go back to my farm. Lindsay Tuckett, one of the selectors, was on the flight with me. At Johannesburg, when he was about to disembark, I went over to say goodbye before travelling on to Salisbury. He just smiled and said: "See you next week at the Wanderers" . . . I knew I was in the Bok side.'

SCORES: Currie Cup A Section, 1966-67.

At Salisbury, 19, 20 and 21 November.

Natal — 330 (D. Gamsy 89, D.B. Pithey 66, D.J. McGlew 57; J.H. du Preez 6/128)

Rhodesia — 112 (M.J. Procter 7/25)
and 212 (J.H. du Preez 76*, N.J. Frangos 31)

Natal won by an innings and 6 runs.

At Johannesburg, 3 and 5 December.

Transvaal — 367 (E.J. Barlow 212; N.R. Williams 3/71)

Rhodesia — 140 (A.J. Pithey 34; D. Mackay-Coghill 6/50)
and 167 (J.H. du Preez 58)

Transvaal won by an innings and 61 runs.

Three Rhodesians who captained Oxford — Barry May, Peter Wilson and Mike Burton — shelter at Lord's from the inevitable English rain.

Du Preez, in only his second over in Test cricket and with the last ball before lunch took his first Test wicket when he bowled Bob Cowper. He followed this up by dismissing Stackpole and returned figures of 14-6-22-2 having not bowled in the first innings. His effort earned him a place in the Fifth and final Test where South Africa again relied on her seam attack to wrap up the series 3-1 and Du Preez bowled a mere ten overs in the match, taking the wicket of Graham McKenzie. And to crown a great year Du Preez was named as Rhodesia's Sportsman of the Year.

Colin Bland played in the First Test against the Australians at the Wanderers but injured his suspect knee on the final day of the Test through crashing into a picket fence. The injury resulted in the removal of a cartilage but fortunately Bland returned quickly because in 1967-68 he was to play a significant role in Rhodesia's cricket progress.

At Port Elizabeth, 9, 10 and 12 December.

Rhodesia — 311 (J.H. du Preez 112, A.J. Pithey 93, K.C. Bland 37; G.M. Den 5/45)
and 183 (J.H. du Preez 70, I.E. Haig 33)

Eastern Province — 300 (R.G. Pollock 134*; J.H. du Preez 3/110)
and 196-9 wkts. (P.L. van der Merwe 67; J.T. Partridge 6/20, N.A. Deudney 3/63)

Eastern Province won by 1 wicket.

In March 1967 a Rhodesian Colts side was scheduled to play against the North-Eastern Transvaal Colts but the fixture was unfortunately cancelled and replaced with a match against a Rhodesian Invitation XI. The Invitation XI was captained by Colin Bland and included popular England opening bowler David Brown, who was holidaying in Rhodesia after a coaching contract earlier in the season. These two experienced players provided the highlights of an enterprising match.

SCORES: at Salisbury, 4 and 5 March.

Rhodesia Invitation XI — 205 (D.J. Brown 39*, N.A. Deudney 30; P.R. McLoughlin 4/33, M. Shacklock 3/45)

and 159-7 dec. (K.C. Bland 84; M. Shacklock 3/56)

Rhodesia Colts — 144 (J.K. Clarke 63, E.D.R. Fuller 34*; D.J. Brown 5/24, V. Jackman 3/35)

and 155-6 wkts. (A. McClelland 39; N.A. Deudney 4/53)

Match drawn.

In the course of Louis Duffus commenting early in the 1966-67 season about the drain on Rhodesian cricket talent he touched upon a very unusual chapter in the history of Oxford University cricket. When former Milton schoolboy and Rhodesian Nuffield captain, Giles Ridley, was named as Oxford's cricket captain in 1967 he began an incredible run of Rhodesians holding this position. The swashbuckling opening batsman, Fred Goldstein (Falcon), took over the captaincy in 1968 and held it for the 1969 season. His brilliant 155 against Cambridge in 1968 must hold pride of place amongst Rhodesian achievements at Oxford and was described in *Wisden* as 'a breathtaking succession of strokes'. He was succeeded as skipper by Mike Burton (Umtali) in 1970, who in turn was followed by Barry May (Prince Edward) in 1971 and Peter Jones (Milton) in 1972. Another Rhodesian, Peter Wilson (Milton) gained his Oxford Blue in 1968 and 1970 whilst Chris Seager (Peterhouse) earned a Cambridge Blue in 1971.

Wilfred Isaacs, a cricket fanatic who had done so much to promote South African cricket, brought a strong side to Rhodesia early in the 1967-68 season. His team blended veterans Roy McLean, Atholl McKinnon and Tiger Lance with up-and-coming stars such as Barry Richards, Mike Procter, Lee Irvine, Ray White, Neil Rosendorff, Elton Chatterton and Chris Dey. They convincingly beat a Mashonaland Country Districts side at Umvukwes in their opening fixture — here John Kitcat provided resolute resistance in an innings of 99 made in only 102 minutes. A Stragglers XI at the Country Club were then comprehensively defeated on the first innings as were a Districts XI at Salisbury South. In the latter match Ross Fuller, Gerald Deary, Robin Kilburn and "Bundu" Waller all made runs but Ray White scored a century in reply to guide the Isaacs XI to a five-wicket win. Finally in a thriller, the tourists tied with a Mashonaland XI at the Police ground. The home side declared at 407-8 — Tony Pithey (107), Jackie du Preez (101) and Brian Davison (84*) all making runs. The Isaacs XI were 262-8 but their "tail" wagged with a vengeance and the last wicket fell with their score at 407.

The Wilfred Isaacs' XI tour had provided a piquant appetizer to a season which was to see Rhodesia once again win the B Section and earn promotion for their efforts. The Currie Cup programme began slowly with a first innings win over Natal B and a loss on first innings to Western Province but once in their stride Rhodesia gained successive outright victories over Border, Orange Free State, Transvaal B and Griqualand West.

The season also began disappointingly in that Tony Pithey, due to his leaving teaching for a career in commerce, withdrew from the side after one match and announced his retirement from first-class cricket. The captaincy, however, was taken over by Colin Bland and his leadership proved an inspiration with the standard of fielding reaching near perfection. Bland also enjoyed a highly successful season — scoring 404 runs (average 57,71) which was bettered only by Ray Gripper (529 runs — average 75,57). Bland for one match held the Rhodesian record for the highest individual score by smashing 197 off Border during which he packed eight sixes and twenty-one fours. In addition he topped the bowling averages (11 wickets at 18,18) and twice opened the attack to telling effect, taking 4/40 against Transvaal B and 3/23 against Border.

The greatest achievement of the season however, belonged to Ray Gripper who established a new Currie Cup record for the highest individual score against the Orange Free State at the Ramblers, Bloemfontein. The Rhodesians mutilated the record books as Gripper (279 not out) put on 268 for the first wicket with Jono Clarke and then continued the onslaught with Rob Ullyett until a new all-wicket record partnership of 281 had been achieved. Gripper's innings eclipsed Eric Rowan's 277 not out for Transvaal against Griqualand West in 1950-51, lasting 6¾ hours and containing four sixes and forty fours. The innings total of 549-1 declared meant subsequently that Rhodesia beat the Free State outright for the loss of only one wicket.

RAY GRIPPER.

RAY GRIPPER.

"JONO" CLARKE.

Two important factors in Rhodesia's success were the arrival of Springbok Peter Carlstein, playing for his fourth province, and the dramatic entry into first-class cricket of Jono Clarke, the bespectacled opening batsman. Carlstein made 125 in his first game for Rhodesia which guided his side to a first innings win over Natal B whilst Clarke made an undefeated 112 in the second innings of his debut match against Western Province. They finished third and fourth respectively in the Rhodesian averages — Carlstein (427 runs — average 53,37) and Clarke (381 runs — average 47,62).

Whilst the gap created by the departure of Lawrence and Partridge was never really bridged, Eddie Parker enjoyed his best season ever with the ball in capturing 25 wickets (average 19,60). Jackie du Preez finished with the most wickets, 28 (average 23,75), proving the mainstay of the attack by bowling 130 overs more than the next man. Inevitably his batting suffered as a result and his only innings of note during the season was his 72 against Transvaal B — for good measure in the same game he finished with a match aggregate of 11/132 to inspire a narrow 39-run victory.

SCORES: Currie Cup B Section, 1967-68.

At Salisbury, 25, 26 and 27 November.
Natal B — 211 (N.R. Williams 3/65)
and 258-5 dec. (R.N. Ireland 152, G.C. Heath 62; E.F. Parker 3/62)
Rhodesia — 309 (P.R. Carlstein 125, B.F. Davison 47, R.A. Gripper 43, K.C. Bland 32)
and 30-0 wkts.
Rhodesia won on first innings.

At Cape Town, 26, 27 and 28 December.
Western Province — 505-8 dec. (R.K. Muzzell 161, A. Bruyns 160, G.P. Pfuhl 65; E.F. Parker 4/110)
Rhodesia — 272 (P.R. Carlstein 89, R.B. Ullyett 37, D.W. Townshend 35, E.F. Parker 31)
and 243-7 wkts. (J.K. Clarke 112*, R.B. Ullyett 42, P.R. Carlstein 37)
Western Province won on first innings.

At East London, 30 December, 1 and 2 January.
Border — 210 (C.P. Wilkins 63; K.C. Bland 3/23)
and 265 (W.S. Farrer 109; J.H. du Preez 5/40)
Rhodesia — 452-7 dec. (K.C. Bland 197, R.B. Ullyett 78, R.A. Gripper 61, J.K. Clarke 48)
and 27-3 wkts.
Rhodesia won by 7 wickets.

At Bloemfontein, 5, 6 and 8 January.
Orange Free State — 252 (N. Rosendorff 120; E.F. Parker 4/50)
and 235 (P. Strydom 75, N. Rosendorff 69; E.F. Parker 6/74, B.F. Davison 3/35)
Rhodesia — 549-1 dec. (R.A. Gripper 279*, J.K. Clarke 130, R.B. Ullyett 126*).
Rhodesia won by an innings and 62 runs.

At Salisbury, 27, 28 and 29 January.
Rhodesia — 149 (H.A.B. Gardiner 34*, P.R. Carlstein 31, K.C. Bland 31)
and 255 (P.R. Carlstein 93, J.H. du Preez 72, B.F. Davison 31)
Transvaal B — 177 (C. Mitchley 66, J.P.D. Flanagan 56; K.C. Bland 4/40, J.H. du Preez 3/40)
and 188 (J.H. du Preez 8/92)
Rhodesia won by 40 runs.

At Bulawayo, 24, 25 and 26 February.
Griqualand West — 196 (J.H. du Preez 6/74, B.F. Davison 3/29)
and 213 (D.J. Schonegevel 98; B.F. Davison 5/52, P.R. McLoughlin 4/53)
Rhodesia — 388 (K.C. Bland 116, J.K. Clarke 56, R.A. Gripper 55, H.A.B. Gardiner 37, P.R. Carlstein 36, B.F. Davison 32)
and 22-1 wkt.
Rhodesia won by 9 wickets.

Dissatisfaction was again expressed at the end of the 1967-68 season with the Currie Cup system as Rhodesia once again made her way back to the A Section after only one year in the lower zone. A growing group suggested that the Australian system of State cricket should be adopted and that there should be no promotion and relegation. This would allow teams with big nurseries of young players to come through lean periods without fear of losing their senior status in the Currie Cup.

To an extent the 1967-68 season showed that there

PETER CARLSTEIN.

were several young cricketers fringing on higher honours in Rhodesian cricket. The Nuffield team was unbeaten in January 1968 and a Rhodesian Colts side had much the better of a match against their Transvaal counterparts. In the latter match an opening stand of 164 by Tommy Dunk and Duncan Fletcher took the Rhodesians past the Transvaal score of 146 and laid the foundation for Jack Heron to thrash an unbeaten 119 in 110 minutes. Heron's innings and his performance for the South African Schools XI were instrumental in his gaining selection for the Rhodesian senior side towards the end of the 1967-68 season.

SCORES: Colts Match, 1967-68.

At Bulawayo, 31 December and 1 January.

Transvaal Colts — 146 (P.R. McLoughlin 3/23, I. Kennedy 3/47)
and 276-7 wkts. (I.W. Finlay 101*, J.R. Cheetham 54; D.A.G. Fletcher 3/13)

Rhodesia Colts — 388-3 dec. (T.W. Dunk 149, J.G. Heron 119*, D.A.G. Fletcher 83)

Match drawn.

Whilst the truncated A Section of 1968-69 ensured that a high standard was maintained, Rhodesia found that the disparity between the standard of play prevailing in this four-team section as compared with that which had occurred in the B Section during the previous season, too difficult to adjust to in one season. Six of the seven matches played during the season resulted in defeat, the remaining game — against Transvaal at Salisbury — was abandoned owing to rain, without an innings being completed. The two matches against Natal were only first innings losses but Rhodesia was beaten outright by Eastern Province twice, Transvaal, and North-Eastern Transvaal in a friendly fixture.

The Rhodesian bowling attack was woefully weak and once again the Lawrence/Partridge penetration of bygone years provided prodding comparison in Press reports. Eddie Parker, who had become an important cog in the Rhodesian side during previous seasons, did not enjoy the same measure of success with the ball but was the leading wicket-taker of the opening bowlers (12 wickets — at an expensive 47,58). Roy McLoughlin, Noel Peck, Brian Davison and Riki Cameron were tried as new-ball bowlers with limited success. It was indeed a pity at such an early stage that the promising McLoughlin should have been put out of action for the remainder of the season through an operation to his right cheekbone. In only the third match of the season he deflected a ball from the Eastern Province pace bowler, Sibley McAdam, on to his face — a great pity because he appeared to be settling down well in the side.

Unlike the other A Section sides, Rhodesia was forced to rely heavily on their spin attack. John Traicos proved a fine off-spin prospect and topped the bowling average (21 wickets — average 25,09) but Jackie du Preez was somewhat expensive (19 wickets — average 46,05). With their serious bowling limitations Rhodesia was consequently only once able to bowl a side out in their first innings for under 300 and that was North-Eastern Transvaal who made 298.

The batting averages revealed that there was not a single century scored by a Rhodesian in their seven matches although Peter Carlstein was bowled by Mike

Procter for 99 against Natal at Kingsmead. Nevertheless, there were some promising batting displays and Colin Bland, Jackie du Preez, Stuart Robertson, Peter Carlstein and Ray Gripper all topped 300 runs for the season. Bland was the leading run-scorer and headed the averages (463 runs — average 38,58) whilst Tony Pithey came out of retirement to contribute a fine 73 against Transvaal and finish with an average of 36,80 for his limited appearances. The find of the season was undoubtedly Stuart Robertson, a classic left-hand bat only twenty years of age, who produced all the shots in the book and scored 319 runs (average 35,44) in the five matches he played. A useful all-rounder at that stage was Brian Davison who scored two good half-centuries including a whirlwind 50 in 14 strokes against North-Eastern Transvaal but was invariably too impetuous.

The most outstanding feature of the 1968-69 Rhodesian side was their high standard of fielding and Louis Duffus wrote at that time: 'Rhodesia have the finest fielding side they have ever possessed. This is perhaps understandable, for once a week most of them spend a session devoted entirely to training and fielding — under the guidance of Colin Bland. The man whose phenomenal fielding captured the imagination of onlookers on three continents has lost little of his genius.'

SCORES: Currie Cup A Section, 1968-69.

At Salisbury, 9, 10 and 11 November.

Natal — 444 (G.C. Heath 78, D. Gamsy 76, B. Versfeld 72, B.L. Irvine 72; J.H. du Preez 6/149)
and 162-4 dec. (B.A. Richards 59)

Rhodesia — 310 (K.C. Bland 82, P.R. Carlstein 50)
and 204-4 wkts. (R.A. Gripper 80, K.C. Bland 53*, A.J. Pithey 40)

Natal won on first innings.

At Salisbury, 7, 8 and 9 December.

Rhodesia — 375-9 dec. (J.H. du Preez 89, E.F. Parker 83*, A.J. Pithey 73, R.A. Gripper 33)

Transvaal — 36-0 wkts.

Match abandoned owing to rain.

At Port Elizabeth, 26, 27 and 28 December.

Rhodesia — 186 (P.R. Carlstein 55, P.R. McLoughlin 37)
and 217 (K.C. Bland 60, E.F. Parker 42, J.K. Clarke 36)

Eastern Province — 322 (A.M. Short 80, A.L. Biggs 71, R.G. Pollock 54; P.R. McLoughlin 4/48)
and 83-1 wkt. (A.L. Biggs 52*)

Eastern Province won by 9 wickets.

At Durban, 31 December, 1 and 2 January.

Natal — 321 (B.L. Irvine 85, B.A. Richards 58; E.F. Parker 3/92, J.H. du Preez 3/116)
and 210-3 dec. (B.A. Richards 112*, B.L. Irvine 60*)

Rhodesia — 212 (R.A. Gripper 70, S.D. Robertson 59, K.C. Bland 36; V.A.P. van der Bijl 5/60)
and 287-6 wkts. (P.R. Carlstein 99, S.D. Robertson 55*, J.K. Clarke 54, K.C. Bland 47)

Natal won on first innings.

At Johannesburg, 17, 18 and 20 January.

Rhodesia — 295 (J.H. du Preez 91, S.D. Robertson 58, R.A. Gripper 38)
and 144 (P.R. Carlstein 41)

Transvaal — 423 (A. Bacher 189, R.K. Muzzell 75; J.H. du Preez 4/104)
and 19-0 wkts.

Transvaal won by 10 wickets.

At Bulawayo, 8, 9 and 10 February.

Rhodesia — 252 (B.F. Davison 57, A.J. Pithey 42, J.D. McPhun 39)
and 181 (R.A. Gripper 32, S.D. Robertson 30; N. Mallett 5/55)

Eastern Province — 344 (R.G. Pollock 166, N. Mallett 54; A.J. Traicos 6/129)
and 90-4 wkts.

Eastern Province won by 6 wickets.

Friendly versus North-Eastern Transvaal.

At Pretoria, 23, 24 and 25 January.

North-Eastern Transvaal — 298 (I.W. Finlay 90; G.N.C. Peck 4/52, E.F. Parker 3/64)
and 265-9 dec. (G.G.M. de Villiers 70; A.J. Traicos 6/66)

Rhodesia — 234 (K.C. Bland 46, R.A. Gripper 37)
and 319 (J.D. McPhun 58, K.C. Bland 54, B.F. Davison 50, S.D. Robertson 47, J.H. du Preez 34)

North-Eastern Transvaal won by 10 runs.

Over the New Year during the 1968-69 season a Rhodesian Colts side made a three-match tour to the Transvaal.

SCORES: Colts Tour to the Transvaal, 1968-69.

At Johannesburg, 31 December and 1 January (Not first-class).

Rhodesia Colts — 229 (W.H. Hodnett 59, E. Laughlin 49; R. van der Knaap 5/29)

Transvaal Colts — 247 (J.P.D. Flanagan 66, D.T. Seccombe 60)
and 119-3 wkts.

Transvaal Colts won by 7 wickets.

At Johannesburg, 2 and 3 January (Not first-class).

Transvaal Nuffield XI — 250 (A.J.S. Smith 51; D. Hinde 7/106)
and 51-2 wkts.

Rhodesia Colts — 406 (J.C. Mitchell 115, J.G. Heron 106)

Match drawn.

At Krugersdorp, 6 and 7 January (Not first-class).

Transvaal Country Districts — 93 (D. Hinde 6/30)
and 159 (J.C. Mitchell 7/44)

Rhodesia Colts — 217-7 dec. (D.A.G. Fletcher 132)
and 39-1 wkt.

Rhodesia Colts won by 9 wickets.

A North-Eastern Transvaal Colts side arrived at the end of the 1968-69 season and played against junior provincial sides before taking on the Rhodesian Colts XI. Bearing in mind that the Rhodesian senior side had suffered an ignominious defeat against B Section North-Eastern Transvaal it did provide some compensation that their junior combination won their encounter by an innings and 21 runs.

SCORES: Colts match, 1968-69.

At Salisbury, 8 and 9 March (Not first-class).

Rhodesia Colts — 269 (T.W. Dunk 71, E. Laughlin 37, R.H. Kaschula 30)

North-Eastern Transvaal Colts — 68 (J.C. Mitchell 4/10, J. Connor 3/16)
and 180 (D.A.G. Fletcher 7/51)

Rhodesia Colts won by an innings and 21 runs.

A practice match was staged early in the 1969-70 season for a Rhodesian XI against Johnny Waite's Wanderers side at the Kent Park Oval, Johannesburg. Fifty-four years earlier Rhodesia had gained a sensational win over a Wanderers XI loaded with Springboks but on this occasion a generous declaration by Colin Bland allowed the home side to record a five-wicket victory.

SCORES: versus Wanderers, 1969-70.

At Johannesburg, 20 and 21 September.

Rhodesia XI — 283-8 dec. (K.C. Bland 67, S.D. Robertson 46, J.H. du Preez 39, H.A.B. Gardiner 31, J.K. Clarke 30)
and 149-4 dec. (J.K. Clarke 73, J.D. McPhun 46)

Wanderers — 263-5 dec. (D. Lindsay-Smith 75, P.R. Carlstein 68, G. Watson 58)
and 172-5 wkts. (J.H. du Preez 3/41)

Wanderers won by 5 wickets.

With Peter Carlstein already in the Transvaal, Colin Bland in the process of emigrating to the Eastern Province, Brian Davison overseas and Tony Pithey no longer available, the middle order of the Rhodesian batting line-up was looking decidedly thin. Ray Gripper's task in handling a Rhodesian team considerably below strength in both the batting and bowling departments was not an enviable one in 1969-70 and in the Currie Cup competition Rhodesia suffered four heavy defeats — three by an innings margin — in a row. Their other first-class match during the season was a friendly against Natal and once again they were swamped — this time by 244 runs. Tragically, Rhodesian cricket appeared to be floundering whilst South Africa was enjoying its most successful season in history.

In 1969-70 the Springboks inflicted a record 4-0 thrashing upon the touring Australians — it was also the first time Rhodesia had been excluded from a touring side's itinerary since Captain R.T. Stanyforth's M.C.C. side missed out the Colony in 1927-28. But whereas Captain Stanyforth's team did not tour because the R.C.U. secretary had never bothered to reply to a South African Cricket Association questionnaire regarding fixtures, Rhodesia was left out of the 1969-70 itinerary for political reasons.

The one happy factor was that John Traicos gained international recognition and in fact became the last man to be capped for South Africa in Test cricket. He played in the last three Tests of the series against the Australians and in his debut took four fine catches in an innings as Australia stumbled to a total of 157 at Kingsmead. Over all he claimed four wickets with his off-spinners but with South Africa relying heavily on speed and seam, he had limited opportunities with the ball.

Because of Rhodesia's selection dilemma, Joe Partridge was recalled to the national team to play against Western Province at the Queens ground in the opening Currie Cup encounter but then withdrew because of a pulled hamstring. Roy McLoughlin was unavailable and it was left to Eddie Parker, Huntsman Williams and Duncan Fletcher to do the seam duties. Fletcher together with Tommy Dunk were the two new caps in the side with their notable efforts the previous season for the Rhodesia Colts side no doubt contributing towards their selection.

The unusual situation arose of newly promoted Western Province being firm favourites against Rhodesia aided by their Springbok acquisition, Mike Procter. Sadly the Rhodesians were humiliated by an innings and 76 runs as they were unable to combat the visitors' sustained barrage of hostile but intelligent bowling.

A better showing at the Police ground saw Rhodesia make Transvaal fight all the way for their 4-wicket

A superb picture sequence of John Traicos in action.

outright victory with Neville Williams bowling impressively. Duncan Fletcher also gave notice of his batting qualities by holding up the Transvaalers in the Rhodesian second innings with a tenacious 49.

After this spirited effort the Rhodesians disappointed on their two-match tour by losing by an innings to both Eastern Province and Natal. South Africa's two master batsmen, Graeme Pollock and Barry Richards, both struck brilliant centuries to set up huge first innings totals for their respective provinces. However, there were some encouraging performances by individual Rhodesians. Duncan Fletcher made a resolute 89 at Port Elizabeth, Stuart Robertson 62 at Durban and Ken Tonkin claimed four wickets for 15 runs in a nine-over spell against Natal which included the prize wicket of Trevor Goddard for a duck.

Goddard praised the raw Rhodesian side at the conclusion of their Currie Cup clash when he said: 'Rhodesians should not be despondent about the efforts of their young cricketers this season. This is a fine team in the making and all they need now is to believe in their own ability.'

Rhodesia had one further first-class match and Trevor Goddard chose the occasion to bow out of first-class cricket with a hat-trick. He claimed the wickets of Duncan Fletcher, Jackie du Preez and Errol Laughlin in successive balls to have the Rhodesians reeling at 55-6 — a position from which they never recovered. Barry Richards made his customary century and Natal coasted to an easy victory.

SCORES: Currie Cup A Section, 1969-70.

At Bulawayo, 8, 9 and 11 November.
Western Province — 371-9 dec. (A. Bruyns 149, C.G. Stephens 88; A.J. Traicos 4/103, J.H. du Preez 4/121)
Rhodesia — 139
and 156 (S.D. Robertson 41, R.A. Gripper 37)
Western Province won by an innings and 76 runs.

At Salisbury, 29 and 30 November, 1 December.
Rhodesia — 221 (R.A. Gripper 73, T.W. Dunk 30)
and 213 (D.A.G. Fletcher 49, E.F. Parker 43, E. Laughlin 36)
Transvaal — 334-7 dec. (A. Bacher 69, D. Mackay-Coghill 52*; A.J. Traicos 3/113, J.H. du Preez 3/115)
and 101-6 wkts. (B.H. Williams 4/56)
Transvaal won by 4 wickets.

At Port Elizabeth, 26, 27 and 29 December.
Rhodesia — 132 (R.A. Gripper 41)
and 249 (D.A.G. Fletcher 89, H.A.B. Gardiner 34, J.H. du Preez 33, B.H. Williams 30)
Eastern Province — 436-5 dec. (R.G. Pollock 138, A.L. Biggs 102, S.J. Bezuidenhout 84)
Eastern Province won by an innings and 55 runs.

At Durban, 1, 2 and 3 January.
Rhodesia — 183 (S.D. Robertson 62)
and 172 (K.J. Tonkin 32)
Natal — 396-9 dec. (B.A. Richards 169, A.M. Short 95; K.J. Tonkin 4/54, J.H. du Preez 3/74)
Natal won by an innings and 41 runs.

Friendly versus Natal.
At Salisbury, 14, 15 and 16 March.
Natal — 324 (B.A. Richards 106, B. Versfeld 69, D.D. Dyer 53; J.C. Mitchell 3/58)
and 201-3 dec. (B.A. Richards 69, B. Versfeld 53*)
Rhodesia — 149 (S.D. Robertson 58, H.A.B. Gardiner 36)
and 132 (S.D. Robertson 39)
Natal won by 244 runs.

At the end of the 1969-70 season the Transvaal Colts side toured, ending their visit with a match against a Rhodesia Colts XI. The home side disappointed and the Transvaalers duly crawled to victory in a somewhat dreary fashion — Richie Kaschula's figures of 24-15-24-3 revealed the snail's pace of the batting.

SCORES: Colts match, 1969-70 (Not first-class).

At Norton, 7 and 8 March.
Rhodesia Colts — 66
and 197 (S.C. Dinsdale 47, E. Laughlin 39)
Transvaal Colts — 190
and 75-5 (R.H. Kaschula 3/24)
Transvaal Colts won by 5 wickets.

RHODESIA, 1969-70.
Back: K. Tonkin, T. Dunk, D. Fletcher, E. Loughlin, H. Williams, J. Mitchell.
Seated: H. Gardiner, S. Robertson, R. Gripper (Captain), A. Pichanick (Manager), J. du Preez, J. Clarke, J. Traicos.

CHAPTER EIGHT

The Mike Procter Era

THE CASTLE BREWERIES double-wicket competition staged at the Police ground, Salisbury, in September 1970, heralded the start of one of the most exciting seasons to date. The two-day festival featured Springboks Eddie Barlow, Mike Procter and Barry Richards who were fresh from their World XI Test series triumph over England, as well as Ali Bacher, Lee Irvine and Jack du Preez. But the man the public flocked to watch was the world's greatest all-rounder, Gary Sobers.

Sobers had been invited by the Mashonaland Cricket Association and the 13 000 crowd which supported the cricket over the week-end loved him. In 1970 he was at his peak and he admitted prior to the double-wicket competition: 'I'm playing far better now than ever before. When I go to the wicket and fail or make mistakes I know exactly what is wrong. Before I had to go to the nets and work it all out. Now I don't have to — in fact I don't like net practices as I waste my energy there.'

No doubt tired after a long, strenuous season in Britain followed by a strength-sapping 6 000-mile flight from London, he might not have been at his best but nevertheless he did show flashes of his true talent. Memories of two deceptively powerful knocks — a scintillating 71 and a brisk 37 not out — stroked in such an effortless manner will long be treasured by the thousands who only ever saw the West Indian captain that week-end at the Police ground.

A standing ovation from the Salisbury crowd as he walked off the field for the last time reflected the high regard these spectators had for Gary Sobers. But back home in the West Indies a great deal of criticism was levelled at him and realising the political implications developing from his action he wrote an apologetic letter to the West Indian cricket administrators expressing '. . . sincere regrets for any embarrassment which my action may have caused.'

The double-wicket competition was won by Mike Procter and Lee Irvine in a fitting end to an action-packed tournament. A glorious 90 not out by Procter — 50 of the runs being struck in the last two overs in a little over eight minutes — was wildly applauded by a hoarse audience in the knowledge that the Springbok all-rounder was Rhodesia's new national coach, having been contracted in a "scoop" achieved by the Rhodesia Cricket Union. In a very short time the value of his arrival was to be proved immeasurable.

Following close on the heels of the double-wicket competition was an amazing finish to a Rothmans National League match between Midlands and Manicaland at the Salisbury Sports Club. A more exciting finish could not have been contrived — Midlands beat Manicaland by three wickets having needed 24 runs off the last over. Gwelo bank employee, John Woods, missed the first ball of that final over but off consecutive deliveries proceeded to hit 6, 4, 4, 6, 6 to register a sensational victory for his side.

The new Rothmans National League was a success although there was some controversy over which side Mike Procter should represent. Initially he turned out for Midlands but then switched to Manicaland where he was to score the century of the season. Playing against Salisbury Sports Club at the Umtali Sports Club ground he struck a superb 159 by way of seven sixes and twenty-five fours to guide Manicaland to victory. Procter ended the season by turning out for Old Hararians who were the inaugural National League champions.

Of Procter's first season in Rhodesia, the 1971 *South African Cricket Annual* commented: 'After two seasons without a single victory Rhodesia could fairly be described as the Team of the Year.' The all-conquering seven-match programme of 1970-71 included four innings victories and a clear-cut 7-wicket margin over the joint Currie Cup holders, Western Province. The inspiration and the example was provided by the great Springbok all-rounder, Mike Procter, and his own achievements were quite magnificent. He compiled 934 runs (average 133,43) in dynamic fashion whilst as an awesomely fast opening bowler he claimed 27 wickets (average 16,11). But Procter's impact on the Rhodesian cricket scene went deeper than that because he brought out the best in his team-mates. John McPhun scored two centuries and enjoyed his best ever season; Howie Gardiner shared the lead in first-class wicket-keeping dismissals; Brian Davison, Ray Gripper, Jackie du Preez and Stuart Robertson all made useful contributions, and slow left-arm bowler, Richie Kaschula, captured 41 wickets in his maiden first-class season.

Mike Procter's most spectacular feat was of course his six successive centuries in first-class matches which equalled the world record held by cricket immortals C.B. Fry who achieved it in 1901, and Sir Donald Bradman in 1938-39. He began his record-equalling

The incomparable Gary Sobers cover-drives Jack du Preez watched by Eddie Barlow, and later chats to Ali Bacher and David Lewis during his visit to Salisbury.

run of innings with 119 in 153 minutes, including a six and nineteen fours, against a competent Natal B team in Bulawayo and followed this with a supremely confident 129 against Transvaal B in Salisbury. The Orange Free State were then on the receiving end of his third (107) and most explosive century scored during the first tour match in the season's fastest time of 72 minutes. At this stage the cricket spotlight began to focus on him and after a brilliantly controlled 174 against North-Eastern Transvaal in Pretoria he had made Currie Cup history. Almost inevitably another century (137) followed against Griqualand West at Kimberley and with one last match to go, a friendly against Western Province, the crowds flocked to Salisbury's Police ground to see if Procter could equal the world record.

Rhodesia, three wickets down for five runs, were in fact in dire trouble when Procter came to the wicket. However, seemingly unaffected by the attention and the situation, the blond maestro despatched Riki

Cameron's first ball into the covers. But when on 3 he snicked a catch into the slips and the crowd froze as the Western Province captain, Andre Bruyns, juggled frantically with the ball. But to the relief of Procter and the vast majority of the crowd the ball popped back over Bruyns' head and went to ground. Thereafter there was no holding him back as he capitalized on his good fortune and proceeded to pulverize the attack for the next 280 minutes in amassing 254 with six sixes and twenty-eight fours.

To summarize briefly a vintage season, Rhodesia began their campaign by thrashing Border at the Police ground by an innings and 168 runs with Procter (5/8 in ten overs) spearheading an attack that saw the visitors rolled for 57. Gripper and McPhun then attacked the Border bowling with the latter reaching his hundred in 163 minutes and enabling the declaration to be made at 384-8 wickets. Richie Kaschula and Jackie du Preez did the rest and Border were enticed out for a slightly more respectable 159.

Natal B put up more of a fight but a Procter century with good batting support from Gripper, McPhun and Errol Laughlin, and steady bowling by Kaschula saw Rhodesia comfortably home by nine wickets. It was certainly a pity that rain then foiled a third successive victory a week later by washing out play on the first day and reducing time on each of the other days in Rhodesia's match against Transvaal B in Salisbury.

The Orange Free State were no match for the Rhodesian side in its first tour game and were dismissed for a paltry 66. The same day McPhun and Procter pressed home the advantage in a batting exhibition of sheer ruthlessness and Gripper was able to declare 282 runs ahead with only six wickets down. The match was completed in one and a half days as Free State, despite a resolute 60 from Neil Rosendorff, were dismissed for 178 in their second innings.

North-Eastern Transvaal and Griqualand West were both thrashed by an innings to complete Rhodesia's domination of the B Section of the Currie Cup. Du Preez and Kaschula put in marathon spells in both games, Howie Gardiner made a couple of hard-hit contributions and Brian Davison made his maiden first-class century at De Beers Stadium, Kimberley. And of course there was Mike Procter.

A two-month wait followed before the eagerly anticipated Western Province match. In that time the selectors saw fit to drop Davison — his last innings was a century — among three changes, with Duncan Fletcher returning and Tommy Dunk and Brian Oldreive gaining selection. The match itself will always be remembered for Procter's historic sixth successive century but there were other notable features. Gardiner (69) put together 166 for the sixth wicket with Procter to take Rhodesia out of trouble; Western Province suffered the indignity of having to follow on; Kaschula sent down 78 overs for his match figures of 8/159; and Gavin Pfuhl and Peter Swart added a defiant 112 for the eighth wicket in an unsuccessful bid to stave off defeat.

SCORES: Currie Cup B Section, 1970-71.

At Salisbury, 14, 15 and 16 November.

Border — 57 (M.J. Procter 5/8, P.R. McLoughlin 3/16) and 159 (N.O. Knight 54; R.H. Kaschula 5/56, J.H. du Preez 4/76)

Rhodesia — 384-8 dec. (J.D. McPhun 124, R.A. Grippei 71, M.J. Procter 45, J.H. du Preez 36*)

Rhodesia won by an innings and 168 runs.

At Bulawayo, 21, 22 and 23 November.

Natal B — 188 (R.H. Kaschula 3/41, M.J. Procter 3/46) and 283 (B.S. Groves 81; R.H. Kaschula 4/61)

Rhodesia — 376 (M.J. Procter 119, J.D. McPhun 79, R.A. Gripper 54, E. Laughlin 47; A. Wood 6/113) and 99-1 wkt. (R.A. Gripper 40, S.D. Robertson 37*)

Rhodesia won by 9 wickets.

At Salisbury, 28, 29 and 30 November.

Rhodesia — 351 (M.J. Procter 129, S.D. Robertson 58, B.F. Davison 31, E. Laughlin 31)

Transvaal B — 119 (J.H. du Preez 6/37, R.H. Kaschula 3/29)
and 89-2 wkts.

Rhodesia won on first innings.

At Bloemfontein, 28, 29 and 30 December.

Orange Free State — 66 (R.H. Kaschula 5/13, M.J. Procter 3/26)
and 178 (N. Rosendorff 60; D.G. Seagrave 4/46)

Rhodesia — 348-6 dec. (J.D. McPhun 154, M.J. Procter 107, S.D. Robertson 46)

Rhodesia won by an innings and 104 runs.

At Pretoria, 1, 2 and 4 January.

Rhodesia — 369-9 dec. (M.J. Procter 174, H.A.B. Gardiner 51, B.F. Davison 42, S.D. Robertson 31)

North-Eastern Transvaal — 187 (G.G.M. de Villiers 73; M.J. Procter 3/20, D.A.G. Fletcher 3/34)
and 164 (R.H. Kaschula 4/43, J.H. du Preez 3/54)

Rhodesia won by an innings and 18 runs.

At Kimberley, 7, 8 and 9 January.

Rhodesia — 386-6 dec. (B.F. Davison 137*, M.J. Procter 106, J.D. McPhun 45, H.A.B. Gardiner 31)

Griqualand West — 87 (M.J. Procter 3/15, R.H. Kaschula 3/16)
and 231 (L.A. McNamara 78, D.J. Taylor 57; J.H. du Preez 4/68)

Rhodesia won by an innings and 68 runs.

Friendly at Salisbury, 5, 6 and 7 March.

Rhodesia — 383 (M.J. Procter 254, H.A.B. Gardiner 69)
and 142-3 wkts. (J.D. McPhun 71*, R.A. Gripper 49)

Western Province — 189 (R.H. Kaschula 5/72)
and 334 (G.P. Pfuhl 117; D.A.G. Fletcher 3/57, J.H. du Preez 3/89)

Rhodesia won by 7 wickets.

Having thrilled huge crowds in England since 1963, the one-day game was introduced officially on an inter-provincial knock-out basis to South Africa during the 1970-71 season. Rhodesia's participation in the competition and the implementation of the different rules which applied soon became a talking point in local cricket circles and a rehearsal match was held prior to Rhodesia's debut against Natal at the Police ground, Salisbury. The practice match was obviously beneficial because when the real thing came about a better start could hardly have been envisaged as the confident Rhodesians kept the runs flowing before an appreciative crowd of 5 500. After rattling up a virtually unassailable 288 the Rhodesians proceeded to run through the Natal batting with the 23-year-old Gwelo farmer, Richie Kaschula, varying his length, pace and direction effectively in twelve steady overs. In addition, team captain Ray Gripper paid tribute to two newcomers in the overall performance: 'It was really good cricket all round by the Rhodesian team. But I was particularly impressed with David McVey (2/37) who bowled tremendously and with Brian Oldreive (53) who had a superb knock after coming in at a most crucial part of our innings when we were 20-2.'

Unfortunately rain intervened in the semi-final at the Wanderers, Johannesburg, and in a major disappointment for the Rhodesians, Transvaal were adjudged the winners through a faster scoring rate over 20 overs. This seemed a little harsh at the time considering that Rhodesia had placed themselves into a match-winning position but it was to be the start of a series of debatable decisions that were to haunt the Rhodesians in the course of their participation in the Gillette Cup and later in the Datsun Shield.

SCORES: Gillette Cup, 1970-71.

At Salisbury, 11 November (Practice Match).

Invitation XI — 213 (J. Clarke 97, G. McPhun 38, A. Paton 30*; E. Laughlin 4/27)

Rhodesia XI — 242-7 wkts. (J.D. McPhun 76, B.F. Davison 42)

Rhodesia XI won by 6 wickets.

At Salisbury, 13 December (First Round).

Rhodesia — 288 (59,5 overs) (M.J. Procter 96, B.H. Oldreive 53, R.A. Gripper 50)

Natal — 108 (39,4 overs) (R.H. Kaschula 3/21)

Rhodesia won by 180 runs.

At Johannesburg, 27 February (Semi-final).

Rhodesia — 194-7 wkts. (60 overs) (S.D. Robertson 39, M.J. Procter 34)

Transvaal — 74-5 wkts. (20 overs)

Transvaal won on faster scoring rate over 20 overs.

The Mashonaland Cricket Association staged another double-wicket competition early in the 1971-72 season starring three Springbok sides, a Rhodesian combination and an English pairing featuring Brian Close and Basil d'Oliveira. The swashbuckling Springbok duo, Eddie Barlow and Denis Lindsay won the tournament which ended with a five-star grand finale match between four of South Africa's cricketing "giants". In a contest which saw sixteen sixes soaring to all parts of the ground, Barry Richards (79* — eight sixes) and Lee Irvine (55) scored 136-1 to beat Graeme and Peter Pollock's tally of 134. They cruised to 100 runs in a mere 26 minutes and through shrewd navigation found they required just three runs off the last ball. Barry Richards nonchalantly pranced down the wicket and drove powerfully for four to highlight a fantastic finish.

Rhodesia's return to the A Section began in an uninspiring manner and by the half-way stage they were languishing at the foot of the league log having collected only 17 points from 4 matches compared with top of the table Transvaal's 40. In a desperate bid to restore morale the selectors named Mike Procter as captain and the team blossomed under his infectious enthusiasm. Three of the last four matches resulted in outright wins — Rhodesia was in fact the only province to win three matches — and in addition they emphasized their superiority by defeating Northern Transvaal and Western Province in friendlies. In the second half of the programme the Rhodesians acquired 56 points to Transvaal's 35 and failed by only 3 points to take the Currie Cup honours for the first time in their history.

Brian Barbour in full flow, drives Natal's Vince van der Bijl, the big Natalian opening bowler who proved the scourge of Rhodesia's batting for many years.

Mike Procter had a tremendous season, achieving the rare "double" of taking 52 wickets in a domestic season whilst scoring 695 runs (average 40,88) with the bat. He did receive considerable support from Fletcher, Du Preez and Kaschula and they accounted for a further 76 wickets. Kaschula was most impressive in the high realms of A Section cricket and he achieved the distinction of dismissing Geoff Boycott, Eddie Barlow and Barry Richards during the season, all without assistance from the field. This in itself was no mean feat.

The selectors, Messrs. Pichanick, Pithey, Mansell and Partridge, adopted a bold but pleasing policy of injecting young blood into the side and to an extent were rewarded for their insight. The season's batting "find" was the 18-year-old left-hander, Brian Barbour, who scored 609 runs (average 32,05) including a maiden century before lunch for Rhodesia against Natal in Bulawayo. His batting was a revelation and looking back on the season one is left pondering over the words of Roy McLean (made at the Wanderers during a match against Transvaal): 'I think Barbour has tremendous potential and I admire his outlook. If he gets going he sets the tempo for the rest of the innings. With experience he'll make his mark in big cricket but he must be left alone. He's got a flair for cricket and he must play his strokes; experienee will teach him a little more discretion — a coach will only ruin him.' Brian Barbour's exciting batting quickly became a point of debate between those cricket pundits who advocated that he curbed his impetuosity and those who remained devout disciples of the Roy McLean outlook.

It is interesting that Clift should make his debut in the same season that Ray Gripper retired in that both were products of the astute Sussex professional at St. George's College, Jim Cornford. Clift gave credit to Jim Cornford for his Rhodesian selection — 'Over the past few years he has speeded up my bowling and has got me using more shoulder,' — whilst a number of years earlier Gripper had benefited from additional private coaching because Cornford had earmarked him as a prospect for the future. Ray Gripper's contribution to Rhodesian cricket was invaluable over a period of fifteen years and when he opted out of the game through business pressure the selectors were faced with an opening partnership dilemma that was to provide much searching and experimenting.

The season began with three drawn matches and then a defeat by 10 wickets at the hands of Natal. Two individual performances stood out during this trying

JOHN McPHUN.

Stuart Robertson batting.

Several promising bowling prospects were introduced. The diminutive Rhodesian rugby fly-half, Terry Bowes, made a sensational debut as an opening bowler when he and Procter were instrumental in Eastern Province plummeting to 9 runs for 4 wickets during an action-packed Saturday afternoon at the Queens ground, Bulawayo. Bowes' contemporary in the 1970 Nuffield side, Vince Hogg, was also introduced to the red-hot cauldron of the A Section only to wait several years before earning a regular spot in the side.

The youngster who was to secure a permanent place in the Rhodesian team was Paddy Clift, an 18-year-old seam bowler who was out of St. George's College a mere few weeks. Ever modest, he said of his selection: 'I just sat stunned for about five minutes and I didn't know what was going on,' but Clift was to reward the selectors many times over in the ensuing seasons.

period for the Rhodesian side. The first was Brian Barbour's superb 97 in the opening match against Transvaal at the Police ground when he failed by 3 runs to become the first Rhodesian to score an 'A' Section hundred on debut. The second occurred when Ray Gripper defied Peter Pollock, Claude Pittaway, Sibley McAdam and Dassie Biggs for 4½ hours in a desperate battle for survival in the match against Eastern Province at St. George's Park, assisted only by Jackie du Preez who contributed 49 in a sixth wicket partnership of 98. These were memorable performances in Rhodesia's otherwise dismal start to the season.

The turning-point came in the return match against Transvaal at the Wanderers when the newly appointed captain, Procter, playing as one possessed, took 10/106 and hit a majestic 83 on his own account to lead his team to victory by 9 wickets. After a long drought of six years and sixteen matches without an A

Mike Procter tossing with Eddie Barlow at Newlands

. . . and bowling to Kev Barbour at the Umtali Sports Club.

Section win, Rhodesia came back with a vengeance. For the scoreboard to read 31-7 wickets — Bacher, Bath, Carlstein, Irvine, McKenzie, Rice and De Vaal all in the pavilion — at the Wanderers or at any other ground for that matter, was almost unbelievable. Gracious in defeat, Ali Bacher, who lost his first match as a captain of Transvaal at the Wanderers, admitted: 'They played very good cricket and we were simply outplayed. We came across a great cricketer at the top of his form and that was that. It could be said that Mike Procter beat Transvaal.'

A hard-fought drawn game against Western Province in Salisbury between two evenly matched sides was followed by a thrilling 22-run win over Natal in Bulawayo. Rhodesia were one run behind Natal on the first innings and at the end of the second day were only 161 ahead with seven wickets down. The following morning they slumped to 173-9 before Richie Kaschula, batting with remarkable restraint, helped Duncan Fletcher add 37 for the last wicket. Kaschula then took the vital wicket of Barry Richards, leg before for 27, and Natal were dismissed for 187 — 22 runs behind. The win gave Rhodesia an outside chance of winning the Currie Cup in Cape Town the following week-end.

At this stage the return of Stuart Robertson must also be given credit for Rhodesia's resurgence. The elegant left-handed batsman had been overseas for the first part of the season when his cricket had been confined to an International Cricket Cavaliers tour to

Procter appealing against Dave Bevan (Eastern Province) at the Police ground.

Devon and Cornwall. He returned to take his place in the line-up for the last five matches and scored 453 runs to top the season's batting averages at 64,71.

At Newlands, Cape Town, Western Province did not take full advantage of winning the toss but a fine half-century by Peter Swart helped to take them from a shaky 184-7 to 272 on the first day. Rhodesia in turn were struggling at 41-3 before Stuart Robertson struck a cultured maiden first-class century helped by Procter and Du Preez who both made sound contributions. However it was an uphill struggle with time running out and Procter's decision to bat on after passing the Western Province total was slated in Cape Town newspapers the following day by unfavourable comments such as 'Rhodesia kill it', 'Rhodesia toss away all chance' and 'Come off it, Mike'. An incensed Procter in retaliation announced during breakfast at the team's Rondebosch hotel: 'The only way to show them is to go out there and win today.'

On a pitch unsuited to pace bowling the Rhodesian captain worked up to top speed. In his first over he shattered Fred Goldstein's stumps, aided a little by the smoke of a South African Railways train that wafted across the pitch. Andre Bruyns went soon afterwards, flashing outside the off-stump; Chris Stephens was beaten neck and crop and Gavin Pfuhl was caught timidly at short leg, whilst Duncan Fletcher accounted for Neville Budge and Peter Denne. When Du Preez removed Bowditch, 18-6 became 32-7 before Richard Morris and Swart delayed the inevitable end with a partnership of 80. But back came Procter to claim Morris, and Westerns were all out for 118 soon afterwards. Rhodesia quickly hit off the required 69 and for a brief time found themselves in top position in the Currie Cup table.

In their two friendlies during the season, Rhodesia gained a narrow two-wicket victory over Western Province and then convincingly defeated a Northern Transvaal side containing the Yorkshire and England opening bat, Geoff Boycott. Mike Procter scored a hundred in 159 minutes in the Rhodesian first innings of the latter match and Boycott reeled off his 56th century of his career. Batting with sleeves buttoned down and a handkerchief round his neck, Northern Transvaal's guest star reached the three-figure mark in a very uncharacteristic fashion with two successive sixes before falling leg before to Kaschula.

Rhodesia's batting inspiration.

SCORES: Currie Cup A Section, 1971-72.

At Salisbury, 30, 31 October and 1 November.

Transvaal — 392 (B.L. Irvine 120, P.D. de Vaal 59, B.F. Bath 53, P.R. Carlstein 51; M.J. Procter 4/76)
and 242-6 dec. (A. Bacher 83, P.D. de Vaal 59*; R.H. Kaschula 3/52)

Rhodesia — 345 (B.D. Barbour 97, J.H. du Preez 64, B.H. Oldreive 40, J.D. McPhun 33, B.F. Davison 30; B.F. Bath 5/56)
and 182-7 wkts. (B.D. Barbour 55, M.J. Procter 50)

Match drawn — Transvaal 8 and Rhodesia 6 bonus points.

At Bulawayo, 13, 14 and 15 December.

Rhodesia — 166 (J.H. du Preez 39, D.A.G. Fletcher 36, B.D. Barbour 36)
and 269-5 dec. (M.J. Procter 84*, B.F. Davison 74, R.A. Gripper 31)

Eastern Province — 165-9 dec. (S.J. Bezuidenhout 58; M.J. Procter 3/25, T.R.C. Bowes 3/38)
and 152-5 wkts. (A.L. Biggs 100)

Match drawn — Eastern Province 5 and Rhodesia 4 bonus points.

At Port Elizabeth, 27, 28 and 29 December.

Eastern Province — 281-6 dec. (R.G. Pollock 129, A.L. Wilmot 76*; D.A.G. Fletcher 4/51)
and 223-6 dec. (S.J. Bezuidenhout 53; J.C. Mitchell 3/45)

Rhodesia — 196 (J.C. Mitchell 73*)
and 205-7 wkts. (R.A. Gripper 116*, J.H. du Preez 49)

Match drawn — Eastern Province 9 and Rhodesia 5 bonus points.

At Durban, 1, 3 and 4 January.

Rhodesia — 111
and 317 (B.F. Davison 91, D.A.G. Fletcher 73*, M.J. Procter 47)

Natal — 385-9 dec. (B.A. Richards 219, M.B. Madsen 66; M.J. Procter 4/97, D.A.G. Fletcher 3/80)
and 47-0 wkts.

Natal (11 bonus points) won by 10 wickets — Rhodesia 2 bonus points.

At Johannesburg, 28, 29 and 31 January.

Transvaal — 124 (M.J. Procter 7/32)
and 315 (B.F. Bath 60, K.A. McKenzie 53; M.J. Procter 3/74, J.H. du Preez 3/96)

Rhodesia — 410 (M.J. Procter 83, B.D. Barbour 58, D.A.G. Fletcher 56, R.A. Gripper 49, S.D. Robertson 43, J.H. du Preez 30)

and 31-1 wkt. (B.D. Barbour 29*)

Rhodesia (10 bonus points) won by 9 wickets — Transvaal 3 bonus points.

At Salisbury, 19, 20 and 21 February.

Rhodesia — 261 (B.F. Davison 66, S.D. Robertson 50, J.C. Mitchell 45*)
and 250-6 dec. (S.D. Robertson 59, B.D. Barbour 57, J.H. du Preez 47*, M.J. Procter 46)

Western Province — 283 (E.J. Barlow 101; M.J. Procter 5/70)
and 68-2 wkts.

Match drawn — Western Province 6 and Rhodesia 5 bonus points.

At Bulawayo, 4, 5 and 6 March.

Rhodesia — 248 (B.D. Barbour 106, M.M. Benkenstein 54*)
and 210 (H.A.B. Gardiner 38, M.M. Benkenstein 36, B.D. Barbour 32, D.A.G. Fletcher 30*)

Natal — 249 (B.A. Richards 76; P.B. Clift 3/43, M.J. Procter 3/62)
and 187 (G.D. Dyer 64; M.J. Procter 4/36, R.H. Kaschula 3/47)

Rhodesia (7 bonus points) won by 22 runs — Natal 7 bonus points.

At Cape Town, 10, 11 and 13 March.

Western Province — 272 (A. Bruyns 71, P.D. Swart 51; M.J. Procter 4/33, P.B. Clift 3/71)
and 118 (R.E.T. Morris 54; M.J. Procter 5/9)

Rhodesia — 322-8 dec. (S.D. Robertson 118, M.J. Procter 86, J.H. du Preez 57)
and 69-3 wkts.

Rhodesia (4 bonus points) won by 7 wickets — Western Province 4 bonus points.

Friendly Inter-provincial matches, 1971-72.

At Cape Town, 7, 8 and 10 January.

Western Province — 263-9 dec. (A. Bruyns 108, M.H. Bowditch 85; B.F. Davison 3/26)
and 180 (R.E.T. Morris 75; R.H. Kaschula 3/30, J.H. du Preez 3/32, M.J. Procter 3/52)

Rhodesia — 325 (M.J. Procter 62, J.C. Mitchell 58, H.A.B. Gardiner 51*, J.D. McPhun 48, B.H. Oldreive 36, B.F. Davison 35)
and 118-8 wkts. (M.J. Procter 31)

Rhodesia won by 2 wickets.

At Pretoria, 3, 4 and 5 February.

Rhodesia — 356-9 dec. (M.J. Procter 107, S.D. Robertson 62, B.F. Davison 60, J.H. du Preez 58)
and 196-4 dec. (J.H. du Preez 70*, S.D. Robertson 63*)

Northern Transvaal — 172 (G. Boycott 107; R.H. Kaschula 4/44)
and 204 (I.W. Finlay 86; R.H. Kaschula 5/60, J.H. du Preez 3/76)

Rhodesia won by 176 runs.

In 1971-72 Rhodesia were drawn to play Transvaal in the first round of the Gillette Cup at the Wanderers, Johannesburg. After Transvaal had won the toss and an opening partnership between Ali Bacher and Brian Bath had realised 87 runs, nothing appeared to be running Rhodesia's way. However, the advent of Jackie du Preez at 102-1 was to have a marked influence on the course of the game. With his first ball he caught and bowled Bacher and then with the last ball of the over he yorked Lee Irvine. He struck again with the second ball of his second over when he had Peter Carlstein leg before — that meant he had dismissed three Springboks in eight balls. Between overs Richie Kaschula momentarily cashed in on the continuing drama when Norman Featherstone spooned up a return catch, before Jackie du Preez had Albie During taken by John McPhun at short leg in his third over. Then with the first ball of his fourth over, he bowled Pat Flanagan which meant he had taken 5/9 in 19 balls — bowling off-spin! Transvaal had meanwhile slumped to 118-7 but Peter de Vaal and Clive Rice staged a minor recovery and they were eventually all out for 178.

Surprisingly this proved enough although rain interference and poor light did not help the Rhodesian cause. In a desperate finish Terry Bowes' run out with three overs remaining and six runs required was a severe blow. It was all left to the last pair — Kaschula played out a maiden to Willie Kerr and a run was taken off the penultimate over bowled by Bath. Unfortunately Jimmy Mitchell drove the first ball of the last over to Bacher who gratefully snapped up the catch.

SCORES: Gillette Cup, 1971-72.

At Johannesburg, 20 November (First Round).

Transvaal — 178 (55,5 overs) (A. Bacher 56; J.H. du Preez 5/42)

Rhodesia — 174 (59,1 overs) (M.J. Procter 41, B.D. Barbour 32)

Transvaal won by 4 runs.

The 1972-73 season will be forever remembered for the famous "walk-off" incident by Lorrie Wilmot and his Eastern Province side — an event which cost Rhodesia their first ever Currie Cup triumph. Yet, whilst this sensational ending to a fascinating encounter overshadowed all else, it was nevertheless an absorbing season.

Ten of the world's leading cricketers assembled at the Police ground for the traditional early season double-wicket competition. Newcomers were Tony Greig, John Snow and the Chappell brothers, Ian and Greg, with Basil d'Oliveira, Eddie Barlow, Barry Richards, Graeme Pollock, Lee Irvine and Mike Procter making welcome reappearances. The Chappells deservedly clinched the $700 first prize by winning three of their four matches and elder brother Ian was the best batsman of the week-end with scores of 32*, 73, 43* and 90*. His last knock was undoubtedly the most memorable innings of the tournament. Chasing 87 by the English pair D'Oliveira and Greig, the Australians were in immediate trouble when Greg Chappell was caught for a duck. The final target became a rather tall order but in a pulsating display Ian Chappell succeeded in hitting off the runs with ten fours and four sixes along the way.

The Rhodesians were well prepared for their Currie Cup programme by an International Wanderers tour in September. The star-studded touring side led by Brian Close contained players of the calibre of John Edrich, John Jameson, Tony Greig, Basil d'Oliveira, Jim Parks, Norman Gifford, Graham McKenzie and Glen Turner and yet were for the most part outplayed by the Rhodesians.

In the opening match at Bulawayo, Close won the toss and sent Rhodesia in to bat only to watch helplessly as the home side went on a run rampage in temperatures of over 35°C. Fletcher, Robertson, Carlstein, Davison, Du Preez and Procter all hit half-centuries to give the wilting visiting attack a torrid time. Declaring at a massive 476-9 wickets, the Rhodesians continued to press home the initiative by dismissing the tourists for 276 and then declaring a second time at 148-4 wickets. Procter left his bowlers four hours in which to dismiss the Wanderers who faced a 348 run target. Kaschula bowled economically to take 4/71 in 35 overs only to be foiled by D'Oliveira, who marshalled all his experience to record a calculated undefeated century and save his team from certain defeat.

In the return match at Salisbury, Rhodesia held the whip hand throughout. The Rhodesian batting in their two innings was highlighted by three top-class centuries against a five-prong international attack. Mike Procter wrote yet another achievement into the pages of Rhodesia's cricket history. He became the first Rhodesian to score a century in both innings of a match and added a lightning 169 with Brian Davison in 135 minutes.

The Wanderers' batting was dismal in contrast particularly on the final day when they were left to chase 523 on a wet and lively pitch after the covers had been carelessly removed. In the first innings the pace attack of Procter and Paddy Clift had shared the eight wickets to fall whilst in the second Jackie du Preez, relishing the role of attacker-in-chief and aided by lethargic batting, spun Rhodesia to victory with 6/39 in 11 overs. The winning margin — an incredible 411 runs.

SCORES: International Wanderers Tour, 1972-73.

At Bulawayo, 23, 24 and 25 September.

Rhodesia — 476-7 dec. (M.J. Procter 99, D.A.G. Fletcher 80, B.F. Davison 79, P.R. Carlstein 74, S.D. Robertson 58, J.H. du Preez 50)
and 148-4 dec. (S.D. Robertson 48*, P.R. Carlstein 35)

International Wanderers — 276 (G.M. Turner 91, B.C. Francis 52; D.A.G. Fletcher 3/31, R.H. Kaschula 3/73)
and 284-8 wkts. (B.L. d'Oliveira 116*, B.C. Francis 65; R.H. Kaschula 4/71)

Match drawn.

At Gwelo, 27 September (Not first-class).

Midlands — 183 (B.F. Davison 70, D.H. Evans 42)

International Wanderers 187-9 wkts. (D.M. Green 40)

International Wanderers won by 1 wicket.

At Salisbury, 29, 30 September and 1 October.

Rhodesia — 273 (M.J. Procter 114, P.R. Carlstein 33)
and 374-7 wkts. (M.J. Procter 131, B.F. Davison 125, M.M. Benkenstein 35)

International Wanderers 124-8 dec. (M.J. Procter 4/20, P.B. Clift 4/53)
and 112 (J.H. du Preez 6/39)

Rhodesia won by 411 runs.

The Wanderers' pathetic 112 was criticized for being an abject batting display, unworthy of the international talent that had been on view. Glen Turner argued in defence: 'Procter was particularly dangerous. He got the ball to lift and fly and it was a wonder nobody was injured.' But such is the versatility of Mike Procter that he created havoc in Transvaal's ranks a month later bowling off-spinners. It was hardly inappropriate that the Transvaal manager Johnny Waite should despondently remark at the conclusion of the game: 'The only thing that surprised me was that Procter didn't come on and bowl left-arm spin. What can you do against a man like that?'

Rhodesia certainly began their Currie Cup programme in fine form with the morale-boosting 113-run victory over Transvaal at Bulawayo. Peter Carlstein in his 17th first-class season held the Rhodesian first innings together with an immaculate 95 on his 34th birthday but it was Mike Procter who again stole the limelight. When he declared at lunch-time on the final day, Transvaal required 310 with 270 minutes remaining. The Rhodesian captain proceeded to have Norman Featherstone caught without scoring but Bacher and Bath consolidated by adding 102 for the second wicket. The irrepressible Procter switched to off-breaks and in a 30-over spell dismissed another eight batsmen to finish with career-best figures of 9/71 and present Rhodesia with 10 points for an outright win.

A drawn match against Natal followed — Barry Richards batted eight hours for his 197, whilst Carlstein scored a fluent 105 in reply — and then came the infamous ''walk-off'' match.

In a high-scoring encounter Rhodesia trailed Eastern Province by 40 runs on the first innings but matters could have been worse if it had not been for a record-breaking ninth wicket partnership by Paddy Clift and Robin Jackman. Eastern Province capitalized on this lead in their second knock with skipper, Lorrie Wilmot, showing the way by hitting five sixes and eleven fours in his 129. He declared 323 runs ahead with four hours remaining — including 20 overs in the final hour.

The Rhodesians went for the runs. Robertson and Mitchell set the pace, Carlstein and Davison followed suit and when the final controversial hour started Procter and Gardiner were well set and heading for their fifties. In his book *Cricket Buccaneer*, Mike Procter wrote: 'Now came the moment of truth which was later to lead to all the controversy. The close of play was scheduled for 5.45 p.m. and the last hour, in which 20 overs had to be bowled, was scheduled to start after 4.45 p.m. when the drinks interval would be held. The umpires Ian Forrest and Chris Sweeting, were in position a minute or so before 4.45 p.m. and according to the laws of the Currie Cup the last over before the interval had to be bowled.

'I was batting with Howie Gardiner at the time and noticed an exchange of words between Wilmot, who was fielding at deep extra cover, Sweeting and the bowler, Claude Pittaway. Lorrie and Claude asked Sweeting if this was the first of the 20 overs and he indicated that he thought it was. Before the over started, Forrest had held up one finger to Sweeting signalling there was one over left before the interval and Sweeting mistakenly thought his colleague was indicating the first of the last 20 overs was to be bowled.

'Although I was concentrating mainly on the job at hand and how many runs we still needed, I gained the impression after a few balls that the start of the 20 overs had been signalled. But I had not been informed of this and knew the 20 overs, under the laws, could only start after the drinks interval. When I got to umpire Forrest's end I asked him what was going on and if the 20 overs had already started.

'He told me not to worry, the 20 overs had not

Two memorable scenes in 1972-73 at the Queens ground, Bulawayo: (*above*) Brian Barbour takes the winning catch against Transvaal off Mike Procter (9 for 71) as umpire, Austin Wilmot, signals the dismissal and (*below*) the aftermath of the infamous Eastern Province ''walk-off'' with Mike Procter making his way back to the pavilion.

started and that the matter would be sorted out during the drinks interval. I was satisfied with the position and left it at that.

'During the drinks interval, Sweeting and Forrest held a short discussion and the reserve umpire was sent to the scorebox to tell the scorers and inform the Press that the first of the compulsory 20 overs was to start immediately after the interval.

'The umpires then called Lorrie and I over and explained their decision. Lorrie replied that they had told him the 20 overs had already started and could not change their minds. They explained the 20 overs could not start until after drinks and when I pointed out that I had never been informed that the 20 overs had started and that the batting side had to be informed as well as the fielding side, Lorrie appeared to me to accept the situation.

'Lorrie denies he agreed to anything during the drinks interval but I was satisfied in my own mind that he accepted the umpires' ruling and never thought to carry the matter any further.

'As far as I was concerned, one of the umpires had

Umpire Ian Forrest prepares to pull up the stumps as Mike Procter and Paddy Clift leave the field.

made a slight mistake and that had consequently been rectified. When the walk-off came I honestly could not believe it. It was so unexpected. Lorrie never said a word to me when he led his side off the field and it was all a little confusing.

'At the end of the 19th over we still needed six runs to win. By this time I was batting with Paddy Clift and walked down the wicket to have a word with him. So busy was I discussing facts, figures and tactics with Paddy that I never noticed Lorrie leading his side off. I had literally taken up my stance when I looked up and saw the Province players disappearing into the distance.

'I just could not credit it. Suddenly the field was almost deserted with only Paddy, myself and the umpires left. The umpires called play two or three times and then I said to them: "Well, that's it then. If they don't want to play, it's our game," and with that Paddy and I walked off the field.

'It was an incredible and sensational end to a magnificent day of cricket.'

Whilst the South African Cricket Association sorted out the problem, the Rhodesians suffered a severe setback to their Currie Cup hopes by losing away matches to Western and Eastern Province. They did recover some lost prestige by beating Natal by five wickets in Durban. Robin Jackman, Rhodesia's professional, completely demoralized an unpredictable Natal batting line-up with career-best figures of 8/40 in 17,4 overs. All out for 86, Natal were never again in the match despite a second innings century from David Orchard and 88 by Barry Richards.

Still in with a chance, Rhodesia threw away a golden opportunity of defeating Transvaal in Johannesburg by a dismal batting display. Procter and Jackman had shared 14 wickets in containing the Transvaal batsmen and the Rhodesians found themselves requiring a mere 184 in their last innings. They failed by 50 runs, unable to play the tall left-hander Don Mackay-Coghill who was in outstanding form in capturing 5/36 in a seventeen-over spell.

It had been a somewhat frustrating season and the Rhodesians vented their feelings in overwhelming Eddie Barlow's Western Province by an innings and 27 runs at the Police ground in the final match of their Currie Cup programme. Procter was again in devastating bowling form to take his tally for Rhodesia over the season to 60. He also weighed in with a useful

Robin Jackman bowling at Newlands.

44 to head his side's overall run tally once again with 870 (average 48,33) whilst the next leading scorer was Peter Carlstein 653 (average 36,27). But in the game in question it was Stuart Robertson's monumental 115 in 390 minutes that provided the backbone to the Rhodesian innings and enabled them to build a commanding lead.

SCORES: Currie Cup A Section, 1972-73.

At Bulawayo, 28, 29 and 30 October.

Rhodesia — 311 (P.R. Carlstein 95, J.H. du Preez 53, D.A.G. Fletcher 45, B.F. Davison 31)
and 242-8 dec. (M.J. Procter 65, H.A.B. Gardiner 64)

Transvaal — 243 (B.F. Bath 50; J.H. du Preez 4/58)
and 197 (A. Bacher 62; M.J. Procter 9/71)

Rhodesia (7 bonus points) won by 113 runs — Transvaal 5 bonus points.

At Salisbury, 11, 12 and 13 November.

Natal — 403-9 dec. (B.A. Richards 197, D.L. Orchard 51; R.D. Jackman 3/81)
and 184-7 dec. (A. Bruyns 107*; R.D. Jackman 3/36)

Rhodesia — 311-9 dec. (P.R. Carlstein 105, B.F. Davison 45, M.J. Procter 34)
and 125-3 wkts. (M.M. Benkenstein 34, D.A.G. Fletcher 32)

Match drawn — Natal 6 and Rhodesia 5 bonus points.

At Bulawayo, 18, 19 and 20 November.

Eastern Province — 301 (A.L. Wilmot 85, S.J. Bezuidenhout 54; M.J. Procter 4/69, R.H. Kaschula 3/66)
and 283-9 dec. (A.L. Wilmot 129, D.J. Brickett 50; R.D. Jackman 3/30, R.H. Kaschula 3/66)

Rhodesia — 261 (P.B. Clift 75*, R.D. Jackman 50, D.A.G. Fletcher 32)
and 318-6 wkts. (S.D. Robertson 67, M.J. Procter 66*, H.A.B. Gardiner 54, P.R. Carlstein 53, B.F. Davison 32)

Match declared a draw by S.A.C.A. — Eastern Province 7 and Rhodesia 4 bonus points.

At Cape Town, 21, 22 and 23 December.

Western Province — 214 (M.H. Bowditch 53; M.J. Procter 6/67)
and 281 (E.J. Barlow 106, P.D. Swart 63; M.J. Procter 4/64, J.H. du Preez 3/55)

Rhodesia — 286 (B.F. Davison 74, J.C. Mitchell 61, J.H. du Preez 43, M.J. Procter 32)
and 164 (P.R. Carlstein 69, J.C. Mitchell 41; E.J. Barlow 7/53)

Western Province (10 bonus points) won by 45 runs — Rhodesia 8 bonus points.

At Port Elizabeth, 26, 27 and 28 December.

Rhodesia — 153 (M.J. Procter 31, H.A.B. Gardiner 30; K.P. Reid 7/50)
and 246 (J.C. Mitchell 76, M.J. Procter 62)

Eastern Province — 347 (A.L. Biggs 131, E. Schmidt 61; R.D. Jackman 3/71)
and 55-3 wkts.

Eastern Province (10 bonus points) won by 7 wickets — Rhodesia 3 bonus points.

At Durban, 30 December, 1 and 2 January.

Natal — 86 (R.D. Jackman 8/40)
and 299 (D.L. Orchard 109*, B.A. Richards 88, D. Gamsy 55; M.J. Procter 5/91)

Rhodesia — 268 (J.C. Mitchell 52, H.A.B. Gardiner 37, S.D. Robertson 36, D.A.G. Fletcher 31; B.D. Gessner 5/58)
and 118-5 wkts. (M.J. Procter 38, S.D. Robertson 38*)

Rhodesia (10 bonus points) won by 5 wickets — Natal 4 bonus points.

At Johannesburg, 9, 10 and 12 February.

Transvaal — 163 (R.D. Jackman 4/41)
and 275 (R.K. Muzzell 110, B.F. Bath 70; M.J. Procter 5/73, R.D. Jackman 3/64)

Rhodesia — 255 (P.R. Carlstein 58, M.J. Procter 43, S.D. Robertson 38, J.C. Mitchell 35; D.F. Becker 5/49)
and 133 (P.R. Carlstein 43; D. Mackay-Coghill 5/36)

Transvaal (6 bonus points) won by 50 runs — Rhodesia 5 bonus points.

At Salisbury, 24, 25 and 26 February.

Western Province — 158 (M.J. Procter 4/43)
and 159 (H.M. Ackerman 57*; J.C. Mitchell 3/12, M.J. Procter 3/23, P.B. Clift 3/45)

Rhodesia — 344 (S.D. Robertson 115, B.F. Davison 66, M.J. Procter 44, J.C. Mitchell 41)

Rhodesia (7 bonus points) won by an innings and 27 runs — Western Province 4 bonus points.

When the murky rain-clouds shut out the sun in drought-stricken Pretoria, cruel luck again played its part as Rhodesia made their exit from the 1972-73 Gillette Cup in the first round against Northern Transvaal at Berea Park, Pretoria. Northern Transvaal appealed against the light at 94-2 after 32 overs when chasing 235 and won through a better runs per wicket count. Northern Transvaal had an average of 47 whereas Rhodesia after 32 overs had scored 125-3, average 41,3. Commented Glen Byrom as a disconsolate Rhodesian side discovered that they had lost through a mathematical equation: 'Two years ago at Wanderers, Rhodesia were well on top but lost to Transvaal on a technicality forced by rain. The issue was then decided on runs per over with wickets not taken into consideration. Because of this game that rule was changed. How ironic. Because if that rule had been in force in Pretoria, Rhodesia would have won.'

SCORES: Gillette Cup, 1972-73.

At Pretoria, 21 October (First Round).

Rhodesia — 235 (59,2 overs) (S.D. Robertson 49, M.M. Benkenstein 49, P.R. Carlstein 44)

Northern Transvaal — 94-2 wkts. (32 overs.)

Northern Transvaal won on a better runs per wicket average.

The double-wicket tournament rules were altered in 1973-74 inasmuch as the batsmen were allowed to bat on if out and the innings was worked out on the basis of an average. In another sunbaked week-end with the stands brightly coloured and the beer flowing freely, nearly 10 000 people enjoyed some carefree cricket. Interesting newcomers were the New Zealand pairing of Bevan Congdon and Bruce Taylor, whilst English batsman Frank Hayes teamed up with Tony Greig to provide for a four-country tournament. Mike Procter and Brian Davison represented Rhodesia and the two South African teams were Lee Irvine and Barry Richards and the eventual winners Eddie Barlow and Graeme Pollock. The Rhodesians, however, provided some of the brightest cricket — Brian Davison hammering 81 in the final match and Mike Procter in merciless fashion slamming four successive sixes off Graeme Pollock who borrowed the umpire's handkerchief to wave in terms of surrender.

The following month the Rhodesians made no mistakes and walked off with the $1 500 first prize and the floating trophy at the Datsun international double-wicket tournament staged at the Wanderers, Johannesburg. Procter and Davison were in fine form to take the competition ahead of England (Greig and Hayes), New Zealand (Congdon and Taylor), Australia (the Chappells), the South African African pair (Habane and Ntikinca) and South Africa (Richards and Barlow). The Rhodesians were unbeaten, shading the Chappells in a tense low-scoring final match.

At home, Standard Bank wrested the Rothmans National League title away from Old Hararians, who had won the championship for the three previous years. The surprise runners-up were Manicaland, captained by former Rhodesian Nuffield player, Barry van Blomestein, with Derbyshire professional Tony Borrington proving an invaluable asset. The relatively unknown Borrington had succeeded the England opening bat, John Jameson, as Manicaland's resident professional.

In the higher sphere of Currie Cup cricket and contrary to all expectations, Rhodesia, on paper a powerful and balanced combination, had a poor season in 1973-74 and finished at the bottom of the A Section table without a single victory. In the Currie Cup programme they lost both matches against Western Province and after a declaration lost at home to Eastern Province. Of the five drawn matches Rhodesia held the advantage in both encounters against Transvaal and against Eastern Province but were fortunate to avoid defeat by a single wicket against Natal. By way of compensation the only success was achieved in a friendly against Northern Transvaal by 108 runs.

Despite the 1973-74 season having been an unsuccessful one, two players were selected for the South African Invitation XI which played against Brian Close's Derrick Robins XI. Mike Procter and Jackie du Preez were both named in the "shadow" Springbok side in what was the first real test for South African cricket since the 1969-70 Australians. Both deserved selection after successful seasons. Procter had scored 563 runs and taken 38 wickets for Rhodesia whilst Du Preez finished with 559 runs and 17 wickets in the nine-match programme.

Although the Rhodesian team was plagued throughout the season by dropped catches, the inconsistent batting must be considered as being primarily responsible for the season's disappointing performances. Only one century was scored — 110 by Mike Procter at Kingsmead, Durban. Jackie du Preez however, was run out for 99 at the Wanderers and in all made five half-centuries. With the side's batting form fluctuating alarmingly at times — Robertson (464 runs — average 27,29), Mitchell (388 runs — average 21,55), Davison (368 runs — average 21,64), Fletcher (341 runs — average 31,00), Barbour (217 runs — average 18,08), Carlstein (201 runs — average 18,27) — all made runs on occasions but frustratingly lacked the consistency necessary for this level of cricket. In addition, to this impressive list of recognized batsmen, Rhodesia was also able to call

RHODESIAN TOURING TEAM, 1973-74.
Back: M. Benkenstein, J. Mitchell, B. Barbour, K. Tattersall, P. Clift, J. Traicos.
Seated: D. Fletcher, J. du Preez, M. Procter (Captain), A. Pichanick (Manager), S. Robertson, B. Davison, R. Jackman.

upon the former Western Province opening bat, Keith Tattersall, after his sojourn at Kariba.

Mike Procter and Robin Jackman again spear-headed the bowling, capturing 70 wickets between them in the course of the season. Veteran Jackie du Preez had a number of tidy spells but his wickets were scattered over the season and the side appeared to miss Richie Kaschula who did not represent Rhodesia at all. Twenty-year-old Paddy Clift returned the season's finest bowling performance when he claimed 7/38 in 15 overs in the opening match against Transvaal at the Police ground. Displaying a maturity that belied his years, Clift took full advantage of the favourable elements — heavy rain-clouds hovering low overhead and intermittent drizzle causing stoppages and interruption of the batsmen's concentration.

The season did produce a few memorable moments. The Natal clash at the Queens ground, Bulawayo, was a notably exciting match. At one stage the visitors' tormentor, Robin Jackman (6/32) had presented Rhodesia with a chance of winning but in the end, Natal's victory hopes hinged on dismissing the Rhodesian last wicket pair, Paddy Clift and Tony de Caila, who defended desperately to put on 24 and thereby salvage a draw. It was certainly an eventful return for De Caila who was recalled after an absence of some five years as Howie Gardiner and Des Evans were both unavailable.

Against Eastern Province at St. George's Park, Port Elizabeth, Rhodesia had the home side eight wickets down and 48 runs in arrears but had only themselves to blame for not winning in that they dropped eight catches on the first two days. And then in the return game at Salisbury, a breath-taking finish with torrential rain only minutes away, saw Eastern Province capitalize on a couple of fielding lapses and squeeze through to an unexpected victory with only two wickets intact and seven balls to spare.

Perhaps fate was never more unkind than to deny Jackie du Preez a century at the Wanderers, Johannesburg. When on 99, he was run out by a brilliant throw from Clive Rice that hit the stumps direct with Du Preez inches from his destination. Some put it down to the cricketers' superstition "The Nelson" — Du Preez's batting partner, Duncan Fletcher, had 33 at the time, the total stood at 333 and their partnership had lasted 111 minutes.

SCORES: Currie Cup A Section, 1973-74.

At Salisbury, 3, 4 and 5 November.

Rhodesia — 285-8 dec. (M.J. Procter 70, S.D. Robertson 52, J.C. Mitchell 47, B.D. Barbour 40, P.R. Carlstein 38)
and 133-4 dec. (B.F. Davison 47*, M.J. Procter 33)

Transvaal — 149-9 dec. (B.L. Irvine 67; P.B. Clift 7/38)
and 211-6 wkts. (B.F. Bath 64; M.J. Procter 4/76)

Match drawn — Rhodesia 8 and Transvaal 2 bonus points.

At Bulawayo, 17, 18 and 19 November.

Natal — 300 (G.A. Katz 69; R.D. Jackman 3/43, A.J. Traicos 3/80)
and 214 (B.A. Richards 60; R.D. Jackman 6/32)

Rhodesia — 264 (J.H. du Preez 68, P.B. Clift 44, B.D. Barbour 40, S.D. Robertson 40; P.P. Henwood 5/68)
and 136-9 wkts. (P.R. Carlstein 39)

Match drawn — Rhodesia 4 and Natal 4 bonus points.

At Johannesburg, 15, 17 and 18 December.

Rhodesia — 372 (J.H. du Preez 99, M.J. Procter 67, B.D. Barbour 55, D.A.G. Fletcher 47*, J.C. Mitchell 42)
and 137 (B.F. Davison 31)

Transvaal — 303 (M.J. Procter 3/64)
and 118-5 wkts.

Match drawn — Transvaal 7 and Rhodesia 6 bonus points.

At Cape Town, 4, 5 and 7 January.

Western Province — 252-9 dec. (A. Bruyns 76; R.D. Jackman 5/58)
and 170 (M.J. Procter 4/43, R.D. Jackman 3/58)

Rhodesia — 110 (S.D. Robertson 46; A.B. Nieuwoudt 5/19)
and 187 (M.J. Procter 53, P.B. Clift 35*; A.B. Nieuwoudt 6/45)

Western Province (9 bonus points) won by 125 runs — Rhodesia 4 bonus points.

At Port Elizabeth, 11, 12 and 14 January.

Rhodesia — 219 (J.H. du Preez 60, S.D. Robertson 42)
and 275-8 dec. (B.F. Davison 54, S.D. Robertson 50, J.C. Mitchell 35)

Eastern Province — 293 (A.M. Short 79, E. Schmidt 71; J.H. du Preez 3/55, P.B. Clift 3/71)
and 153-8 wkts. (R.G. Pollock 51)

Match drawn — Rhodesia 6 and Eastern Province 5 bonus points.

At Durban, 19, 20 and 21 January.

Rhodesia — 200 (J.C. Mitchell 70)
and 316-7 wkts. (M.J. Procter 110, S.D. Robertson 78, J.H. du Preez 38, D.A.G. Fletcher 38*)

Natal — 242 (G.A. Katz 73, R.A. Woolmer 71; M.J. Procter 4/42)

Match drawn — Natal 6 and Rhodesia 3 bonus points.

At Salisbury, 2, 3 and 4 February.

Rhodesia — 272-9 dec. (J.C. Mitchell 58, S.D. Robertson 50, J.H. du Preez 34)
and 154-4 dec. (D.A.G. Fletcher 71, B.F. Davison 49)

Eastern Province — 142 (P.B. Clift 4/43)
and 288-8 wkts. (K.S. McEwan 90, S.J. Bezuidenhout 53; M.J. Procter 3/59)

Eastern Province (3 bonus points) won by 2 wickets — Rhodesia 8 bonus points.

At Bulawayo, 2, 3 and 4 March.

Western Province — 162 (M.J. Procter 3/19, A.J. Traicos 3/36)
and 274 (H.M. Ackerman 80, F.S. Goldstein 63; R.D. Jackman 3/33)

Rhodesia — 81 (B.F. Davison 30; D.L. Hobson 6/28)
and 207 (D.A.G. Fletcher 52, J.H. du Preez 34)

Western Province (5 bonus points) won by 148 runs — Rhodesia 5 bonus points.

Friendly at Pretoria, 20, 21 and 22 December.

Rhodesia — 324 (M.J. Procter 73, J.H. du Preez 70, B.F. Davison 68, J.C. Mitchell 37; J.D. Sparks 5/50)
and 192-7 dec. (P.R. Carlstein 59, J.H. du Preez 54, D.A.G. Fletcher 31*)

Northern Transvaal — 193 (A. Mostert 59; R.D. Jackman 4/19)
and 216 (K.D. Verdoorn 81; P.B. Clift 4/24)

Rhodesia won by 107 runs.

Imported Rhodesian captain, Mike Procter (*above*) appeals for a lbw decision against Rhodesian "export", Fred Goldstein, and (*below*) the roles are reversed as former Rhodesian, Riki Cameron is convinced he has trapped Procter in front of his wickets.

For some years Rhodesians had bemoaned the fact that they did not have a B team which would help bridge the disparity between club and Currie Cup cricket. In November 1973, the R.C.U. arranged a friendly for a Rhodesian B side against Transvaal B and in a brave decision decided to play the game in Gwelo. Although this was a financial risk it did give one of the smaller centres the opportunity to stage a major match. The outcome of the R.C.U.'s effort was a highly entertaining drawn game highlighted by an exhilarating 144 by Keith Tattersall and some fine off-spin bowling by the Rhodesian B skipper, John Traicos. Perhaps the success of the fixture could be drawn from the comment of national selector Alwyn Pichanick: 'It was a real eye-opener for us.'

SCORES: Rhodesia B versus Transvaal B.

At Gwelo, 24, 25 and 26 November, 1973-74 (Not first-class).

Rhodesia B — 288 (T.W. Dunk 112, M.M. Benkenstein 64, K. Tattersall 34)
and 231-7 dec. (K. Tattersall 144)

Transvaal B — 277 (V. Greve 76; A.J. Traicos 5/98, K.J. Tonkin 3/56)
and 99-6 (A.J. Traicos 3/27)

Match drawn.

In an opening show of power in their first round Gillette Cup encounter, Rhodesia overwhelmed a plucky Orange Free State side by 7 wickets at the Ramblers ground, Bloemfontein. Although county players Mike Buss and Roger Prideaux made the lion's share of the runs, steady bowling by Paddy Clift and Robin Jackman restricted their scoring rate. Jackman in fact polished off the Free State tail with three wickets in his last two overs, two of them with the last two balls of the innings.

Natal was a different proposition and the Rhodesians were on the receiving end of the season's biggest thrashing. A David Dyer century and the controlled seam attack of Natal's formidable duo, Vince van der Bijl and Pat Trimborn were the decisive factors.

SCORES: Gillette Cup, 1973-74.

At Bloemfontein, 20 October (First Round).

Orange Free State — 187 (60 overs) (M.A. Buss 78; P.B. CLift 4/44, R.D. Jackman 3/46)

Rhodesia — 188-3 wkts. (42,5 overs) (S.D. Robertson 82*, J.C. Mitchell 48, B.F. Davison 40)

Rhodesia won by 7 wickets.

At Durban, 9 February (Semi-final).

Natal — 286-8 wkts. (59,5 overs) (D.D. Dyer 135; P.B. Clift 3/40)

Rhodesia — 99 (36,4 overs) (B.F. Davison 35)

Natal won by 187 runs.

A knee injury prevented Mike Procter from playing any real part in Rhodesia's Currie Cup bid in 1974-75. He played one match in September against the International Wanderers but twisted his knee playing touch rugby prior to Rhodesia's opening encounter against Western Province in Salisbury. He did attempt to make an early comeback in the return match at Newlands, batting in considerable pain to score 64 in a partnership of 125 with Keith Tattersall, but then bowed out of the game for the rest of the season.

The International Wanderers under Brian Close visited again but played just one first-class match in Salisbury — the second fixture, originally scheduled for Bulawayo was transferred to the Wanderers, Johannesburg. They did, however, play four limited-over matches in Bulawayo, Gwelo, Umtali and Salisbury. The last of these games, which was played in the capital, was a $1 100 challenge match and for this contest Graeme Pollock and Ian Chappell joined the touring side. The brilliant South African left-hander unanimously won the "man of the match" award for a glorious century made in 123 minutes.

In the only first-class fixture, the game was evenly poised after the first innings with Mike Procter and Stuart Robertson notching half-centuries for Rhodesia and the veteran former England captain, Brian Close, hitting 102 in reply for the tourists. However, a fine all-round performance by the effervescent West Indian, John Shepherd (4/37 and 71 not out), swung the match second time round, firmly in favour of the International Wanderers. It was sweet revenge for Brian Close and his men following their humiliating defeat in 1972-73 and to add to their laurels they ended the short tour unbeaten.

SCORES: International Wanderers' Tour, 1974-75.

At Bulawayo, 12 September (50 overs-a-side) (Not first-class).

International Wanderers — 193-6 wkts. (G.R.J. Roope 53*; A.J. Traicos 3/29)

Rhodesia XI — 127 (J.C. Mitchell 42)

International Wanderers won by 66 runs.

At Salisbury, 14, 15 and 16 September.

Rhodesia — 224 (M.J. Procter 68, S.D. Robertson 51)
and 219 (P.B. Clift 73, P.R. Carlstein 55)

International Wanderers — 235 (D.B. Close 102; R.D. Jackman 3/52)
and 214-3 wkts. (J.N. Shepherd 71*, E.J. Barlow 52)

International Wanderers won by seven wickets.

At Gwelo, 17 September (50 overs-a-side) (Not first-class).

International Wanderers — 266-7 wkts. (G.M. Turner 114, M. Harris 54; B. Wishart 3/41)

Rhodesia XI — 195-8 wkts. (R.D. Jackman 37, D.B.E. Bawden 33, B.F. Davison 33)

International Wanderers won by 71 runs.

At Umtali, 21 September (50 overs-a-side) (Not first-class).

International Wanderers — 272-4 wkts. (G.M. Turner 76, R.W. Tolchard 72*, P.R. Carlstein 54*)

Rhodesia XI — 215-8 wkts. (R.D. Jackman 71*, J.C. Mitchell 36, K. Tattersall 31)

International Wanderers won by 57 runs.

At Salisbury, 22 September (50 overs-a-side) (Not first-class).

International Wanderers — 267-6 wkts. (R.G. Pollock 102, E.J. Barlow 61)

Rhodesia XI — 174 (P.R. Carlstein 42*, S.D. Robertson 38, M.J. Procter 36)

International Wanderers won by 93 runs.

Embarking on the Currie Cup trail, Rhodesia made a fine start under their new skipper, Brian Davison. Leading the way Davison struck a powerful 81 to lay the foundation for a useful 246 total against Western Province in Salisbury. Fellow professional Robin

Jackman, in association with the promising Paddy Clift, led the bowling onslaught and Province were routed 132 runs behind.

In their second visit to the crease the Rhodesians shaped poorly, with the exception of Paddy Clift, and at 74-7 prospects looked ominous for the home side. Wicket-keeper Howie Gardiner joined Clift at this stage and in a magnificent rearguard battle hoisted Rhodesia out of trouble. Their record-breaking partnership boosted the total by 152 runs and it was indeed unfortunate that Gardiner should have been dismissed a mere single away from his maiden first-class century.

Davison declared leaving Province a fair if daunting challenge with a good seven hours to score the required 400 runs for victory — a situation tailor-made for the visiting skipper Eddie Barlow. As anticipated, Province went for the runs and Fred Goldstein led the way by hitting four sixes and eight fours in his 66. Davison relied on Jackie du Preez and the little leg-spinner worked his way through the batting order to finish with 6/102 and bring 18 valuable points to his province.

After such an encouraging start the Rhodesians struggled, drawing matches against Natal and Western Province at home and losing to the same sides away. Matters worsened prior to the match against Eastern Province at St. George's Park, Port Elizabeth, because Mike Procter withdrew for the remainder of the season and a jaded Robin Jackman was rested. For the first time in four years the Rhodesians were without a professional in their side.

Perhaps it was due to the fact that a virtually home-grown Rhodesian side (only Peter Carlstein could not be considered in this category) realized its heavy responsibility that the team suddenly started to come right. A superb second innings 107 by Brian Davison allowed the Rhodesians back into the game after an inauspicious start and on the last afternoon, Eastern Province were 155-7 with 12 overs remaining before Graeme Pollock and Arthur Short (batting at number 9) steered them clear of possible defeat.

At the Wanderers, Johannesburg, the finish was even more dramatic with Rhodesia again in the driving-seat. Transvaal faced the task of finding 264 runs for victory in 135 minutes plus the mandatory 20 overs but lost wickets at an alarming rate. With their score at 97-9 last man Derick Adams faced just two balls before the heavens opened 65 minutes from the close and Rhodesia were denied a deserved victory. Those ten points in the final outcome would have meant that Rhodesia would have finished top of the A Section with a margin of 5 clear points.

The 1974-75 Wanderers side and the local welcoming committee at Aloe Park, Umtali: Graham McKenzie, Jimmy Mitchell, Peter Sainsbury, "Jock" Holden, Brian Close (Captain), Brian Wishart, Mrs. F. Twiselton, Tommy Dunk, Keith Tattersall, Mr. Frank Twiselton (Manager), Mike Harris, Robin Jackman and Phil Berridge.

Although it was a keyed-up Rhodesian side that faced Eastern Province in Bulawayo they started badly and declared at a modest 182-9. When Eastern Province went in to lunch on the second day at 144-4 the game seemed to be slipping badly for Rhodesia but in five action-packed overs immediately after the break, Duncan Fletcher altered the course of the game. He claimed five wickets for 4 runs and Eastern Province were all out for 158. However, that was not the end because Fletcher returned on the third day to inspire a Rhodesian victory as Eastern Province failed miserably in their endeavour to chase the required 268. Said team manager, Alwyn Pichanick, of the Rhodesian victory soon after the match had ended: 'It was an outstanding performance. As in the game in

Johannesburg we lost an important toss and batted when the wicket was most responsive on the first day. We then fought back from a difficult first innings position to outplay Eastern Province conculsively.

'The good results of the last three games were encouraging, especially considering having lost Procter, who was our best bowler and best batsman and we really needed two men to replace him.'

SCORES: Currie Cup A Section, 1974-75.

At Salisbury, 2, 3 and 4 November.

Rhodesia — 246 (B.F. Davison 81, H.A.B. Gardiner 31*)
and 267-9 dec. (H.A.B. Gardiner 99, P.B. Clift 74*)

Western Province — 114 (R.D. Jackman 6/51, P.B. Clift 3/16)
and 286 (F.S. Goldstein 66; J.H. du Preez 6/102)

Rhodesia (10 bonus points) won by 113 runs — Western Province 5 bonus points.

Duncan Fletcher batting (*above*) against Natal during the 1974-75 season and bowling (*below*) watched by local umpire, Austin Wilmot.

At Bulawayo, 16, 17 and 18 November.

Rhodesia — 272 (P.R. Carlstein 60, D.A.G. Fletcher 54, J.H. du Preez 43; D.R. Neilson 5/82)
and 208 (B.F. Davison 47, J.H. du Preez 44, D.A.G. Fletcher 40; D.S. van der Knapp 6/61)

Transvaal — 299 (S.J. Cook 104; D.A.G. Fletcher 5/48)
and 78-2 wkts.

Match drawn — Rhodesia 7 and Transvaal 5 bonus points.

At Salisbury, 23, 24 and 25 November.

Rhodesia — 135 (K. Tattersall 32; P. Henwood 5/32)
and 308 (P.B. Clift 55, B.F. Davison 47, K. Tattersall 43, J.C. Mitchell 40, J.H. du Preez 32, S.D. Robertson 30)

Natal — 284 (B.A. Richards 162; P.B. Clift 7/79)
and 24-1 wkt.

Match drawn — Natal 8 and Rhodesia 3 bonus points.

At Pietermaritzburg, 13, 14 and 15 December.

Rhodesia — 181 (B.D. Barbour 40, S.D. Robertson 38, J.C. Mitchell 31; V.A.P. van der Bijl 6/46)
and 221 (B.F. Davison 109)

Natal — 379-6 dec. (D.D. Dyer 87, D. Bestall 78, G.A. Katz 60*, H.R. Fotheringham 57)
and 28-1 wkt.

Natal (8 bonus points) won by 9 wickets — Rhodesia 3 bonus points.

At Cape Town, 17, 18 and 20 January.

Western Province — 317-8 dec. (E.J. Barlow 152, A. Bruyns 58; A.J. Traicos 3/78)
and 174-7 dec. (D.A.G. Fletcher 3/30)

Rhodesia — 245 (K. Tattersall 70, M.J. Procter 64, B.F. Davison 42)
and 161 (J.H. du Preez 33, P.B. Clift 32*)

Western Province (7 bonus points) won by 85 runs — Rhodesia 5 bonus points.

At Port Elizabeth, 24, 25 and 27 January.

Rhodesia — 202 (S.D. Robertson 72, M.M. Benkenstein 31)
and 306-7 dec. (B.F. Davison 107, M.M. Benkenstein 55, J.H. du Preez 36, P.B. Clift 32*, S.D. Robertson 32)

Eastern Province — 274-9 dec. (S.J. Bezuidenhout 117, R.K. Muzzell 64; J.H. du Preez 3/75)
and 210-7 wkts. (R.G. Pollock 75*, D.A.G. Fletcher 5/87)

Match drawn — Eastern Province 8 and Rhodesia 6 bonus points.

At Johannesburg, 31 January, 1 and 3 February.

Rhodesia — 175 (P.R. Carlstein 66, B.F. Davison 40, K. Tattersall 31; D.R. Neilson 5/39)
and 298-9 dec. (M.M. Benkenstein 84, D.A.G. Fletcher 49, H.A.B. Gardiner 43)

Transvaal — 210 (R.D. Jackman 4/60, P.B. Clift 3/48)
and 97-9 wkts. (J.H. du Preez 3/16, R.D. Jackman 3/23)

Match drawn — Transvaal 7 and Rhodesia 6 bonus points.

At Bulawayo, 22, 23 and 24 February.

Rhodesia — 182-9 dec. (S.D. Robertson 52, M.M. Benkenstein 33)
and 243 (S.D. Robertson 74, P.R. Carlstein 33; J.W. Gleeson 6/63)

Eastern Province — 158 (C.P. Wilkins 59; D.A.G. Fletcher 6/31, A.J. Traicos 4/27)
and 166 (D.A.G. Fletcher 5/61, A.J. Traicos 3/39)

Rhodesia (6 bonus points) won by 101 runs — Eastern Province 4 bonus points.

In the Gillette Cup competition Rhodesia again drew Orange Free State in their first round match and Natal in their semi-final clash. Whilst it was accepted that the B Section side was given a home fixture it was pleasant news and to Rhodesia's advantage that they played Natal at the Police ground, Salisbury.

Brian Davison batted 123 minutes (fifteen fours and one six) against the Free State to score a century and ensure that Rhodesia made their way into the semi-final. It was Rhodesia's first-ever Gillette Cup hundred and Davison deservedly received the batting award for his effort.

Surprisingly Rhodesia went down to Natal despite Stuart Robertson registering the second Rhodesian Gillette Cup century. But there were no complaints from an appreciative crowd which saw a magnificent day's cricket with Natal edging ahead in the last over of the day. In a match that could have gone either way, 551 runs were scored, and even the most rabid Rhodesian supporter could not argue against cricket being the winner.

SCORES: Gillette Cup, 1974-75.

At Bloemfontein, 19 October (First Round).

Rhodesia — 266-9 wkts. (60 overs) (B.F. Davison 102, D.A.G. Fletcher 38, H.A.B. Gardiner 38*, J.C. Mitchell 30)

Orange Free State — 161 (57 overs) (M.A. Buss 50; A.J. Traicos 3/43)

Rhodesia won by 105 runs.

At Salisbury, 8 February (Semi-final).

Rhodesia — 275-7 wkts. (60 overs) (S.D. Robertson 100, B.F. Davison 65, D.A.G. Fletcher 35*, J.C. Mitchell 34)

Natal — 276-8 wkts. (59,1 overs) (H.R. Fotheringham 90, D. Bestall, 66; R.D. Jackman 3/55)

Natal won by two wickets.

An historic tour was made in March 1975 by the Eric Ellerine African XI. The side was captained by former England cricketer, Don Wilson, and was further bolstered by all-rounder, Phil Carrick — both men having been employed as coaches in Soweto. Wilson, who had spent the past four years coaching Africans in the Transvaal, said on the side's arrival: 'This is a very important tour and it is a real breakthrough for African cricket. We don't expect miracles but in the past three years the improvement has been unbelievable.'

For most of the players it was their first experience of turf wickets although Edward Habane and Edmund Ntinkina had played in international double-wicket competitions at the Wanderers. Habane made a fine half-century against the President's XI in Salisbury but it was the team's vice-captain, Zimasi Mtabani, who was the most consistent of the African batsmen. Phil Carrick made 130 against the Rhodesian Country Districts but for the most part the side's batting let the team down. It was the bowling which impressed throughout and although the team did not win a match on their travels across the country, they managed to contain successfully some fully

Stuart Robertson is congratulated on his century in the 1974-75 Gillette Cup semi-final against Natal by excited spectators whilst umpire, Ken Poole, walks to his mark.

A historic photograph taken during the tea interval of the Manicaland versus Eric Ellerine's XI match at the Umtali Sports Club. *Left to Right:* Zimasa Mbatini, Bridgeman Mokoena, Samuel Nontshinga, Don Wilson (Eric Ellerine's XI captain), Mike Griffiths (Manicaland Captain), William Magitshima, Terry Wallace and Edward Habane.

Jimmy Mitchell in action against Eric Ellerine's XI.

representative provincial batting line-ups.

New Zealand's prodigious run-maker, Glenn Turner, led the 1975-76 International Wanderers on their tour of Rhodesia. He brought a powerful side with him — English Test players Barry Wood, Roger Tolchard, Graham Roope, John Snow, Phil Edmonds, Chris Old and Frank Hayes, West Indian John Shepherd, Pakistanis Mohammed Ilyas and Younis Ahmed, veteran Indian star Buddy Kunderan and leading county player Geoff Greenidge.

They were immediately tested against a strong Rhodesian combination in a 50 overs-a-side match at the Police ground and went down by 12 runs in a run romp. Brian Davison showed tremendous form to notch a century but was outpaced by a free scoring Keith Tattersall in a 164-run third wicket partnership that took a mere 104 minutes.

Davison continued his sparkling form against the International Wanderers, firstly for a Midlands Invitation XI by scoring 91 and then for Rhodesia in the opening first-class match in Bulawayo. By hammering two half-centuries the belligerent Davison kept the Rhodesians firmly in the latter game but the end result could have gone either way. The International Wanderers went into the final twenty overs at 156-3, chasing 254. They fell behind, scoring 44 in the first ten overs but with Chris Old and Younis Ahmed hitting out purposefully the pendulum swung in favour of the tourists. Victory was in sight when both fell at the last hurdle and numbers 10 and 11, Phil Edmonds and John Snow, were left to score eleven runs off the final over. Amid tremendous excitement they got six runs off the first four balls before Snow was caught behind to the faintest of touches and Rhodesia won a great victory by 4 runs. But full credit was due to the International Wanderers for continuing to go for the runs in fading light when the Queens ground became a gloomy dust bowl late on the final afternoon.

Another schoolboy storybook finish occurred at the Umtali Sports Club when a Manicaland Invitation XI required 18 runs off the last two overs against a formidable Test attack. Derrick Townshend took one run off English pace bowler Chris Old's first ball of the penultimate over to give Stuart Robertson the strike. Robertson swung the next ball over mid-wicket for six and then hit the third for an effortless straight six. Four runs came off the fifth and the home side had won with seven balls remaining. It was a grand climax to a game that had begun sensationally enough when Eddie Hough had dismissed both Barry Wood and Geoff Greenidge in the opening over of the innings.

A stung International Wanderers won their last match comfortably against Rhodesia in a three-day fixture at the Police ground, Salisbury. But even this game had its moments. Roger Tolchard, Phil Edmonds and John Snow retrieved the International Wanderers' position, from 115-8 to 284-9 declared, in their first innings and then Paddy Clift, new cap Brendon Boyd and John Traicos proved almost as frustrating to the visitors in dogged, last ditch stands during the final afternoon.

The tour provided some great contests and the President of the R.C.U., David Lewis, commented on its conclusion: 'It was a great success from the cricketing point of view — the Wanderers were a fine bunch who play in a professional and positive manner which we have now come to expect of them.'

SCORES: International Wanderers Tour, 1975-76.

At Salisbury, 21 September (50 overs-a-side) (Not first-class).

Rhodesia — 235-7 wkts. (B.F. Davison 101, K. Tattersall 88)

International Wanderers — 223-7 wkts. (G.M. Turner 51; R.D. Jackman 3/37)

Rhodesia won by 12 runs.

A cartwheeling stump brings to an end a magnificent century by Brian Davison against the 1975-76 International Wanderers. Graham Roope is the delighted bowler.

At Gwelo, 24 September (50 overs-a-side) (Not first-class).

International Wanderers — 262-6 wkts. (G.M. Turner 68, G.R.J. Roope 59)

Midlands Invitation XI — 183 (B.F. Davison 91; J.A. Snow 3/9)

International Wanderers won by 79 runs.

At Bulawayo, 27, 28 and 29 September.

Rhodesia — 244 (B.F. Davison 66, S.D. Robertson 39, H.A.B. Gardiner 33, D.A.G. Fletcher 31)
and 230 (B.F. Davison 78, S.D. Robertson 54, K. Tattersall 40; C.M. Old 5/38)

International Wanderers — 221 (G.R.J. Roope 77; A.J. Traicos 4/67, J.H. du Preez 3/61)
and 249 (G.M. Turner 74, G.R.J. Roope 63; D.A.G. Fletcher 4/78)

Rhodesia won by 4 runs.

At Umtali, 1 October (50 overs-a-side) (Not first-class).

International Wanderers — 213-6 wkts. (F. Hayes 93*, R.W. Tolchard 50*)

Manicaland Invitation XI — 215-5 wkts. (T.W. Dunk 65, K. Tattersall 49, S.D. Robertson 40*, J.G. Heron 35)

Manicaland Invitation XI won by 2 wickets.

At Salisbury, 4, 5 and 6 October.

Rhodesia — 210 (D.A.G. Fletcher 70, S.D. Robertson 38)
and 181 (P.B. Clift 64)

International Wanderers — 284-9 dec. (P.H. Edmonds 73, R.W. Tolchard 72*; A.J. Traicos 3/68)
and 108-1 wkt. (B. Wood 56*)

International Wanderers won by 9 wickets.

Prior to the Currie Cup season a Standard Bank Invitation XI played against a Rhodesia XI in a limited overs match. Guest stars for the Invitation XI were the England fast bowler, John Snow, the Pakistan batsman, Younis Ahmed, and the dynamic South African wicket-keeper batsman, Denis Lindsay. On an easy-paced wicket, Snow could not extract much venom and two strong candidates for the national side, Robin Jones and Barry Dudleston, both enhanced their reputations. Jones, a former Rhodesian and South African Schools player had been serving as Bacup's professional in the Lancashire League whilst Dudleston was an experienced Leicestershire professional.

SCORES: At Salisbury, 20 October, 1975-76 (55 overs-a-side) (Not first-class).

Standard Bank Invitation XI — 171-9 (J.H. du Preez 3/33)

Rhodesia XI — 177-4 (B. Dudleston 51, S.D. Robertson 48*, J.G. Jones 47; K.J. Tonkin 3/31)

Rhodesia XI won by 6 wickets.

In the Currie Cup, Rhodesia again finished in fourth place in 1975-76 but very nearly improved on their previous season's record for they came within an ace of beating Western Province at the Police ground, Salisbury. At the same time Rhodesia did win two matches in dramatic finishes. They made heavy weather of beating Transvaal at the Wanderers as the game hinged on the last pair, Du Preez and Hogg, who had to scrape together the required three runs. And they beat Eastern Province in Bulawayo with only two wickets standing and two balls of the final over to go when Clift lifted a ball over mid-off's head to the boundary. By contrast, Rhodesia's two defeats were heavy ones, by an innings at Newlands and by ten wickets at Kingsmead when they were dismissed for 83.

Rhodesia's greatest problem during the season was the lack of an opening bowling partnership. It was only a couple of seasons before that they had the best opening attack in the Currie Cup in the form of Mike Procter and Robin Jackman. However, with Procter unable to bowl at pace and Jackman showing indifferent form, problems were created. To add to the bowling difficulties, Duncan Fletcher, who had headed the Currie Cup averages in the previous season captured a mere eight wickets at an expensive 38,25 each. Hogg bowled well to take 6/78 against Natal early in the season before being discarded and in the last match against Eastern Province, Bernie Horton, in only his second game for Rhodesia, took 7/76 in 31 overs. Whilst the selectors continuously experimented with the pace and seam attack hoping for a change in fortune, they must have been thankful for the quite considerable service given by Paddy Clift. He bowled far more overs than anyone else in the side and his ability to move the ball both ways and to keep one end going for long periods was invaluable. He claimed 31 wickets in the Currie Cup competition (37 in all matches) to head comfortably the Rhodesian averages at 22,93 and at the end of the season travelled overseas to begin a cricket contract with Leicestershire.

The Rhodesian batting relied heavily on Jack Heron, who had been given several opportunities in the national side since his debut in 1967-68 without much success. Establishing himself with a century against Border in a Gillette Cup match early on in the season, he proceeded to become the first Rhodesian to score 700 runs in a Currie Cup season and ended with an impressive 747 runs in eight matches (average 49,80). His most valuable innings was against Eastern Province at Bulawayo when he made 153 of the 274 required for victory, the next highest score being John Shepherd's 33 late in the innings.

There was a touch of humour in this cliff-hanger. With the 2 200 crowd sitting nervously awaiting the final over to commence and Rhodesia needing three runs to win, Lorrie Wilmot began leading the Eastern Province side off the field just as he had done three seasons before. The crowd watched in open-mouthed disbelief as history appeared to be repeating itself but this time it ended in laughter as the Eastern Province players stopped, turned round and went back to play the final over.

Brendon Boyd cover-drives John Shepherd whilst Glen Turner (slip), Roger Tolchard (wicket-keeper) and Austin Wilmot (umpire) look on. (Rhodesia versus International Wanderers, Salisbury 1975-76.)

On a more serious note were the unfortunate problems that surrounded John Shepherd, the West Indian Test all-rounder who was coaching in Salisbury, and was selected to play against Transvaal at the Police ground where he made a cavalier half-century. As Rhodesia were restricted to one professional he was dropped for the Currie Cup tour in that he had taken no wickets against Transvaal and the selectors felt that Jackman would be of the greater value in this sphere. The decision gave rise to a regrettable controversy arising from the suggestion that Shepherd had been excluded 'for reasons other than cricket'. As it happened Jackman did not take a single wicket in the two matches in the Cape but redeemed himself at the Wanderers. At home for the last two matches of the season Shepherd was recalled, did little with the ball but made needed runs quickly.

Brian Davison continued to captain the side after returning from a highly successful overseas season

A lofted on-drive by Jack Heron.

where he finished fifth in the overall English averages and had capped a great season by hammering 189 for Leicestershire against the Australians. Sadly he had a relatively disappointing season for Rhodesia, scoring 307 runs with a modest 23,61 average but on 25 January 1976, he became the first Rhodesia-born batsman to reach 10 000 first-class runs. It was an historic occasion for a dedicated cricketer who thrives on continuous, six-days-a-week cricket, and since the offer of a first contract in 1970, has represented

Robin Jackman and Mike Procter celebrate with John Shepherd the news of his Rhodesian selection in November, 1975.

Leicestershire in the County Championship with distinction.

Honour also came Jackie du Preez's way when he gained his 100th cap for Rhodesia against Natal at Kingsmead, Durban. He became the first Rhodesian to reach this milestone — a remarkable achievement for a player who had given so much to Rhodesian cricket since his debut against John Reid's New Zealanders in 1961-62. He had come a long way since learning his cricket at Highlands Junior School where former Springbok, Chris Duckworth, noticed every ball he delivered was a leg break and encouraged him to start spin bowling. He then came under Sussex professional, Jim Cornford, made the junior school 1st XI, represented the Rhodesian Fawns and in time was selected for the Prince Edward 1st XI and the 1961 Nuffield side.

Success of a different nature was achieved by Dave Bawden when he was named for the Rhodesian side against Western Province at the Police ground. He became a double Rhodesian representative, having played on the wing for the national rugby side during the 1966-69 seasons but admitted: 'It's always been my greatest ambition to play cricket for Rhodesia.' To crown a great year Bawden married the former Rhodesian swimming star, Caroline Fairbairn, in April.

Sadly the season was Mike Procter's last for Rhodesia. It had been a relatively quiet one for him in that he took only 10 wickets in limited spells. However, he did produce some notable performances with the bat, including 121* and 77 against Eastern Province at Port Elizabeth. His century enabled him once again to enter the record books — on this occasion he and Stuart Robertson in a third-wicket partnership of 226 in 229 minutes broke Jimmy Dell and David Lewis's 23-year-old record stand of 211 made against Border in 1952-53.

Procter's contribution as the national coach and player since 1970-71 had been priceless, not only in the many great deeds he performed on the field of play but in that he had created a resurgence of interest in the game at all levels. Said Alwyn Pichanick, then vice-president of the R.C.U.: 'He was responsible for injecting completely new thinking into Rhodesian cricket and gave the other players confidence in themselves. From my relationship with him as manager of the Rhodesian team when he was captain I know we could never have asked for a player who gave more for Rhodesia. He always gave everything he had and he's going to be a terrible loss.'

Natal's Robert Cheetham ducks under a bouncer bowled by Robin Jackman during the 1975-76 Currie Cup encounter at Bulawayo — Barry Richards watches from the non-striker's end.

SCORES: Currie Cup A Section, 1975-76.

At Bulawayo, 8, 9 and 10 December.

Natal — 368 (B.A. Richards 159, H.R. Fotheringham 71, K.M. Hosken 58*; V.R. Hogg 6/78)
and 246-4 dec. (B.A. Richards retired ill 69, R.A. Woolmer 66, A.J.S. Smith 55)

Rhodesia — 334-6 dec. (M.J. Procter 84, J.G. Heron 51, S.D. Robertson 42, B.F. Davison 38, H.A.B. Gardiner 37*, J.H. du Preez 32*)
and 73-1 wkt. (D.A.G. Fletcher 42*)

Match drawn — Rhodesia 4 and Natal 7 bonus points.

At Salisbury, 29, 30 November and 1 December.

Rhodesia — 387-7 dec. (J.G. Heron 175, J.N. Shepherd 51, M.J. Procter 46, D.A.G. Fletcher 32)

Transvaal — 197 (C.E.B. Rice 58; P.B. Clift 4/39, J.H. du Preez 3/20, A.J. Traicos 3/40)
and 329-4 wkts. (N.G. Featherstone 101, C.E.B. Rice 93*, D.D. Dyer 66)

Match drawn — Rhodesia 9 and Transvaal 3 bonus points.

At Cape Town, 5, 6 and 8 December.

Rhodesia — 146-9 dec. (J.G. Heron 47, J.H. du Preez 30)
and 149 (D.A.G. Fletcher 43, H.A.B. Gardiner 38)

Western Province — 352-4 dec. (P.N. Kirsten 128*, A. Bruyns 93, H.M. Ackerman 60)

Western Province (7 bonus points) won by an innings and 57 runs — Rhodesia 1 bonus point.

At Port Elizabeth, 12, 13 and 15 December.

Rhodesia — 293-3 dec. (S.D. Robertson 136, M.J. Procter 121*)
and 420-7 dec. (J.G. Heron 136, M.J. Procter 77, B.F. Davison 66, D.A.G. Fletcher 55, H.A.B. Gardiner 35)

Eastern Province — 387-7 dec. (S.J. Bezuidenhout 126, C.P. Wilkins 99, K.S. McEwan 54; P.B. Clift 4/83)
and 159-3 wkts. (C.P. Wilkins 65)

Match drawn — Eastern Province 9 and Rhodesia 7 bonus points.

At Johannesburg, 16, 17 and 19 January.

Transvaal — 144 (R.D. Jackman 5/52, P.B. Clift 4/44).
and 133 (P.B. Clift 4/34, R.D. Jackman 3/37, D.A.G. Fletcher 3/39)

Rhodesia — 152.
and 126-9 wkts. (S.D. Robertson 39; D.R. Neilson 6/38)

Rhodesia (5 bonus points) won by 1 wicket — Transvaal 5 bonus points.

At Durban, 24, 25 and 26 January.

Rhodesia — 158 (J.G. Heron 61; V.A.P. van der Bijl 5/39)
and 83 (J.G. Heron 33)

Natal — 178 (A.J.S. Smith 68; V.R. Hogg 3/35, R.D. Jackman 3/46, P.B. Clift 3/55)
and 64-0 wkts.

Natal (6 bonus points) won by 10 wickets — Rhodesia 5 bonus points.

At Salisbury, 7, 8 and 9 February.

Rhodesia — 410-9 dec. (B.F. Davison 74, J.N. Shepherd 65, B.D. Barbour 44, D.A.G. Fletcher 43, M.J. Procter 41, J.H. du Preez 41, D.B.E. Bawden 36)
and 120-7 wkts. (J.N. Shepherd 33, B.D. Barbour 32)

Western Province — 170-9 dec. (H.M. Ackerman 52; J.N. Shepherd 3/34, J.H. du Preez 3/56)
and 374 (P.N. Kirsten 123, E.J. Barlow 104; M.J. Procter 4/109, J.H. du Preez 4/116)

Match drawn — Rhodesia 7 and Western Province 2 bonus points.

At Bulawayo, 21, 22 and 23 February.

Eastern Province — 290-9 dec. (S.J. Bezuidenhout 115, K.S. McEwan 70; P.B. Clift 6/71)
and 220 (K.S. McEwan 61; B. Horton 7/76)

Rhodesia — 238 (D.A.G. Fletcher 44, D.B.E. Bawden 40)
and 274-8 wkts. (J.G. Heron 153, J.N. Shepherd 33)

Rhodesia (7 bonus points) won by 2 wickets — Eastern Province 10 bonus points.

In January 1976 a Transvaal Colts side played two matches in Rhodesia on a short tour.

SCORES: Transvaal Colts Tour, 1975-76.

At Salisbury, 15 and 16 January (Not first-class).

Rhodesia Colts — 196 (B. Thorn 58, P. Curran 33)
and 262-9 dec. (D.W. Hornby 80, L.L. de Grandhomme 69, M. Dunk 38)

Transvaal Colts — 229-6 dec. (Sher 58*; L.L. de Grandhomme 3/47)
and 231-5 wkts. (K. Dollery 68, T. van Beuge 64)

Transvaal Colts won by 5 wickets.

At Umtali, 17 and 18 January. (Not first-class).

Rhodesia B — 154
and 233-4 dec. (D.B.E. Bawden 86, B.D. Barbour 46, T.J. Townshend 36)

Transvaal Colts — 157 (A. du Preez 51; B. Horton 6/49)
and 120-3 wkts. (I. Carruthers 63)

Match drawn.

The 1975-76 Gillette Cup competition reflected Rhodesian cricket at its best and at its very worst. The Rhodesians failed to bowl out lowly Border within the 60 overs in their first-round encounter but thanks to a powerful, undefeated 148 by Jack Heron scored the necessary runs with little difficulty. In sharp contrast against Northern Transvaal in the second round a middle-order collapse saw Rhodesia reeling at 121-7 before Howie Gardiner and Robin Jackman staged a rescue stand worth 84. Tight bowling resulted in Northerns producing a pitiful 103 in reply.

The semi-final was a disaster. After a reasonable start the Eastern Province middle order of Ken McEwan, Graeme Pollock, Lorrie Wilmot and Darryl Bestall could only muster 18 between them but the later batsmen hit out to reach a moderate total of 213. Unfortunately the Rhodesian side, packed with batsmen, put up an abysmal display which saw Rhodesia record their lowest-ever Gillette Cup score and exit from the competition.

SCORES: Gillette Cup, 1975-76.

At East London, 18 October (First Round).

Border — 235-9 wkts. (60 overs) (R. Kent 70, R.C. Ontong 55; R.D. Jackman 3/45)

Rhodesia — 237-2wkts. (49,2 overs) (J.G. Heron 148*, K. Tattersall 46)

Rhodesia won by 8 wickets.

At Pretoria, 25 October (Second Round).

Rhodesia — 221 (59,3 overs) (R.D. Jackman 44, D.A.G. Fletcher 42, H.A.B. Gardiner 41, S.D. Robertson 34)

Northern Transvaal — 103 (36,3 overs) (R.D. Jackman 3/18, J.H. du Preez 3/37)

Rhodesia won by 118 runs.

At Port Elizabeth, 31 January (Semi-final).

Eastern Province — 213 (51 overs) (S.J. Bezuidenhout 61; D.A.G. Fletcher 4/69)

Rhodesia — 88 (36,5 overs) (D.J. Brickett 5/23)

Eastern Province won by 125 runs.

CHAPTER NINE

The Transition

WHILST THE NATIONAL selectors spent the winter pondering over the difficulties likely to confront their aspirations for 1976-77 two Rhodesians were making a great impression on the English County Championship. They were Brian Davison, destined to become Rhodesia's next national coach, who was in his eighth season in England, and Paddy Clift, who was experiencing his first season at the Grace Road ground, Leicester. Both were praised frequently in Press reports for their outstanding deeds throughout the demanding Championship season. Tony Greig, who was named as the M.C.C. captain for the Indian tour during the English winter, wrote: 'Between them they have given Leicester a tremendous boost. Davison has been steadily developing into one of the most attractive and forceful batsmen in world cricket. Clift has made a big impact in his first season with his medium-pace bowling. We probably have yet to see the best of him.'

Perhaps the greatest tributes they received came from the Leicestershire and England captain, Ray Illingworth, one of the most knowledgeable men in the game. He said of Brian Davison: 'I've said again and again he is one of the finest batsmen in the County Championship. What more can I say of a player of his talents? He fails so rarely, yet he makes his runs in a fierce, entertaining style. His cover-drive is one of the finest in the English game. I see no weaknesses in his game.' And of Paddy Clift, who had arrived in England comparatively unknown, to replace the famous Australian opening bowler Graham "Garth" McKenzie, Illingworth said: 'Paddy is similar to Garth in build, bowling ability and even temperament. He began the season sensationally with eight wickets against the M.C.C. and he has consistently been around the top of the national averages. His greatest asset is that he bowls straight, making the batsmen play every ball. He is also a powerful, clean-hitting batsman but has not yet had the opportunity to confirm his promise.'

Unfortunately the grass was not as green on the other side of the Equator and both Davison and Clift were to find the next Currie Cup season to be harder going and less rewarding. Rhodesia were not expected to do well in the 1976-77 season but the end results were far worse than even anticipated. No fewer than five of the eight matches were lost outright, four of them in the last five matches, and there was not a single victory to record. Rhodesia finished bottom of the Currie Cup table, 18 points behind Eastern Province, who in turn were no fewer than 39 points behind Transvaal and Western Province. When it is considered that the Rhodesian batsmen could average only 24 runs per wicket, that it cost the bowlers almost 40 runs to take a wicket and that they were only able to capture 81 wickets in eight matches, then it is hardly surprising they should have had such a poor playing record.

The season began under handicap. Mike Procter had left, Robin Jackman's coaching contract debarred him from playing Currie Cup and John Shepherd did not return. In addition Jackie du Preez needed an operation which kept him out of the first five matches while Howie Gardiner, through back trouble, was unable to play at all. John Traicos broke a thumb stopping a hard drive at the Wanderers and effectively missed the last three matches, Stuart Robertson was suddenly struck with appendicitis the night before the Newlands match and once again military service continued to hamper team building and match fitness.

There were other telling features which lessened Rhodesia's hopes of success during the season. Jack Heron suffered an alarming loss in form and apart from a century at Port Elizabeth he could only manage another 127 runs in ten innings. There was also a disturbing fall in Robertson's form after his operation and his last six innings brought him no more than 44 runs. In addition, Brian Davison again could not reproduce his overseas batting form and eventually he was replaced as captain by Robertson for the last two matches in the hope that this would have a beneficial effect on his batting. Davison promised so much by hitting 201 in a national league match for B.A.C. and then 250* in a Logan Cup encounter for Matabeleland against Mashonaland but could only average 26,60 in first-class matches.

The bowling created even greater problems. Robin Jackman was released for the two opening home matches but then played no further part in the Currie Cup competition. Unfortunately the search to find an opening bowler to replace him proved fruitless. Bernie Horton headed the bowling averages and was the leading wicket taker with 19 but was expensive at 33,21 runs per wicket. Clift and Fletcher were tried in

BRIAN DAVISON.

the opening role but neither was fast enough to be effective and both ended up having disappointing seasons.

There were a couple of bright spots amid the encroaching problems. The Leicestershire professional, Barry Dudleston, came into the team in the second half of the season and provided some reliability in the batting line-up. Scoring a century on his first appearance against Western Province at Newlands, he made 393 runs (average 49,12) in the four matches he played as well as hitting a sparkling half-century, which included four sixes in the last Gillette Cup encounter against Natal.

The other pleasing factor was the improvement in Jimmy Mitchell's batting. Having returned from a season in the Transvaal, Mitchell scored 480 runs (average 32,00) with four half-centuries. Towards the end of the season he had matured into a consistent opening bat and invariably gave his side a good start from his end.

Having retired a couple of seasons earlier before moving to Johannesburg, Peter Carlstein returned in fine fettle, hitting 152 in his first league match for Old Hararians against a Salisbury Sports Club attack which included Robin Jackman and John Traicos. He was recalled to the Rhodesian side for the opening Currie Cup match against Western Province but in his enthusiasm dislocated his shoulder whilst fielding during a limited overs match for Rhodesia B and was forced to miss the main game. He was selected again for the Rhodesian team later in the season but met with little success apart from a half-century against Eastern Province at Port Elizabeth.

In an endeavour to counter the poor run being suffered by the national side, the R.C.U. stepped up their efforts to promote the game and the Rhodesia B players were provided with several opportunities to prove their worth. Initially they were given two one-day fixtures against Western Province and Transvaal at home prior to the Currie Cup encounters. These provided invaluable opportunities for Currie Cup "fringers" to gain attention and later in the season, during the New Year period, a successful short tour was made to the Transvaal.

Players on trial such as Vince Hogg, Trevor Townshend, Barry Dudleston, Brian Thorn, Keith Tattersall, Denis Streak, Robin Brown, Pat Curran and Dave Alers all gave notice that they were in form at different stages for the B team and were subsequently given their chances to represent the senior side in the Currie Cup and Gillette Cup competitions. The B side was therefore serving an invaluable purpose and obviously the selectors hoped to establish a pool of home-grown players experienced in this higher class of cricket.

An interesting addition to the Rhodesian side during the 1976-77 season was Allan Fletcher who batted with tremendous determination but earned little success with his promising leg-spin bowling. On one memorable occasion against Eastern Province, he stayed for over an hour to stave off imminent defeat — twenty minutes of this time was spent in a desperate last wicket stand with Bernie Horton. Allan's elder brother Duncan, however, did not enjoy a successful season and his one moment of brilliance was performed in the lower realms of Salisbury First League cricket. Batting for Old Hararians against Sunrise he hit a double century before lunch and in a staggering run spree totalled 246 when he was out fifteen minutes before the break. In all he struck twenty-four fours and twelve sixes and batted for 210 minutes.

Whilst Rhodesia struggled through the frustrating season with their somewhat innocuous attack, Mike Procter performed wonders for Natal. Denys Heesom wrote in his *Wisden* report: 'Natal deserved to win the Currie Cup if only because of Procter's superlative bowling. Looking trimmer and fitter than in recent years, he bowled off his longest run again and then, as a change, bowled his off-spinners very effectively. Altogether he collected 59 Currie Cup wickets to create a new record, beating the 55 of J.T. Botten in 1958-59. Almost simultaneously he became the highest Currie Cup wicket taker of all time finishing the season with 335 wickets; the previous record was 317 by J. Waddington also in 1958-59. Natal needed his exceptional bowling because their batting was sometimes suspect.'

SCORES: Currie Cup A Section, 1976-77.

At Bulawayo, 6, 7 and 8 November.

Rhodesia — 136 (P.B. Clift 40*, A.W.R. Fletcher 33) and 237 (S.D. Robertson 79, B.F. Davison 44)

Dave Bawden hooks Eddie Barlow during Rhodesia's match against Western Province at Bulawayo in 1976-77.

A mighty six by Keith Tattersall off left-arm spinner Phil Carrick during the 1976-77 encounter with Eastern Province. Another left-hander, Graeme Pollock, looks on in admiration.

Western Province — 361 (A.J. Lamb 109, H.M. Ackerman 94; R.D. Jackman 4/66, B. Horton 4/72) and 13-0 wkts.

Western Province (8 bonus points) won by 10 wickets — Rhodesia 2 bonus points.

At Salisbury, 13, 14 and 15 November.

Transvaal — 304-9 dec. (B.L. Irvine 112; P.B. Clift 3/63)
and 149-3 wkts. (D.D. Dyer 92*)

Rhodesia — 375 (S.D. Robertson 97, B.F. Davison 83, J.C. Mitchell 61, D.B.E. Bawden 42; P.D. de Vaal 7/76)

Match drawn — Rhodesia 6 and Transvaal 4 bonus points.

At Durban, 18, 19 and 20 December.

Rhodesia — 178-9 dec. (B.F. Davison 63, J.C. Mitchell 33, S.D. Robertson 30)
and 161 (S.D. Robertson 49; V.A.P. van der Bijl 6/58)

Natal — 235 (M.J. Procter 59; P.B. Clift 4/70, V.R. Hogg 3/40)
and 105-4 wkts. (A.J. Traicos 3/36)

Natal (7 bonus points) won by 6 wickets — Rhodesia 5 bonus points.

At Cape Town, 7, 8 and 10 December.

Western Province — 387-7 dec. (K.C. Wessels 136, A.J. Lamb 60; D.A.G. Fletcher 3/73)
and 166-6 wkts. (K.C. Wessels 71; A.J. Traicos 4/48)

Rhodesia — 202-9 dec. (B. Dudleston 49, J.G. Heron 39, A.J. Traicos 38; D.L. Hobson 7/99)
and 347 (B. Dudleston 142, J.C. Mitchell 66, D.A.G. Fletcher 64, B.F. Davison 37)

Western Province (10 bonus points) won by 4 wickets — Rhodesia 4 bonus points.

At Port Elizabeth, 10, 11 and 13 December.

Eastern Province — 376-5 dec. (K.S. McEwan 92, R.G. Pollock 90, K.P Reid 78)
and 286-4 dec. (S.J. Bezuidenhout 122*, C.P. Wilkins 55)

Rhodesia — 347-8 dec. (J.C. Heron 122, P.R. Carlstein 50, A.W.R. Fletcher 39*, S.D. Robertson 35)
and 197-9 wkts. (S.D. Robertson 68, J.C. Mitchell 35; P. Carrick 5/59)

Match drawn — Eastern Province 8 and Rhodesia 5 bonus points.

At Johannesburg, 11, 12 and 14 February.

Rhodesia — 184 (P.B. Clift 60*)
and 235 (B. Dudleston 84, J.C. Mitchell 77; P.D. de Vaal 6/27)

Transvaal — 237 (K.A. McKenzie 65; J.H. du Preez 3/72)
and 185-5 wkts. (B.L. Irvine 61, C.E.B. Rice 52*)

Transvaal (8 bonus points) won by 5 wickets — Rhodesia 6 bonus points.

At Salisbury, 26, 27 and 28 February.

Rhodesia — 233 (J.C. Mitchell 52, J.H. du Preez 46, K. Tattersall 40)
and 268-8 dec. (B. Thorn 66, B.F. Davison 61, J.H. du Preez 45*, K. Tattersall 33; P. Carrick 5/96)

Eastern Province — 302-7 dec. (G.S. Cowley 90*; B. Horton 3/89)
and 116-4 wkts. (B. Horton 3/46)

Match drawn — Eastern Province 7 and Rhodesia 4 bonus points.

At Bulawayo, 12, 13 and 14 March.

Natal — 352-6 dec. (H.R. Fotheringham 90, B.S. Groves 65, M.J. Procter 55*)

Rhodesia — 177 (D.A.G. Fletcher 37, B. Dudleston 33)
and 157 (B. Dudleston 41; M.J. Procter 5/61)

Natal (9 bonus points) won by an innings and 18 runs — Rhodesia 3 bonus points.

The Rhodesia B matches during the season were as follows:

At Bulawayo, 4 November (60-overs-a-side) (Not first-class).

Western Province — 307-3 wkts. (K.C. Wessels 132, H.M. Ackerman 118*)

Rhodesia B — 2-0 wkts.

Match abandoned owing to rain.

At Salisbury, 11 November (60-overs-a-side) (Not first-class).

Rhodesia B — 188-8 (T.J. Townshend 56, T.W. Dunk 40)

Transvaal — 190-4 (R.K. Muzzell 51)

Transvaal won by 6 wickets.

At Bulawayo, 12 December (60-overs-a-side) (Not first-class).
versus Nuffield XI — see Schools section.

At Pretoria, 12 and 13 December (Not first-class).

Rhodesia B — 301 (T.W. Dunk 75, B. Thorn 60, K. Tattersall 52, R.D. Brown 40)
and 132-6 (B. Thorn 51, T.J. Townshend 40)

Northern Transvaal B — 200 (A.M. Ferreira 54; D.H. Streak 4/57, M. Morgan 3/54)
and 306-7 dec. (M. Mellor 101, C. Fletcher 78; P.J. Allan 4/92)

Match drawn.

At Johannesburg, 15 and 16 January (Not first-class).

Rhodesia B — 302 (K. Tattersall 78, T.W. Dunk 73, B. Thorn 32, R.D. Brown 31).
and 135-8 (R.D. Brown 56)

Transvaal C — 137 (D.G.W. Alers 7/68)
and 298-9 dec. (G.E. McMillan 79*, R.W. Berry 56; P.J. Allan 3/63)

Rhodesia B won by 2 wickets.

Rhodesia made a tremendous start to their Gillette Cup programme of 1976-77 by thrashing Northern Transvaal for the second consecutive year. The match was dominated by Jack Heron's batting — in leading Rhodesia to victory he scored 119 out of the total of 158-2. He monopolized the run scoring to such an extent that in a partnership of 133 for the second wicket with Dave Bawden, the latter's contribution was a mere 27.

However, Rhodesia's Gillette Cup aspirations were cut short by Natal's three-pronged pace attack. Mike Procter (1/14), Vince van der Bijl (3/27) and Aubrey Lilley (3/41) bowled so tightly within their allocated 12 overs each that Rhodesia were hard pressed to average three runs an over. In reply Paddy Clift bowled superbly but his efforts were not sufficient to prevent Natal progressing towards the final.

Barry Dudleston sweeps in the course of a hard-hit half-century against Natal in the 1976-77 Gillette Cup. Wicket-keeper, Tich Smith, looks on.

SCORES: Gillette Cup 1976-77.

At Pretoria, 23 October (First Round).

Northern Transvaal — 156 (56 overs) (D.A.G. Fletcher 3/45)

Rhodesia — 158-2 wkts. (44,3 overs) (J.G. Heron 119*)

Rhodesia won by 8 wickets.

At Salisbury, 30 January (Semi-final).

Rhodesia — 180-8 wkts. (60 overs) (B. Dudleston 54, T.J. Townshend 41, J.G. Heron 35)

Natal — 181-7 wkts. (55,1 overs) (P.B. Clift 3/26)

Natal won by 3 wickets.

Trevor Townshend adopts a strange stance during his aggressive innings of 41 in the 1976-77 Gillette Cup match against Natal at Salisbury.

In April 1977, Brian Davison and Paddy Clift represented Rhodesia in the fourth Datsun International Double-Wicket Competition. Teams from Australia (Alan Turner and Ross Edwards), New Zealand (Bevan Congdon and Richard Hadlee) and England (Graham Barlow and John Lever) provided testing competition for four South African sides and the Rhodesians. The strong New Zealand combination beat Rhodesia on the first day but Davison and Clift then provided the fireworks by holding the pre-tournament favourites, South Africa A (Eddie Barlow and Mike Procter), to a 27-run tie. There were some thrilling contests and towards the end of the second day Rhodesia and South Africa A finished jointly at the top, each with five victories, one defeat and a tie. This necessitated a play-off which proved to be intensely exciting and *The South Africa Cricket Annual* reported: 'Barlow and Procter scored a very reasonable 44 in their innings, a considerable task to improve upon in extremely bad light and with Procter bowling off his longest run. However, whilst Clift was virtually a spectator, Davison was in terrific form to make a splendid 37. Thus a team which scored only one point in its first two matches ultimately came through to win and the excitement held a large crowd right to the end . . . Each of the winning team received a new Datsun 1200 car as his prize.'

The 1977-78 season was fortunately an improvement on the doleful 1976-77 performance in that Rhodesia finished in fourth place above Natal. But the highlight of the season was undoubtedly the Datsun Shield victory when luck at last seemed to run Rhodesia's way. A comfortable victory over Border in East London was followed by two abandoned matches against Transvaal in the semi-final. The rules stated that the outcome would have to be based on the drawing of a name out of a hat. To the delight of the home side Mr. Varachia, the President of the S.A.C.U., drew Rhodesia.

The weather continued to mar the Datsun Shield progress and the final against Eastern Province, originally scheduled for mid-February had to be postponed because the ground was unplayable until March. When the fixture was played at the Wanderers, Johannesburg, it had to be called off through very bad light when the Rhodesians were still 12 runs short of outright victory with six wickets to fall and 20 balls to be bowled. Thus if play could have continued Rhodesia would have had little difficulty reaching the target and therefore were worthy winners of the Shield even if the final decision was based on a calculated runs-per-wicket ratio.

Rhodesia owed everything to Brian Davison and

The moment of truth. South African Cricket Union president, Mr. Rashid Varachia, draws Rhodesia's name out of the hat to decide the outcome of their 1977-78 Datsun Shield semi-final with Transvaal.

Stuart Robertson, captain of the winning Rhodesia team, receives the Datsun Shield from Mr. Peter Whitfield, Managing Director of Datsun-Nissan, after the Final at the Wanderers, Johannesburg.

Brian Barbour, who pulled the match out of a seemingly impossible position after their side was floundering at 27-3 and 81-5 in reply to Eastern Province's 227-8 wickets. In a tremendous unbeaten partnership of 135 they hammered the Province attack to all parts of the vast Wanderers stadium with the 11 000 crowd applauding every run of the gallant fight-back. So much on top were the two Rhodesian batsmen that at the end they were scoring at the rate of six runs per over so, indeed, it was a pity that they were not able to bring off a real, instead of technical, victory.

Always the senior partner, Davison's 102 won him the batting prize and a special award for making a century, but Barbour's mature 57 gave him splendid support. Rhodesian captain, Stuart Robertson won the fielding prize, holding a brilliant slip catch to dismiss Simon Bezuidenhout, but on the whole, Rhodesia's fielding was of the highest order and some great catches were held.

In the Currie Cup, Rhodesia were never anywhere near being contenders for the title though they did have moments of success. A satisfying six-wicket win over Natal at the Police ground gave them their first victory in two seasons whilst they were not far off winning against Transvaal at the Wanderers. They also held their own in a couple of the drawn matches, displaying pleasing fighting qualities. However, they were somewhat lucky to scrape a draw against Natal when skipper Stuart Robertson appealed against the conditions at Kingsmead, Durban. With rain falling steadily the home side were within four runs of victory, had eight wickets in hand and 34 balls were still to be bowled. The appeal provoked a strong reaction from a demonstrating crowd but it was noticeable that in Press comments two former Natal captains, Jackie McGlew and Pat Trimborn, both came out strongly in favour of Robertson's decision.

Whilst it was harsh justice for the Natal side that the game was drawn, it was remembered that only nine months earlier Natal had won the Currie Cup at a waterlogged Queens ground. Robertson in only his second match as captain had then been criticized for not playing the game hard enough in that he had not called for an appeal against the conditions when last man, Bernie Horton, walked to the wicket in mounting drizzle. Under fire at Durban for his "questionable sportsmanship", a more experienced Robertson argued: 'We played strictly according to the rules. We also owe it to the rest of the Currie Cup teams, as well as ourselves, to play it hard.'

Jack Heron catches Peter Kirsten (Western Province) off Richie Kaschula's bowling for 37 as Stuart Robertson and Gerald Peckover roar their appeals (at Salisbury, 1977-78).

For Barry Dudleston the season was a continuing success story. His aggregate of 678 runs added to his 393 runs made in the second half of the previous season, meant that he exceeded 1 000 runs for Rhodesia in only twelve matches. There was also a welcome return to form by Brian Davison — his 527 runs (average 43,91) was a great improvement on his previous season's figure. Stuart Robertson remained a model of consistency scoring 552 runs (average 39,42) whilst Brian Barbour, given another chance, returned to score a century against Natal at the Police ground, Salisbury. In fact Barbour regarded by many as too unsound in method since his remarkable debut season of 1971-72, topped the batting averages with 203 runs — average 50,75. One other achievement of note was an impressive debut innings by the world-rated hockey player, Gerald Peckover. Coming in as night-watchman against Eastern Province at Bulawayo, Peckover stayed on the following day to register 93 runs during a determined 3½ hours at the wicket.

Paddy Clift's injury, sustained during the 1977 English season was a great blow and prevented him from playing except in the last two matches. Immediately he returned, his blend of seam and off-spin bowling brought him 6/36 in an innings against Natal which underlined his value to the team and did much to set up the victory. The huge left-arm spinner Richie Kaschula had returned to the side at the start of the season in place of Clift and his 307 overs were one hundred overs more than the next man, Duncan Fletcher. He did claim 27 wickets at the rather expensive rate of 28,18 runs but only Clift and Vince Hogg were ahead of him in the bowling averages.

SCORES: Currie Cup A Section, 1977-78.

At Bulawayo, 5, 6 and 7 November.

Eastern Province — 308-7 dec. (R.G. Pollock 134, S.J. Bezuidenhout 75; R.H. Kaschula 3/88)
and 357-5 dec. (R.G. Pollock 120*, K.S. McEwan 64)

Richie Kaschula loves his cricket whether batting or bowling.

Rhodesia — 372-8 dec. (G.E. Peckover 93, B.F. Davison 86, B. Dudleston 58, S.D. Robertson 57)
and 62-2 wkts.

Match drawn — Rhodesia 7 and Eastern Province 5 bonus points.

At Salisbury, 11, 12 and 13 November.

Rhodesia — 160 (J.H. du Preez 37*, B. Dudleston 36, B.F. Davison 33; G.S. le Roux 5/29)
and 335-8 dec. (B.F. Davison 100*, B. Dudleston 98, S.D. Robertson 49, J.C. Heron 35)

Western Province — 266 (H.M. Ackerman 83; R.H. Kaschula 3/71)
and 28-0 wkts.

Match drawn — Western Province 7 and Rhodesia 3 bonus points.

At Port Elizabeth, 26, 27 and 28 December.

Eastern Province — 239 (G.S. Cowley 83; R.H. Kaschula 4/44, B. Horton 3/68)
and 330-8 dec. (R.G. Pollock 190*, D.J. Brickett 70; V.R. Hogg 3/52)

Rhodesia — 269 (B. Dudleston 118, J.C. Mitchell 61, S.D. Robertson 30; M.J. Macaulay 5/80)
and 90 (M.J. Macaulay 6/36)

Eastern Province (8 bonus points) won by 210 runs — Rhodesia 9 bonus points.

At Durban, 31 December, 1 and 2 January.

Rhodesia — 159 (B. Dudleston 58; V.A.P. van der Bijl 8/56)
and 168 (B. Dudleston 35, G.E. Peckover 33; A.R. Lilley 5/48)

Natal — 289-8 dec. (H.R. Fotheringham 119; V.R. Hogg 5/89, B. Horton 3/85)
and 35-2 wkts.

Match drawn — Natal 9 and Rhodesia 3 bonus points.

At Cape Town, 27, 28 and 30 January.

Rhodesia — 202 (S.D. Robertson 37, B.F. Davison 36; D.L. Hobson 6/49)
and 259 (T.W. Dunk 78, S.D. Robertson 74, J.C. Mitchell 35; R.E.T. Morris 5/44)

Western Province — 372 (M.J. Nel 86, R.A. Drummond 76; R.H. Kaschula 6/124, B. Horton 3/61)
and 92-2 wkts.

Western Province (8 bonus points) won by 8 wickets — Rhodesia 2 bonus points.

At Johannesburg, 3, 4 and 6 February.

Rhodesia — 340-6 dec. (S.D. Robertson 98, B.F. Davison 82, B.D. Barbour 51*, J.C. Mitchell 38)
and 312-8 dec. (B.F. Davison 91, D.A.G. Fletcher 51, T.W. Dunk 47, G.E. Peckover 35, J.C. Mitchell 34)

Transvaal — 355-7 dec. (D.D. Dyer 111, L.J. Barnard 106, C.E.B. Rice 71; R.H. Kaschula 3/96)
and 171-8 wkts. (N.T. Day 60; B. Horton 3/54)

Match drawn — Transvaal 10 and Rhodesia 7 bonus points.

At Salisbury, 11, 12 and 13 February.

Natal — 292-9 dec. (H.R. Fotheringham 72, A. Barrow 55; R.H. Kaschula 3/86)
and 143 (P.B. Clift 6/36, D.A.G. Fletcher 3/37)

Rhodesia — 239-8 dec. (J.C. Mitchell 59, B.F. Davison 46, G.E. Peckover 30)
and 197-4 wkts. (B.D. Barbour 102*, J.C. Mitchell 43)

Rhodesia (5 bonus points) won by 6 wickets — Natal 5 bonus points.

Kaschula appealed in vain for Graeme Pollock's dismissal because umpire, Willem Stander, was not sympathetic.

At Bulawayo, 4, 5 and 6 March.

Rhodesia — 159 (B. Dudleston 38)
and 277 (B. Dudleston 132, S.D. Robertson 48)

Transvaal — 340 (S.J. Cook 84, A.J. Kourie 84*; D.A.G. Fletcher 4/89, V.R. Hogg 3/70)
and 98-2 wkts.

Transvaal (12 bonus points) won by 8 wickets — Rhodesia 5 bonus points.

SCORES: DATSUN SHIELD, 1977-78.

At East London, 22 October (First Round).
(Rain restricted play to 31-overs-a-side).

Border — 142-7 wkts. (31 overs) (G.W. Nelson 59; B. Horton 4/42)

Rhodesia — 144-2 wkts. (27,2 overs) (J.G. Heron 66, B. Dudleston 54*)

Rhodesia won by 8 wickets.

At Salisbury, 14 January (Semi-final).

Rhodesia — 171-5 dec. (51 overs) (J.C. Mitchell 60, B. Dudleston 36)

Transvaal — 37-0 wkts. (18 overs)

Match abandoned.

At Salisbury, 15 January (Semi-final Replay).

Rhodesia — 72-2 (B. Dudleston 37*) versus Transvaal

Rhodesia won on the drawing of lots.

At Johannesburg, 11 March (Final).

Eastern Province — 227-8 wkts. (60 overs) (D.A.G. Fletcher 3/47)

Rhodesia — 216-5 wkts. (56,2 overs) (B.F. Davison 102*, B.D. Barbour 57*)

Rhodesia won on a better runs/wicket ratio.

Rhodesia B's debut full season in first-class cricket in the Castle Bowl competition was unsuccessful in that the side failed to win any of its matches but the position could so easily have been different. They lost their two matches against Natal B by the narrow margins of 2 runs and 4 runs respectively and might well have won both. They certainly should have won the match at Pinetown if their batsmen had kept their heads as they had had much the better of the match until the final stages.

The B team did give a number of young players the opportunity to experience first-class cricket as well as serving as a recuperation trial for first team players who had been out of form or perhaps had been showing indifferent form. Of those who profited from their matches in the B team, the most impressive were Brian Barbour and Tommy Dunk who were both promoted to the first team where they performed creditably. Peter Wallace, who came into the team straight from obtaining a South African Schools Cap, showed promise and also gained a place in the A Section side whilst Brian Thorn, the regular opening batsman, showed up well in the matches against Transvaal B.

SCORES: Rhodesia B: Castle Bowl competition 1977-78.

At Lenasia, 11, 12 and 14 November.

Rhodesia B — 164 (T.W. Dunk 43; D.S. van der Knaap 5/37)
and 296 (T.W. Dunk 74, B. Thorn 53, R.M. Ervine 33)

Transvaal B — 455-5 dec. (R.V. Jennings 168, C.G. Stephens 150*, M. van Wyk 60*; D.H. Streak 3/113)

Transvaal B (11 bonus points) won by an innings and 5 runs — Rhodesia B, 2 bonus points.

Brian Thorn cuts during his innings of 49 for Rhodesia B in their Castle Bowl match against Transvaal B at the Salisbury Sports Club in 1977-78.

At Bulawayo, 26, 27 and 28 November.

Natal B — 293-1 dec. (M.G. Mathews 145*, K.N. Hosken 122*)
and 199-8 dec. (N.H. Harvey 63; J.C. Mitchell 6/68)

Rhodesia B — 231-8 dec. (B.D. Barbour 86, P.R. Carlstein 50, A.J. Traicos 38; D.K. Pearse 5/29)
and 259 (B.D. Barbour 82, A.J. Traicos 43, J.C. Mitchell 42, T.W. Dunk 34; N.H. Harvey 5/106)

Natal B (6 bonus points) won by 2 runs — Rhodesia B, 3 bonus points.

At Salisbury, 21, 22 and 23 January.

Transvaal B — 352-9 dec. (S.J. Cook 146, C.G. Stephens 63; D.H. Streak 4/81, J.A. Carse 3/89)
and 148-6 dec. (A.J. Traicos 4/50)

Rhodesia B — 213 (P.D. Wallace 49, M.S. Hogge 34, B. Thorn 33; A.J. Kourie 7/68)
and 112-3 wkts. (B. Thorn 49, R.D. Brown 36)

Match drawn — Transvaal B, 7 and Rhodesia B, 4 bonus points.

At Pinetown, 11, 12 and 13 February.

Natal B — 151 (F.B. Hill 62; V.R. Hogg 3/39, J.H. du Preez 3/59)
and 185 (A.A. Hipkin 58; J.H. du Preez 5/75, V.R. Hogg 4/59)

Rhodesia B — 212 (J.G. Heron 59, M.H. Gibb 34, R.D. Brown 30)
and 120 (P.D. Wallace 43, J.H. du Preez 36)

Natal B (4 bonus points) won by 4 runs — Rhodesia B, 6 bonus points.

Rhodesia continued to struggle in 1978-79, a season that provided little for local supporters to enthuse over. It began with the humiliating defeat in the first round of the Datsun Shield to Griqualand West — an unexpected upset for the holders although they had been denuded of their opening attack (Hogg, Clift and Fletcher) just prior to the match. The final score had been tied (both 164 for 8) and Griquas had won on account of their faster scoring rate over the first twenty overs. Team Manager, Ian Davidson, pointed out that the awarding of 4 runs for a wide had cost Rhodesia heavily: 'When you realise that Griquas were given 16 runs in that first twenty overs, and we lost the match by 8 runs on the count-out, their batting total never actually exceeded ours — the runs were just given to them.'

The problems of the Currie Cup season, however, were largely the result of vulnerable batting. But misfortune did hit the team from the outset in that skipper, Stuart Robertson, was unable through injury to play again after the first match. The unusual situation arose of three different captains in the opening three games because Brian Davison took over in the next match before giving way to Jack Heron.

Heron inherited numerous difficulties. The batting successes of the previous season failed to repeat their achievements and a meagre eight bonus batting points were earned. Seven of these points came in two matches and in five of the eight matches not a single point was achieved. Only one century partnership was made throughout the season — 118 for the third wicket by Jack Heron and Brian Davison at Port Elizabeth against Eastern Province.

Jack du Preez topped the batting averages (110 runs — average 55,00) but only played two matches whilst Brian Davison was the leading run scorer (488)

Vince Hogg pictured (*top*) at the Wanderers, Johannesburg, and (*bottom*) in Salisbury, at different stages of his bowling action.

although his average (34,85) dropped by 9 runs an innings from the previous year. Rob Bentley, the most promising cricketer of the new generation scored 205 runs (average 34,15) to finish third with skipper Heron next (405 runs — average 31,16). Barry Dudleston suffered an unfortunate drop in form and made less than half his previous season's aggregate with 331 runs. Paddy Clift did reasonably well in compiling 327 runs but Brian Barbour, apart from a century against Transvaal, struck a frustrating patch and scored a mere 53 runs in eleven innings.

Fortunately the return of Paddy Clift inspired the bowling attack to greater deeds. In four matches the full quota of 5 bowling points was obtained and the total of 34 compared favourably with the 37 achieved by Transvaal who had the best all-round attack in the competition. Clift took 33 wickets at 21,72 runs each and made all the difference in what was at times a makeshift attack.

After drawing their first five matches, Rhodesia then lost badly to Transvaal at the Wanderers before achieving their sole success of the season — beating Eastern Province by 5 wickets at the Police ground. It was a fine team performance by the Rhodesians with Brian Davison (92 not out) dominating the last stage of the match. Providing comic relief, Lorrie Wilmot again staged a mock walk-off two runs from the end, a reminder of the occasion in 1972-73 when he did so in earnest. But such was the delight of the Rhodesian supporters to win this match that when victory came they hoisted Wilmot on to their shoulders and carried him off the field.

Unfortunately the jubilation was short lived because a month later at the same ground the Rhodesians were thrashed by Western Province to the tune of 194 runs. Protective helmets were seen for the first time at the Police ground as the Rhodesians, facing Garth le Roux at his most menacing, were bundled out twice cheaply to end the season on a rather dismal note.

SCORES: Currie Cup A Section, 1978-79.

At Bulawayo, 4, 5 and 6 November.

Natal — 255 (D. Bestall 88; P.B. Clift 4/69, A.J. Traicos 3/55)

Rhodesia — 181 (J.H. du Preez 75*; V.A.P. van der Bijl 5/44)

Match drawn — Natal 7 and Rhodesia 5 bonus points.

At Salisbury, 11, 12 and 13 November.

Rhodesia — 143 (J.G. Heron 63)
and 337-9 wkts. (B.D. Barbour 104, B.F. Davison 48, P.B. Clift 46, A.J. Traicos 37)

Transvaal — 285 (A.J. Kourie 94*, R.G. Pollock 67; A.J. Traicos 4/43, P.W.L. Geach 3/48)

Match drawn — Transvaal 6 and Rhodesia 3 bonus points.

At Port Elizabeth, 9, 11 and 12 December.

Rhodesia — 173 (B.F. Davison 57, J.G. Heron 53, W.K. Watson 5/32)
and 290-9 dec. (B.F. Davison 129, J.G. Heron 47, R.M. Bentley 31*)

Eastern Province — 253 (A.L. Wilmot 62*; D.A.G. Fletcher 4/60, P.B. Clift 3/65)
and 100-5 wkts. (D.A.G. Fletcher 3/33)

Match drawn — Eastern Province 6 and Rhodesia 3 bonus points.

At Pietermaritzburg, 15, 17 and 18 December.

Natal — 301 (C.P. Wilkins 91, B.S. Groves 77; J.C. Mitchell 6/54)
and 158 (D. Bestall 85; C.B. Jonker 4/32)

Rhodesia — 248 (B. Dudleston 59, R.M. Bentley 55*, B.F. Davison 45, P.B. Clift 34; V.A.P. van der Bijl 5/59)
and 75-3 wkts. (B. Dudleston 42)

Match drawn — Natal 10 and Rhodesia 8 bonus points.

At Cape Town, 6, 8 and 9 January.

Western Province — 249 (S.D. Bruce 109*; C.B. Jonker 3/43, P.B. Clift 3/48)
and 254-7 dec. (A.J. Lamb 107, P.N. Kirsten 65)

Rhodesia — 241 (J.C. Mitchell 47*, D.L. Houghton 33)
and 215-7 wkts. (J.G. Heron 122*, P.B. Clift 33)

Match drawn — Western Province 5 and Rhodesia 4 bonus points.

At Johannesburg, 12, 13 and 15 January.

Transvaal — 190 (A.J. Kourie 50; P.B. Clift 5/63, V.R. Hogg 3/49)
and 195-6 dec. (R.G. Pollock 112; V.R. Hogg 3/44)

Rhodesia — 114 (P.B. Clift 49*)
and 112 (B. Dudleston 56, B.F. Davison 34)

Transvaal won by 159 runs.

At Salisbury, 3, 4 and 5 February.

Eastern Province — 275 (V.R. Hogg 3/62, P.B. Clift 3/71)
and 185 (R.J.D. Whyte 58; D.A.G. Fletcher 3/34, B. Dudleston 3/43)

Rhodesia — 270-9 dec. (D.A.G. Fletcher 77, R.M. Bentley 50)
and 191-5 wkts. (B.F. Davison 92*)

Rhodesia (9 bonus points) won by 5 wickets — Eastern Province 9 bonus points.

At Salisbury, 3, 4 and 5 March.

Western Province — 204 (P.N. Kirsten 52; B. Dudleston 3/14, P.B. Clift 3/48)
and 169-5 dec. (S.D. Bruce 51*; P.B. Clift 3/52)

Rhodesia — 115 (B. Dudleston 35)
and 64

Western Province (7 bonus points) won by 194 runs — Rhodesia 5 bonus points.

SCORES: Datsun Shield, 1978-79.

At Kimberley, 28 October (First Round).

Griqualand West — 164-8 wkts. (60 overs) (J.A. Carse 3/33, D.H. Streak 3/42)

Rhodesia — 164-8 wkts. (60 overs) (J.C. Mitchell 41)

Griqualand West won on a faster scoring rate over first 20 overs.

The President's Competition provided an interesting series of matches against the B sides of the A Section provinces but continuity was hindered by the fact that after the first two home matches in November there was a gap of over two months before the southern tour. Such were changes in form that only three players were retained over this period of time. One of these was Eddie Parker who came out of a retirement which had lasted for nine years to captain the side most efficiently. Rhodesia B lost on three occasions but the highlight of the season was the team's first-ever victory when they thrashed Eastern Province B by an innings and 49 runs. The main feature of this annihilation was the batting of Robin Brown and debutant,

An interesting sequence of shots involving Paddy Clift: (*above*) he is well positioned to drive Rupert Hanley; (*below*) he hooks confidently against Eastern Province; and (*on opposite page*) he ducks under a bouncer from Garth le Roux.

Peter Allan. A record fourth-wicket partnership of 300 was achieved by these two — the first time this figure had been attained by a Rhodesian pair in first-class cricket. Brown hit twenty-six fours and a six in just over five hours at the wicket for an unbeaten double century, whilst Allan (138) notably started his first-class career with a six over the long-on boundary. Two other newcomers began their careers with distinction — Billy Houghton had match figures of 9/115 and Rob Bentley, apart from scoring 39 not out had a useful match analysis of 6/88.

SCORES: Rhodesia B (President's Competition), 1978-79.

At Salisbury, 18, 19 and 20 November.

Eastern Province B — 258 (D.H. Howell 110, G.C.G. Fraser 61; W.J. Houghton 4/65, C.B. Jonker 3/71) and 201 (W.J. Houghton 5/50, R.M. Bentley 4/50)

Rhodesia B — 508-4 dec. (R.D. Brown 200*, P.J. Allan 138, T.W. Dunk 55, D.L. Houghton 40, R.M. Bentley 39*)

Rhodesia B (8 bonus points) won by an innings and 49 runs — Eastern Province B, 6 bonus points.

At Bulawayo, 24, 25 and 26 November.

Western Province B — 284 (A.P. Kuiper 95, N.P. Daniels 73; R.M. Bentley 4/80, C.B. Jonker 4/84) and 267-5 dec. (S.D. Bruce 83; C.B. Jonker 3/81)

Rhodesia B — 146 (R.D. Brown 41; E.S. Gordon 5/42) and 254 (D.L. Houghton 72, W.J. Houghton 65)

Western Provincc B (10 bonus points) won by 151 runs — Rhodesia B, 5 bonus points.

At Johannesburg, 3, 5 and 6 February.

Transvaal B — 302-8 dec. (N.T. Day 109, R.W. Adair 50)
and 183-4 dec. (N.E. Wright 72*, R.F. Pienaar 57; G.C. Wallace 3/61)

Rhodesia B — 146 (P.J. Allan 55*; N.V. Radford 5/50) and 222 (E.F. Parker 61, G.C. Wallace 42)

Transvaal B (11 bonus points) won by 117 runs — Rhodesia B, 4 bonus points.

At Pinetown, 8, 9 and 10 February.

Natal B — 291-7 dec. (I.R. Tayfield 86, P.H. Williams 77, T.M. Roberts 50*; I.S. Friend 3/95)
and 218-5 dec. (I.R. Tayfield 70 ; A.J. McCallum 3/108)

Rhodesia B — 198 (P.R. Carlstein 75, A.J. McCallum 33, P.J. Allan 33)
and 274 (G.E. Peckover 71, P.R. Carlstein 67, A.J. McCallum 43, M.A.J. Seager 41)

Natal B (8 bonus points) won by 37 runs — Rhodesia B, 5 bonus points.

The 1979-80 season began with Jackie du Preez's benefit match in September which made him the first Rhodesian player to be honoured in this manner. Two limited overs matches were played during the weekend with the second clash basically matching Du Preez's Rhodesia XI against Mike Procter's South African XI. The result was purely academic but an appreciative crowd of 2 000 saw some glorious hitting and 659 runs were scored in 101 overs against fine bowling and fielding. Paddy Clift, Duncan Fletcher and Chris Wilkins scored centuries while big Vince van der Bijl took the bowling honours. Du Preez himself had a quiet match and it is appropriate to note here that he was to play his last two matches for Rhodesia in the course of the season. These brought his career total to a record 112 appearances — his tallies of 3 988 runs and 277 wickets put him unquestionably into the position of being statistically the country's foremost cricket all-rounder.

The national team's season got under way with a friendly against Border which was later declared to be not first-class. This was a pity in that Richie Kaschula took a hat-trick which was acclaimed at the time as the first ever for Rhodesia. The match was also notable for a century by Tommy Dunk and a fine innings of 73 by the Prince Edward schoolboy, Kevin Arnott.

SCORES: versus Border, 1979-80 (Not first-class).

At Salisbury, 29 and 30 September and 1 November.

Rhodesia — 352-4 dec. (T.W. Dunk 114*, K.J. Arnott 73, J.G. Heron 52, P.J. Allan 36, R.M. Bentley 35*, P.B. Clift 35)
and 210-8 dec. (P.J. Allan 50, D.A.G. Fletcher 50, D.L. Houghton 31)

Border — 173 (R.H. Kaschula 4/28, R.D. Jackman 3/48)
and 157 (R.D. Jackman 5/58, R.H. Kaschula 3/8)

Rhodesia won by 232 runs.

Three weeks later Rhodesia suffered an ignominious Datsun Shield first round defeat at the hands of the Transvaal B side at the Wanderers, Johannesburg. Barry Dudleston and Paddy Clift put together 81 runs for the fifth wicket but received little other support and the Rhodesians went down by a fairly substantial margin.

Fortunately, the Datsun Shield disappointment was quickly shrugged off and Rhodesia won her opening Currie Cup match against Northern Transvaal but it was a close thing. They had to chase 283 runs at a run-a-minute and victory came with just seven balls remaining in rapidly fading light. At different stages of the innings with the scoreboard reading 55-4 and 117-5 the odds were loaded heavily against a Rhodesian victory. However a resolute stand between Robin Brown and Duncan Fletcher of 116 in 110 minutes put them back firmly on the rails and well on their way towards a fine victory.

That remained Rhodesia's sole success. Matches were lost against Transvaal (twice) and against both Western and Eastern Province at home. The remaining fixtures were drawn with Rhodesia finishing on top against Eastern Province at Port Elizabeth and Northern Transvaal at Pretoria.

The end of the season match at Bulawayo against Eastern Province marked the final chapter in Rhodesia's 76-year-old Currie Cup cricket history. Sadly the Rhodesian second innings folded up pathetically which was surprising after a first-innings lead had been established, and the curtain was brought down finally on the Currie Cup association by Lorrie Wilmot belting a towering six off Paddy Clift to win the match for the visitors.

Inevitably there were a number of reasons for Rhodesia's poor record, not least being the security situation, which meant that match preparations were again seriously affected. With military call-ups being heaviest during the election period, Rhodesia's leading cricketers could hardly be blamed for their unavoidable lack of net and centre wicket practice. But there were other factors militating against Rhodesia's Currie Cup hopes.

The Rhodesian side suffered considerably from the loss of Brian Davison who had accepted a contract to captain Tasmania in the Australian Sheffield Shield competition. In his career for Rhodesia spanning the seasons 1967 to 1978, Davison had gained 90 caps, scored 4 480 runs and made a career highest of 137 not out against Griqualand West in 1970-71. By the time of his departure he had scored more runs for Rhodesia than any other cricketer in its history — testimony of his immense contribution to the game in this country.

Smiles all round at the airport from members of the 1979-80 Zimbabwe side: Jack Heron, Ian Davidson (Manager), Andy Pycroft, James Carse, Rob Bentley, Dave Bawden, Richie Kaschula, Graham Clinton and Robin Jackman.

A further blow was dealt to the side's hopes with Stuart Robertson being unable to play more than three matches in the course of the season. As the second most prolific run scorer in Rhodesia's cricket history his experience and talents were understandably severely missed. To add to the side's troubles, Barry Dudleston played in only two matches, injured himself in a shooting accident and then left for England early in the new year in order to prepare for his benefit season.

Robin Jackman returned to Rhodesia having been the third highest wicket-taker in the 1979 English County Championship and began well by taking eight wickets in the opening friendly against Border. However, he bowled a mere 37 overs in the entire Currie Cup season and Rhodesia, tragically, were denied their opportunity of making use of an opening bowler of international stature. The following summer Jackman was flown out to the West Indies by the M.C.C. as a replacement and immediately became embroiled in a political storm but at the same time fittingly crowned his career by gaining selection for England in three Tests.

Andy Pycroft was a welcome addition to the country's cricket ranks, having gained recognition as a member of the South African Schools XI, the South African Universities side and the Western Province B team. As a youngster he had come under the guidance (as did Henry Fotheringham and Rob Bentley) of Bryan Curtis, headmaster of Ruzawi School, and it was in those formative years that Pycroft had scored over 1 000 runs, including 6 centuries, in a junior school cricket year. Unfortunately he was to have an unhappy first season for Rhodesia in the Currie Cup scoring only 111 runs in 10 innings.

Graham Clinton who had arrived in Rhodesia on a contract with the Matabeleland Cricket Association, made an immediate impact in league cricket. He was a very sound opening batsman and had represented Surrey during the 1979 season scoring over 1 000 runs, but unfortunately managed only 138 runs in eight Currie Cup innings.

Perhaps the most interesting local cricketer to emerge during the season was James Carse. Young and athletic, he possessed plenty of enthusiasm and fire but was invariably uncontrolled, struggling throughout the season with his run-up, no-balls and wides. However, he made an impression because he tested the batsmen by his pace and the famed Springbok Neil Adcock, told Glen Byrom that Rhodesians should not '. . . pressurize him with theories of how to bowl more accurately; just let him have his head. I feel sure he will develop into a shock bowler of great value.'

1979-80 had its individual successes but over all the averages reflected the season's struggle to overcome the various problems. Rob Bentley underlined his outstanding potential by scoring 578 runs and topping the batting averages (36,13). He frequently took on the sheet anchor role for the side and it was indeed a pity that he would be lost to Zimbabwe cricket in future years because of the continuation of his studies at Natal University.

For Tommy Dunk the season was memorable in that he was given a regular berth in the side and fully justified his place by finishing second in the averages with 446 runs (average 34,31). After years of uncertainty through being in and out of the Currie Cup team, Dunk's retention for the season gave him increased confidence and his unwavering concentration was an invaluable asset in providing some stability to the brittle batting line-up.

Of the other batsmen, Duncan Fletcher (416 runs — average 27,73) did admirably considering the added responsibilities of the captaincy and his usual bowling load. Karoi farmer Robin Brown (347 runs — average 21,69), began the season well but his performances tailed off whilst there were only the odd supporting innings from Paddy Clift, Jack Heron and Graham Clinton who all averaged under 20 runs for the season.

Rhodesia again lacked a front-line bowler capable of doing major damage and this was reflected by the fact that no bowler took 5 wickets in an innings at any stage of the Currie Cup programme. Richie Kaschula (32), Paddy Clift (29) and Duncan Fletcher (18) did capture a relatively large haul of wickets but were more expensive than they had been in the past. Possibly Robin Jackman summed up the frustrations of this final season when he remarked in *The Herald* 'Go back to the times when Mike Procter was here — no one would complain and we were expected to win. Now the attitude seems to be that it will be a good effort if we don't lose.

'Since then, too, the War has taken its toll with more call-ups. It has been a tremendous problem. I remember in Procter's day that we would always have everyone out at practice. There was more time for preparation. Without making excuses we have not had the time for proper practice and preparation. We are

ROB BENTLEY.

also short of young players because they are invariably lost to national service the moment they leave school. By the time they finish, very often their enthusiasm for cricket has been blunted — they have other things on their minds.

'Had there not been a War it might have been different. It's not just the physical effort. There has also been a mental effect on the players.'

SCORES: Currie Cup A Section, 1979-80.

At Salisbury, 26, 27 and 28 October.

Northern Transvaal — 267 (R.C. Ontong 60, H.W. Raath 51*)
and 239 (B. Dudleston 3/57, R.H. Kaschula 3/74)

Rhodesia — 224 (T.W. Dunk 51, R.D. Brown 38, B. Dudleston 36)
and 283-7 wkts. (R.D. Brown 89, D.A.G. Fletcher 68, R.M. Bentley 30)

Rhodesia (6 bonus points) won by 3 wickets — Northern Transvaal 7 bonus points.

At Bulawayo, 3, 4 and 5 November.

Transvaal — 291-9 dec. (K.A. McKenzie 79, A.J. Kourie 53; R.H. Kaschula 4/74, D.A.G. Fletcher 4/82)
and 209-5 dec. (R.V. Jennings 70, D.D. Dyer 58; P.B. Clift 3/83)

Rhodesia — 226 (R.D. Brown 68, D.L. Houghton 38, T.W. Dunk 35)
and 192 (J.G. Heron 59, D.A.G. Fletcher 39; R.W. Hanley 6/52)

Transvaal (8 bonus points) won by 82 runs — Rhodesia 7 bonus points.

At Johannesburg, 26, 27 and 28 December.

Rhodesia — 121
and 183 (R.M. Bentley 51, D.A.G. Fletcher 36)

Transvaal — 338-7 dec. (H.R. Fotheringham 127, D.D. Dyer 50)

Transvaal (10 bonus points) won by an innings and 34 runs — Rhodesia 4 bonus points.

At Durban, 1, 2 and 3 January.

Natal — 332 (V.A.P. van der Bijl 87, A.J.S. Smith 60; R.D. Jackman 4/62, J.A. Carse 3/77)
and 161-6 dec.

Rhodesia — 234 (R.M. Bentley 79, P.B. Clift 51; M.J. Procter 5/65)
and 198-8 wkts. (R.M. Bentley 74, D.L. Houghton 38*)

Match drawn — Natal 8 and Rhodesia 5 bonus points.

At Salisbury, 26, 27 and 28 January.

Rhodesia — 186 (R.M. Bentley 60, G.S. Clinton 38)
and 177 (R.M. Bentley 34)

Western Province — 330 (L. Seeff 71, A.J. Lamb 54, P.D. Swart 52)
and 34-1 wkt.

Western Province (12 bonus points) won by 9 wickets — Rhodesia 6 bonus points.

At Port Elizabeth, 1, 2 and 4 February.

Rhodesia — 254 (R.M. Bentley 122, D.A.G. Fletcher 79*)
and 206 (T.W. Dunk 40, J.G. Heron 37, D.A.G. Fletcher 36)

Eastern Province — 219 (R.L.S. Armitage 82; P.B. Clift 3/25, R.H. Kaschula 3/55)
and 183-8 wkts. (R.H. Kaschula 3/32)

Match drawn — Rhodesia 8 and Eastern Province 6 bonus points.

At Pretoria, 8, 9 and 11 February.

Rhodesia — 277 (T.W. Dunk 90, D.A.G. Fletcher 54)
and 264 (S.D. Robertson 55*, J.A. Carse 44, T.W. Dunk 43, A.J. Pycroft 32; W.F. Morris 6/105)

Northern Transvaal — 320-7 dec. (A. Jordaan 70, A.M. Ferreira 68, P.D. de Vaal 64; P.B. Clift 3/128)
and 86-8 wkts. (R.H. Kaschula 4/24, P.B. Clift 4/56)

Match drawn — Northern Transvaal 5 and Rhodesia 4 bonus points.

At Bulawayo, 15, 16 and 17 March.

Rhodesia — 261 (T.W. Dunk 98*, D.A.G. Fletcher 41; R.L.S. Armitage 5/71)
and 76 (R.L.S. Armitage 5/25)

Eastern Province — 201 (D.J. Brickett 58*; P.B. Clift 4/75)
and 137-3 wkts. (K.P Reid 52*)

Eastern Province (5 bonus points) won by 7 wickets — Rhodesia 6 bonus points.

Tommy Dunk, the experienced Zimbabwean opening batsman, demonstrates his watertight technique to national colleagues, Jack Heron, Duncan Fletcher and Dave Houghton.

SCORES: Datsun Shield, 1979-80.

At Johannesburg, 20 October (First Round).

Transvaal B — 201-8 wkts. (60 overs) (R.M. Bentley 3/24, P.B.Clift 3/36)

Rhodesia — 159 (55,1 overs) (B. Dudleston 46, P.B. Clift 42)

Transvaal B won by 42 runs.

During the 1979-80 season the B team's programme in the Castle Bowl was increased to six matches. Of these Rhodesia B gained one outright win, lost to Natal B and the Orange Free State outright and drew the remainder. The sole victory came in the last match of the season at Bulawayo and provided a pleasant swan-song for skipper Eddie Parker who scored a match-winning half century. Parker's experience and reliability in the lower order of the batting line-up frequently pulled his team out of trouble and he topped his side's batting averages (416 runs — average 46,22).

A more concerted effort was made than in the past to use the B side as a platform on which to ''blood'' promising youngsters. Four batsmen emerged of note — Gary Wallace (427 runs — average 38,82), Allan McCallum (327 runs — average 36,33), Jannie Meyer (252 runs — average 31,50) and Lawrence de Grandhomme (229 runs — average 32,17). In contrast the bowling proved expensive and revealed little. Vince Hogg, relegated to the B side for the most part of the season, and Cedric Jonker bore the brunt of the attack but worked hard for their wickets. Terry Coughlan began the season well when he so nearly brought about Border's demise with some vicious leg-spin bowling off an awkward length but thereafter he gained few opportunities. Although Coughlan still topped the bowling averages, it was Lawrence de Grandhomme who shouldered the spin bowling department for the remainder of the season.

SCORES: Rhodesia B: Castle Bowl 1979-80.

At Triangle, 17, 18 and 19 November.

Rhodesia B — 259 (E.F. Parker 82, G.E. Peckover 51, M.M. Benkenstein 47)
and 182-7 dec. (G.C. Wallace 47, A.J. McCallum 40, L.L. de Grandhomme 31)

Border — 282 (M. McGill 59, D.C. McKenna 51; L.L. de Grandhomme 3/61)
and 79-9 wkts. (T.D. Coughlan 5/16)

Match drawn — Border 4 and Rhodesia B 4 bonus points.

At Pietermaritzburg, 18, 19 and 20 January.

Rhodesia B — 194 (A.J. McCallum 106*)
and 201 (E.F. Parker 76*, M.M. Benkenstein 44; I.R. Ault 7/52)

Natal B — 282 (D. Turner 69, C.L. Smith, 57; C.B. Jonker 4/55)
and 116-4 wkts. (V.R. Hogg 3/35)

Natal B (10 bonus points) won by 6 wickets — Rhodesia B 5 bonus points.

RHODESIA B, 1979-80.
Back: G. Wallace, A. McCallum, S. Kuhn, J. Meyer, T. Coughlan, L. de Grandhomme, K. Arnott.
Seated: V. Hogg, E. Parker (Captain), C. Wallace (Manager), D. Bawden (Vice-Captain), C. Jonker.

At Port Elizabeth, 22, 23 and 24 January.

Eastern Province B — 357 (T.B. Reid 92, J.W. Stephenson 84; V.R. Hogg 4/98, L.L. de Grandhomme 3/75) and 222-6 dec. (D.H. Howell 74, R.J.D. Whyte 71)

Rhodesia B — 242-7 dec. (J. Meyer 69, D.B.E. Bawden 64, A.J. McCallum 53)
and 227-6 wkts. (L.L. de Grandhomme 57*, E.F. Parker 53*, G.C. Wallace 40)

Match drawn — Eastern Province B 9 and Rhodesia B 6 bonus points.

At Bloemfontein, 26, 28 and 29 January.

Orange Free State 227-8 dec. (A. Lloyd 68, R.A. le Roux 57; L.L. de Grandhomme 3/56)
and 285-4 dec. (R.J. East 108, R.A. le Roux 80*, E. Schmidt 60*; V.R. Hogg 3/109)

Rhodesia B — 225-7 dec. (G.C. Wallace 111, J. Meyer 30)
and 155 (G.C. Wallace 33, D.B.E. Bawden 32)

Orange Free State (2 bonus points) won by 132 runs — Rhodesia B 4 bonus points.

In April 1980, after fourteen years of lonely isolation and seven years of bloody civil war, a new nation, Zimbabwe, emerged with world recognition following independence. This major development ensured that the country's various sports could once again take their places in the international sphere. It also inevitably meant that ties with South Africa were to be cut so the Z.C.U. withdrew from the various South African competitions on the completion of the 1979-80 season. The Currie Cup of course had been the lifeblood of Rhodesian cricket and followers of the sport anxiously awaited the proposed alternatives. They were to be pleasantly surprised by the efforts of the Z.C.U., and in the first cricket season as Zimbabwe, two English counties and a Kenyan national team toured. Public support was for the most part disappointing but fortunately a sponsor was found to underwrite the loss of the first tour. It is a testimony of the Z.C.U.'s determination that they have adopted a policy of positivism and they have continued to be ambitious in their efforts to promote the game.

Robin Brown in determined mood.

At Salisbury, 15, 16 and 17 March.

Rhodesia B — 314 (J.G. Heron 77, L.L. de Grandhomme 60, C.B. Jonker 37, K.J. Arnott 35, E.F. Parker 35)
and 230-5 dec. (G.C. Wallace 79*, J. Meyer 48, E.F. Parker 46)

Transvaal B — 259-5 dec. (N.T. Day 111*, R.F. Pienaar 52)
and 71-1 wkt.

Match drawn — Transvaal B 7 and Rhodesia B 5 bonus points.

At Bulawayo, 22, 23 and 24 March.

Griqualand West — 205 (E.F. Parker 3/32, M. Jarvis 3/49)
and 226 (M.J.D. Doherty 101; V.R. Hogg 4/32, C.B. Jonker 3/36)

Rhodesia B — 209 (J.G. Heron 58, A.J. McCallum 32, V.R. Hogg 30; G.K. Funston 5/46)
and 224-6 wkts. (E.F. Parker 58*, J. Meyer 55, D.L. Houghton 41)

Rhodesia B (5 bonus points) won by 4 wickets — Griqualand West 6 bonus points.

The first side to take advantage of the country's return to legality were the English County and Gillette Cup champions, Middlesex. They were captained by the astute Mike Brearley, who a few months later was to return as captain of England and lead his country to one of the most dramatic Test series triumphs in history. Also in the Middlesex team were three other members of the England side that ultimately retained the Ashes in 1981 in a series that will surely become an unforgettable legend — they were Mike Gatting, Paul Downton and John Emburey. In addition Clive Radley, an experienced England batsman, Mike Selvey, the former England seam bowler and Roland Butcher, who was about to embark on the M.C.C. tour to the West Indies during 1980-81, were all in the Middlesex squad.

It was Mike Selvey who said of Middlesex's opening 38-overs-a-side game against a Zimbabwe XI: 'It's set the tour up'. The result was a tie — Middlesex had initially scored a rapid 237-4 but Duncan Fletcher in scoring a century of great power had put his team into a wonderful position. With one over left the Zimbabwe XI needed only three runs off spinner, John Emburey, to win, but failed at the last hurdle.

JOHN TRAICOS.

The opening first-class match produced some tremendous cricket but with the batsmen very much on top. All the Middlesex top order batsmen made runs in their total of 317-7 declared but Richie Kaschula (5/98) had the satisfaction of having Brearley caught by Lawrence de Grandhomme and of bowling Gatting and Butcher. In reply Zimbabwe batted impressively and overtook the Middlesex score before declaring. Fletcher and Dunk set the Zimbabweans off to a great start with a stand of 103 but it was Robin Brown who took on the lead role with relish. He was in fine form and peppered the field with a varied array of attacking shots, reaching his 50 with a six over mid-wicket off teenage left-arm spinner, Rajesh Maru. So dominant was he that he overtook Dunk in the nineties and reached his century first with a hook to the fence off quick bowler, Simon Hughes.

Middlesex made another big second innings score but with a result not in the offing, the match ended in a comical manner — Zimbabwe declined the rather stiff target that they were set of scoring 272 in 170 minutes and consequently batted out time.

In Umtali, Brearley sent Zimbabwe in to bat on a wicket affected by the overnight rain. Mike Selvey exploited the damp patches to good effect and the early Zimbabwe XI batsmen had a torrid time contending with some lively bowling. Schoolboy Colin Robertson hooked opening bowler Bill Merry for six over backward square leg and Cedric Jonker struck a bold 37 but there was little else to enthuse over in the Zimbabwe XI's miserable total which Middlesex passed without losing a wicket.

Bulawayo saw an enthralling struggle. Two fine innings by Gatting and Selvey propped up the Middlesex innings of 231 against some penetrative bowling by Richie Kaschula. The visitors fought back and Zimbabwe were dismissed for the same score placing the match in an intriguing position. Relying again on their spin attack of Kaschula and Traicos, the Middlesex second innings wickets were gradually whittled away and Zimbabwe were left to score 213 to win. It was a score they duly managed for the loss of six wickets with Jack Heron scoring an invaluable 66 whilst John Emburey toiled admirably on a stifling hot day to take another five wickets.

Middlesex were hardly extended in thrashing a Zimbabwe XI at Gwelo in a 50-overs-a-side fixture before making their way back to Salisbury for the decisive third and final first-class match.

The game was in effect lost by Zimbabwe through their first-innings collapse. Only Rob Bentley was not at sea against Mike Selvey who varied his pace cleverly to record figures of 7/45. Behind by 171 runs on the first innings Zimbabwe were ultimately left with a mammoth fourth innings score of 416 to chase. They made a great fight of it — openers Brown and Fletcher put together 107 before the latter was tragically run out and thereafter Heron and Pycroft kept Zimbabwe in the picture but it was to no avail. Middlesex deservedly came out on top and shared the honours in the three-match series.

SCORES: Middlesex tour, 1980-81.

At Salisbury, 25 September (38-overs-a-side) (Not first-class).

Middlesex — 237-4 (W.N. Slack 84, M.W. Gatting 51)

Zimbabwe XI — 237-4 (D.A.G. Fletcher 108, J.G. Heron 58, R.D. Brown 38)

Tie.

At Salisbury, 27, 28 and 29 September.

Middlesex — 317-7 dec. (W.N. Slack 60, J.M. Brearley 76, M.W. Gatting 63; R.H. Kaschula 5/97).
and 310-8 dec. (M.W. Gatting 79, J.E. Emburey 79*, R.O. Butcher 52; R.H. Kaschula 4/132)

Zimbabwe — 345-4 dec. (R.D. Brown 108, T.W. Dunk 106, D.A.G. Fletcher 46, J.G. Heron 38*)
and 181-6 (A.J. Pycroft 61*, D.A.G. Fletcher 40)

Match drawn.

At Umtali, 1 October (50-overs-a-side) (Not first-class).

Zimbabwe XI — 132 (C.B. Jonker 37)

Middlesex — 133-0 wkts. (J.M. Brearley 77*, P. Downton 53*)

Middlesex won by 10 wickets.

At Bulawayo, 4, 5 and 6 October.

Middlesex — 231 (M.W. Gatting 71, M.W.W. Selvey 67; R.H. Kaschula 6/68)
and 211 (M.W. Gatting 54; R.H. Kaschula 4/99, A.J. Traicos 3/58)

Zimbabwe — 231 (R.D. Brown 39, R.M. Bentley 39, D.A.G. Fletcher 38; J.E. Emburey 5/76)
and 213-6 wkts. (J.G. Heron 66, D.A.G. Fletcher 40, R.M. Bentley 34; J.E. Emburey 5/70)

Zimbabwe won by 4 wickets.

At Gwelo, 8 October (50-overs-a-side) (Not first-class).

Middlesex — 255-6 wkts. (P. Downton 100, C. Radley 71)

Zimbabwe XI — 167-7 wkts. (G. Liddiard 34*, D.A.G. Fletcher 32)

Middlesex won by 88 runs.

At Salisbury, 11, 12 and 13 October.

Middlesex — 289 (M.W. Gatting 99, R.O. Butcher 50; D.A.G. Fletcher 5/48)
and 244 (W.N. Slack 94, I.J. Gould 57; A.J. Traicos 4/62, V.R. Hogg 3/63)

Zimbabwe — 118 (R.M. Bentley 65; M.W.W. Selvey 7/45)
and 333 (R.D. Brown 78, A.J. Pycroft 76, J.G. Heron 53, D.A.G. Fletcher 40; S. Hughes 6/78)

Middlesex won by 82 runs.

Contact was renewed with Kenya on the advent of independence and they made a welcome tour over the New Year period. After the considerable time lapse there was no really accurate barometer against which to measure standards but the Zimbabweans justifiably felt confident. Their Currie Cup background — perhaps the toughest provincial testing ground in the world — and their encouraging performances against Middlesex placed them firm favourites.

Nevertheless, Kenya made a promising start in their opening three-day encounter on a pitch surprisingly unaffected by the heavy rains. They had four Zimbabwean wickets down for 78 before Pycroft, Meyer and Curran dug the side out of trouble. Hitesh Mehta, a member of the 1979 East African World Cup team in England who proved Kenya's mainstay in Zimbabwe, clean bowled both Robin Brown and Jannie Meyer and finished with 4/102. But Zimbabwe's 359-8 declared turned out to be too formidable a task for the visitors to match and the home side helped themselves to a clear-cut ten-wicket victory. It was a fitting start for Zimbabwe in her first international cricket match. Pycroft's century, Curran's highly promising all-round display and Kaschula's bowling were key factors backed up by some superb fielding with De Grandhomme's one-handed catch low down at backward short leg to dismiss Bharat Desai, quite brilliant.

Zimbabwe B had the better of a two-day fixture at Gwelo against the tourists before the second first-class fixture over the ensuing week-end at the Queens ground, Bulawayo. Zimbabwe won this match in no uncertain manner with John Traicos mesmerising the batsmen in the course of his match analysis of 11/83. Enforcing Zimbabwe's domination Robin Brown and Andy Pycroft both scored centuries and batted just over two hours for their partnership of 156. For good measure Richie Kaschula was promoted in the interests of quick runs prior to the declaration and swung mightily at every ball to collect a robust 29. Zimbabwe's 398-7 declared was sufficient to ensure that the match was over a day early with the home side victorious by an innings.

Kenya next ventured several miles outside the capital to the Salisbury South Country Club where plenty of runs were scored and wickets fell with regularity during the space of two entertaining days. There the tourists encountered the Zimbabwe Country Districts XI in a match played in a festival spirit with the new Zimbabwean all-rounder, Kevin Curran, stamping his personality indelibly upon the proceedings. The son of the former Rhodesian batsman and stalwart Country Districts player, Kevin Curran senior, the younger Curran scored a century and took wickets but was unable to inspire a victory as Districts made a valiant but vain second innings effort to score 156 in 13 overs.

Whilst Kenya were a very ordinary side, Zimbabwe B's victory in a three-day affair cannot be entirely ignored. It did illustrate depth of talent even though the home side experienced an alarming middle order collapse during their first innings. The headline in the local Press following the opening day complimented the "(Hough)ton" combination — brothers-in-law Eddie Hough and Dave Houghton took wickets and scored runs respectively to put Zimbabwe B in a good position. Youngsters, Malcolm Jarvis and Gary Scott then took over the protagonist roles to bring about a five-wicket victory.

Finally the Kenyans played a one-day match at the Salisbury Sports Club against the Zimbabwe Schools XI. They won their first match of the tour in extraordinary circumstances. To all but their last pair, Chotai and Opondo, defeat was imminent with the scoreboard showing 110-9 in reply to the Schools XI's

162. Somehow they cut, carved and swept their way to the required victory total leaving the schoolboys that much wiser in their defeat.

SCORES: Kenya tour, 1980-81.

At Salisbury, 26, 27 and 28 December.

Zimbabwe — 359-8 dec. (A.J. Pycroft 115, K. Curran 56*, D.A.G. Fletcher 42, J. Meyer 40, G. Wallace 36) and 23-0 wkts.

Kenya — 160 (V.R. Hogg 4/23, R.H. Kaschula 4/65) and 221 (H. Mehta 56; R.H. Kaschula 4/67, K. Curran 3/42)

Zimbabwe won by 10 wickets.

At Salisbury, 10, 11 and 12 January (Not first-class).

Kenya — 124 (C. Cox 3/20, E.J. Hough 3/30) and 247 (M. Jarvis 7/79)

Zimbabwe B — 182 (D.L. Houghton 48) and 194-5 wkts. (G. Scott 82, M. Seager 45*)

Zimbabwe B won by 5 wickets.

At Salisbury, 14 January (Not first-class).

versus Zimbabwe Schools — see Schools section.

The Leicestershire county side which toured at the end of the season included two guest stars — Jackie Hampshire the Yorkshire captain and former England batsman, and David Steele of Derbyshire, who had made a belated but highly successful entrance into Test cricket during the latter half of the 1970s. The three former Zimbabwean players who had served Leicestershire for a number of seasons — Brian Davison, Paddy Clift and Barry Dudleston — did not accompany them but Tim Boon, who was serving a coaching contract in Zimbabwe, was drafted into the side.

Leicestershire brought with them some typically English weather and the entire first day's cricket (the Saturday) of the opening three-day encounter against Zimbabwe at the Harare Sports Club was washed out. Earlier that day Duncan Fletcher had won the toss, prior to when play was thought possible. With the pitch dry but the outfield wet and the bowlers' run-ups sodden he had elected to bat but fate directed that Zimbabwe should only begin batting on the Sunday. Their innings was a shambles, lasting two hours and a mere 25 overs. The Leicestershire pace attack handled the conditions with aplomb and Zimbabwe's total of 56 was their fourth lowest in history.

Leicestershire also struggled and were all out for 121 which meant that they had a lead of 65. But the

ANDY PYCROFT.

At Gwelo, 31 December and 1 January (Not first-class).

Kenya — 204 (H. Mehta 53; M. Jarvis 5/60) and 71-0 wkts.

Zimbabwe B — 297 (D.L. Houghton 81, G. Scott 57, C. Robertson 46, R. Ervine 43)

Match drawn.

At Bulawayo, 3, 4 and 5 January.

Kenya — 147 (A.J. Traicos 5/33) and 148 (A.J. Traicos 6/50)

Zimbabwe — 398-7 wkts. (R.D. Brown 108, A.J. Pycroft 102, T.W. Dunk 41, D.A.G. Fletcher 41, G. Wallace 31)

Zimbabwe won by an innings and 103 runs.

At Salisbury, 7 and 8 January (Not first-class).

Kenya — 224 (H. Patel 91, S. Patel 58; R. Ervine 4/40, K. Curran 3/38)

and 146-8 dec. (S. Patel 30)

Zimbabwe Country Districts — 215-6 dec. (K. Curran 109, B.H. Oldreive 48) and 95-5 wkts. (K. Curran 30)

Match drawn.

pitch was easing up and Zimbabwe, thanks to the efforts of Andy Pycroft and Gary Wallace, managed to build up sufficient runs to enable Fletcher to offer a reasonable second innings declaration. Set 165 in 102 minutes Leicestershire managed 120-5 by the close of play.

A Zimbabwe XI won a thriller by one run at the Umtali Sports Club and then the tourists made the long haul across country to Bulawayo for their second three-day encounter. The game was unfortunately called off through drizzle and poor light after Zimbabwe had been set 172 runs at seven runs an over on the last afternoon. Bulawayo cricket fans nevertheless saw a feast of good batting over the three days with England batsmen Jack Balderstone, David Steele and Jackie Hampshire scoring half-centuries for Leicestershire and Jack Heron, Duncan Fletcher and Andy Pycroft doing likewise for the home side.

Leicestershire won their first tour fixture three days later when they beat a Zimbabwe XI in a limited overs match at Queens. But their most exciting clash was reserved for the final three-day fixture against Zimbabwe at the Salisbury Sports Club.

On the first day a crowd of 2 000 saw Zimbabwe recover remarkably well after having been 86-5 wickets. Andy Pycroft gave full vent to his talents by scoring an undefeated century and added 148 in an unbroken sixth wicket partnership with Kevin Curran. Zimbabwe declared at 234-5 wickets and did well to dismiss the tourists for 163 — opener, Tim Boon, kept his wicket intact throughout the innings and was left undefeated on 75.

A fine half-century by Robin Brown on the third morning enabled Zimbabwe to set Leicestershire 304 to win in four hours. It was a difficult but not impossible task and the visitors fared admirably to keep up with the required 4,5 runs per over. Pencil-slim Tim Boon (41) continued his good run and set Leicestershire well on the trail with Jack Balderstone (20). The greying and bespectacled David Steele (29), thereafter gave flashes of his ability but it was Jackie Hampshire (112) who took control of the bowling. In an innings of classical, rugged and improvised batting he took Leicestershire to within striking distance of the required target. As the hulking frame of Richie Kaschula moved in to bowl the last over eight runs were required with two wickets in hand. Two runs came off the first two balls, two off the fourth and three off the fifth. Dave Werlock hammered the last ball which Kaschula brilliantly plucked out of the air and Nick Cook was run out. The scores were tied and the match declared a draw.

This fixture brought the season to an end on a particularly high note. Zimbabwe could look back on a very impressive baptism as an independent cricket nation and the season provided a solid foundation for future aspirations. It was also a particularly triumphant one for Andy Pycroft who scored 683 runs (average 68,30) and amply rewarded the selectors for the faith they had placed in him during the previous season. In addition, Robin Brown, 503 runs (average 41,91) and Duncan Fletcher, 466 runs (average 35,84) were heavy run scorers whilst Richie Kaschula (45) and John Traicos (32) were the leading wicket takers.

Zimbabwe seam bowler, "Mac" Dudhia, in action during his first-class debut against Leicestershire. The batsman backing up is Tim Boon who had just completed a coaching contract in Salisbury whilst the umpire is Father Ken Nixon.

SCORES: Leicestershire tour, 1980-81.

At Salisbury, 7, 8 and 9 March.

Zimbabwe — 56.
and 229-9 dec. (A.J. Pycroft 81*, G. Wallace 71)

Leicestershire — 121 (V.R. Hogg 3/23)
and 120-5 wkts. (J.H. Hampshire 51*)

Match drawn.

At Umtali, 11 March (50-overs-a-side) (Not first-class).

Zimbabwe XI — 154 (G. Scott 41, D.A.G. Fletcher 38)

Leicestershire — 153-9 wkts. (D.A.G. Fletcher 4/27)

Zimbabwe XI won by 1 run.

At Bulawayo, 13, 14 and 15 March.

Leicestershire — 209 (J.C. Balderstone 79, D.S. Steele 52; K.M. Curran 4/33)
and 260-5 dec. (J.C. Balderstone 70, N.E. Briers 60*, J.H. Hampshire 58)

Zimbabwe — 298 (J.G. Heron 83, D.A.G. Fletcher 66, A.J. Pycroft 54)
and 54-3 wkts. (R.D. Brown 30*)

Match drawn.

At Bulawayo, 18 March (50 overs-a-side) (Not first-class).

Zimbabwe XI — 152 (J. Brent 30)

Leicestershire — 153-5 wkts. (T. Boon 96*)

Leicestershire won by 5 wickets.

At Salisbury, 20, 21 and 22 March.

Zimbabwe — 234-5 dec. (A.J. Pycroft 104*, K.M. Curran 55*)
and 232-9 dec. (R.D. Brown 61*, D.A.G. Fletcher 49, J.G. Heron 42; J. Agnew 6/70)

Leicestershire — 163 (T. Boon 75*; K.M. Curran 3/26)
and 303-9 wkts. (J.H. Hampshire 112, R.W. Tolchard 54; A.J. Traicos 3/110)

Match drawn with the scores level when stumps were pulled up.

'The Windies are coming' was splashed across local headlines to herald the arrival of a team of exciting young players from the Caribbean. In past years glimpses had been seen in what was formerly Rhodesia of some of the world's greatest cricketers who hailed from the West Indies — Gary Sobers, Wes Hall, Chester Watson, Sonny Ramadhin, Everton Weekes and Rohan Kanhai had all visited at some stage. Now a team that represented the first West Indian side to visit an African country was to undertake a three-week tour of Zimbabwe. Cammie Smith, himself a former Test player, managed the side which he described as 'one of the best possible teams of young players the West Indies could have chosen.'

They included six of the players who had been chosen for the full West Indies tour to Australia — Faoud Bacchus, Jeffrey Dujon, Desmond Haynes, Harold Joseph, Gus Logie and Malcolm Marshall. The Zimbabwe visit was, therefore, of importance to them in their preparations for Test selection and of the remainder, Mr. Smith said that the short tour was '. . . obviously an opportunity for them to shine as they will be competing with senior cricketers for places when they return — and their performances will be considered for any major event'.

The young West Indians certainly lived up to expectations and produced the type of cricket associated with the "islands of calypsos, rum and cricket". They created a tremendous impression, rejuvenating enthusiasm throughout the country and the President of the Z.C.U., Alwyn Pichanick, said at the conclusion of the tour: 'We could not expect better cricket. They have played with the skill and exuberance for which they are renowned. Our players have risen to the occasion.'

The tour began at the Salisbury South Country Club where the West Indies played against the Zimbabwe Country Districts before a crowd of 500. Attention was inevitably focused on the West Indian pacemen and the manner in which the Zimbabweans stood up to the

ZIMBABWE COUNTRY DISTRICTS v. YOUNG WEST INDIES, 1981-82.
Back: K. Curran, A. Waller, G. Paterson, R. Staunton, R. Barker, N. Ervine, D. Dolphin.
Front: M. Seager, R. Ervine, P. Carr (M.C.D. Chairman), B. Oldreive (Captain), P. King (Manager), D. Streak, R. Brown.

anticipated barrage. As it turned out, Robin Brown (23) and Grant Paterson (31) opened well, dealing competently with the flying thunderbolts of openers Hartley Alleyne and Winston Davis. This boded well for Zimbabwe's chances even though the West Indies had little difficulty in notching their first victory.

Zimbabwe's opening first-class performance was somewhat disappointing with regard to the batting collapses which enabled the West Indies to coast to a convincing seven-wicket victory. However, there were some notable individual displays and several players emerged with credit. High on the list was Andy Pycroft who scored a defiant, unbeaten first innings 61 and then snapped up two fine catches, all on the opening day — his effort to get rid of the West Indian captain, Faoud Bacchus, was superb. Another great catch was taken by wicket-keeper David Houghton who dived spectacularly to get rid of the experienced Test batsman, Desmond Haynes, off Kevin Curran.

Houghton was also the batting hero of the Rhodesian second innings. He led a gallant fight-back with Vince Hogg (21) that saw Zimbabwe recover from 110-8 to be 197-9 and then all out for 201. Houghton slammed twelve fours in his 87 and might well have reached his century had he not been struck on the cheek-bone trying to hook a short ball from Wayne Daniel late in his innings — an accident which obviously shocked him and affected his concentration.

The third local player to stand out was John Traicos who took 5/73 in 26 overs and three balls of controlled off-spin and he caused Everton Mattis and Jeffrey Dujon to treat him with the utmost respect as they guided the tourists to 302. In the West Indian second innings the ubiquitous Traicos again came to light when he dived full-length to hold a magnificent one-handed catch at backward point which got rid of Timur Mohamed.

In the one-day matches the West Indies won with little trouble at the Police ground, despite another Pycroft half-century, and then gained a convincing 91-run win over a Zimbabwe XI at Gwelo.

At the Queens ground, Bulawayo, the Zimbabweans did well to dismiss the West Indies for 215 — not one of the visitors was allowed to get into his stride and none of the batsmen reached 30. Particularly effective was Vince Hogg (4/33 in 16,4 overs) who was rapidly becoming a real threat to the top order West Indian batsmen.

In reply, Robin Brown scored a gallant century for Zimbabwe. Dropped four times in his innings, Brown paid his libation to the gods of cricket by riding his luck and guiding his side past the West Indian total.

ZIMBABWE v. YOUNG WEST INDIES, 1981-82.
Back: D. Houghton, H. Alleyne, K. Curran, J. Dujon, A. Pycroft, I. Cadette, G. Paterson, G. Wallace.
Third Row: M. Neita, T. Mohamed, R. Brown, M. Marshall, J. Traicos, E. Mattis, V. Hogg, H. Joseph, L. de Grandhomme, M. Tucker.
Seated: W. Daniel, J. Heron, D. Haynes, D. Fletcher (Zimbabwe Captain), C. Smith (Y.W.I. Manager), J. Mitchell (Zimbabwe Manager), F. Bacchus (Y.W.I. Captain), R. Kaschula.
Front: W. Davis, A. Logie.

Jeffrey Dujon, who impressed as a batsman/wicket-keeper for the Young West Indies, is caught behind by Robin Brown.

Compiling his runs largely through cover drives and square cuts, Brown's five-hour stay at the wicket was admirable in its determination and with Dave Houghton he was associated in a 102-run partnership in even time.

The West Indies took no chances in their second innings and batted out the remaining time. They were not keen to let the game slip particularly after losing the limited overs match the same week-end. With one-day fixtures being held on the Sunday during the three-day encounter the Zimbabweans had surprised the visitors by winning the second clash of the three-match series. It was a splendid achievement, particularly after the West Indies had for the most part looked set for another win. Tommy Dunk, Duncan Fletcher and Gary Wallace made runs to enable the Zimbabweans to reach a satisfactory but far from unassailable total of 227-5. In reply, the West Indies, after being comfortably placed at 140-2, collapsed against an attack well-marshalled by Duncan Fletcher. Wallace and Curran each took two boundary catches to get rid of the first four batsmen, including Desmond Haynes who scored a whirlwind 48. Brown then caught four of the last five batsmen behind the stumps to initiate the final slump as Hogg and Denis Streak with their tails up captured 7 wickets between them for 88 runs.

At Umtali a hat-trick by Timur Mohamed and a century by Desmond Haynes saw the West Indians win easily by 116 runs and then it was back to the Salisbury Sports Club for the final round of first-class and limited overs matches against Zimbabwe.

In the three-day match the tourists established a first innings lead but the Zimbabweans wiped this out as they raced to a big second innings total before declaring. Unfortunately a tame draw resulted because the final target of chasing 236 to win in an hour plus the mandatory 20 overs proved too difficult. The game was called off with the West Indians 116 for 2 and 14 overs to go.

In the limited overs match the tourists made short work of the Zimbabweans to win the one-day series 2-1. Only Vince Hogg came out of the game with his reputation enhanced, beginning his bowling spell with three successive maidens whilst continuously beating the bat in an impressive ten overs. This over all was the worst of the Zimbabwean performances but nevertheless it did not detract from the fact that much had been gained from the tour.

Obviously Zimbabwe could not hope to imitate the carefree West Indian type of game but they learnt quickly and Cammie Smith commented: 'The tour was harder than we thought it would be and the standard was higher than we expected.'

In *The Herald*, Duncan Fletcher stated that he was impressed with his team's performances and singled out Vince Hogg and Andy Pycroft whilst mentioning the invaluable contributions of several other players: 'Once we got over the initial experience of the quick bowling we coped pretty well.

'Vince Hogg did a tremendous job, continuously opening up the West Indian batting and achieving more than his final figures (14 wickets at 18,21) suggest. They didn't like facing him . . .

'Andy Pycroft showed he thinks a lot about the game. He played very well under pressure and

Zimbabwe captain, Duncan Fletcher, has his off-stump uprooted by a Winston Davis "snorter".

continued to attack, never altering his game or closing up. He will improve even more.'

The most important aspect of all, however, was that the West Indies with their flair and belligerence swelled the attendance figures for they were a priceless drawcard. West Indian cricket is so unaffected by modern trends of stifling entertainment with systematic, mechanical play and Duncan Fletcher remarked: 'When they were in trouble they never tried to block it out — they just carried on. With this attacking style I always thought we were either going to annihilate them or they would annihilate us.'

SCORES: West Indies Tour, 1981-82.

At Salisbury, 7 October (40 overs-a-side) (Not first-class).

Zimbabwe Country Districts — 132-6 (G. Paterson 31)

West Indies — 134-3 (E. Mattis 55*)

West Indies won by 7 wickets.

At Salisbury, 9, 10 and 12 October.

Zimbabwe — 163 (A.J. Pycroft 61*)
and 201 (D.L. Houghton 87; M. Tucker 5/50)

West Indies — 302 (E. Mattis 107, J. Dujon 60; A.J. Traicos 5/73)
and 63-6 wkts. (V.R. Hogg 3/23)

West Indies won by 7 wickets.

At Salisbury, 11 October (50-overs-a-side) (Not first-class).

Zimbabwe — 183-6 (A.J. Pycroft 63, G. Paterson 39)

West Indies — 189-7 (F. Bacchus 51)

West Indies won by 3 wickets.

At Gwelo, 14 October (50-overs-a-side) (Not first-class).

West Indies — 270-4 (D. Haynes 89, E. Mattis 78, T. Mohamed 59)

Zimbabwe XI — 179-7 (G.C. Wallace 48, S. Kuhn 35*, J.G. Heron 35)

West Indies won by 91 runs.

At Bulawayo, 16, 17 and 19 October.

West Indies — 215 (V.R. Hogg 4/33, R.H. Kaschula 3/78)
and 318-9 wkts. (M. Marshall 109, D. Haynes 69; R.H. Kaschula 4/115, V.R. Hogg 3/50)

Zimbabwe — 279 (R.D. Brown 102, D.L. Houghton 46, D.A.G. Fletcher 35, A.J. Pycroft 30)

Match drawn.

At Bulawayo, 18 October (50-overs-a-side) (Not first-class).

Zimbabwe — 227-5 (D.A.G. Fletcher 54, J.G. Heron 44, G.C. Wallace 40*, T.W. Dunk 33)

West Indies — 174 (D.H. Streak 4/45, V.R. Hogg 3/43)

Zimbabwe won by 53 runs.

At Umtali, 21 October (50-overs-a-side) (Not first-class).

West Indies — 283 (D. Haynes 122; M. Jarvis 3/40, K.M. Curran 3/56)

Zimbabwe XI — 165 (G. Scott 44, J. Meyer 31, A.J. Pycroft 30)

West Indies won by 118 runs.

At Salisbury, 23, 24 and 26 October.

Zimbabwe — 194 (A.J. Pycroft 94*)
and 255-5 dec. (A.J. Pycroft 59, D.L. Houghton 45, G. Paterson 43*, G.C. Wallace 35*)

West Indies — 214 (T. Mohamed 59; V.R. Hogg 3/68)
and 116-2 wkts. (T. Mohamed 54)

Match drawn.

At Salisbury, 25 October (50-overs-a-side) (Not first-class).

West Indies — 231-7 (G. Logie 73)

Zimbabwe — 105

West Indies won by 126 runs.

The Pakistan International Airlines side which arrived at the end of the season was managed by Hanif Mohammad, the legendary Pakistan batsman who had visited Rhodesia with the Commonwealth XI in 1961-62. Hanif's equally famous brother Mushtaq, captained the strong P.I.A. team and was undoubtedly the tour's big drawcard. A player of vast experience, Mushtaq made his first-class debut at 13 years 41 days and then became the youngest-ever Test cricketer when he represented Pakistan against the West Indies in the Third Test at Lahore in March 1959, at the tender age of 15 years 124 days. Less than two years later he became the youngest century-maker in Test cricket, scoring 101 against India at Delhi.

Three other Test players were named in the Pakistan touring side. The most interesting of these was Aftab Baloch who was the second youngest Test player in history — 16 years 191 days — when he made his debut against New Zealand in 1969-70. Baloch again made the record books during the 1973-74 season when he became only the seventh player to pass the 400-run mark in an innings, scoring 428 for Sind against Baluchistan. The other two Test players in the touring party were Ghulam Abbas, who represented Pakistan against England in 1967, and opening bowler, Liaqat Ali, who made his debut against the West Indies in 1974.

Aftab Baloch captained the tourists in their opening limited overs match against a well-balanced Zimbabwe Country Districts side at the Salisbury South Country Club. Zimbabwe's farming community could certainly put together a formidable combination spearheaded

Desmond Haynes awaits the outcome of a jubilant appeal by Vince Hogg, Duncan Fletcher, Richie Kaschula and Robin Brown as umpire, Kantilal Kanjee, sums up the situation.

by past and present national players Brian Oldreive, Robin Brown, Grant Paterson, Iain Butchart and Denis Streak. To back them up were the varied talents of Rory Ervine, Roger Staunton, Mike Seager, Dave Dolphin and the Waller cousins — the fact that the Districts scored a fine 32-run victory after a day of absorbing cricket was not altogether surprising. Nevertheless, the Pakistanis gave warning that they would be a difficult side to dismiss once acquainted with local conditions whilst Mushtaq Mohammad's arrival would obviously strengthen the team considerably and provide it with the necessary direction.

absence Baloch resumed the captaincy at the Umtali Sports Club where local batsman, Greg Langlois, was the hero in helping a Zimbabwe Select XI force an enthralling tie against the visitors.

Two limited overs matches were played at Bulawayo instead of the usual first-class match and these produced a feast of runs. In the first, Craig Hodgson, batting as a "makeshift" opener, gave Zimbabwe a fine start with a swashbuckling 52, and with Robin Brown, Andy Pycroft, Ali Shah and Gary Scott providing useful support the home side won by three wickets. The following day the scoring was fast and

Sharp fielding by Duncan Fletcher as Mushtaq Mohammad, the veteran Pakistani star, turns a ball to leg — wicket-keeper, Robin Brown, looks on.

Mushtaq's immense batting skills were brought to the fore at the Salisbury Sports Club ground during the opening three-day and one-day encounters with Zimbabwe. Although internationally acclaimed as a free scoring stroke-maker, Mushtaq subordinated his attacking propensities for the most part in order to restore the balance and lay the vital foundations for his team's innings on two memorable occasions. In the three-day game he compiled a masterful century to enable Pakistan to claw their way back into the contest and ultimately earn a draw with the honours even. And then in the limited overs fixture he virtually secured victory for the tourists single-handed with a superb 95 not out. Displaying a tremendous array of shots, Mushtaq was rarely in trouble and caused gasps of amazement with his unique "reverse sweeps" struck through the slips area.

Shortly after the team had moved on to Umtali, Mushtaq was unfortunately forced to fly home to England on account of his wife's illness. This resulted in him missing three one-day fixtures before he returned to Zimbabwe the following week. In his

furious and over 500 runs were amassed in the course of the two 50-over innings. Robin Brown and Andy Pycroft made half-centuries for Zimbabwe and Ghulam Abbas for the P.I.A. side, but bad light prevented an outright decision with the visitors needing 37 runs from the remaining three overs.

Mushtaq Mohammad flew back to Salisbury in time to catch the flight to Triangle for another limited overs fixture. Once again the veteran Pakistani stamped his personality indelibly on the proceedings — this time as the master tactician. All out for 178, the visitors were in dire trouble but tight bowling and astute field placing saw the Zimbabwe Select XI crumble from 94-3 to 140 all out in their 45th over. It was a fine win for the tourists with Mushtaq deservedly being named "man of the match" and Shahid Mohammad (59) and Liaqat Ali (3/14) taking the batting and bowling prizes respectively.

The stage was set for some great cricket at the Salisbury Sports Club in the final first-class and one-day matches. And cricket enthusiasts were to be well rewarded for their support because Zimbabwe rose to the occasion and gave two five-star performances. In the three-day match the Zimbabweans bowled and batted superbly to register an overwhelming victory by an innings and 45 runs. It was a tremendous morale booster with the overseas tour looming up in front of them and there were a number of pleasing individual performances. The in-form batsmen, Dave Houghton and Andy Pycroft, continued their devastating run-making mood whilst Craig Hodgson smashed five sixes and seven fours in a powerful 87, adding 160 for the fifth wicket with Pycroft. Equally encouraging was the pace and seam attack of Vince Hogg, Eddie Hough and Duncan Fletcher which remained in firm control throughout. They displayed admirable stamina, perseverance and competitiveness without ever resorting to a quick bowler's moments of theatrical gesture or self-conscious by-play. Hough certainly grabbed his chances with both hands and several fine performances against the Pakistanis included clean bowling Mushtaq for 9 with a disconcerting delivery in the second innings of the opening first-class match.

The one-day match contained all the ingredients of a thrilling contest only to be dashed by an unexpected rain storm in the latter part of the afternoon. At that moment the Pakistanis were 200-6 in their 37th over chasing Zimbabwe's 272-6. "Man of the match" was undoubtedly Duncan Fletcher (95 and 3/33) but there were other sterling batting performances from Mushtaq Mohammad, Asif Mohammad, Craig Hodgson, Andy Pycroft and Kevin Curran. Curran's spectacular lofted drive high into the pine trees bordering the North Avenue stands was perhaps the highlight of a day that saw some big but always calculated hitting.

SCORES: Pakistan International Airlines Tour, 1981-82.

At Salisbury, 21 March.

Zimbabwe Country Districts — 250-8 (50 overs) (G. Paterson 60, I. Butchart 55, B. Oldreive 34, M. Seager 34)

P.I.A. — 218 (47 overs) (Asif Mohammad 54; M. Seager 5/56)

Zimbabwe Country Districts won by 32 runs.

At Salisbury, 19, 20 and 22 March.

Zimbabwe — 299 (A.J. Pycroft 71, D.L. Houghton 62, D.A.G. Fletcher 56)
and 193-4 dec. (A.J. Pycroft 42*, J.G. Heron 41, D.A.G. Fletcher 39*, D.L. Houghton 36)

P.I.A. — 246-9 dec. (Mushtaq Mohammad 101; V.R. Hogg 3/50)
and 163-4 wkts. (Asif Mohammad 100*; E.J. Hough 3/51)

Match drawn.

At Umtali, 24 March.

P.I.A. — 200 (Naeem Ahmed 74, Ghulam Abbas 58; G.C. Wallace 4/14)

Zimbabwe Select XI — 200 (G. Langlois 42, K.M. Curran 31)

Tie.

At Bulawayo, 27 March.

P.I.A. — 205 (47,5 overs) (Hasan Jamil 65; D.A.G. Fletcher 3/30, K.M. Curran 3/34)

Zimbabwe — 208-7 (46,4 overs) (C. Hodgson 52, R.D. Brown 42, A.J. Pycroft 31)

Zimbabwe won by 3 wickets.

At Bulawayo, 28 March.

Zimbabwe — 275-8 (50 overs) (A.J. Pycroft 66, R.D. Brown 63, I. Butchart 41)

P.I.A. — 239-8 (46,1 overs) (Ghulam Abbas 77; V.R. Hogg 3/33)

Match drawn.

At Triangle, 31 March.

P.I.A. — 178 (49,5 overs) (Shahid Mohammed 59; P. Rawson 3/31)

Zimbabwe Select XI — 140 (44 overs) (J.G. Heron 38)

P.I.A. won by 38 runs.

At Salisbury, 2, 3 and 5 April.

P.I.A. — 159 (Mushtaq Mohammad 46; D.A.G. Fletcher 3/28)
and 195 (Aquil Memon 55; E.J. Hough 4/48)

Zimbabwe — 399-7 dec. (A.J. Pycroft 133, C. Hodgson 87, D.L. Houghton 83, J.G. Heron 43)

Zimbabwe won by an innings and 45 runs.

At Salisbury, 4 April.

Zimbabwe — 272-6 (50 overs) (D.A.G. Fletcher 95, C. Hodgson 59, A.J. Pycroft 42, K.M. Curran 38*)

P.I.A. — 200-6 (37 overs) (Mushtaq Mohammad 59; D.A.G. Fletcher 3/33)

Match drawn.

At a cocktail party held in honour of the Pakistani tourists after their final match at the Salisbury Sports Club, the Zimbabwe squad to tour England was named. It consisted of:

D.A. Ellman-Brown — Manager
L.N. Watson — Assistant Manager
D.A.G. Fletcher — Captain
A.J. Traicos — Vice-Captain
J.G. Heron — Member of Tour Committee

R.D. Brown	E.J. Hough
I.P. Butchart	D.L. Houghton
K.M. Curran	A.J. Pycroft
M.H.E.M. Dudhia	P.W.E. Rawson
C.A.T. Hodgson	G.M. Scott
V.R. Hogg	G.C. Wallace

Non-travelling reserves:
L. de Grandhomme, G. Paterson and A. Shah.

Mr. David Ellman-Brown, the tour manager reports that the tour by a fully representative Zimbabwean team was the first encounter by our cricketers outside Africa. Following the break with South Africa and our subsequent acceptance as an Associate Member of the International Cricket Conference in July 1980, Zimbabwe became eligible to participate in the Associate Members World Cup. This is held prior to the Prudential World Cup with the first competition being held in 1979. The competition was the brain-child of John R. Gardiner who designed and presented the magnificent trophy. Based in the West Midlands of England with the headquarters at St. John's Hotel, Solihull, the 1982 tournaments started with friendly fixtures on 2 June and ended with the final at the County ground, Grace Road, Leicester on 10 July.

The only teams not to participate were Argentina who were forced to withdraw as a result of the Falklands crisis and Denmark who declined to accept the invitation. The competition was run on a league

ZIMBABWE TOURING SIDE, 1982.
Back: D. Houghton, C. Hodgson, I. Butchart, G. Scott, E. Hough, P. Rawson, M. Dudhia, K. Curran, G. Wallace.
Seated: A. Pycroft, J. Heron, D. Ellman-Brown (Manager), D. Fletcher (Captain), A. Pichanick (President Z.C.U.), J. Traicos (Vice-Captain), L.. Watson (Manager), R. Brown, V. Hogg.

and knockout basis with the teams being divided into two groups for the preliminary matches with the top two teams in each section participating in the semi-finals and final which were played on a knockout basis.

The Board of Control of the Zimbabwe Cricket Union very wisely decided that the team should arrive in England early and play four matches against County sides to enable them to become acclimatized to the English conditions. They left Harare on 28 May.

The tour started on 2 June with a three-day match against Worcestershire at the delightful County ground with the picturesque setting of the Cathedral in the background. Rain interfered considerably with the game which resulted in a draw. The wicket turned out to be flat and slow but nevertheless the players proved their worth on a wicket which had been affected by heavy rain the previous day.

SCORES: versus Worcestershire.

At the County ground, Worcester, 2, 3 and 4 June.

Worcestershire — 222-9 dec. (Younis Ahmed 63, M.J. Weston 63; A.J. Traicos 5/56)
and 181-7 dec. (Younis Ahmed 75*; P.W. Rawson 5/42)

Zimbabwe — 156-3 dec. (A.J. Pycroft 62*, D.A.G. Fletcher 56*)
and 52-2 wkts.

Match drawn.

The next match was against Leicestershire at the County ground, Grace Road, Leicester. This was a three-day match and the Leicester side was captained by the England player David Gower and included home-grown Zimbabweans Brian Davison and Paddy Clift.

Again rain interfered with the game which ended in a draw very much in favour of Zimbabwe. Leicestershire found themselves with 78 runs for 5 wickets in their second innings chasing 251 runs when bad light stopped play on the third day. Our players again used the match to acquaint themselves with the English conditions. Traicos had the distinction of capturing the prize wicket of David Gower in both innings with a magnificent caught and bowled in the second innings off the first ball Gower faced.

The tour selectors decided to give all the players two matches against the County sides which resulted in balanced sides being selected for each game rather than the strongest team being selected for any particular match.

SCORES: versus Leicestershire.

At Grace Road, Leicester, 5, 7 and 8 June.

Zimbabwe — 249-9 dec. (I.P. Butchart 54, R.D. Brown 51, C.A.T. Hodgson 47, G.C. Wallace 34)
and 286-9 dec. (J.G. Heron 83, A.J. Pycroft 50, G.C. Wallace 43, C.A.T. Hodgson 33)

Leicestershire — 284-7 dec. (J.F. Steele 64, R.F. Cobb 64; A.J. Traicos 3/71)
and 78-5 wkts. (A.J. Traicos 3/5)

Match drawn.

Trent Bridge was the venue for the one-day game against Nottinghamshire on 9 June and again rain delayed the start. Eventually at 12.50 p.m. a 44-over match was started. Clive Rice showed our players how limited overs cricket should be played when Duncan Fletcher won the toss and put Nottinghamshire in to bat. Rice scored a hard-hitting 60 in 57 minutes and helped Nottinghamshire score 218 runs for 3 wickets off 44 overs at an average of 4,95 runs per over.

Zimbabwe batted badly and were all out for 142 runs with only Pycroft scoring 41 and Curran 23 runs in a 52-run partnership showing any application.

Zimbabwe could have performed better had they held vital catches, but in the end analysis the 1981 County Champions had given Zimbabwe an invaluable lesson in how to play one-day cricket.

SCORES: versus Nottinghamshire.

At Trent Bridge, Nottingham, 9 June.

Nottinghamshire — 218-3 (C.E.B. Rice 60, J.D. Birch 58*)

Zimbabwe — 142 (A.J. Pycroft 41)

Nottinghamshire won by 76 runs.

John Traicos in action against Bangladesh.

The final County match prior to the ICC Trophy competition was against Yorkshire at Abbeydale Park, Sheffield. Yorkshire was captained by Ray Illingworth who subsequently took over the captaincy for the remainder of the season and Geoff Boycott was included in the side.

Zimbabwe batted first and scored 202 all out in 56,3 overs. The lower order batting failed and Zimbabwe slumped from 172 for 4 to 202 all out. The top order batsmen all made runs with the exception of Brown, whilst Duncan Fletcher batted well to score 53.

Yorkshire batted very slowly due mainly to Boycott who struggled to 50 in 42 overs. Eventually Yorkshire passed the Zimbabwe tally with 7 wickets down and 3 balls to spare with Duncan Fletcher taking 2 wickets for 30 runs in 10,3 overs.

The Zimbabweans had a good match and made many friends with their aggressive brand of cricket which kept Yorkshire tied down to the last over.

SCORES: versus Yorkshire.

At Abbeydale Park, Sheffield, 10 June.

Zimbabwe — 202 (D.A.G. Fletcher 53, K.M. Curran 33)

Yorkshire — 203-7 (G. Boycott 98*)

Yorkshire won by 3 wickets.

In all the County matches the standard of fielding produced by the Zimbabwean side was of the highest order and favourable comment was received in this regard from the English Press. The many hours of training prior to the tour were reaping its rewards.

ICC TROPHY TOURNAMENT MATCHES

The competition involved 60 trophy matches and some 165 friendly matches against clubs. Only Bangladesh and Zimbabwe had planned warm-up matches prior to the competition and whilst Bangladesh played against weak club sides Zimbabwe had played two three-day matches and two one-day matches against County sides including Leicestershire who were eventually to finish second to Middlesex in the Schweppes County Championships.

The tournament was split into two groups with pre-tournament favourites Zimbabwe in Group 1 and close rivals Bermuda in Group 2.

The composition of the two groups was as follows:

GROUP 1	GROUP 2
Gibraltar	East Africa
Zimbabwe	Fiji
Hong Kong	Bermuda
Kenya	Malaysia
Papua New Guinea	West Africa
Israel	Holland
USA	Bangladesh
Canada	Singapore

Rain interfered with the preliminary matches and at one stage threatened to disrupt the entire competition. Zimbabwe were extremely lucky in having only two matches washed out — against Canada and Gibraltar. Other sides were not so lucky with West Africa losing five matches to the weather, Singapore, Gibraltar and United States each losing four matches whilst Canada, Holland, Fiji, East Africa and Malaysia each lost three matches.

Not all matches were played on the same day and no

provision was made for the matches to be played on alternative days. When it is considered that the preliminary rounds consisted of seven matches, to have five matches washed out by rain gives a team no chance of qualifying for the semi-finals.

It became very apparent early in the competition that Zimbabwe's main opposition would be Bermuda with a threat from Canada and Bangladesh. As it turned out, Zimbabwe won Group 1 with five victories and two matches washed out with an average run rate

The final log for the preliminary matches was as follows:

	WON	LOST	NO RESULT	POINTS	TOTAL RUNS	TOTAL OVERS	SCORING RATE
GROUP 1							
Zimbabwe	5	0	2	24	882	159,8	5,50
Papua New Guinea	4	2	1	18	828	214,5	3,85
Canada	3	1	3	18	475	119,1	3,98
Kenya	3	2	2	16	668	198,4	3,35
Hong Kong	2	3	2	12	735	242,3	3,03
USA	1	2	4	8	394	109	3,61
Gibraltar	0	3	4	8	264	110,9	2,38
Israel	0	5	2	4	473	180,1	2,62
GROUP 2							
Bermuda	6	0	1	26	1 179	225,5	5,22
Bangladesh	4	1	2	20	745	231	3,22
Holland	3	1	3	18	865	240	3,60
Singapore	1	2	4	12	449	149,4	3,00
Fiji	1	3	3	10	532	147,5	3,59
East Africa	1	3	3	10	639	226,2	2,82
West Africa	0	2	5	10	170	60	2,83
Malaysia	0	4	3	6	489	163	2,98

David Houghton, three times nominated "man of the match", in action against U S A at Mosely Cricket Club ground.

of 5,50 runs per over. Bermuda won Group 2 with six victories and one match washed out with an average run rate of 5,22 runs per over. The overall run rate was important as the rules provided for an eventual winner in the semi-finals or final being decided on the higher run rate if a result could not be obtained due to adverse weather conditions.

The tournament provided for "man of the match" at each game and Zimbabwe collected six such awards. Dave Houghton collected three awards: against USA for scoring 135 runs, against Kenya for scoring 71 runs and against Israel for scoring 43 runs out of a total of 66 for 1 wicket. Andy Pycroft collected two awards: against Hong Kong for scoring 83 not out and against Bermuda for scoring 82. Kevin Curran collected one award in the semi-final against Bangladesh for scoring 44 runs, taking 4 wickets for 31 runs in 12 overs and for a magnificent run out.

Zimbabwe started the ICC Trophy campaign in sensational fashion by thrashing the United States by 191 runs in a 60-over match. Opening batsman David Houghton, struggling to find form on tour, found it in no uncertain manner as he slammed a six and nine fours in a brilliant 135 to collect the "man of the match" award. Hot on his heels was Harare Sports Club all-rounder Kevin Curran with a fine 126 not out batting at No. 3, hitting two sixes and eleven fours in his mammoth 213-run partnership with Houghton which set Zimbabwe on their way to a huge 332 for 4. Peter Rawson, generating tremendous pace and lift off the wicket, snapped up four wickets for 34 runs in 11,5 overs as the United States tumbled to 141 all out in 37,5 overs.

The US captain Kahn won the toss and put Zimbabwe in to bat on a perfect wicket prepared by former Bulawayo Queens groundsman Steve Rouse, who knew just what the side from Africa wanted.

Zimbabwe lost Jack Heron — run out for 18 in the

12th over — with the total on 38 through a fine throw and direct hit on the stumps from square leg fielder Lashkari.

Houghton was joined by Curran and they set about the American bowling which, in fact, included an excellent accurate spell by Durami of 0 wickets for 25 runs in 12 overs.

However, the remaining bowlers suffered at the hands of the two young Zimbabweans who kept up a brisk pace which accelerated as the innings wore on. The Zimbabwe total stood at a solid 164-1 after 40 overs but at the end of the 60 overs an additional 168 runs had been added at a run rate of 8,4 runs per over.

SCORES: versus USA.

At Mosley, 16 June.

Zimbabwe — 332-4 (D.L. Houghton 135, K.M. Curran 126*)

USA — 141 (P.W. Rawson 4/34)

Zimbabwe won by 191 runs.

Against Kenya, opening batsman David Houghton spearheaded a mighty onslaught on their bowlers to see Zimbabwe trounce them by 121 runs in a rain-shortened match.

Houghton collected his second successive "man of the match" award for flaying the Kenya attack for a scintillating 71 runs.

Opening partner Jack Heron continued his run of good form to score a sound 50 in an opening partnership of 92 in 14 overs to set Zimbabwe on their way to 192-4 in 25 overs.

The match was reduced to 25 overs because of rain for most of the day and the start was delayed until 3.35 p.m. with Zimbabwe being put in to bat first by the Kenyan captain who won the toss.

In almost impossible conditions the Zimbabwean opening pair took advantage of the Kenyans' inability to hold the slippery ball and scored at a cracking pace, running up 72 in the first 10 overs and 152 by the end of the 20th over.

After the 92-run opening stand Zimbabwe lost three quick wickets with Duncan Fletcher and Andy Pycroft falling on 120 and Houghton eventually departing at 163.

Middle-order men Kevin Curran and Craig Hodgson made merry for a brief spell to run up to 192 in 25 overs with Curran finishing on 27 not out and Hodgson 23 not out.

Kenya never attempted the scoring rate, hoping for more rain, and once the inevitable Traicos had made the breakthrough it was a back-to-the-wall battle for the Kenyans who were pinned down by accurate bowling and superb fielding.

Kenya bowled their 25 overs at a very disappointing rate of 13,64 overs per hour whilst Zimbabwe bowled at 24,19 overs per hour in their endeavour to beat the rain. This was a well deserved victory in very difficult conditions against negative opponents who did everything to try to ensure that there would be no result.

SCORES: versus Kenya.

At Wolverhampton, 18 June (25-overs-a-side).

Zimbabwe — 192-4 (D.L. Houghton 71, J.G. Heron 50)

Kenya — 71-4.

Zimbabwe won by 121 runs.

SCORES: versus Gibraltar.

at Brewood, 21 June.

Match abandoned without a ball being bowled.

SCORES: versus Canada.

At Leamington, 25 June.

Canada — 9-0 (9 overs)

Match abandoned owing to rain.

While Zimbabwe lost only two matches to the weather it was evident that inadequate covers were used to protect the wickets. In fact at Brewood no covers were used at all with the exception of the batting creases.

Future management of this competition should arrange for better covers and provision for playing the match on a second day. With sixteen countries participating in the largest cricket competition of its kind in the world and with high costs involved of getting the teams to England, it is imperative that the weather does not dictate the outcome of the competition and its eventual winner who is then eligible to participate in the World Cup with the seven Test-playing countries.

In the match against Israel, opening batsman David Houghton set an ICC record when for the third successive occasion he was named "man of the match". Houghton was in devastating form with the bat as Zimbabwe routed their opponents who won the toss and decided to bat and were bowled out for 65 runs in 33 overs with only Perlman reaching double figures.

Bowlers shared the honours, with "Mac" Dudhia taking 2/4, Peter Rawson 3/22, John Traicos 4/22 and Vince Hogg 1/12.

It took Zimbabwe seven overs and two balls to pass the Israeli tally with Houghton slamming three sixes and four boundaries in a hurricane 43. Heron batted quietly with an injured shoulder for an undefeated 12 and all-rounder Kevin Curran slammed a huge six into the local steelworks from the only ball he faced to complete the slaughter.

Houghton added two catches and two stumpings — one, a brilliant effort off the lively seamers of Dudhia — to make his mark on the match.

SCORES: versus Israel.

At Bloxwich, 28 June.

Israel — 65 (A.J. Traicos 4/22, P.W. Rawson 3/22)

Zimbabwe — 66-1 (D.L. Houghton 43)

Zimbabwe won by 9 wickets.

Zimbabwe moved on in their relentless hunt for the ICC Trophy with another emphatic victory against Papua New Guinea who were at this stage of the competition lying second in the log, only two points behind Zimbabwe.

High-riding Papua New Guinea had just beaten the rated Canadian side, thanks to a swashbuckling 100 by No. 7 batsman Vavine Pala.

Zimbabwe were naturally apprehensive about this game and Duncan Fletcher having won the toss put Papua in to bat.

A large crowd saw Papua lose their first wicket to Vince Hogg's second ball. Papua never really recovered thereafter and were all out for 94 in 32 overs with only Vavine Pala scoring a quick 21 and opener Agonia a painstaking and laborious 31 to be last man out.

Hogg took two wickets for 19 but it was the

devastating combination of spinner John Traicos 3/16 and speedy Peter Rawson 3/24 that destroyed their chances.

Eleven without loss at lunch, Zimbabwe found the wicket decidedly lively after the lunch break, and Heron, after being hit on the cheek by a lifter, was bowled for 18. After that David Houghton shone again with a brisk 44 not out, and Curran, hitting five fours in an undefeated 30, batted brilliantly on the lively wicket to take the score to 96 for victory in the 20th over.

SCORES: versus Papua New Guinea.

At Wombourne, 30 June.

Papua New Guinea — 94 (A.J. Traicos 3/16, P.W. Rawson 3/24)

Zimbabwe — 96-1 (D.L. Houghton 44*, K.M. Curran 30*)

Zimbabwe won by 9 wickets.

Zimbabwe qualified for a place in the semi-final against Bangladesh with a victory against Hong Kong at Bewdley Cricket Club on that most attractive ground which borders the Severn River. Zimbabwe won by seven wickets thanks to a fine undefeated 83 by Andy Pycroft who was awarded the "man of the match" award.

The Zimbabweans were made to work for victory for the first time in the competition with Hong Kong scoring 192 for 4 off their 60 overs.

Zimbabwe started their innings slowly, losing David Houghton, run out for 6 and Kevin Curran for 18, and at tea the score was 52 for 2 after 25 overs. Jack Heron scored a patient 51 and it was left to Andy Pycroft and Duncan Fletcher to see Zimbabwe to victory with Pycroft scoring a brilliant 83 not out and Fletcher 33 not out.

Peter Rawson, who helped destroy Papua New Guinea's chances.

Andy Pycroft, declared "man of the match" against Hong Kong.

SCORES: versus Hong Kong.

At Bewdley, 5 July.

Hong Kong — 192-4 (A. Lorimer 72*; V.R. Hogg 3/34)

Zimbabwe — 196-3 (A.J. Pycroft 83*, J.G. Heron 51, D.A.G. Fletcher 33*)

Zimbabwe won by 7 wickets.

Zimbabwe earned their place in the final of the International Cricket Conference Trophy competition by defeating Bangladesh at West Bromwich Dartmouth Cricket Club by 8 wickets.

Bangladesh were dismissed for 124 having been asked to bat, and Zimbabwe passed their total for the loss of only 2 wickets.

The Bangladesh batsmen had no answer to the accurate Zimbabwe attack led by Kevin Curran.

After the openers Vince Hogg and Eddie Hough had brushed aside the top order, Curran's lively seamers tore the heart out of the middle order to end with the most creditable figures of 4 wickets for 31 runs off 12 overs. Raqibul Hassan had a brief middle-order "flutter" with a 49-run stand of which he scored 35 and Badshah 19 before both were dismissed by Curran.

Zimbabwe started their innings by losing Dave Houghton for 1 before Heron (63 not out) and Curran (44) added 103 for the second wicket and made victory certain.

The Zimbabwe all-round performance was magnificent with a very professional attitude beginning to show. Again the fielding was of the highest order with Curran contributing with a magnificent run out.

SCORES: Semi-final versus Bangladesh.

At West Bromwich Dartmouth, 7 July.

Bangladesh — 124 (K.M. Curran 4/31)

Zimbabwe — 126-2 (J.G. Heron 63*, K.M. Curran 44)

Zimbabwe won by 8 wickets.

On 10 July in glorious weather reminiscent of home for both teams, Fletcher followed fashion and put Bermuda in to bat on winning the toss at the County ground, Grace Road, Leicester, trim with its rows of young trees and colourful flower beds looking good enough to stage a Royal Show.

Brown, opening the innings, helped to lay a sound foundation by putting 135 runs on the board with the help of Reid, Lightbourne and Gibbons. Bermuda had good cause to be grateful to Brown for he had stood firm as Fletcher dealt a lethal double blow taking the wickets of Lightbourne and Gibbons in three deliveries.

Whilst the Bermuda batsmen were comfortable enough against the pace it was John Traicos who really tied them down. An off-spinner born at Zag-a-Zig, Egypt, and who played Test cricket for South Africa in 1970 against Australia, he tied down the Bermuda batsmen who remained anchored and strokeless as he bowled 11 overs before lunch for 16 runs.

They did their best to break out of it after lunch despite a deep-set field with six men on the boundary. With overs running out, the tempo increased and one way or another 70 runs came in the last 10 overs to lift the total to a respectable 231 for 8 wickets at the end of 60 overs. Brown and skipper Colin Blades not only began to miss the fielders with their strokes but also

Vince Hogg (*above*) and Eddie Hough (*below*) brushed aside the top order in the semi-final against Bangladesh.

ran for everything. Brown made 48 whilst Blades made 45 and Allan Douglas a brisk 36 not out.

The determination of Zimbabwe to win this match was demonstrated by the fielding, with Heron throwing in marvellously to run out James, and Kevin Curran off his own bowling, flinging himself about the pitch

Gazi-Ashraf Hossain, the Bangladesh No. 3 batsman is out lbw bowled Vince Hogg. Duncan Fletcher, Jackie Heron and wicket-keeper David Houghton appeal successfully.

Duncan Fletcher dealt Bermuda a lethal blow when he took the wickets of Lightbourne and Gibbons in three deliveries.

saving fours and singles with equal abandon, once nearly running out Blades from point as he followed through at speed. John Traicos ended Brown's innings with a brilliant diving catch at gully.

As Zimbabwe started out requiring 232 runs to win at a rate of a little more than three and a half runs an over, an eventful climax lay in prospect. An impressive start from Heron and Houghton would have given Zimbabwe the edge. As the openers settled in, Bermuda suffered a cruel blow when their tall fast-medium bowler, King, pulled up with ligament trouble and retired.

The disappointment was offset immediately, however, when Houghton fell lbw to Trott in the seventh over. The 13th over proved to be unlucky for Heron who mis-hit Gibbons's first ball and was caught by the bowler. By tea, when Curran had also fallen lbw to Blades, the equation was still the same. Andy Pycroft and Duncan Fletcher continued the attack but on 110 Fletcher was caught by Lightbourne off Gibbons for 13.

Pycroft and Hodgson took command after these set-backs and with an enterprising 82 Pycroft set his team well on their way to victory. When he was out at 177, only 45 runs were required with 16 overs to get them in and five wickets in hand. He made only two mistakes in a feast of drives, pulls, glances and cuts. At 31 he played a tired-looking stroke and was dropped by Brown and the second mistake, a lapse of concentration, cost him his wicket when he was caught by Lightbourne off Gibbons.

Victory was assured in an unbroken sixth wicket stand of 55 in 11 overs by Craig Hodgson who assumed command and Robin Brown, a dedicated cricketer who makes a round trip of more than 250 miles from his farm every week-end to play the game.

Hodgson scored the winning run in the 55th over and ended with 57 not out showing a mature approach to the game and proving that he had learnt a great deal from the tour.

The ICC Trophy was presented to Duncan Fletcher by Gubby Allen, and Andy Pycroft was named "man of the match" by Leicester President, Charles Palmer.

TEAM

Fletcher — Captain	Hodgson
Traicos — Vice-Captain	Brown
Heron	Rawson
Houghton	Hough
Curran	Hogg
Pycroft	

RESULT — Won by 5 wickets.

BERMUDA

G.A. Brown c Traicos b Rawson	48
W.A. Reid b Hogg	13
S. Lightbourne b Fletcher	32
N.A. Gibbons b Fletcher	1
C. Blades c Curran b Rawson	45
E.G. James run out	8
J. Tucker lbw b Hogg	18
A.C. Douglas not out	36
J.L.O. Bailey c Hough b Fletcher	4
A. King not out	5
Extras (nb 4, w 1, lb 15, b 1)	21
Total (8 wickets 60 overs)	231

W. Trott did not bat.

Fall of wickets:
1-27, 2-74, 3-78, 4-135, 5-151, 6-161, 7-197, 8-210

Bowling:
Hogg 10-0-35-2, Hough 8-3-28-0, Rawson 12-1-48-2, Traicos 12-3-25-0, Fletcher 9-1-34-3, Curran 9-1-40-0

ZIMBABWE

D.L. Houghton lbw b Trott	8
J.G. Heron c and b Gibbons	9
K.M. Curran lbw b Blades	30
A.J. Pycroft c Lightbourne b Gibbons	82
D.A.G. Fletcher c Douglas b Blades	13
C.A.T. Hodgson not out	57
R.D. Brown not out	12
Extras (nb 2, w 10, lb 8, b 1)	21
Total (5 wickets 54,4 overs)	232

P.W. Rawson, A.J. Traicos, E.J. Hough and V.R. Hogg did not bat.

Fall of wickets:
1-22, 2-30, 3-78, 4-110, 5-177

Bowling:
Trott 11.4-1-27-1, King 3-0-10-0, James 11-1-41-0, Gibbons 12-0-64-2, Blades 12-2-39-2, Bailey 5-0-30-0

Zimbabwe now take their place alongside the seven Test-playing countries in the 1983 Prudential World Cup and are included in a draw with West Indies, Australia and India.

In October/November 1982, while this history was being made ready to go to Press, Zimbabwe were hosts to the Sri Lanka touring side. Two four-day and two one-day games were played, the honours being shared with one win each in the one-day matches. The first of the four-day games was drawn and Zimbabwe had a convincing victory by an innings and 119 runs in the second encounter. Zimbabwe will have the opportunity to gain further experience in its quest for full Test status at the Prudential World Cup contest in the United Kingdom in mid-1983, when it plays against the visiting Young Australian side in Zimbabwe in April 1983.

Jackie Heron in action during his innings of 63 not out in the game against Bangladesh.

Andy Pycroft, "man of the match", during his match-winnings innings of 82 in the final against Bermuda.

Jubilation at the moment of victory when Hodgson scored the winning run. Eddie Hough, John Traicos, Kevin Curran (Manager), David Ellman-Brown and Larry Watson (Assistant Manager) give vent to their feelings.

The ICC Trophy is presented to Duncan Fletcher by Gubby Allen.

U.K. TOUR — BATTING

	MATCHES PLAYED				COUNTY			
	County	ICC	Friendly	Total	No. of ins.	N.O.	Runs	Ave.
Pycroft	4	8	4	16	5	1	188	47,00
Hodgson	2	8	5	15	3	—	99	33,00
Curran	3	8	5	16	3	1	56	28,00
Heron	4	8	2	14	6	—	146	24,33
Scott	2	0	5	7	1	—	2	2,00
Fletcher	4	8	4	16	5	1	152	38,00
Brown	4	6	6	16	6	—	91	15,17
Houghton	3	8	4	15	5	1	49	12,25
Butchart	3	1	5	9	4	—	77	19,25
Wallace	2	2	6	10	3	—	77	25,67
Traicos	4	8	3	15	4	2	24	12,00
Rawson	4	8	4	16	3	1	20	10,00
Hough	3	5	4	12	3	2	16	16,00
Dudhia	2	2	5	9	1	—	1	1,00
Hogg	1	8	4	13	—	—	—	—

BOWLING

	COUNTY				ICC			
	O	M	R	W	O	M	R	W
Traicos	108	31	252	14	68	16	148	11
Rawson	72	13	209	8	68,1	15	177	14
Hogg	23	5	72	0	60	10	151	10
Hough	48	11	156	2	36	10	99	4
Curran	12	0	66	2	23	3	75	4
Butchart	29	4	102	3	—	—	—	—
Fletcher	49,3	9	170	4	39	7	147	6
Dudhia	23	5	60	3	18	6	39	2
Wallace	3	1	8	0	—	—	—	—
Houghton	—	—	—	—	—	—	—	—

JUNE-JULY, 1982

AVERAGES

ICC				FRIENDLY				TOTAL			
No. of ins.	N.O.	Runs	Ave.	No. of ins.	N.O.	Runs	Ave.	No. of ins.	N.O.	Runs	Ave.
5	2	184	61,33	4	—	225	56,25	14	3	597	54,27
3	3	84	—	5	—	179	35,80	11	3	362	45,25
7	4	276	92,00	4	—	53	13,25	14	5	385	42,78
7	2	221	44,20	2	—	135	67,50	15	2	502	38,62
—	—	—	—	5	1	172	43,00	6	1	174	34,80
4	1	82	27,33	3	—	112	37,33	12	2	346	34,60
1	1	12	—	6	2	234	58,50	13	3	337	33,70
7	1	308	51,33	4	—	91	22,75	16	2	448	32,00
—	—	—	—	4	1	95	31,67	8	1	172	24,57
—	—	—	—	6	1	60	12,00	9	1	140	17,50
—	—	—	—	3	—	49	16,33	7	2	73	14,60
—	—	—	—	2	—	17	8,50	5	1	37	9,25
—	—	—	—	2	1	2	2,00	5	3	18	9,00
—	—	—	—	4	2	22	11,00	5	2	23	7,67
—	—	—	—	3	3	6	—	3	3	6	—

AVERAGES

FRIENDLY				TOTAL			
O	M	R	W	O	M	R	W
12	3	28	3	188	50	428	28
28	10	62	3	168,1	38	448	25
44	16	103	11	127	31	326	21
30,5	9	71	8	114,5	30	326	14
38,3	7	115	8	73,3	10	256	14
35	12	66	9	64	16	168	12
14	2	50	1	102,3	18	367	11
42	14	90	5	83	25	189	10
21,3	9	31	8	24,3	10	39	8
7,3	0	38	2	7,3	0	38	2

Duncan Fletcher with the trophy.

FRIENDLY MATCHES:

versus Broadway C.C.

At Snowshill Road, 13 June.

Zimbabwe — 205-9 (D.A.G. Fletcher 69, I.P. Butchart 39*, D.L. Houghton 30; F. Caranza 5/22)

Broadway — 93 (V.R. Hogg 5/38)

Zimbabwe won by 112 runs.

versus Blossomfield C.C.

At Blossomfield, 14 June.

Zimbabwe — 235-5 (J.G. Heron 82, R. Brown 38*, A.J. Pycroft 36)

Blossomfield — 70 (E.J. Hough 4/13, K.M. Curran 3/19)

Zimbabwe won by 165 runs.

versus Bromsgrove C.C.

At Bromsgrove, 20 June.

Zimbabwe — 273-9 (R.D. Brown 123, A.J. Pycroft 75 ret. hurt)

Bromsgrove — 126 (G.C. Wallace 3/18, V.R. Hogg 3/19)

Zimbabwe won by 147 runs.

versus Pickwick C.C., 23 June. Game washed out by heavy overnight rain.

versus Cannock and Rugeley C.C.

At Cannock and Rugeley, 27 June.

Zimbabwe — 278-5 (C.A.T. Hodgson 113, R.D. Brown 34*, D.A.G. Fletcher 33, A.J. Pycroft 30)

Cannock and Rugeley — 104 (G.C. Wallace 5/6)

Zimbabwe won by 174 runs.

versus Fiji.

At Lucas (Solihull) C.C., 2 July.

Zimbabwe — 265 (G.M. Scott 91, A.J. Pycroft 84)

Fiji — 176 (E.J. Hough 3/13, I.P. Butchart 3/21)

Zimbabwe won by 89 runs.

versus Ludlow and South Shropshire C.C.

At Ludlow, 4 July.

Zimbabwe — 279-9 (J.G. Heron 53, G.M. Scott 46, A.J. Traicos 40)

Ludlow — 150 (I.P. Butchart 3/22, A.J. Traicos 3/28)

Zimbabwe won by 129 runs.

SUMMARY OF RESULTS

	Scheduled Matches	Won	Drawn	Lost	Washed Out
County	4		2	2	
ICC Trophy	9	7			2
Friendlies — Clubs	7	6			1
	20	13	2	2	3

CHAPTER TEN
Schools Cricket

CRICKET HAS PLAYED an integral part in the history of what were formerly European schools in this country. It was played as early as the 1897-98 season by St. George's College when that school entered the Bulawayo Second League. In 1902 the arrival of the English Jesuit, Fr. Gardner, saw an increased interest and the acquiring of a serviceable ground of ten hectares about half a mile from the school. Progress was such that in the 1908-09 season, St. George's was admitted to the First League to join issue with Queens, B.A.C. and Gwelo. Jock Thompson recorded in his book: 'The schoolboys were remarkably good fielders and Basil Howard, Pat and Sonny Walsh, were all good bats, and the last a useful bowler. No less worthy of record was a slim youth, a good bat and bowler and a brilliant slip-field, known as "Doc" Campbell. The Doc, one of the most popular sportsmen in Bulawayo, had played for both Cape Town and Edinburgh Universities, obtained Scottish Trials and subsequently played for and captained Rhodesia.'

The first inter-school match was played in November 1907, between Plumtree and St. John's College at Plumtree. St. John's won by seven wickets due to two fine batting displays by their captain, Lionel Bell, who scored 137* and 23*. J.B. Clarke records in his book *Plumtree School — A history of the school from inception to 75th Anniversary* that Bell in later years returned to the area as the Church of England Chaplain and playing for the Village XI, scored another century against the school.

A firm rivalry began between St. John's College (later Milton School) and Plumtree and soon these two schools became the Alma Mater of so many of Rhodesia's cricketers, particularly after the First World War. Their traditional two-day fixture is the only one of its kind between schools in this country and to date (1982) Plumtree have won 61, Milton 36, 38 have been drawn and one tied.

Plumtree's first century-maker against Milton and their finest cricketer of the 1920s was Hamish Campbell-Rodger who scored 2 311 runs and took 144 wickets in his school 1st XI career during 1921-25. As a 17-year-old schoolboy he was selected to play for Rhodesia against Solly Joel's English tourists in the 1924-25 season.

Milton produced two great cricketers in Victor Hepker and Jack Hayward. Hepker captained the Milton side that Colonel Brady took to South Africa on an historic two-match tour in 1927 and hit 80 in the drawn game against Hilton College and made top score in both innings when Milton went down heavily to King Edward VII School. Hepker went on to represent Transvaal in subsequent seasons whilst Hayward made a name for himself in local circles. The latter captained Bulawayo Schools in 1928 in a two-day match at Queens against a Transvaal team containing Springboks, Jack Christy and Bruce Mitchell. As a schoolboy, Hayward made his debut for Rhodesia against Transvaal in 1928 and top-scored with a superb 72 in the first innings.

Prince Edward also had two fine schoolboy cricketers in their 1st XI at this time and co-incidentally both were destined to make their international debuts on the victorious 1935 Springbok tour to England. Denis Tomlinson captained the Prince Edward side and in one school term in 1928 represented Mashonaland and Rhodesia against the Transvaal tourists and was selected for the South African Schools team which played against Capt. R.T. Stannyforth's M.C.C. tourists. Crisp, who represented the Prince Edward 1st XI during 1926-28 gained selection for the Mashonaland senior side in his last year at school.

Umtali played their first inter-school match in 1927 against Prince Edward and were well beaten but two years later gained their first victory, beating St. George's by 145 runs. Ronnie Michell, who became Umtali's first Rhodesian representative, hit 90 in this match and in 1930 hammered 163* against Town which remains the highest individual score recorded for the Umtali 1st XI.

Mark Napier (Plumtree) was chosen for the South African Schools side which played against Percy Chapman's M.C.C. tourists in 1930-31. He made 17 in the schools' 15-man total of 130 and according to a report from Grahamstown 'shaped up well' against the terrors of Voce, Tate and Goddard.

In 1930 Umtali visited Plumtree — the round trip of over 1 000 miles was acknowledged at that time as being a world record for one match by the former M.C.C. captain "Plum" Warner. Umtali went down by an innings to their hosts and had to wait nineteen years before they evened matters by beating a Plumtree side at home in 1949.

In 1935, Plumtree decided to spread their wings

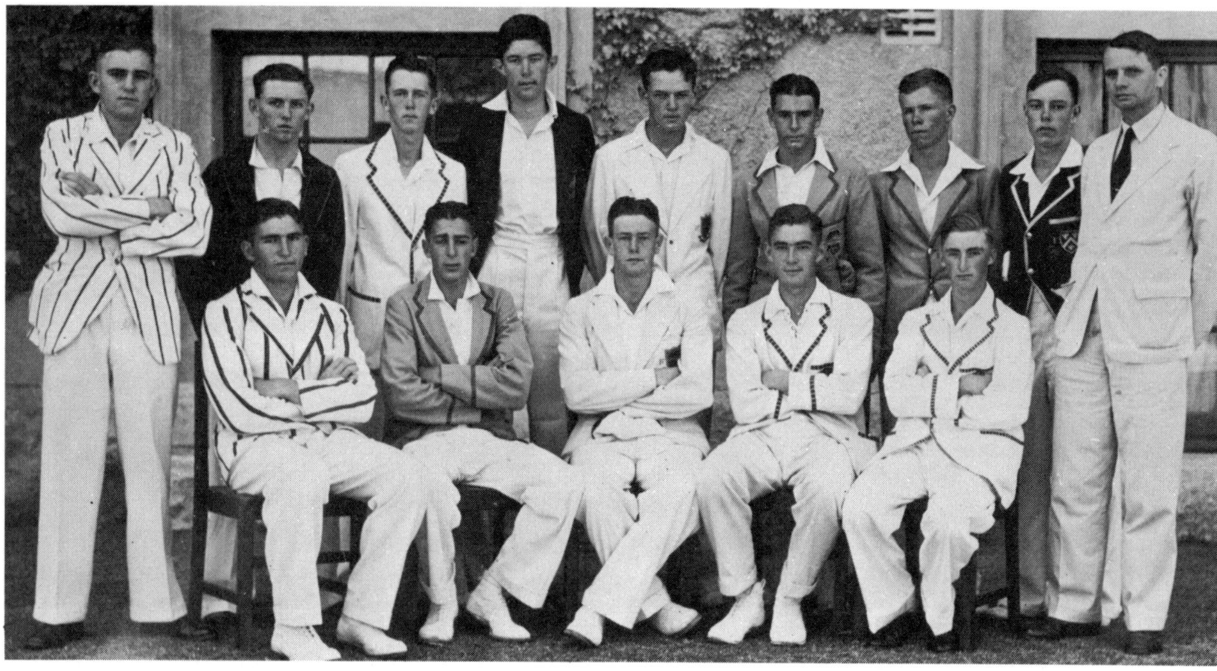

NUFFIELD XI, 1941.
Back: H. Montgomery, B. Kitto, K. Forrest, P. Uren, E. Cutter, C. Harris, D. Wood, B. Carew, Mr. R. Rolfe (Manager).
Seated: B. Chimowitz, M. Harris, R. McAdam (Captain), N. Dyer, A. Green.

and test their skills on a South African tour. In the course of an unbeaten three-match programme they avenged Milton's earlier defeat at the hands of King Edward VII school when a fine all-round performance by Reg Noble, a future Rhodesian player, saw Plumtree win that match by 62 runs. Another Rhodesian player in the making, Forbes McDonald, starred in the other two matches — scoring 161 against St. John's and 114 against St. Andrew's.

Percy Mansell inspired Milton almost single-handedly to a 5-wicket win over Plumtree in 1935 and the following year gained Rhodesian senior selection whilst still at school.

Cricket was making giant strides at schoolboy level at this time and Rhodesia was well prepared for the advent of the Nuffield Week. This was undoubtedly the most significant factor in the history of schoolboy cricket and the Rhodesians entered a side in the first Week in January 1940. Connie Pretorius (Chaplin) and David Thomas (Prince Edward) were the outstanding performers in a side that acquitted itself well, winning all four matches although they lost an unofficial fixture against Mr. N.V. Bellville's XI.

The following year, in 1941, Rhodesia set up a record innings score which still stands of 399-9 against Orange Free State whilst the 123 made by Paddy Green (Prince Edward) was at that time the highest individual score.

Two noteworthy performances during this period were achieved at school level. Bernard Carew (Bulawayo Tech.) took 7/47 and 9/25 and scored 89 and 18* in his school's sound win over Plumtree in 1941 — taking ten wickets (let alone 16) and scoring one hundred runs in a match does not occur often. Nor does Robert Kennedy's feat of a century (102) and a hat-trick in the same match which was accomplished during Plumtree's 'derby' fixture with Milton in 1942.

Nuffield Week went into recess for the War years, 1939-45, but a Combined Rhodesian Schools XI captained by Doug Pechey (St. George's) played against a Mashonaland XI on New Year's day, 1945. When the Nuffield tournament was re-established in 1946 David Lewis (Plumtree) captained a powerful side containing several names that were to become synonymous with this country's cricket — Curran, Johnson, and O'Connell-Jones. But the most sensational achievement of the late 1940s occurred in Port Elizabeth in 1948 when superb bowling by Gerald Ziehl (Bulawayo Tech.), who took 6/20 in 9 overs, saw a Natal side containing names such as McGlew, McLean, Goddard, Waite, Melle and Tayfield bundled out for a paltry 51 — Rhodesia won easily and ended the tournament undefeated.

The following year Salisbury was the host centre and Rhodesia, under the management of (Senator) "Coney" Fleming, were again unbeaten in a very successful week — not only were all costs met for the tournament but £1 000 was handed over to the capital fund. Said Mr. C.J. Offord, the organizing secretary, at a civic luncheon on the final day: 'Rhodesia has reached the pinnacle of success.'

The Rhodesian schoolboys of 1951 were a great deal wiser after bungling their match against Border. With the third last ball of the day, Border's century-maker was dismissed which meant Border required 6 runs in two balls. They took two off the first and the next ball was delivered well outside the off-stump in order to make things difficult for the batsman. However, the problems came Rhodesia's way as a wide was called, the wicket-keeper could only partially stop it, the batsmen ran, an overthrow followed, mid-on backing up shied at the bowler's stumps, the bowler was not looking and another run was added to the score. That ball was entered as three wides. One run was still needed and almost before

NUFFIELD XI, 1946.
Back: K. Green, J. Marais, D. McDonald, D. Black, G. Bain, R. Harris, D. O'Connell-Jones.
Seated: K. Curran, E. Passaportis, D. Lewis (Captain), Mr. F. Batchelor (Manager), P. Johnson (Vice-Captain), R. Salmon, K. Teague.

Gerald Ziehl (*crouching, second from right*) inspects the Pirates ground wicket prior to his fine bowling performance against Natal during the 1948 Nuffield Week. His Rhodesian team-mates are (*standing*): R. Rosselli, E. Gous, T. Anderson, J. Baldwin, T. Butts and (*crouching*): P. Green, T. Lange and M. Hanley.

the last ball had left the bowler's hand the batsmen were running — the wicket-keeper standing three metres back could not get up in time and Border raced through for the winning bye.

Tony Pithey (Plumtree), perhaps the greatest schoolboy batsman this country has produced, played his first Nuffield Cricket Week in 1950, being run out for 0 in his debut against Griqualand West. He scored 2390 runs in 58 matches (average 58,29) for Plumtree, represented the Nuffield side for four years producing well over 600 runs, and gained selection on three occasions for the South African Schools XI. In 1952 he hit 106 against the Border senior side to guide the South African Schools to a fine four-wicket victory. Vernon Dickinson (St. George's), who hit 45 not out in the same match, had represented the Rhodesian Schools side with distinction for three years and in 1952 had added 148 for the 5th wicket with Pithey in a Rhodesian Nuffield record stand.

Tony's brother David, who was later to gain his Oxford Blue, and Rob Ullyett (Chaplin) were great successes in 1954. Ullyett compiled scores of 69*, 71 and 34 before crowning his week with a brilliant 104 against Natal whilst Pithey, one of those rare cricketers who could bowl at any pace with either hand, ensured himself of a place in the South African Schools combination by taking wickets as well as making runs. Both were back the following year when Rhodesia had

TONY PITHEY, 1950-51-52-53 and brother DAVID, 1953-54-55.

NUFFIELD XI, 1952.
Back: C. Duckworth, D. Allies, M. Micklesfield, D. Napier, B. Hefer, M. Timms, T. van Rooyen.
Middle: A. Pithey, A. Todd (Captain), Mr. D. Whaley (Manager), P. Walshe (Vice-Captain), V. Dickinson.
Front: E. Deftereos, R. Ault.

VERNON DICKINSON.

S.W. "PIP" NELSON.

one of their strongest sides but the Week was cancelled due to the polio epidemic.

David Parker (St. George's), an aggressive fast bowler, who sadly lost his life in a helicopter crash when Officer Commanding R.L.I., was selected for the 1954-55 Nuffield sides. Whilst at school in 1954 he took 129 wickets for 779 runs and in 1955 he seemed well on his way to improving this record with 66 wickets at 4,9 runs apiece before his departure for Sandhurst.

Churchill's entrance into the 1st XI arena came in 1954 and it is recorded in the Books of Zimbabwe publication *Some Renowned Rhodesian Senior Schools* that the school's first century was scored by D. Penfold in a match against the "Vampires" in February 1955. The page of the Scorebook was signed by the legendary English cricketer, Sir Jack Hobbs, who watched the game.

Ray Gripper (St. George's) set a batting record for his school by scoring 1 159 runs in 1955 and gained selection for the South African Schools in 1956. Colin Bland (Milton) made his debut in 1956 and skippered the Rhodesian side the following year when the tournament was held in Bulawayo — to the delight of his home crowd he was named vice-captain of the South African Schools side. However, "Pip" Nelson (Prince Edward) stole the show that year when he ran through a strong Rhodesian senior side to record figures of 6/21 in 11 overs — still the best bowling

NUFFIELD XI, 1956.
Back: R. Grey, C. Pafitis, R. Robertson, D. Erskine, E. Parker, T. Cockcroft, R. Gripper, B. Ashley-Cooper, P. Ciapparelli.
Seated: B. Jones, G. Deary (Captain), Mr. J. Buchanan (Manager), J. Pluke (Vice-Captain), C. Bland.

EDDIE PARKER, 1955-56-57-58.

performance by a South African Schools player.

Eddie Parker (Milton) making his fourth Nuffield appearance and Gordon Den, who took a record 128 wickets in one year for Prince Edward, were notable selections for the Nuffield side in 1958 but after being unbeaten for two years Rhodesia did not win a game during that Week. However, they came back well in 1959 for another undefeated tournament. In one incredible match against Western Province, Rhodesia were all out for a meagre 22 (6 ducks) but fought back to win outright by three wickets. Brian Baxter (Churchill) who had taken 7/31 in Province's first innings recorded figures of 6/64 in 21 overs against the Natal senior side for the South African Schools XI.

Great honour came Prince Edward's way when in successive years two of their products — John McPhun in 1959 and Nick Frangos in 1960 — captained South African Schools. In the latter Week 15-year-old Graeme Pollock annihilated the Rhodesian bowling for the first time when he smote 101 not out for Eastern Province.

Huntsman Williams (Plumtree) captured all 10 Milton wickets for 42 runs in 1961 and with Chris Nourse (Peterhouse) gained selection two years running (1961-62) for the South African Schools. Williams took 24 wickets (average 5,91) at the two Weeks he attended. Ross Fuller (Plumtree) captained the powerful 1961 Rhodesian Schools team which also included Jackie du Preez (Prince Edward) and Fred Goldstein (Falcon).

Once again the Rhodesians finished unbeaten in 1962 and proceeded to embark on their first tour to England. They were known as the Fawns — the 'brain child' of cricket stalwarts, "Weary" Maxwell and George Wells. The Fawns had begun in a small way in 1951, initially on a local basis, but after Rex McCulloch (now at Prince Edward) had brought up a Transvaal side in 1958 the Rhodesian Fawns U-15 side made a reciprocal visit in 1959. Included in that team were Jack du Preez, Ken Tonkin, Dave McVey and Ross Fuller amongst other future Nuffield players. The Fawns organization continued to work tirelessly in the promotion of junior cricket and the English tour was the high point of their progress, providing the schoolboys with an opportunity of playing at such hallowed grounds as Lord's and The Oval. Finance was raised through an appeal to individuals and firms with the biggest donation of £750 coming from Ndola Lotteries. Managed by Harry Birrell with George Wells travelling as secretary, the Fawns toured England for nearly seven weeks and crammed 25 matches into that time. The tour objective was 'mainly to learn' and the team excelled themselves, returning unbeaten with 20 victories and 5 drawn matches. Dubbed the "Fabulous Fawns" by the Press, the former President of the M.C.C., Harry Altham, praised the team at a luncheon in their honour at the Lord's Tavern: 'On this really astonishing tour these Fawns have shown the schools they met in England just how this game of cricket should be played.'

SCORES: Fawns Tour to England, 1962.

At the Oval.
Fawns — 262-3 dec. (W. Hodnett 143*, S. Barbour 62)
XL Club — 135 (E. Bedser 48; D. Northcroft 5/13)
Fawns won by 127 runs.

At Leatherhead.
Fawns — 247-3 dec. (R. McTavish 96, B. May 71, T. Wells 50*)
St. John's — 89 (D. Northcroft 5/26, A. Suleman 3/30)
Fawns won by 158 runs.

At Croydon.
Fawns — 224-8 dec. (S. Barbour 97, A. Carlisle 48; D. Dewar 29, B. May 28)
Trinity School — 85 (A. Suleman 3/19, T. Wells 3/22)
Fawns won bv 139 runs.

At Dulwich.
Fawns — 164-3 dec. (S. Barbour 50*, T. Wells 40*, D. Dewar 38, R. McTavish 25)
Dulwich College — 44 (M. Burton 4/11, D. Northcroft 4/16)
Fawns won by 120 runs.

At Epsom.
Fawns — 196-4 dec. (D. Dewar 63, B. May 51, T. Wells 44)
Epsom College — 81 (M. Burton 7/24)
Fawns won by 115 runs.

At Elmer's End, Kent.
Fawns — 164-6 (P. Rennie 76, H. Capon 42, C. Nourse 26)
Standard Bank — 89 (M. Burton 5/16)
Fawns won by 75 runs.

NUFFIELD XI, 1959.
Back: W. Hogg, R. Mitchell, B. Lendrum, P. Densem, S. Cunningham, N. Frangos, G. Vaughan.
Seated: D. Beets, I. Godden, J. McPhun (Captain), Mr. C. Silcock (Manager), A. Kimble (Vice-Captain), B. Baxter, C. Purchase.

RHODESIAN FAWNS TOUR TO ENGLAND, 1962.
Back: G. Ridley, D. Northcroft, B. May, C. Nourse, W. Hodnett, M. Burton, S. Barbour, R. McTavish.
Seated: Mr. H. Birrell (Manager), A. Suleman, T. Wells (Captain), Mr. H. Pichanick, P. Rennie (Vice-Captain), H. Capon, Mr. G. Wells (Secretary).
Front: G. Linden, A. Carlisle, D. Dewar.

At Rochester.
Fawns — 208-7 (T. Wells 56, R. McTavish 51, W. Hodnett 30)
King's School — 35 (G. Ridley 4/11, H. Capon 4/12)
Fawns won by 173 runs.

At Canterbury.
Fawns — 216-9 dec. (T. Wells 100, R. McTavish 70)
King's Schools — 96 (D. Northcroft 4/24, M. Burton 4/30)
Fawns won by 120 runs.

At Eastbourne.
Fawns — 265-4 dec. (S. Barbour 159*)
Eastbourne College — 134 (M. Burton 4/20, A. Suleman 4/31)
Fawns won by 131 runs.

At Cranleigh.
Cranleigh School — 154 (D. Northcroft 7/31)
Fawns — 155-5 (R. McTavish 62, C. Nourse 23, D. Dewar 25*)
Fawns won by 5 wickets.

At Malvern.
Fawns — 232-2 dec. (R. McTavish 136*, P. Rennie 51, D. Dewar 31)
Malvern — 177-5
Match drawn.

At Cheltenham.
Fawns — 198-6 dec. (T. Wells 86, R. Dewar 46)
Dean Close School — 61 (A. Suleman 4/10, M. Burton 4/18)
Fawns won by 137 runs.

At Radley.
Fawns — 239-2 dec. (B. May 85*, R. McTavish 71, A. Carlisle 51, C. Nourse 27*)
Radley College — 128 (M. Burton 4/26, D. Northcroft 3/45)
Fawns won by 111 runs.

At Haywards Heath, Sussex.
Fawns — 211-5 (A. Carlisle 71*, P. Rennie 51, D. Dewar 52)
Ardingly College — 90 (H. Capon 5/20, G. Ridley 3/26)
Fawns won by 121 runs.

At Dauntsey's School.
Dauntsey's School — 117
Fawns — 118-5 (W. Hodnett 61, T. Wells 22)
Fawns won by 5 wickets.

At Blandford, Dorset.
Fawns — 246-2 dec. (R. McTavish 137*, T. Wells 71, S. Barbour 30*)
Bryanston School — 110 (M. Burton 4/25, A. Suleman 3/45)
Fawns won by 136 runs.

At Salisbury.
Fawns — 209-7 dec. (A. Carlisle 61, D. Northcroft 30, G. Ridley 31)
Bishop Wordsworth School — 64 (M. Burton 4/8)
Fawns won by 145 runs.

At Millfield, Somerset.
Fawns — 290-3 dec. (S. Barbour 121*, W. Hodnett 95*, D. Dewar 44)
Millfield School — 196-9 (A. Suleman 4/90)
Match drawn.

Colin Bland demonstrates an off-drive to Derek Collett, a member of the 1967 Rhodesian Fawns U-13 side.

Michael Kerwin (Lord Malvern School) bowling, watched by Mike Procter and Dave Coughlan the Lord Malvern 1st XI coach.

Robin Jackman presents a merit certificate to Ian Scutt, captain of the 1979 Partridges (Zimbabwe Rhodesia's primary schools team). Looking on are other team members (*left to right, top to bottom*): Andrew Playford, Colin Sayer, Kevin Butler, Darryl de Jager, Blair Hutchings, Chris James, Garrick Mullin, Graeme du Preez, Wayne Robertson, Johnny van Heerden, Gary Carlisle.

At Canford.
Fawns — 205-3 dec. (P. Rennie 100*, C. Nourse 63)
Canford School — 105 (G. Ridley 5/26)
Fawns won by 100 runs.

At Bath.
Fawns — 227-5 dec. (W. Hodnett 80*, R. McTavish 47)
Kingswood School — 121 (M. Burton 5/21, D. Northcroft 3/31)
Fawns won by 106 runs.

At Clifton.
Fawns — 218-4 dec. (P. Rennie 56*, S. Barbour 50, T. Wells 42, W. Hodnett 28)
Clifton — 104 (M. Burton 5/34)
Fawns won by 114 runs.

At Bath.
Fawns — 208-7 dec. (S. Barbour 61, A. Carlisle 45)
Lansdown Club — 146-6.
Match drawn.

At Cheltenham.
Fawns — 212-5 dec. (G. Linden 48, R. McTavish 43, T. Wells 37*, B. May 37*)
Cheltenham College — 151-6 (G. Ridley 3/25)
Match drawn.

At Bath.
Marlborough College — 233 (M.G. Griffith 121; G. Ridley 5/70, D. Northcroft 3/40)
Fawns — 218-6 (S. Barbour 115, A. Carlisle 55)
Match drawn.

At Norbury, Surrey.
Barclays Bank — 79 (D. Northcroft 9/26) and 72 (D. Northcroft 4/31)
Fawns — 189-1 dec. (D. Dewar 104*, G. Linden 54*)
Fawns won by an innings and 38 runs.

In December 1962, the Nuffield side suffered what might be termed an ignominious defeat when they were beaten by a Schoolmasters XI. However, there were some pretty useful cricketers amongst Messrs. Mallett (captain), Clarance, Ashley-Cooper, Duckworth, Lamond, Robertson, Meyer, Snyder, Todd, van Blomestein and Whiley.

The 1963 side lost once during the Week and that was in a 'thriller' to Natal when they were beaten by three wickets with three minutes remaining. Richards, Procter and Irvine all made runs in Natal's 187-7 but they were made to fight all the way by off-spinner, Mike Burton (Umtali), who took 5/34. The same year Giles Ridley (Milton) made his second cricket tour to England, this time alongside the likes of Richards, Procter, Ackerman, Watson, Morris, Biggs and Rosendorff in the powerful South African Schools side. Ridley headed both the batting (63,00) and the bowling averages (11,73) and with 46 wickets took almost twice as many as the next highest.

For the three following years (1964-66) Rhodesia remained undefeated which was a remarkable achievement considering the wealth of schoolboy cricketing talent in South Africa during that period — Richards, Greig, Procter, Biggs, Ackerman, Rosendorff, Dyer to name a few. Perhaps the most outstanding Rhodesian performance was in dismissing the star-studded Natal combination in 1965 for 62 — Peter Swart (Jameson)

GRAHAM HOBBINS, 1964-65.

10,3-6-14-6 and Graham Hobbins (Umtali) 10-2-28-4 doing the damage in an impressive win. Swart notably followed this performance by returning figures of 23-11-24-5 against Western Province.

Graham Hobbins, Nuffield captain in January 1965, had also captained Rhodesia's first Craven Week side in 1964. Perhaps his leaving school had a marked effect initially on the Umtali 1st XI because in their opening match of the following season they were 12 runs for 9 wickets against Mount Pleasant. But playing true to the old adage of 'a match is never won until the last wicket falls', the Umtali tail-enders, John Caswell and Gary Gold, added 69 to set up a dramatic victory as Mount Pleasant were then bowled out for 67. (Frank Richmond 7 for 8.)

Richmond, in more recent years a well-known cricket commentator, finished the 1966 tournament, top of the Nuffield batting averages in a Week which saw Rhodesia and the M.C.C. Schools as the only sides with unblemished records. When they clashed the Rhodesians declared at 223-5 with Rob Berry (St. George's) 70* and then had the M.C.C. battling at 74-4 — John Traicos (Thornhill) and Jimmy Mitchell (Churchill) bowled 18 maidens in 19 overs. Said team manager, Mike Whiley: 'There was no team competing that was better than the Rhodesian side. Their team spirit was terrific and their fielding and running between the wickets was one of the highlights of the Week.'

NUFFIELD XI, 1966.
Back: F. Richmond, P. Wilkinson, J. Ford, R. Kaschula, N. Davidson, R. McLoughlin, J. Traicos.
Seated: R. Berry, J. Mitchell, C. Fletcher (Captain), Mr. M. Whiley (Manager), E. Gilmour, S. Robertson, T. Dunk.

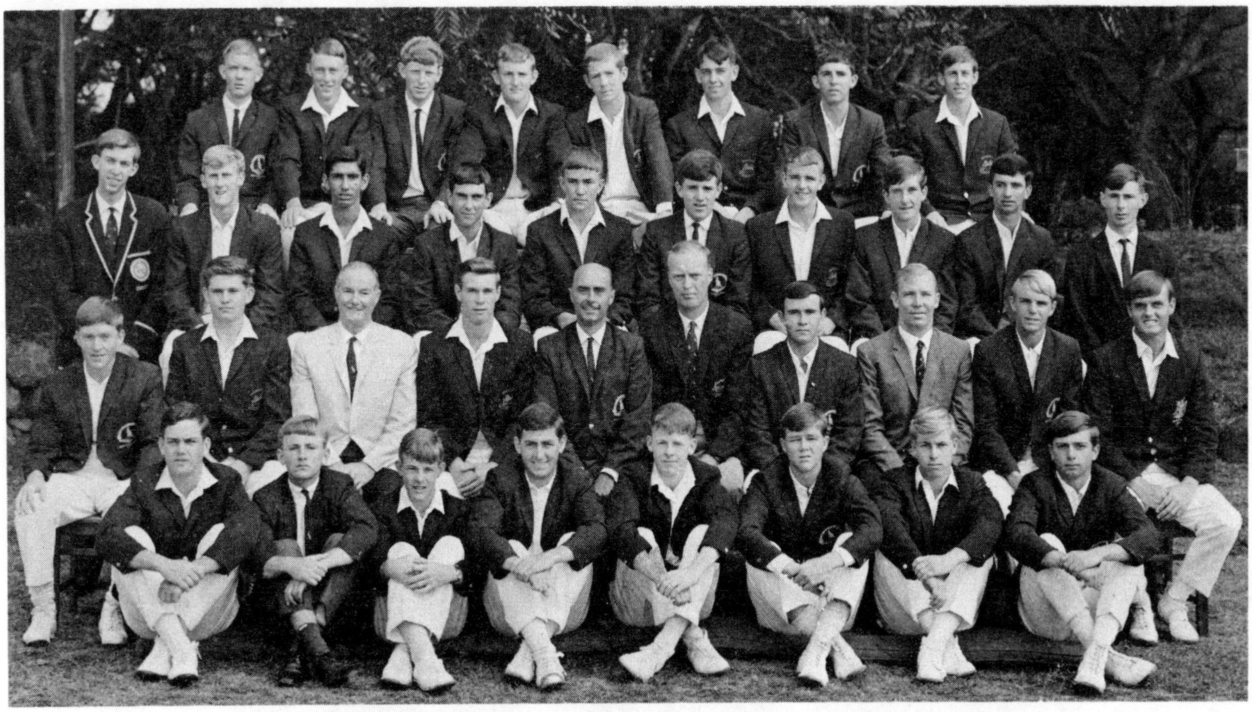

RHODESIAN SCHOOLS v. AUSTRALIAN SCHOOLS, 1967.
Back: J. Ryan (A), K. Moore (R), B. House (A), G. Ogilvie (R), G. Bailey (A), K. Cantrell (R), M. Malone (A), R. Cameron (R).
Third: R. Norman (Scorer), W. Palmer (A), K. Gokal (R), A. Turner (A), P. O'Donovan (R), A. Oliver (A), M. Benkenstein (R), R. Mehegan (A), C. Aldams (A), B. Shine (Scorer).
Seated: P. Dodd (A), R. Ferreira (R Vice-Captain), Mr. P. Le Mesurier (Assistant Manager), J. Heron (R Captain), Mr. A. Gifford (A Manager), Mr. M. Whiley (Organizing Chairman), K. Thompson (A Captain), T. Bourdillon (R Manager), G. House (A Vice-captain), R. McLoughlin (R).
Front: R. Jones (R), H. Timperley (A), D. Evans (R), G. Harrington (A), M. Baldwin (R), A. Irvine (A), L. Ashley (R), W. King (A).

In 1967 it was Salisbury's turn to host the Nuffield Week and for Rhodesia the outstanding cricket achievement was possibly the record 4th wicket stand of 154 between Jack Heron (Churchill) and Richard Ballance (Umtali) — the last 104 runs coming in a hurricane 40 minutes. In an upset result on the final day the South African Schools XI beat the senior Rhodesian side. Rob Berry gained his second South African Schools' cap whilst the schoolboy side's opening pace attack that year consisted of Roy McLoughlin (Hamilton) and the future Springbok rugby captain, Morné du Plessis.

McLoughlin toured England with the South African Schools team in 1967 — also in the side was an Umtali boy, Frik Bredenkamp, who attended school in the Northern Transvaal but later returned to represent Manicaland for several years.

In December 1967, the Australian Schools visited Salisbury and the home side amassed 256-9 declared — Robin Jones (Prince Edward) (61) and Jack Heron (52) before the match petered out in a tame draw. Heron also made top score (41) for the South African Schools against the tourists in South Africa's four-wicket victory. Kishu Gokal (Morgan) had an eventful day for the Rhodesians against the Aussies. He shared in a partnership of 89 in 75 minutes with Jones, bagged two wickets with his off-spinners, went off to hospital to have three stitches in a cut left hand after stopping a hard throw at the stumps, came back an hour later and bagged two more wickets before the close.

Robin Jones scored 1025 runs including four centuries (average 60,3) and played his part in Prince Edward being unbeaten in 22 matches during 1968. Jones made the South African Schools XI in 1969 and

ROBIN JONES, 1968-69.

DES EVANS, 1968-69-70.

was joined by Riki Cameron (Mount Pleasant) who took 20 wickets during the Nuffield Week.

With the Rhodesian Nuffield side unbeaten for another three years (1970-72) further honours were bestowed on Prince Edward cricketers when Dave Rawlings was selected as the South African Schools captain in 1970 and Mike Mathews in 1972. The 1972 Rhodesian side was a particularly strong combination and Marshall Page (Churchill) and Paddy Clift (St. George's) joined Mathews in the South African Schools XI. Said team manager, John Pluke, of the Rhodesian performance during the Week: 'It was a splendid team effort. My only disappointment is that many in the team were unable to show their talents because the top-order batsmen did so well. This is proved when one studies the score-sheets. Rhodesia lost only eleven wickets in the entire Week while we captured 55.'

Mathews, a fine all-round sportsman, who captained the Rhodesian Nuffield XI in 1971-72, captained the Rhodesian Craven Week XV in 1971 and represented the Rhodesian Schools at hockey in 1970, set up a new Prince Edward batting record in 1971 by compiling 1171 runs (average 53,23). At the 1972 Week he was only dismissed twice in scoring 232 runs and played a leading role in Rhodesia's 9-wicket victory over a Western Province side which included Allan Lamb, Peter Kirsten, and Stephen Bruce.

In the first term of 1972, Peter Chingoka made history by becoming the first African to represent St. George's when he made his one and only 1st XI appearance against Peterhouse. On leaving school he was to reappear in the record books when he captained the South African Bantu XI in their Gillette Cup debut against Natal in 1975-76.

In the third term of 1972, Simon Kerr (St. George's) hit a record four consecutive undefeated centuries for the St. George's 1st XI, was dismissed cheaply at Umtali, then hit 102* against Prince Edward and 91 against a Composite Schools XI in the season's remaining matches. Wisden recognized Kerr's outstanding achievement by devoting a full page to his deeds and his selection as the 1973 Nuffield captain came as no surprise.

Bulawayo hosted the 1973 tournament and Rhodesia fielded two sides for the first time. The B XI actually did as well as their senior combination and Trevor Williams (Hamilton) with scores of 96*, 45, and 92 came into consideration for a place in the South African Schools XI.

DAVID RAWLINGS, 1969-70.

MIKE MATHEWS, 1970-71-72.

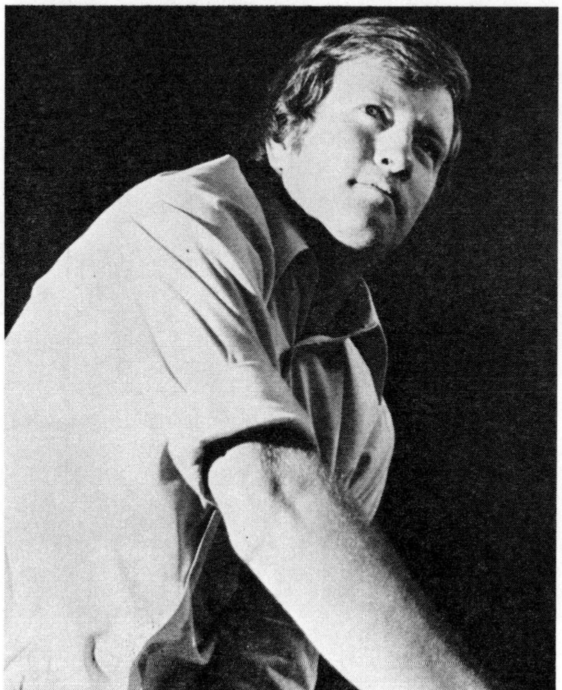

ALLAN FLETCHER, 1970-71.

Gerald Peckover scored 1073 runs (average 76,64) for Churchill in 1973 and made his third Nuffield appearance in 1974, scoring an unbeaten century against Griqualand West.

The 1974 side became only the second Rhodesian team to emerge with a Nuffield record of three losses but Billy Houghton (Prince Edward) had the amazing analysis against the Orange Free State of 21-15-7-6. However, such has been the wealth of schoolboy talents in this country that a lean year was usually followed by several prosperous seasons and between 1975-78, Rhodesia won 12, drew 6 and tied once in 20 matches.

Prince Edward School is renowned for its family contributions and in 1975, Dave Houghton became the third brother to have represented the Nuffield side, following Billy (1974) and Ken (1971), thus equalling the achievement of the Fletcher clan. The Fletchers went one better in that Colin (1966) and Duncan (1967) were both named as Nuffield captains although the latter had to withdraw through illness. Allan represented the Nuffield side in 1970-71, eldest brother, John, played for the Fawns and a fifth brother, Gordon, was a Nuffield reserve in 1969.

January 1976 saw a particularly thrilling victory for Rhodesia by 6 runs over Western Province. Western Province seemed to have the game in hand when they needed 11 runs to win with 4 wickets in hand and the best part of seven overs to do it in. In an incredible finish two batsmen were caught going for completely

Peter Chingoka, captain of the 1975-76 S.A. African XI, appeals unsuccessfully for lbw against Alan Barrow (Natal) in a Gillette Cup match at Kingsmead, Durban.

NUFFIELD XI, 1972.
Back: G. Peckover, N. Calvert, M. Page, M. McGinty, R. Staunton, I. Ault, C. Kuhn.
Seated: J. Oosthuizen, P. Clift, M. Mathews (Captain), Mr. J. Pluke (Manager), A. MacCallum (Vice-Captain), B. Phillips, S. Kerr.
Front: K. White (Scorer).

unnecessary big hits and two others were run out — there were altogether four run-outs in the Western Province innings which reflected Rhodesia's outstanding ground fielding and throwing.

David Alers, a nephew of the former Rhodesian player Charles Wooler, made his fourth appearance at this Week and his South African Schools Cap climaxed an outstanding career in schoolboy cricket. He scored 3647 runs in 95 innings (average 46,75) for Plumtree with a highest score of 172 made against Milton in 1975 and took 326 wickets (average 9,17). Of further interest at the January 1976 tournament, two Rhodesians attending Hilton College were included in the Natal Schools side. They were John Robinson who is a grandson of the former Rhodesian batsman, Victor Robinson, and Rob Bentley, who had captained the Rhodesian Partridges (a national side selected from primary schools) for two years.

In December 1977, Kevin Arnott (Prince Edward), and Peter Wallace (Milton), both emulated their fathers by gaining selection for the South African Schools — this rare occurrence had only happened twice before in Nuffield history — in the cases of W.C. and M.J. Procter and P.B. and J. During. Mention should also be made here of Stuart Forrest (Prince Edward) — Nuffield 1976J-76D-77) whose father Ken Forrest (Prince Edward) had represented the 1941 Rhodesian Nuffield side. And in 1977 Kevin Curran (Jnr.) not only followed in his father's footsteps — Kevin Curran (Snr. — Milton) was Vice-Captain of the 1947 side — but he became Marandellas's first Nuffield representative. The captain of the 1977 side was Neil Ervine (Prince Edward) whose father, Mike Ervine (Plumtree), played in 1951 and brother, Rory, in 1976J.

At the 1977 Week, Wallace scored 278 runs (average 69,50) and set up a record 155-run third-wicket stand with Kevin Curran against Western Province.

NEIL BOONZAIER, 1973-74-75.

In December 1979, Mike Griffiths managed the last Rhodesian Nuffield side which played in Port Elizabeth. No Rhodesians were selected for the South African Schools XI but Derek Hawtrey (Prince Edward), Colin Robertson (Umtali) and Chris Cox (Marlborough) were selected for the Nuffield Invitation XI which played the Western Province Colts early the following year.

The first Zimbabwe Schools side played a series of four matches during which they beat Zimbabwe B in a one-day game and lost to Kenya by one wicket with the visitors putting on a match-winning last-wicket partnership of 53. Colin Robertson was the star performer, hitting 52* against the Zimbabwe senior side and 61 against Kenya, whilst Kenyon Ziehl (Prince Edward) followed his father, Ken Ziehl (Bulawayo Tech. — 1951) and uncle Gerald Ziehl (Bulawayo Tech. — 1948) into the side.

Colin Robertson made his third appearance in 1982 and Jeremy Weatherall (Jameson) who was a non-travelling reserve in 1979, gained his first cap. Graham Hick gained selection as a 15-year-old — a prolific run-scorer in the junior ranks, he amassed 1082 runs (average 216,40) in his first year at Prince Edward whilst playing in a higher age group.

The English Dragons made a three-week tour in January 1982 which enabled the various provincial sides to play against them as well as the Zimbabwe Schools XI. Unfortunately, the Dragons fared poorly and were overwhelmed by the Zimbabwe Schools side in their second encounter.

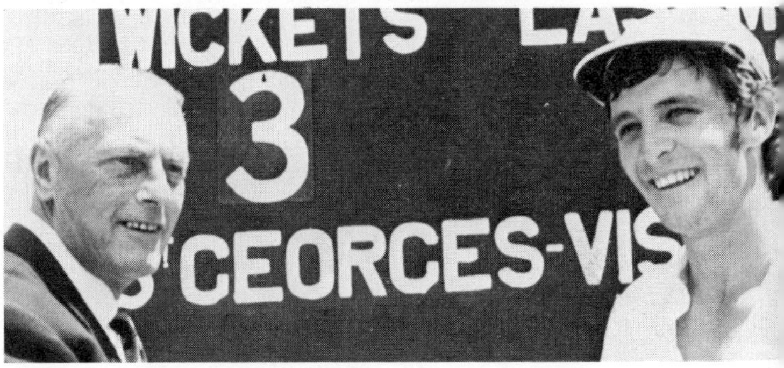

Simon Kerr pictured with Jim Cornford during the course of his century against Old Georgians in 1972.

BARRY ACUTT, 1973-74.

NUFFIELD XI, JANUARY, 1976.
Back: G. Wallace, H. Wallace, K. Lawler, O. Dods, P. Geach, P. Rawson, R. Ervine.
Middle: G. Weatherall, S. Forrest, L. de Grandhomme (Captain), Mr. K. Harris (Manager), D. Alers (Vice-Captain), M. Gibb, A. Keith.
Front: C. Phillips (Scorer).

Peter Wallace (Nuffield 1976-77), captain of the 1975 Rhodesian Fawns, receives a presentation from his Headmaster, Mr. R.K. Gracie, in recognition of his cricket feats at Milton High School.

KEVIN ARNOTT, 1977-78-79.

IAIN BUTCHART, 1977-78-79.

THE NUFFIELD XI, 1979.
Back: Mr. A.M. Griffiths (Manager), C. Robertson, D. Hawtrey, P. Candler, G. Symmonds, C. Cox, B. Currin, D. Tennick, A. Gibson, Mr. K.J.R. Wither (Asst. Manager).
Front: J. Meyer, K. Arnott (Vice-Captain), P. Roche (Captain), B. Roberts, I. Butchart.

NUFFIELD WEEK
BEST PERFORMANCES

CENTURIES

163	P. Wilson (Milton) v. North-Eastern Transvaal 1963.
127*	J. McPhun (Prince Edward) v. North-Eastern Transvaal 1959.
125*	M. Davies (Plumtree) v. Orange Free State 1949.
124*	P. Wallace (Milton) v. Western Province 1977.
116	R. Jones (Prince Edward) v. Natal 1969.
114	B. Roberts (Prince Edward) v. Western Province 1978.
113	K. Tattersall (Prince Edward) v. Western Province 1964.
105	C. Bland (Milton) v. Orange Free State 1956.
104	R. Ullyett (Chaplin) v. Natal 1954.
103*	G. Peckover (Churchill) v. Griqualand West 1974.
102*	J. Heron (Churchill) v. Composite XI 1967.
100	P. Lishman (Gifford) v. Griqualand West 1963.

BOWLING

8/36	R. Lobban (Milton) v. Natal 1950.
8/42	D. Wood (Milton) v. Orange Free State 1941.
8/46	E. Parker (Milton) v. Natal 1957.
7/20	H. Williams (Plumtree) v. Eastern Province 1962.
7/30	R. Cameron (Mount Pleasant) v. Transvaal 1969.
7/31	B. Baxter (Churchill) v. Western Province 1959.
7/56	E. Parker (Milton) v. Transvaal 1958.
6/7	W. Houghton (Prince Edward) v. Orange Free State 1974.
6/11	J. Annandale (Guinea Fowl) v. Transvaal 1953.
6/14	P. Swart (Jameson) v. Natal 1965.
6/16	P. Rudd (Falcon) v. Orange Free State 1973.
6/20	G. Ziehl (Bulawayo Tech.) v. Natal 1948.

ZIMBABWE SCHOOLS, 1982.
Back: G. Hick, I. Stewart, D. Dismore, B. Botha, G. Elworthy, J. Weatherall, A. Elliott.
Seated: S. Lawler, C. Foster-Archibald, S. Carroll (Captain), Mr. R. Gordon (Manager), J. Roche (Vice-Captain), C. Robertson, S. Elworthy.

NUFFIELD WEEK PLAYERS

Acutt B.	(Plumtree) 1973-74 (Capt. '74)
Alers D.	(Plumtree) 1973-74-75-76J (V. Capt. '76), S.A. 1976J
Allan P.	(Hamilton) 1976D, S.A. 1976D
Allies D.	(St. George's) 1952
Amos D.	(Umtali) 1949
Anderson P.	(Prince Edward) 1948-49-50
Anderson T.	(Gifford) 1947-48
Annandale J.	(Guinea Fowl) 1953, S.A. 1953
Archer J.	(Milton) 1962 (V. Capt. '62)
Arnott D.	(Plumtree) 1954-55, S.A. 1955
Arnott K.	(Prince Edward) 1977-78-79 (V. Capt. '78-'79), S.A. 1977-78
Ashley L.	(Ellis Robins) 1968
Ashley-Cooper B.	(Prince Edward) 1956
Ault B.	(Milton) 1952
Ault I.	(Milton) 1972
Austin H.	(Churchill) 1978, S.A. 1978
Austin J.	(St. George's) 1960
Austin P.	(Oriel) 1981
Bailey D.	(Chaplin) 1954
Bain G.	(St. George's) 1946
Baines G.	(Peterhouse) 1978
Baldwin J.	(Plumtree) 1947-48
Baldwin R.	(St. George's) 1968
Ballance R.	(Umtali) 1967
Barber G.	(Plumtree) 1951
Barbour B.	(Milton) 1970-71
Barbour S.	(Milton) 1962 (V. Capt. '62)
Barrett P.	(Plumtree) 1950-51 (Capt. '51)
Bashall M.	(Falcon) 1973 B
Baxter B.	(Churchill) 1959-60, S.A. 1959-60
Beets D.	(Milton) 1959-60
Benatar M.	(Prince Edward) 1949
Benkenstein M.	(Churchill) 1968-69 (V. Capt. '69)
Bennett B.	(Christian Brothers College) 1961
Berrington J.	(St. George's) 1942
Berry R.	(St. George's) 1965-66-67 (Capt. '67), S.A. 1966-67
Bitter B.	(Milton) 1967
Black D.	(Plumtree) 1946
Bland C.	(Milton) 1956-57 (Capt. '57), S.A. 1956-57 (V. Capt. '57)
Bone M.	(Allan Wilson) 1973 B
Boonzaier N.	(Hamilton) 1973-74-75 (V. Capt. '75)
Botha W.	(Fort Victoria) 1982
Bowes T.	(Hamilton) 1970-71
Boyce J.	(Plumtree) 1958 (Capt. '58)
Bradshaw R.	(St. George's) 1969
Bredenkamp L.	(Cranborne) 1971
Bredenkamp M.	(Prince Edward) 1954
Broom G.	(Plumtree) 1951
Brown G.	(Prince Edward) 1947
Brown R.	(Umtali) 1970
Brownlee-Walker A.	(Plumtree) 1964
Broughton G.	(Prince Edward) 1981
Buckley R.	(Umtali) 1975
Burton M.	(Umtali) 1962-63, S.A. 1963
Butchart I.	(Plumtree) 1977-78-79
Butts A.	(St. George's) 1947-48
Calvert N.	(Prince Edward) 1972
Cameron R.	(Mount Pleasant) 1968-69, S.A. 1969
Campher F.	(Fort Victoria) 1973 B
Candler D.	(Gifford) 1940-42
Candler P.	(Plumtree) 1979
Cantrell K.	(Hamilton) 1968
Capon H.	(Milton) 1962-63
Carew B.	(Gifford) 1941-42
Carlisle A.	(Prince Edward) 1963
Carroll S.	(Umtali) 1981-82 (Capt. '81-'82)
Chandler J.	(Hamilton) 1978
Chevallier F.	(Umtali) 1942
Chimowitz B.	(Chaplin) 1941
Ciapparelli P.	(Chaplin) 1956
Clarke D.	(Umtali) 1978
Clift P.	(St. George's) 1971-72, S.A. 1972
Cochrane P.	(Umtali) 1973 B
Cockroft T.	(St. George's) 1956-57
Conway M.	(Gifford) 1955
Cooper S.	(Northlea) 1960
Coventry D.	(Chaplin) 1942
Cox C.	(Marlborough) 1979-81
Cruger J.	(Umtali) 1973 B
Cumming G.	(Chaplin) 1960
Cunningham R.	(Gifford) 1957
Cunningham S.	(St. George's) 1959
Curran K.	(Milton) 1946-47 (V. Capt. '47)
Curran K.	(Marandellas) 1977
Curran S.	(Chaplin) 1973 B-74
Currin B.	(Chaplin) 1979
Cutter E.	(Plumtree) 1941-42
Davies M.	(Plumtree) 1948-49, S.A. 1949
Davidson N.	(Falcon) 1966
Davison B.	(Gifford) 1964-65
Deane-Williams E.	(Umtali) 1958
Deary G.	(Prince Edward) 1954-55-56 (Capt. '56)
De Caila A.	(Northlea) 1958
Deftereos E.	(Umtali) 1952-53
Deftereos G.	(Umtali) 1949
De Grandhomme L.	(Churchill) 1975-76J (Capt. '76J)
Delport J.	(Sinoia) 1969-70
Den G.	(Prince Edward) 1958
Densem P.	(Prince Edward) 1959
Dick P.	(Prince Edward) 1973 B
Dickinson V.	(St. George's) 1950-51-52, S.A. 1952
Dismore D.	(Prince Edward) 1982
Dives W.	(Prince Edward) 1942
Dods O.	(Milton) 1976J
Dollar N.	(Chaplin) 1955
Drysdale J.	(Umtali) 1950-51
Duckworth C.	(Chaplin) 1950-51-52
Duncan H.	(Prince Edward) 1961 (V. Capt. '61)
Dunk M.	(Northlea) 1969
Dunk T.	(Northlea) 1965-66
Du Preez J.	(Prince Edward) 1961
Dyer N.	(Prince Edward) 1940-41, S.A. 1941
Edwards J.	(Churchill) 1962 (Capt. '62)
Ellis B.	(Prince Edward) 1942
Elliott A.	(Prince Edward) 1982
Elworthy G.	(Chaplin) 1982
Elworthy S.	(Chaplin) 1982
Erskine D.	(Prince Edward) 1956-57
Ervine M.	(Plumtree) 1951
Ervine N.	(Prince Edward) 1976D-77 (V. Capt. '76D, Capt. '77)
Ervine R.	(Plumtree) 1954 (Capt. '54)
Ervine R.	(Prince Edward) 1976J
Evans D.	(Prince Edward) 1968-69-70, S.A. 1970
Faasen N.	(Chaplin) 1948, S.A. 1948
Fallon P.	(St. George's) 1949
Ferreira R.	(Guinea Fowl) 1968 (V. Capt. '68)

Fletcher A.	(Prince Edward) 1970-71
Fletcher C.	(Prince Edward) 1966 (Capt. '66)
Fletcher D.	(Prince Edward) 1967 (Capt. '67)
Flowerdew M.	(Churchill) 1958
Ford J.	(St. George's) 1966-67
Forrest K.	(Prince Edward) 1941
Forrest S.	(Prince Edward) 1976J-76D-77
Foster-Archibald C.	(Oriel) 1982
Frampton S.	(Mount Pleasant) 1973
Frangos N.	(Prince Edward) 1959-60 (Capt. '60), S.A. 1960 (Capt. '60)
Fuller R.	(Plumtree) 1961 (Capt. '61)
Furber C.	(Que Que) 1974
Galloway S.	(Oriel) 1976D
Gardiner H.	(Christian Brothers College) 1962
Geach P.	(Lord Malvern) 1976J-76D
Gibb M.	(Hamilton) 1976J-76D (Capt. '76D)
Gibson A.	(Falcon) 1979-81 (V. Capt. '81)
Gillfillan J.	(Prince Edward) 1960
Gilmour E.	(Chaplin) 1965-66
Giri M.	(St. George's) 1942
Godden I.	(Prince Edward) 1959
Godfrey J.	(Umtali) 1940
Gokal K.	(Morgan) 1968
Goldstein F.	(Falcon) 1961
Gous E.	(Chaplin) 1948-49 (Capt '49)
Graham B.	(Hamilton) 1974
Green K.	(St. George's) 1946
Green P.	(Prince Edward) 1941
Green P.	(Plumtree) 1947-48
Grey R.	(Churchill) 1956
Gripper R.	(St. George's) 1956, S.A. 1956
Grundy G.	(Churchill) 1973
Gubb R.	(Gifford) 1961
Hadingham P.	(Umtali) 1964
Hall C.	(Hamilton) 1967
Hanley M.	(St. George's) 1947-48 (V. Capt. '48)
Hanssen K.	(Milton) 1940
Hardwick A.	(Prince Edward) 1978
Harris C.	(Milton) 1940-41-42
Harris M.	(Milton) 1941-42, S.A. 1942
Harris R.	(Milton) 1946
Harris R.	(Gifford) 1960
Havnar G.	(Umtali) 1967
Hawtrey D.	(Prince Edward) 1979-81
Hayes L.	(Plumtree) 1940
Hayes S.	(Peterhouse) 1982
Hefer B.	(Chaplin) 1952
Henderson N.	(Milton) 1958
Hepker G.	(St. George's) 1958
Hepple E.	(Chaplin) 1953
Heron J.	(Churchill) 1967-68 (Capt. '68), S.A. 1968 (V. Capt. '68)
Hick G.	(Prince Edward) 1982
Hill F.	(Falcon) 1969-70 (V. Capt. '70)
Higgins D.	(Umtali) 1981
Hobbins G.	(Umtali) 1964-65 (V. Capt. '64, Capt. '65)
Hodnett W.	(Jameson) 1962-63
Hogg V.	(Alan Wilson) 1969-70, S.A. 1970
Hogg W.	(Prince Edward) 1959
Hornby D.	(Churchill) 1973-74-75 (Capt. '75)
Hough N.	(Prince Edward) 1981
Houghton D.	(Prince Edward) 1975
Houghton K.	(Prince Edward) 1971
Houghton W.	(Prince Edward) 1974
Huckle M.	(Plumtree) 1957
Ingram R.	(Prince Edward) 1950
Jacobson S.	(Peterhouse) 1969-70
James M.	(Churchill) 1967
Jameson J.	(Guinea Fowl) 1975
Jarvis M.	(Que Que) 1975

Jellicoe L.	(Umtali) 1947
Johnson P.	(St. George's) 1946 (V. Capt. '46)
Jones B.	(Milton) 1956
Jones G.	(Prince Edward) 1964
Jones P.	(Milton) 1967
Jones R.	(Prince Edward) 1968-69, S.A. 1969
Kaschula R.	(Chaplin) 1965-66
Keith A.	(Guinea Fowl) 1976J
Kelley P.	(Milton) 1960
Kendall C.	(Northlea) 1960
Kemp C.	(Guinea Fowl) 1953-54 (V. Capt. '54)
Kemp R.	(Guinea Fowl) 1958
Kerr S.	(St. George's) 1971-72-73 (Capt. '73)
Kimble A.	(Plumtree) 1959
Kitto B.	(Chaplin) 1941
Kuhn C.	(Hamilton) 1972
Lachenicht L.	(Falcon) 1973 B
Lamond H.	(Falcon) 1967
Lange T.	(Gifford) 1947-48 (Capt. '48)
Langham C.	(Plumtree) 1953
Laughlin E.	(Milton) 1964-65
Lawler K.	(St. George's) 1976J
Lawler S.	(St. George's) 1982
Leask D.	(St. George's) 1955
Lendrum B.	(Northern Rhodesia) 1959-60
Lewis D.	(Plumtree) 1946 (Capt. '46), S.A. 1946 (V. Capt. '46)
Lindsay D.	(Ellis Robins) 1963
Lishman P.	(Gifford) 1963
Lloyd H.	(Chaplin) 1957
Lobban R.	(Milton) 1950
Locke D.	(Guinea Fowl) 1953
Lothian K.	(Chaplin) 1977
Lunderstedt D.	(Umtali) 1973 B (Capt. B '73)
Macdonald I.	(Prince Edward) 1971
Maggs R.	(Umtali) 1981
Marais J.	(Prince Edward) 1946-47
Martin F.	(Prince Edward) 1948
Martin J.	(Gifford) 1949, S.A. 1949
Mason R.	(Gifford) 1976D
Masson R.	(Plumtree) 1972
Mathews M.	(Prince Edward) 1970-71-72 (Capt. '71-'72), S.A. 1972 (Capt. '72)
McAdam R.	(Plumtree) 1941 (Capt. '41)
McCallum A.	(Milton) 1972
McDonald D.	(Milton) 1946
McGinty M.	(St. George's) 1972
McKechnie P.	(Gifford) 1953-54
McKenzie P.	(Chaplin) 1961
McLoughlin R.	(Hamilton) 1966-67-68, S.A. 1967-67(E)-68
McPhun J.	(Prince Edward) 1957-58-59 (V. Capt. '58, Capt. '59), S.A. 1959 (Capt. '59)
McTavish R.	(Mount Pleasant) 1962-63
Meyer A.	(Gifford) 1950
Meyer J.	(Cranborne) 1977-78-79
Micklesfield M.	(Milton) 1952
Millar T.	(Umtali) 1974
Minter-Brown A.	(Milton) 1971
Mitchell J.	(Churchill) 1964-65-66
Mitchell R.	(Chaplin) 1959
Montgomery H.	(Plumtree) 1941-42
Moore K.	(Plumtree) 1968
Moore N.	(Milton) 1974
Morgan M.	(Churchill) 1976D
Muir A.	(Hamilton) 1973 B
Murray D.	(Plumtree) 1947
Mushava J.	(St. George's) 1982
Napier D.	(Plumtree) 1951-52
Napier R.	(Plumtree) 1955
Nelson S.	(Prince Edward) 1957 (V. Capt. '57), S.A. 1957

Ness R.	(Oriel) 1975
Northcroft D.	(Prince Edward) 1963
Nourse C.	(Peterhouse) 1961-62, S.A. 1961-62
O'Connell-Jones D.	(Plumtree) 1946-47 (Capt. '47)
O'Donovan P.	(Guinea Fowl) 1968
Ogilvie G.	(Churchill) 1968
Oldham H.	(Milton) 1953
Oldreive B.	(Mount Pleasant) 1963
Olivier E.	(Prince Edward) 1974
Oosthuizen J.	(Umtali) 1971-72
Page M.	(Churchill) 1971-72, S.A. 1972
Pafitis C.	(Prince Edward) 1956, S.A. 1956
Parker D.	(St. George's) 1954-55 (V. Capt. '55)
Parker E.	(Milton) 1955-56-57-58, S.A. 1957-58
Passaportis E.	(Prince Edward) 1946
Passaportis T.	(Prince Edward) 1940
Paton A.	(Oriel) 1969
Pearce W.	(Plumtree) 1976D-77
Pechey A.	(St. George's) 1973
Peckover G.	(Churchill) 1972-73-74
Phillips B.	(Churchill) 1971-72
Picken W.	(Chaplin) 1940
Pithey A.	(Plumtree) 1950-51-52-53 (Capt. '53), S.A. 1951-52-53 (V. Capt. '53)
Pithey D.	(Plumtree) 1953-54-55, S.A. 1954
Playford D.	(Milton) 1950 (V. Capt. '50)
Plenderleith D.	(Guinea Fowl) 1973
Pluke J.	(Plumtree) 1956
Postlethwayt C.	(Prince Edward) 1955
Pretorius C.	(Chaplin) 1940, S.A. 1940
Pretorius J.	(Chaplin) 1947
Purchase C.	(Plumtree) 1959-61
Rawson P.	(Churchill) 1976J
Rawlings D.	(Prince Edward) 1969-70 (Capt. '69-'70), S.A. 1970 (Capt. '70)
Rennie P.	(Umtali) 1963 (V. Capt. '63)
Richmond F.	(Umtali) 1966
Rider G.	(Prince Edward) 1973
Ridley G.	(Milton) 1962-63-64 (Capt. '64), S.A. 1963(E)-64
Rigby S.	(Umtali) 1977
Rippon G.	(Guinea Fowl) 1953
Ristow G.	(Allan Wilson) 1969-70
Roberts B.	(Prince Edward) 1978-79, S.A. 1978
Robertson C.	(Umtali) 1979-81-82
Robertson R.	(Churchill) 1956-57
Robertson S.	(Churchill) 1964-65-66
Roche J.	(St. George's) 1982 (V. Capt. '82)
Roche P.	(St. George's) 1978-79 (Capt. '79)
Rogan M.	(St. George's) 1975
Rogers B.	(Churchill) 1974-75
Rosselli R.	(St. George's) 1948
Rudd P.	(Falcon) 1973
Russell B.	(Hamilton) 1967
Salmon R.	(Plumtree) 1946
Sanderson M.	(Plumtree) 1940
Scott G.	(Cranborne) 1976D-77
Seager C.	(Peterhouse) 1970
Senar E.	(Chaplin) 1961-62
Shadwell D.	(Christian Brothers College) 1973 B
Simmonds D.	(Gifford) 1961
Slater G.	(Gifford) 1949
Slaven F.	(St. George's) 1949-50 (V. Capt. '49, Capt. '50)
Smith L.	(Milton) 1978
Snyman C.	(Chaplin) 1950
Sprague W.	(Milton) 1949
Springer M.	(Hamilton) 1973
Stacey H.	(Umtali) 1960 (V. Capt. '60)
Staunton R.	(Plumtree) 1972
Stedall J.	(Plumtree) 1949
Stewart I.	(Sinoia) 1982
Steyn T.	(Umtali) 1967
Storey J.	(St. George's) 1940-41 (V. Capt. '41)
Surgey P.	(Plumtree) 1973 B
Swart P.	(Jameson) 1964-65, S.A. 1965
Symmonds G.	(Ellis Robins) 1979-81
Tattersall K.	(Prince Edward) 1964-65 (V. Capt. '65), S.A. 1965
Teague K.	(Prince Edward) 1946
Tennick D.	(Falcon) 1979-81
Thomas D.	(Prince Edward) 1940 (Capt. '40), S.A. 1940
Thorn B.	(Churchill) 1971 (V. Capt. '71)
Timms M.	(Prince Edward) 1951-52
Todd A.	(Chaplin) 1951-52 (Capt. '52)
Tonkin K.	(Churchill) 1962, S.A. 1962
Townshend D.	(Milton) 1964
Travers A.	(Peterhouse) 1978 (Capt. '78)
Traicos J.	(Thornhill) 1966
Turner G.	(Umtali) 1977 (V. Capt. '77)
Ullyett R.	(Chaplin) 1953-54-55 (Capt. '55), S.A. 1954
Uren P.	(Umtali) 1941
Van Blomestein B.	(Guinea Fowl) 1954
Van Rooyen T.	(Milton) 1952
Vaughan G.	(Prince Edward) 1959-60
Vawdrey M.	(Umtali) 1978
Vincent B.	(Chaplin) 1953-55
Viviers J.	(Northern Rhodesia) 1963
Wallace D.	(Churchill) 1964
Wallace G.	(St. George's) 1976J-'76D
Wallace H.	(Milton) 1976J
Wallace J.	(Churchill) 1961
Wallace P.	(Milton) 1976D-77
Walsh W.	(St. George's) 1940
Walshe A.	(Milton) 1951-52 (V. Capt. '52), S.A. 1951-52
Walton K.	(Peterhouse) 1975
Waspe J.	(Hamilton) 1977
Watson D.	(Umtali) 1957-58
Watson R.	(St. George's) 1942 (Capt. '42)
Weatherall G.	(Jameson) 1975-76J (Churchill) 1976D
Weatherall J.	(Jameson) 1982
Wentzel V.	(Northlea) 1957
Wilkins D.	(St. George's) 1949-50
Wilkinson K.	(Hamilton) 1965-66
Wilkinson P.	(Hamilton) 1965-66
Williams H.	(Plumtree) 1961-62, S.A. 1961-62
Williams M.	(Chaplin) 1954-55
Williams T.	(Hamilton) 1973 B
Wilson G.	(Milton) 1953-54
Wilson P.	(Milton) 1963 (Capt. '63), S.A. 1963
Winton J.	(Churchill) 1957-58
Wishart B.	(Ellis Robins) 1967
Wither K.	(Guinea Fowl) 1962
Wood D.	(Milton) 1941, S.A. 1941
Wood W.	(Jameson) 1958
Wooler C.	(Plumtree) 1948-49, S.A. 1949
Ziehl G.	(Gifford) 1948
Ziehl K.	(Gifford) 1951
Ziehl K.	(Prince Edward) 1981

The following players, who are included in the above list, were selected but for various reasons were unable to participate in the Nuffield Week:

J. Storey (1941), M. Davies (1948), J. Stedall (1949), P. McKechnie (1953), J. Archer (1962), D. Fletcher (1967), J. Ford (1967), T. Bowes (1971), R. Masson (1972).

RHODESIA — ZIMBABWE SCHOOLS
OVERALL RECORD

Nuffield	Played	Won	Lost	Drew/ Aban-doned	Tie
1940	4	4	—	—	—
1941	5	3	2	—	—
1942*	5	2	—	3	—
1946	4	—	1	3	—
1947	4	1	3	—	—
1948	4	4	—	—	—
1949	5	2	—	3	—
1950	4	2	2	—	—
1951	5	1	1	3	—
1952	4	1	1	2	—
1953	4	1	1	1	1
1954	4	3	1	—	—
1955		Cancelled			
1956	5	3	—	2	—
1957	4	2	—	2	—
1958	4	—	2	2	—
1959	4	3	—	1	—
1960	5	2	2	1	—
1961	4	3	1	—	—
1962	4	1	—	3	—
1963	4	1	1	2	—
1964	4	3	—	1	—
1965	5	2	—	3	—
1966	4	3	—	1	—
1967	5	2	2	1	—
1968	5	4	—	1	—
1969	5	2	1	2	—
1970	5	1	—	4	—
1971	5	2	—	3	—
1972	5	3	—	2	—
1973 A	5	1	1	3	—
1973 B	5	2	2	1	—
1974	5	1	3	1	—
1975	5	4	1	—	—
1976 J	5	2	—	2	1
1976 D	5	3	—	2	—
1977	5	3	—	2	—
1978	5	—	1	4	—
1979	5	2	2	1	—
	174	79	31	62	2

*A match against Transvaal at Johannesburg on the way home from Durban has been included here.

NOTE: The 1979 side played as Zimbabwe Rhodesia.

RHODESIA SCHOOLS OTHER MATCHES

	Played	Won	Lost	Drew/ Aban-doned	Tie
Mr. N.V. Bellville's XI (1940)	1	—	1	—	—
M.C.C. Schools (1966)	1	—	—	1	—
Australian Schools (1968)	1	—	—	1	—
Rhodesia B (1976 D)	1	—	1	—	—
	4	—	2	2	—

ZIMBABWE SCHOOLS

	Played	Won	Lost	Drew/ Aban-doned	Tie
1981	4	1	3	—	—
1982	3	1	1	1	—
	7	2	4	1	—

FAWNS TOUR TO ENGLAND 1962

Played 25; Won 20; Lost 0; Drew 5.

	Played	Won	Lost	Drew/ Aban-doned	Tie
ALL MATCHES	210	101	37	70	2

RHODESIA/ZIMBABWE SCHOOLS' SCORES 1940-82

N.B.: Only opponents' individual scores of interest have been included.

1940 at Durban.

Rhodesia — 202 (T. Passaportis 77, C. Pretorius 29, D. Thomas 26)
North-Eastern Transvaal — 66 (J. Godfrey 3/6, L. Hayes 3/25)

Won by 136 runs.

Rhodesia — 168 (D. Thomas 33, W. Picken 32, C. Pretorius 29)
Orange Free State — 104 (W. Picken 3/16, D. Thomas 3/23)

Won by 64 runs.

Rhodesia — 179 (D. Thomas 68, C. Pretorius 51*)
Western Province — 123 (T. Passaportis 6/34)

Won by 56 runs.

Rhodesia — 78 (C. Pretorius 35)
and 56
Mr. N.V. Bellville's XI — 242-8 (W. Picken 3/40)

Lost by an innings and 108 runs.

Rhodesia — 183 (D. Thomas 59, T. Passaportis 23, W. Picken 23, D. Candler 21)
Border — 163 (L. Hayes 6/44, T. Passaportis 3/58)

Won by 20 runs.

1941 at Cape Town.

Orange Free State — 169 (P. During 114; D. Wood 8/42)
Rhodesia — 399-9 (P. Green 123, M. Harris 69, D. Wood 59, N. Dyer 36*, K. Forrest 24, C. Harris 21)
Won by 7 wickets.

Griqualand West — 73 (M. Harris 5/33, D. Wood 4/25)
and 97 (M. Harris 4/9, P. Green 3/8)
Rhodesia — 130 (K. Forrest 55, E. Cutter 25)
Won by 6 wickets.

Rhodesia — 79 (H. Montgomery 20)
and 125-9 (B. Carew 45, H. Montgomery 28)
Natal — 175-6 dec. (M. Harris 3/30)

Lost by 8 wickets.

Transvaal — 193 (H. Montgomery 4/28, M. Harris 3/43)
Rhodesia — 136 (D. Wood 59, N. Dyer 31)

Lost by 57 runs.

Rhodesia — 200 (P. Green 82, M. Harris 44, B. Chimowitz 31*)
North-Eastern Transvaal — 100 (H. Montgomery 5/29)

Won by 100 runs.

1942 at Durban.

Eastern Province — 89 (B. Carew 4/17, H. Montgomery 3/30)
and 83-6
Rhodesia — 139 (M. Harris 48, E. Cutter 28, D. Candler 26)

Won by 5 wickets.

Rhodesia — 28-2
versus Orange Free State

Rain — Match abandoned.

Rhodesia — 65-8
versus Western Province
Rain — Match abandoned.

Rhodesia — 205-5 dec. (C. Harris 69, B. Carew 36*, M. Harris 32, R. Watson 24)
Griqualand West — 69 (H. Montgomery 5/26, D. Candler 3/4)

Won by 136 runs.

1946 at Johannesburg.

Rhodesia — 41
and 61-4 (D. Lewis 31*)
Eastern Province — 228-9 dec.

Lost by 8 wickets.

Rhodesia — 144-3 (D. Lewis 45, D. O'Connell-Jones 44*, D. Black 26)
versus Orange Free State

Rain — Match abandoned.

versus Transvaal

Rain — No play possible.

Border — 143 (D. O'Connell-Jones 4/37, P. Johnson 3/31)
Rhodesia — 115-8 (K. Curran 27, R. Harris 21, D. Black 20)

Draw.

Transvaal — 182 (P. Winslow 40; P. Johnson 6/43)
Rhodesia — 139-7 (E. Passaportis 40, G. Bain 30*, R. Harris 25)

Draw.

1947 at Cape Town.

Rhodesia — 108 (D. O'Connell-Jones 52)
Natal — 175 (D. Murray 3/28, J. Pretorius 3/32)

Lost by 4 wickets.

Rhodesia — 105 (M. Hanley 33)
and 40
Eastern Province — 97 (D. Murray 4/24)
and 42-3

Won by 8 runs.

Rhodesia — 101 (M. Hanley 27, L. Jellicoe 21)
Border — 167 (T. Anderson 4/40, K. Curran 3/29)
Rhodesia — 62-6

Lost by 5 wickets.

Western Province — 149 (D. Murray 3/48)
Rhodesia — 117 (M. Hanley 26)

Lost by 32 runs.

1948 at Port Elizabeth.

Western Province — 96 (T. Anderson 6/45, N. Faasen 4/12)
Rhodesia — 137-8 (N. Faasen 31, A. Butts 22, E. Gous 21)

Won by 4 wickets.

Orange Free State — 84 (G. Ziehl 3/19, T. Anderson 3/24)
Rhodesia — 211-5 (E. Gous 86*, M. Hanley 61, P. Green 38*)

Won by 6 wickets.

Natal — 51 (G. Ziehl 6/20)
and 59-4 (B. Pfaff 24, J. McGlew 18*; G. Ziehl 2/28)
Rhodesia — 73 (E. Gous 18; T. Goddard 3/12)

Won by 3 wickets.

North-Eastern Transvaal — 137 (M. Hanley 3/18, N. Faasen 3/48)
Rhodesia — 151 (E. Gous 39, G. Ziehl 23, F. Martin 20)

Won by 1 wicket.

1949 at Salisbury.

Orange Free State — 104 (C. Wooler 3/17, M. Benatar 3/36)
Rhodesia — 264-7 (M. Davies 125*, C. Wooler 38, W. Sprague 27, G. Deftereos 27)

Won by 6 wickets.

Border — 178-7 (J. Martin 3/28)
Rhodesia — 117-7 (E. Gous 48*, M. Davies 33)

Draw.

Rhodesia — 163 (W. Sprague 33, C. Wooler 37, E. Gous 25, D. Amos 25)
Western Province — 88-9 (C. Wooler 3/22, J. Martin 4/23)

Draw.

Transvaal — 105 (J. Martin 4/20, P. Anderson 3/20)
Rhodesia — 127 (W. Sprague 27, F. Slaven 55)

Won by 2 wickets.

Rhodesia — 171-2 (W. Sprague 85, D. Amos 36)
Eastern Province — 4-0

Rain — Match abandoned.

1950 at Kimberley.

Griqualand West — 200-8 (C. Snyman 3/29)
Rhodesia — 108 (P. Anderson 25)

Lost by 92 runs.

Rhodesia — 185 (V. Dickinson 47, P. Anderson 32, A. Pithey 27, C. Duckworth 20)
Natal — 134 (C. Tayfield 60; R. Lobban 8/36)

Won by 51 runs.

Rhodesia — 219 (V. Dickinson 48, D. Playford 41, P. Barrett 27)
North-Eastern Transvaal — 60 (C. Snyman 4/19, P. Anderson 3/21)

Won by 159 runs.

Rhodesia — 182 (A. Pithey 49, P. Barrett 31, D. Playford 27, V. Dickinson 21)
Western Province — 190-2.

Lost by 8 wickets.

1951 at Durban.

Western Province — 226 (K. Ziehl 4/65)
Rhodesia — 128-8 (P. Barrett 37, A. Pithey 33, V. Dickinson 25)

Draw.

Rhodesia — 153 (G. Barber 39, A. Pithey 29, V. Dickinson 23*)
Transvaal — 145 (G. Ritchie 70; V. Dickinson 4/46)

Won by 8 runs.

Rhodesia — 194-7 (A. Pithey 94, V. Dickinson 54)
Border — 195-4 (R. Geach 120)

Lost by 6 wickets.

Rhodesia — 167 (C. Duckworth 56, A. Pithey 31)
Orange Free State — 60-6 (V. Dickinson 4/7)

Draw.

Griqualand West — 171-8 (V. Dickinson 3/60, J. Drysdale 3/77)
Rhodesia — 139-9 (A. Walshe 32*, J. Drysdale 30)

Draw.

1952 at East London.

Natal — 168 (V. Dickinson 4/30)
Rhodesia — 2-0

Rain — Match abandoned.

Rhodesia — 204-8 (C. Duckworth 87, B. Ault 36)
Transvaal — 75-7 (D. Napier 3/29, M. Micklesfield 3/16)

Draw.

Rhodesia — 222-7 (A. Pithey 96, V. Dickinson 89)
North-Eastern Transvaal — 112 (T. van Rooyen 5/26, M. Micklesfield 3/30)

Won by 110 runs.

Western Province — 248-8 (D. Napier 3/53, V. Dickinson 3/82)
Rhodesia — 107 (D. Allies 35, B. Hefer 25)

Lost by 141 runs.

1953 at Pretoria.

Transvaal — 88 (J. Annandale 6/11)
Rhodesia — 88 (G. Wilson 37*, R. Ullyett 22)

Tie.

Rhodesia — 191-9 (A. Pithey 54, D. Locke 34*, E. Hepple 22*, J. Annandale 22)
Griqualand West — 35-6 (C. Langham 4/14)

Draw.

Rhodesia — 85-4 (J. Annandale 27*, A. Pithey 20)
Eastern Province — 24-6 (J. Annandale 4/13)

Draw.

Rhodesia — 179 (D. Pithey 57, A. Pithey 50, E. Deftereos 34)
Border — 200-8 (C. Kemp 3/28)

Lost by 4 wickets.

Natal — 167 (J. Annandale 4/33, C. Langham 3/39, H. Oldham 3/42)
Rhodesia — 171-5 (E. Deftereos 54, C. Kemp 40*, A. Pithey 27, G. Wilson 26)

Won by 5 wickets.

1954 at Cape Town.

Rhodesia — 222-7 (R. Ullyett 69*, G. Wilson 49, D. Parker 37, D. Pithey 21)
Western Province — 223-6 (R. Ervine 3/47)

Lost by 4 wickets.

North-Eastern Transvaal — 68 (M. Williams 4/16, D. Pithey 4/23)
Rhodesia — 213-5 (D. Pithey 89, R. Ullyett 71)

Won by 7 wickets.

Transvaal — 142 (M. Williams 4/37, D. Pithey 3/53)
Rhodesia — 178 (R. Ervine 34, R. Ullyett 34, G. Wilson 28)

Won by 5 wickets.

Rhodesia — 299-9 (R. Ullyett 104, R. Ervine 45, D. Parker 42, B. van Blomestein 36, D. Bailey 32)
Natal — 161 (C. Burger 42; M. Williams 4/55, G. Deary 3/45)

Won by 138 runs.

1955 at Bloemfontein.

Week cancelled due to polio epidemic.

1956 at Bloemfontein.

Western Province — 265-8 (B. Ashley-Cooper 4/93, E. Parker 3/47)
Rhodesia — 198-6 (C. Bland 69, R. Gripper 49, B. Ashley-Cooper 35*)

Draw.

Rhodesia — 184 (R. Robertson 67, E. Parker 42)
Eastern Province — 156 (B. Jones 4/32)

Won by 28 runs.

Rhodesia — 280-8 (C. Pafitis 82, G. Deary 57, B. Ashley-Cooper 33, C. Bland 26, R. Grey 26, R. Gripper 22)
Griqualand West — 63 (E. Parker 5/9, B. Ashley-Cooper 3/28)
and 86-8 (P. Ciapparelli 4/25)

Won by 217 runs.

Rhodesia — 192 (C. Bland 105, B. Ashley-Cooper 25)
Orange Free State — 165 (P. Carlstein 31; T. Cockroft 4/44, B. Ashley-Cooper 4/58)

Won by 27 runs.

Rhodesia — 216 (R. Gripper 65, D. Erskine 41*, R. Grey 35, B. Ashley-Cooper 21)
Border — 118-8 (B. Ashley-Cooper 3/39)

Draw.

1957 at Bulawayo.

Rhodesia — 127 (S. Nelson 40*, J. McPhun 29; J. Botten 7/52)
North-Eastern Transvaal — 117 (J. Botten 38, H. Lance 26; E.F. Parker 4/40, C. Bland 3/15)

Won by 10 runs.

Rhodesia — 234-6 (C. Bland 66, R. Robertson 46, S. Nelson 34*, E. Parker 30, R. Cunningham 27*)
Eastern Province — 109-4

Draw.

Border — 132 (E.F. Parker 4/53, S. Nelson 4/31)
Rhodesia — 191-5 (R. Cunningham 58, C. Bland 50*, V. Wentzel 35)

Won by 7 wickets.

Rhodesia — 108-5 (V. Wentzel 29*, C. Bland 20)
Western Province — 38-7 (S. Nelson 3/17)

Draw.

Natal — 149-9 (E. Parker 8/46)
Rhodesia — 25-2

Rain — Match abandoned.

1958 at East London.

Rhodesia — 141-5 (J. Winton 56, C. Hepker 48)
Border — 88-1

Draw.

Eastern Province — 146 (M. Flowerdew 4/53, G. Den 3/48)
Rhodesia — 111 (N. Henderson 39, J. Boyce 30)

Lost by 35 runs.

Transvaal — 152 (E. Parker 7/56, J. Boyce 3/15)
Rhodesia — 50 (E. Deane-Williams 17)
and 21-1

Lost by 102 runs.

Rhodesia — 122-4 (J. McPhun 55*, J. Boyce 25, N. Henderson 23)
Western Province — 55-3

Draw.

1959 at Pietermaritzburg.

Rhodesia — 239-4 (J. McPhun 127*, P. Densem 37, C. Purchase 28)
North-Eastern Transvaal — 97-6 (B. Lendrum 3/24)

Draw.

Western Province — 61 (B. Baxter 7/31)
and 62 (D. Beets 6/32)
Rhodesia — 22
and 104-8 (J. McPhun 34, C. Purchase 20)

Won by 3 wickets.

Rhodesia — 160 (R. Mitchell 40, N. Frangos 23, D. Beets 21*)
Griqualand West — 96 (B. Lendrum 4/8, B. Baxter 3/38)

Won by 64 runs.

Natal — 64 (B. Baxter 5/18)
and 90-6
Rhodesia — 152-7 (J. McPhun 43, N. Frangos 48)

Won by 8 wickets.

1960 at Johannesburg.

Eastern Province — 224-8 (G. Pollock 101*; G. Vaughan 3/44)
Rhodesia — 105 (P. Kelly 32, N. Frangos 21, G. Vaughan 20)

Lost by 119 runs.

Rhodesia — 219-4 (N. Frangos 81*, G. Vaughan 37, J. Gilfillan 30, D. Beets 27, G. Cumming 26)
Orange Free State — 140 (B. Baxter 5/26)

Won by 79 runs.

Rhodesia — 213-6 (N. Frangos 75, G. Cumming 55, P. Kelly 22, J. Gilfillan 20)
Transvaal — 141-3 (A. Bacher 38; J. Austin 3/44)

Draw.

Rhodesia — 155 (J. Gilfillan 38, G. Vaughan 27, G. Cumming 23, D. Beets 21)
Western Province — 199-8 (P. Kelly 6/47)

Lost by 6 wickets.

Border — 143 (B. Baxter 3/36, G. Vaughan 3/49)
Rhodesia — 145-9 (S. Cooper 45*, N. Frangos 29, J. Gilfillan 26)

Won by 1 wicket.

1961 at Port Elizabeth.

North-Eastern Transvaal — 35 (H. Williams 5/14, P. Mackenzie 5/16)
and 62-4
Rhodesia — 181-5 (J. Wallace 46, E. Senar 45, J. du Preez 32*, H. Duncan 31)

Won by 9 wickets.

Rhodesia — 93 (F. Goldstein 29, J. Wallace 24)
and 16-0
Natal — 142 (C. Purchase 5/46, R. Fuller 4/36)

Lost by 3 wickets.

Rhodesia — 163 (J. du Preez 65, C. Purchase 32, D. Simmonds 27)
Transvaal — 121 (H. Williams 5/41, B. Bennett 4/32)

Won by 42 runs.

Rhodesia — 201 (C. Nourse 53*, C. Purchase 38, H. Duncan 29, J. du Preez 20)
Griqualand West — 55 (H. Williams 5/8, J. du Preez 3/6)
and 39 (R. Fuller 4/4, H. Williams 3/8)

Won by an innings and 107 runs.

1962 at Johannesburg.

Eastern Province — 57 (H. Williams 7/20)
and 110-2
Rhodesia — 129 (S. Barbour 56, C. Nourse 23)

Won by 7 wickets.

Rhodesia — 139 (W. Hodnett 60, R. McTavish 34, S. Barbour 26)
Border — 100-7 (K. Tonkin 3/22)

Draw.

Rhodesia — 166 (W. Hodnett 65, R. McTavish 39)
Transvaal — 93-9 (H. Williams 3/24, M. Burton 3/20)

Draw.

Orange Free State — 174 (K. Tonkin 4/42, K. Wither 3/49)
Rhodesia — 163-9 (E. Senar 35, W. Hodnett 24, K. Tonkin 24)

Draw.

Western Province — 181 (K. Tonkin 4/24)
Rhodesia — 145-4 (S. Barbour 64, R. McTavish 27, W. Hodnett 21*)

Draw.

1963 at Cape Town.

Rhodesia — 292-4 (P. Wilson 163, W. Hodnett 57, R. McTavish 46, P. Lishman 21)
North-Eastern Transvaal — 87-2

Draw.

Rhodesia — 226-3 (P. Lishman 100, R. McTavish 70, W. Hodnett 41*)
Griqualand West — 125 (J. Viviers 3/12, G. Ridley 3/34)

Won by 101 runs.

Rhodesia — 186 (G. Ridley 38, B. Oldreive 36, R. McTavish 27, P. Lishman 23)
Natal — 187-7 (B. Irvine 55, B. Richards 50, M. Procter 23; M. Burton 5/34)

Lost by 3 wickets.

Eastern Province — 209-9 (M. Burton 5/75)
Rhodesia — 176-8 (P. Wilson 46, G. Ridley 44, W. Hodnett 26, R. McTavish 23, M. Burton 20*; A. Biggs 4/37)

Draw.

1964 at Pretoria.

Border — 152 (H. Ackerman 46; G. Hobbins 5/16)
Rhodesia — 176 (K. Tattersall 49, G. Jones 37, B. Davison 21; H. Ackerman 3/11, A. Greig 2/34)

Won by 5 wickets.

Orange Free State — 187 (P. Swart 3/28, J. Mitchell 3/35)
Rhodesia — 175-8 (B. Davison 45, D. Wallace 45, G. Ridley 24, P. Swart 22, K. Goodwin 6/73)

Draw.

Transvaal — 96 (B. Davison 5/24, A. Brownlee-Walker 3/5)
and 73-3 (G. Watson 51*)
Rhodesia 115-7 (P. Swart 27*, G. Ridley 25*, D. Wallace 24, B. Davison 20)

Won by 3 wickets.

Western Province — 215-4 (G. Pfuhl 101*, J. Cheetham 64)
Rhodesia — 216-3 (K. Tattersall 113, D. Townshend 71)

Won by 7 wickets.

1965 at Kimberley.

Rhodesia — 245-7 (K. Tattersall 75, T. Dunk 48*, P. Swart 36, B. Davison 29, R. Berry 26)
Griqualand West — 86-7 (J. Mitchell 3/22)

Draw.

North-Eastern Transvaal — 118 (J. Mitchell 5/45, R. Kaschula 3/18)
Rhodesia — 130 (E. Gilmour 26, R. Berry 20)

Won by 3 wickets.

Rhodesia — 133 (K. Tattersall 58, T. Dunk 21; P. Henwood 8/41)
and 142-5 (E. Gilmour 62*, R. Berry 38*; P. Henwood 3/42)
Natal — 62 (D. Dyer 15, A. Hipkin 15; P. Swart 6/14, G. Hobbins 4/38)
and 81-6 (M. Procter 27; R. Kaschula 3/24)

Won by 71 runs.

Western Province — 131 (J. Cheetham 55; P. Swart 5/24, P. Wilkinson 4/46)
Rhodesia — 16-4

Rain — Match abandoned.

Eastern Province — 90-4 (A. Biggs 37)

Rain — Match abandoned.

1966 at Cape Town.

Rhodesia — 223-5 (C. Fletcher 57, R. Berry 70*, S. Robertson 49, F. Richmond 27*)
M.C.C. Schools — 74-4

Draw.

Transvaal — 185-6 (P. Wilkinson 3/40)
Rhodesia — 189-6 (S. Robertson 71, C. Fletcher 40*, R. Berry 22)

Won by 4 wickets.

Rhodesia — 198 (E. Gilmour 74, N. Davidson 31, R. Berry 21, R. Kaschula 20)
Natal — 165-7

Draw.

Rhodesia — 195-8 (F. Richmond 82, S. Robertson 31)
Griqualand West — 137 (J. Traicos 5/34, J. Ford 4/49)

Won by 58 runs.

Orange Free State — 153 (J. Traicos 6/40)
Rhodesia — 155-1 (S. Robertson 70*, E. Gilmour 42*, P. Wilkinson 31)

Won by 9 wickets.

1967 at Salisbury.

Rhodesia — 195-9 (T. Steyn 86; V. van der Bijl 3/39)
Western Province — 95-4

Draw.

Composite XI — 104 (P. Jones 3/27, G. Havnar 3/28)
and 110-5
Rhodesia — 203-3 (J. Heron 102*, R. Ballance 69*)

Won by 7 wickets.

Rhodesia — 143 (R. Ballance 46, J. Heron 23, P. Jones 23)
Natal — 145-9 (B. Wishart 5/50, R. McLoughlin 4/35)

Lost by 1 wicket.

North-Eastern Transvaal — 103 (F. Bredenkamp 39*; R. McLoughlin 6/25, B. Wishart 3/28)
Rhodesia — 125 (B. Wishart 46, F. Bredenkamp 4/51)

Won by 22 runs.

Eastern Province — 188 (M. James 4/31, B. Wishart 3/21, P. Jones 3/70)
Rhodesia — 91 (T. Steyn 33, B. Wishart 26)

Lost by 97 runs.

1968 at East London.

Rhodesia — 184-8 (L. Ashley 77*, R. Ferreira 44)
Border — 184-6

Draw.

Rhodesia — 94 (M. Benkenstein 46)
Western Province — 48 (R. McLoughlin 5/21, R. Cameron 4/26)

Won by 46 runs.

Griqualand West — 125 (R. McLoughlin 5/41)
Rhodesia — 181-3 (J. Heron 76, R. Ferreira 75)

Won by 9 wickets.

Rhodesia — 198 (R. McLoughlin 84, J. Heron 35, M. Benkenstein 25; D. Neilson 4/61, N. Featherstone 4/52)
Transvaal — 124 (R. McLoughlin 4/28)

Won by 74 runs.

Orange Free State — 125 (K. Cantrell 3/21, R. Cameron 3/33, R. Baldwin 3/43)
Rhodesia — 128-3 (J. Heron 52*, R. Ferreira 22, P. O'Donovan 20)

Won by 7 wickets.

Australian Schoolboys' Tour 1967-68.

At Salisbury, 19 December.

Rhodesian Schools — 256-9 dec. (R. Jones 61, J. Heron 52, K. Gokal 44, M. Benkenstein 30, L. Ashley 30*)
Australian Schools — 168-5 wkts. (G. Bailey 57; K. Gokal 4/47)

At Salisbury, 20 and 21 December.

Rhodesia U-23 — 395-8 dec. (E. Gilmour 97, D. Fletcher 77, J. Heron 55, T. Dunk 46, J. Wallace 45)
Australian Schools — 214 (G. House 91*; E. Gilmour 3/26, I. Kennedy 3/39)
and 106-4 wkts. (S. Robertson 3/26)

Match drawn.

1969 at Pietermaritzburg.

North-Eastern Transvaal — 82 (R. Cameron 3/14, J. Delport 3/17)
Rhodesia — 153 (R. Jones 65, A. Paton 42)

Won by 7 wickets.

Transvaal — 112 (R. Cameron 7/30)
and 92-3
Rhodesia — 132 (R. Jones 41, G. Ristow 30, D. Evans 20)

Won by 3 wickets.

Eastern Province — 228-6 (R. Cameron 4/93)
Rhodesia — 164-2 (G. Ristow 52, M. Benkenstein 47*, R. Jones 45*)

Draw.

Rhodesia — 202-5 (R. Jones 116, M. Benkenstein 42)
Natal — 99-6 (D. Rawlings 3/18)

Draw.

Rhodesia — 136 (G. Ristow 35, R. Cameron 30, F. Hill 26)
Composite XI — 144-5 (R. Cameron 4/58)

Lost by 5 wickets.

1970 at Bloemfontein.

Border — 209-9
Rhodesia — 184-6 (A. Fletcher 46, G. Ristow 31, D. Rawlings 30, C. Seager 26, F. Hill 26)

Draw.

Griqualand West — 176-6 (T. Bowes 3/38)
Rhodesia — 135-5 (G. Ristow 49, D. Rawlings 30)

Draw.

Natal — 185-3 (D. Bestall 100*, H. Fotheringham 53*; T. Bowes 3/36)
Rhodesia — 82-4 (F. Hill 40*, D. Rawlings 29)

Draw.

Rhodesia — 173-8 (D. Rawlings 38, A. Fletcher 87)
Orange Free State — 67 (D. Rawlings 4/13, S. Jacobson 3/15)

Won by 106 runs.

Rhodesia — 165 (D. Rawlings 47, G. Ristow 45, F. Hill 27)
Transvaal — 151-9 (T. Bowes 4/46)

Draw.

1971 at Port Elizabeth.

Composite XI — 173-5
Rhodesia — 175-5 (B. Phillips 56, M. Mathews 33, P. Clift 25*, B. Barbour 24)

Won by 5 wickets.

Eastern Province — 214-3 (P. Clift 3/53)
Rhodesia — 144-5 (B. Phillips 54*, B. Barbour 47, M. Mathews 21)

Draw.

Border — 254-4 (K. McEwan 156)
Rhodesia — 148-6 (M. Mathews 64, S. Kerr 33*, B. Barbour 20)

Draw.

Rhodesia — 80 (Mathews 28)
North-Eastern Transvaal — 73 (S. Kerr 3/17, J. Oosthuizen 3/36)

Won by 7 runs.

1972 at Johannesburg.

Rhodesia — 157-4 (S. Kerr 47, M. Mathews 37, C. Kuhn 28*)
Natal — 117-5

Draw.

Transvaal — 98 (M. Page 6/23, P. Clift 4/21)
Rhodesia — 15-2

Rain — Match abandoned.

Orange Free State — 124 (M. Mathews 3/23)
Rhodesia — 127-3 (B. Phillips 41*, S. Kerr 41, M. Mathews 23)

Won by 7 wickets.

Griqualand West — 88 (M. Page 3/2)
and 31 (J. Oosthuizen 5/14, P. Clift 3/14)
Rhodesia — 195-1 (M. Mathews 73*, B. Phillips 60*, N. Calvert 46)

Won by an innings and 76 runs.

Western Province — 142 (P. Clift 4/40)
Rhodesia — 149-1 (M. Mathews 96*, N. Calvert 35)

Won by 9 wickets.

1973 at Bulawayo.

Rhodesia — 192 (R. Rudd 47, G. Peckover 34, M. Springer 54)
Western Province — 197-2 (A. Lamb 122, P. Kirsten 65*)

Lost by 8 wickets.

Transvaal — 191-9
Rhodesia B — 96

Lost by 95 runs.

Western Province — 177 (D. Lunderstedt 6/21)
Rhodesia B — 83 (A. Muir 30)

Lost by 94 runs.

Eastern Province — 195-5 (R. Armitage 90)
Rhodesia — 119-8 (A. Pechey 26, D. Hornby 21*, G. Grundy 21)

Draw.

Orange Free State — 182-5 (K. Wessels 60)
Rhodesia B — 187-9 (T. Williams 96*, A. Muir 25)

Won by 1 wicket.

Rhodesia — 213-5 (G. Grundy 76, A. Pechey 48, S. Frampton 33, M. Springer 22*)
Natal — 161-8 (N. Boonzaaier 5/55)

Draw.

Rhodesia — 203 (B. Acutt 55, G. Grundy 44)
Border — 134-8 (I. Foulkes 39, D. Alers 4/57)

Draw.

Rhodesia B — 248 (D. Shadwell 53, T. Williams 45, D. Lunderstedt 43)
Griqualand West — 123 (M. Bone 5/26)

Won by 125 runs.

Rhodesia — 244-8 (S. Kerr 52, M. Springer 44*, G. Peckover 34, P. Rudd 25)
Orange Free State — 70 (P. Rudd 6/16, D. Hornby 3/22)

Won by 174 runs.

Rhodesia B — 196 (T. Williams 92, P. Dick 44)
Eastern Province — 166-6 (M. Bone 3/40)

Draw.

1974 at Pretoria.

Transvaal — 163 (D. Hornby 4/51, D. Alers 4/58)
Rhodesia — 96 (L. Barnard 4/17)

Lost by 67 runs.

Rhodesia — 240-1 (G. Peckover 103*, B. Graham 67, B. Acutt 43*)
Griqualand West — 79-7 (E. Olivier 4/18)

Draw.

Rhodesia — 139 (N. Boonzaaier 64, G. Le Roux 2/33)
Western Province — 144-3 (P. Kirsten 98*)

Lost by 7 wickets.

Rhodesia — 180 (N. Boonzaaier 70)
Orange Free State — 63 (W. Houghton 6/7)

Won by 117 runs.

Rhodesia — 117 (S. Curran 34, G. Peckover 22, N. Boonzaaier 20)
Natal — 118-3

Lost by 7 wickets.

1975 at Kimberley.

Transvaal — 128 (M. Rogan 4/31, D. Alers 4/31)
Rhodesia — 129 (K. Walton 45)

Won by 1 wicket.

Transvaal B — 88 (M. Jarvis 4/27)
Rhodesia — 161-3 (D. Houghton 51*, K. Walton 31, L. de Grandhomme 31, N. Boonzaaier 30*)

Won by 8 wickets.

Orange Free State — 91 (D. Hornby 4/7, M. Jarvis 4/19)
Rhodesia — 141-8 (R. Buckley 22, J. Jameson 21, D. Houghton 21, M. Jarvis 20)

Won by 5 wickets.

Rhodesia — 208-7 (K. Walton 65, N. Boonzaaier 33, D. Houghton 29, D. Alers 26, L. de Grandhomme 20)
Border — 77 (M. Jarvis 4/13, N. Boonzaaier 3/20, B. Rogers 3/21)

Won by 131 runs.

Eastern Province — 203-7 (D. Alers 5/46)
Rhodesia — 116 (G. Weatherall 36, K. Walton 27)

Lost by 87 runs.

1976 at Cape Town (January).

Natal — 162-4
Rhodesia — 162 (K. Lawler 63)

Tie.

Rhodesia — 166 (G. Weatherall 42, D. Alers 37, P. Rawson 22)
Northern Transvaal — 142-7

Draw.

Rhodesia — 121-8 (P. Rawson 42*, R. Ervine 23, K. Lawler 21)
Western Province A — 115 (R. Ervine 3/16, G. Wallace 3/32)
Won by 6 runs.

Rhodesia — 205-9 (D. Alers 64, H. Wallace 47, K. Lawler 29)
Transvaal — 155-4
Draw.

Griqualand West — 74 (D. Alers 4/19)
Rhodesia — 79-2 (K. Lawler 32*)
Won by 8 wickets.

1976 at East London (December).

Eastern Province — 197 (M. Morgan 3/51)
Rhodesia — 102-5 (P. Allan 34, G. Scott 26*)
Draw.

Rhodesia — 145 (P. Allan 49)
Natal — 104 (P. Allan 6/40)
Won by 41 runs.

Border 165-9 (R. Mason 5/35, M. Morgan 3/45)
Rhodesia — 169-6 (P. Allan 68, M. Morgan 33*, M. Gibb 23)
Won by 4 wickets.

Rhodesia — 178-3 (G. Weatherall 73, M. Gibb 69, P. Allan 31*)
Transvaal — 98-4
Draw.

Rhodesia — 231-6 (M. Gibb 57, N. Ervine 46, S. Forrest 40*, S. Galloway 36, P. Wallace 23*)
Northern Transvaal — 87 (P. Geach 4/13, M. Morgan 3/15)
Won by 144 runs.

The side also played a limited overs match against a full strength Rhodesia B side:

Rhodesia B — 298-5 (T.W. Dunk 73 retired, R.D. Brown 73, K. Tattersall 61, P. Allan 3/101)
Nuffield XI — 196-7 (M. Gibb 61, G. Weatherall 54, G. Scott 36)
Lost by 102 runs.

1977 at Durban.

Griqualand West — 153 (W. Pearce 5/89)
Rhodesia — 155-4 (P. Wallace 39)
Won by 6 wickets.

Natal — 160 (G. Turner 5/66)
Rhodesia — 166-3 (K. Arnott 66, P. Wallace 57)
Won by 7 wickets.
Transvaal — 175 (N. Ervine 3/43)
Rhodesia — 148-9 (K. Curran 43, S. Forrest 27, P. Wallace 22)
Draw.

Natal B — 184-6 (W. Pearce 3/61)
Rhodesia — 185-5 (K. Curran 55*, K. Arnott 46, P. Wallace 36)
Won by 5 wickets.

Rhodesia — 256-3 (P. Wallace 124*, K. Curran 52, K. Arnott 33, S. Forrest 20*)
Western Province — 161-3 (A. Kuiper 71*)
Draw.

1978 at Bloemfontein.

Rhodesia — 265-7 (B. Roberts 114, P. Roche 38, K. Arnott 32, H. Austin 27, A. Travers 21)
Western Province — 232-7
Draw.

Eastern Province — 195 (H. Austin 4/66, M. Vawdrey 3/42)
Rhodesia — 150-6 (H. Austin 64*, K. Arnott 37, P. Roche 32)
Draw.

Transvaal — 207 (R. Pienaar 101; G. Baines 5/43)
Rhodesia — 128-8 (K. Arnott 31, B. Roberts 28*, P. Roche 21)
Draw.

Rhodesia — 160 (H. Austin 34, B. Roberts 33, J. Chandler 29, I. Butchart 23)
Orange Free State — 154-8
Draw.

Rhodesia — 133 (H. Austin 43, J. Meyer 37)
Northern Transvaal — 138-8 (M. Vawdrey 3/30)
Lost by 2 wickets.

1979 at Durban.

Border — 187-6
Rhodesia — 188-3 (K. Arnott 72, J. Meyer 58, I. Butchart 23*)
Won by 7 wickets.

S.A. Country — 128 (G. Symmonds 3/12)
Rhodesia — 129-9 (J. Meyer 40, B. Currin 30)
Won by 1 wicket.

Rhodesia — 235-9 (D. Hawtrey 83, J. Meyer 33, C. Robertson 31, B. Currin 23, C. Cox 21)
Transvaal — 157-6 (D. Hawtrey 3/44)
Draw.

Rhodesia — 129 (P. Roche 33, I. Butchart 23)
Eastern Province — 130-4
Lost by 6 wickets.
Rhodesia — 202 (C. Robertson 72, I. Butchart 41, A. Gibson 33)
Natal — 203-6 (I. Butchart 3/56)
Lost by 4 wickets.

1981

At Salisbury.

Zimbabwe Schools — 179-5 (C. Robertson 52*, R. Maggs 42, D. Broughton 36, D. Hawtrey 31; A.J. Traicos 3/42)
Zimbabwe — 180-4 (T.W. Dunk 55, G.C. Wallace 44*, D.A.G. Fletcher 30, D. Higgins 3/53)
Lost by 6 wickets.

At Salisbury.
Zimbabwe B — 301-7 (G. Paterson 85, J. Meyer 69, S. Kuhn 53*, L. de Grandhomme 47; C. Cox 4/113)
Zimbabwe Schools — 138 (K. Ziehl 42; K. Curran 3/24) and 111 (D. Hawtrey 29, K. Ziehl 27; R. Ervine 3/22, L. de Grandhomme 3/18)
Lost by an innings and 52 runs.

At Salisbury.

Zimbabwe Schools — 131 (G. Symmonds 36, D. Hawtrey 26; R. Buckley 3/14)
Zimbabwe B — 121 (G. Scott 48; G. Symmonds 4/33, D. Hawtrey 3/42)
Won by 10 runs.

At Salisbury.

Zimbabwe Schools — 162 (C. Robertson 61, R. Maggs 34, D. Hawtrey 20; D. Patel 4/50, H. Mehta 3/35)
Kenya — 163-9 (A. Patel 45, A. Chotai 36*, J. Opondo 20*; C. Cox 4/51)
Lost by 1 wicket.

1982

At Salisbury.

Zimbabwe Schools — 213 (C. Robertson 76, J. Roche 29, J. Weatherall 22, J. Mushava 21; P. Rawson 5/38, J. Agnew 4/22)

Jack Heron's XI — 218-2 (P.R. Carlstein 63*, A.J. Pycroft 63*, D.L. Houghton 57)

Lost by 8 wickets.

At Salisbury.

Dragons — 205-9 dec. (C. Foster-Archibald 3/21)
Zimbabwe Schools — 160-5 (S. Elworthy 87*, C. Foster-Archibald 31)

Draw.

At Salisbury.

Dragons — 89 (S. Lawler 5/10)
Zimbabwe Schools — 93-2 (C. Foster-Archibald 38, C. Robertson 29*)

Won by 8 wickets.

FAWNS TOUR TO ENGLAND 1962
(4 May to 23 June)

The team: T. Wells (Prince Edward — Captain), P. Rennie (Umtali — Vice-Captain), S. Barbour (Milton), M. Burton (Umtali), H. Capon (Milton), A. Carlisle (Prince Edward), R. Dewar (Northlea), W. Hodnett (Jameson), G. Linden (Hamilton), R. McTavish (Mt. Pleasant), B. May (Prince Edward), D. Northcroft (Prince Edward), C. Nourse (Peterhouse), G. Ridley (Milton), A. Suleman (Morgan).

H. Birrell (Manager); G. Wells (Founder/Secretary).

TOUR AVERAGES

BATTING	INNS	NO	RUNS	HS	AVGE
Northcroft	5	4	88	31	88,00
Barbour	16	5	836	159*	76,00
McTavish	15	3	788	137*	65,66
Wells	15	4	611	100	55,54
Carlisle	16	7	457	71*	50,27
Hodnett	14	2	515	143*	42,91
Linden	7	3	171	59*	42,75
Dewar	15	3	511	104*	42,50
Rennie	13	2	406	100*	36,91
Suleman	4	2	69	27*	34,50
May	16	4	392	85*	32,66
Ridley	5	3	57	30	28,50
Capon	2	0	51	42	25,50
Nourse	10	1	176	63	19,55
Burton	6	2	42	16*	10,30

BOWLING	O	M	R	W	AVGE
Barbour	9	2	22	3	7,33
Wells	10	2	22	3	7,33
Burton	269	97	451	57	7,91
Northcroft	214	68	461	53	8,69
Ridley	221	81	391	34	11,50
Suleman	103	18	290	25	11,66
Capon	172	60	302	25	12,08
Rennie	64	22	131	9	13,46
Hodnett	3	1	14	1	14,00
Linden	104	49	182	9	20,22
McTavish	134	54	264	11	24,00
Carlisle	5	0	30	1	30,00

Note: In 17 matches the Fawns declared at a total of over 200 and were never fully dismissed. In their 25 matches they scored an aggregate of 5 324 runs for the loss of only 114 wickets, an average of 212 runs per match and 46,70 per individual innings.

SOUTH AFRICAN SCHOOLS VERSUS RHODESIA MATCHES

At Salisbury, 15 January 1949.

Rhodesia — 230 (C.D. Franklin 93*, C.J. Pretorius 37; A. Tayfield 6/85, T.L. Goddard 3/62)

S.A. Schools — 87-5 (A. Bowman 39; H.J. Tayfield 3/33)

Draw.

At Bulawayo, 10 January 1957.

S.A. Schools — 166 (E.F. Parker 40*; D.B. Pithey 5/38, J.T. Partridge 3/48)

Rhodesia — 113-9 (C.A.R. Duckworth 36, D.B. O'Connell-Jones 34; S.W. Nelson 6/21)

Draw.

At Salisbury, 14 January 1967.

Rhodesia — 156 (J.D. McPhun 56, A.J. Pithey 46; D.S. van der Knapp 4/69)

S.A. Schools — 163-9 (K.A. McKenzie 46, D.J. Morgan 32; N.A. Deudney 3/37, J.H. du Preez 3/65)

S.A. Schools won by 1 wicket.

At Bulawayo, 6 January 1973.

Rhodesia — 332-3 dec. (P.R. Carlstein 102, B.F. Davison 77*, S.D. Robertson 59, J.C. Mitchell 49)

S.A. Schools — 177 (K.D. Verdoorn 69, C. van Niekerk 35; R.H. Kaschula 4/76, M.I. Procter 3/27)

Rhodesia won by 155 runs.

A S.A. Schools XI on tour in January 1971 played against a Rhodesia Colts XI.

At Salisbury, 7 and 8 January.

Rhodesian Colts — 387-9 dec. (J.K. Clarke 120, J.C. Mitchell 63, T.W. Dunk 35; R. Rogers 4/56)

S.A. Schools — 223 (D.L. Hobson 65*, G.S. Cowley 50; A.J. Traicos 4/68, D.P. Cameron 3/62)

Rhodesian Colts XI on first innings.

Addendum

The visit of the Young Australians and the announcement of the Zimbabwe Team for the Prudential World Cup Competition occurred as the book was going to Press, providing a last-minute opportunity for the inclusion of the following additional information.

SRI LANKA TOUR OF ZIMBABWE — 1982

SCORES:

At Bulawayo, 5, 6, 7 and 8 November.

Zimbabwe — 416 (A. Pycroft 128, K. Curran 96, D. Houghton 45, C. Hodgson 40, J. Traicos 32*) and 221-6 (A. Pycroft 81, D. Houghton 77)

Sri Lanka — 335 (R. Dias 85; P. Rawson 6/82) and 126-2 (R. Dias 61*)

Match drawn.

At Harare, 12, 13 and 14 November.

Zimbabwe — 365 (A. Pycroft 96, J. Heron 72, P. Rawson 63*, D. Houghton 50)

Sri Lanka — 104 (K. Curran 4/24, D. Fletcher 3/30) and 221 (D. Mendis 67; V. Hogg 6/26)

Zimbabwe won by an innings and 40 runs.

ONE-DAY MATCHES (50 OVERS)

At Harare, 30 October.

Zimbabwe — 196-6 (50 overs) (K. Curran 59, D. Fletcher 45, J. Heron 35)

Sri Lanka — 197-7 (45,5 overs) (D. Mendis 53)

Sri Lanka won by 3 wickets.

At Harare, 31 October.

Sri Lanka — 161 (48,5 overs) (D. Fletcher 3/24)

Zimbabwe — 162-4 (43 overs) (D. Fletcher 60*, A. Pycroft 50)

Zimbabwe won by 6 wickets.

OTHER ONE-DAY MATCHES (50 OVERS)

At Harare South, 27 October.

Zimbabwe Country Districts — 213-9 (50 overs) (I. Butchart 66, R. Brown 65)

Sri Lanka — 214-3 (44 overs) (R. Dias 102*, D. Mendis 50; K. Curran 2/33, I. Butchart 1/19)

Sri Lanka won by 7 wickets.

At Mutare, 3 November.

Sri Lanka — 284 (50 overs) (D. Mendis 87; V. Hogg 3/54)

A Zimbabwe XI — 118 (38,4 overs)

Sri Lanka won by 166 runs.

At Triangle, 10 November.

A Zimbabwe XI — 165-9 (50 overs) (T. Dunk 42, Ali Shah 36)

Sri Lanka — 169-5 (46,3 overs)

Sri Lanka won by 5 wickets.

YOUNG AUSTRALIA TOUR OF ZIMBABWE — 1983

SCORES:

At Harare, 1, 2, 3 and 4 April.

Young Australia — 408 (D. Boon 148, G. Ritchie 69, W. Philips 58; J. Traicos 5/103, P. Rawson 3/92)

Zimbabwe — 164 (Ali Shah 42, A. Pycroft 33) and 190 (Ali Shah 55, D. Houghton 55; M. Whitney 5/29)

Young Australia won by an innings and 55 runs.

At Harare, 14, 15, and 16 April.

Zimbabwe — 127 (D. Fletcher 44) and 308-9 dec. (Ali Shah 105, D. Fletcher 56, I. Butchart 48*, A. Pycroft 35)

Young Australia — 126 (P. Rawson 7/55, J. Traicos 3/22) and 216 (D. Boon 108; P. Rawson 6/88, J. Traicos 3/44)

Zimbabwe won by 93 runs.

50-OVERS MATCHES

At Harare, 30 March.

Young Australia — 164-4 (50 overs) (G. Shipperd 75*)
Zimbabwe Colts — 43 (25,5 overs)

Young Australia won by 121 runs.

At Mutare, 6 April.

Young Australia — 236-5 (D. Jones 66)

Zimbabwe Colts — 214 (48,5 overs) (G. Paterson 47, K. Curran 46)

Young Australia won by 22 runs.

At Bulawayo, 9 April.

Zimbabwe — 234-8 (50 overs) (D. Fletcher 79, D. Houghton 36)

Young Australia — 222-6 (46,4 overs) (W. Philips 75, D. Boon 65*)

Young Australia won — higher average per wicket.

At Harare, 12 April.

Young Australia — 242-5 (50 overs) (G. Shipperd 67, D. Boon 53*)

Zimbabwe Country Districts — 105 (36,1 overs) (M. Seager 31, R. Ervine 27*; P. Blizzard 4/7)

Young Australia won by 137 runs.

At Harare, 17 April.

Zimbabwe — 242-7 (50 overs) (J. Heron 82, Ali Shah 68)

Young Australia — 246-4 (49 overs) (W. Philips 135)

Young Australia won by 6 wickets.

ZIMBABWE TEAM FOR THE PRUDENTIAL WORLD CUP COMPETITION — MAY AND JUNE 1983

D. Fletcher — Captain	I. Butchart	G. Hick	D. Houghton	A. Pycroft
J. Traicos — Vice-Captain	K. Curran	C. Hodgson	G. Paterson	P. Rawson
R. Brown	J. Heron	V. Hogg	G. Peckover	Ali Shah

APPENDIX

Rhodesian and Zimbabwean First-Class Records

THE OVERALL RECORD

YEAR	PLAYED	WON	LOST	DREW
1904-05	1	—	1	—
1909-10	2	—	1	1
1922-23	2	—	1	1
1924-25	1	—	1	—
1927-28	2	—	2	—
1929-30	5	—	5	—
1930-31	1	—	—	1
1931-32	5	4	1	—
1935-36	1	—	—	1
1936-37	1	—	1	—
1938-39	2	—	—	2
1945-46	2	—	1	1
1946-47	7	1	3	3
1947-48	5	1	4	—
1948-49	2	—	—	2
1949-50	2	—	2	—
1950-51	6	2	3	1
1951-52	6	3	2	1
1952-53	6	3	2	1
1953-54	1	—	—	1
1954-55	6	3	2	1
1955-56	6	6	—	—
1956-57	3	—	2	1
1957-58	6	3	2	1
1958-59	6	1	—	5
1959-60	8	3	3	2
1960-61	7	2	3	2
1961-62	6	1	2	3
1962-63	8	4	—	4
1963-64	5	4	—	1
1964-65	4	1	2	1
1965-66	5	1	1	3
1966-67	5	—	5	—
1967-68	6	4	—	2
1968-69	7	—	4	3
1969-70	5	—	5	—
1970-71	7	6	—	1
1971-72	10	5	1	4
1972-73	10	4	3	3
1973-74	9	1	3	5
1974-75	9	2	3	4
1975-76	10	3	3	4
1976-77	8	—	5	3
1977-78	8	1	3	4
1978-79	8	1	2	5
1979-80	8	1	4	3
1980-81	8	3	1	4
1981-82	5	1	1	3
1982	2	—	—	2
	255	75	90	90

TEAM RECORDS

HIGHEST INNINGS TOTALS

570-6d	v.	Griqualand West	at Bulawayo	1955-56
560-6d	v.	North-Eastern Transvaal	at Pretoria	1962-63
551	v.	Orange Free State	at Salisbury	1955-56
549-1d	v.	Orange Free State	at Bloemfontein	1967-68
483	v.	Griqualand West	at Kimberley	1955-56
476-7d	v.	International Wanderers	at Bulawayo	1972-73
473	v.	Griqualand West	at Kimberley	1950-51
471	v.	Griqualand West	at Kimberley	1954-55
468-7d	v.	North-Eastern Transvaal	at Bulawayo	1955-56
452-7d	v.	Border	at East London	1967-68
450	v.	Eastern Province	at Salisbury	1965-66

NOTE: Rhodesia B compiled 508-4d against Eastern Province B at Salisbury in 1978-79.

LOWEST INNINGS TOTALS

47	v.	North-Eastern Transvaal	at Pretoria	1963-64
52	v.	Cavaliers	at Salisbury	1960-61
55	v.	Transvaal	at Johannesburg	1904-05
56	v.	Leicestershire	at Salisbury	1980-81
57	v.	M.C.C.	at Salisbury	1956-57
60	v.	Border	at King Williamstown	1929-30
61	v.	M.C.C.	at Salisbury	1948-49
64	v.	Transvaal	at Salisbury	1949-50
64	v.	Western Province	at Salisbury	1978-79
68	v.	Transvaal	at Salisbury	1952-53
71	v.	Australians	at Bulawayo	1949-50

BATTING

INDIVIDUAL SCORES OF 150 OR MORE

279	R.A. Gripper	v. Orange Free State at Bloemfontein	1967-68
254	M.J. Procter	v. Western Province at Salisbury	1970-71
197	K.C. Bland	v. Border at East London	1967-68
179	B.J. Carew	v. North-Eastern Transvaal at Pretoria	1952-53
175	J.G. Heron	v. Transvaal at Salisbury	1975-76
174	M.J. Procter	v. North-Eastern Transvaal at Pretoria	1970-71
170*	D.J. Lewis	v. North-Eastern Transvaal at Salisbury	1954-55
166	D.B. Pithey	v. North-Eastern Transvaal at Pretoria	1962-63
162	K.C. Bland	v. North-Eastern Transvaal at Pretoria	1962-63
161*	A.J. Pithey	v. Transvaal at Johannesburg	1958-59
154	P.N.F. Mansell	v. Griqualand West at Kimberley	1955-56
154	J.D. McPhun	v. Orange Free State at Bloemfontein	1970-71
153*	R.A. Gripper	v. Eastern Province at Bulawayo	1975-76
153	J.G. Heron	v. Natal at Salisbury	1964-65

NOTE: R.D. Brown scored 200* for Rhodesia B against Eastern Province B at Salisbury in 1978-79.

HUNDRED ON DEBUT

128	A.H. Pattison	v.	Orange Free State	at Johannesburg	1931-32
124*	T.A. Chapman	v.	Griqualand West	at Salisbury	1952-53
125	P.R. Carlstein	v.	Natal B	at Salisbury	1967-68
112*	J.K. Clarke	v.	Western Province	at Cape Town	1967-68
142	B. Dudleston	v.	Western Province	at Cape Town	1976-77

NOTE: Only J.K. Clarke was making his debut in first-class cricket.

P.J. Allan scored 138 for Rhodesia B against Eastern Province B at Salisbury in 1978-79 in his first-class debut.

TWO SEPARATE HUNDREDS IN A MATCH

114/131 M.J. Procter v. International Wanderers at Salisbury 1972-73

FASTEST HUNDRED

Mins.
65 E.S. Newson (114) v. Griqualand West at Kimberley 1946-47
72 M.J. Procter (107) v. Orange Free State at Bloemfontein.............................. 1970-71

HUNDRED BEFORE LUNCH

ON THE FIRST DAY OF A MATCH
P.N.F. Mansell (111) v. Griqualand West at Kimberley 1954-55
D.B. O'Connell-Jones (121) v. Orange Free State at Salisbury 1955-56
B.D. Barbour (106) v. Natal at Bulawayo... 1971-72
ON OTHER DAYS
T.A. Chapman (124*) v. Griqualand West at Salisbury 1952-53
(Score increased from 5* to 124* on third morning)
B.F. Davison (129) v. Eastern Province at Port Elizabeth.................................... 1978-79
(Score increased from 18* to 118* on third morning)

SIX HUNDREDS IN SUCCESSIVE INNINGS

M.J. procter (1970-71) equalled the world record held jointly by C.B. Fry (1901) and D.G. Bradman (1938-39). Procter's scores were: 119 v. Natal B at Bulawayo; 129 v. Transvaal B at Salisbury; 107 v. Orange Free State at Bloemfontein; 174 v. North-Eastern Transvaal at Pretoria; 106 v. Griqualand West at Kimberley and 254 v. Western Province at Salisbury.

MOST RUNS SCORED OFF ONE OVER

26 (606644) E.F. Parker off F.T.M. Drummer v. Transvaal at Salisbury.................. 1968-69

HIGHEST AVERAGE EACH SEASON
(Qualification: 200 runs)

		M	I	N.O.	R	H.S.	AV.	100	50
1929-30	C.J.R. Hayward	5	10	—	318	86	31,80	—	3
1931-32	H. Campbell-Rodger	5	9	1	385	108	48,13	2	1
1946-47	P.N.F. Mansell	7	13	2	508	111*	46,18	1	4
1947-48	C.J. Pretorius	5	10	—	328	104	32,80	1	2
1950-51	D. Rees	4	7	1	273	105	45,50	1	1
1951-52	D.J. Lewis	5	10	2	414	100*	51,77	1	4
1952-53	D.J. Lewis	6	11	2	420	114	46,67	1	2
1954-55	P.N.F. Mansell	6	7	—	427	131	61,00	2	3
1955-56	P.N.F. Mansell	5	6	—	393	154	65,50	2	1
1957-58	D.B. Pithey	3	5	2	230	99*	76,67	—	2
1958-59	A.J. Pithey	6	11	2	497	161*	55,22	2	1
1959-60	R.A. Gripper	6	12	2	256	73	25,60	—	1
1960-61	A.J. Pithey	7	13	2	418	111	38,00	1	2
1961-62	K.C. Bland	5	10	1	449	91	49,89	—	4
1962-63	A.J. Pithey	8	15	3	638	141	53,17	2	4
1963-64	J.D. McPhun	3	5	2	318	131	106,00	1	2
1964-65	A.J. Pithey	3	6	2	385	98	96,25	—	4
1965-66	D.B. Pithey	5	9	1	332	143	41,50	1	1
1966-67	J.H. du Preez	5	10	1	394	112	43,78	1	3
1967-68	R.A. Gripper	6	11	4	529	279*	75,57	1	2
1968-69	K.C. Bland	7	13	1	463	82	43,53	—	4
1969-70	S.D. Robertson	5	10	—	313	62	31,30	—	2
1970-71	M.J. Procter	7	7	—	934	254	133,43	6	—

		M	I	N.O.	R	H.S.	AV.	100	50
1971-72	S.D. Robertson	5	10	3	453	118	64,71	1	4
1972-73	M.J. Procter	10	19	2	841	131	49,47	2	4
1973-74	J.H. du Preez	9	16	1	559	99	37,27	—	5
1974-75	M.M. Benkenstein	3	6	—	226	84	37,66	—	2
1975-76	J.G. Heron	8	15	—	747	175	49,80	3	2
1976-77	B. Dudleston	4	8	—	393	142	49,13	1	1
1977-78	B.D. Barbour	3	6	2	203	102*	50,75	1	1
1978-79	B.F. Davison	8	15	1	488	129	34,85	1	2
1979-80	R.M. Bentley	8	16	—	578	122	36,13	1	4
1980-81	A.J. Pycroft	8	14	4	683	115	68,30	3	4
1981-82	A.J. Pycroft	5	8	2	507	133	84,50	1	4

HIGHEST AGGREGATES IN A SEASON: OVER 600 RUNS

		M	I	N.O.	R	H.S.	AV.	100	50
1970-71	M.J. Procter	7	7	—	934	254	133,43	6	—
1972-73	M.J. Procter	10	19	2	841	131	49,47	2	4
1975-76	J.G. Heron	8	15	—	747	175	49,80	3	2
1971-72	M.J. Procter	10	19	2	695	107	40,88	1	5
1980-81	A.J. Pycroft	8	14	4	683	115	68,30	3	4
1977-78	B. Dudleston	8	16	1	678	132	45,20	2	3
1972-73	P.R. Carlstein	10	18	—	653	105	36,28	1	5
1962-63	A.J. Pithey	8	15	3	638	141	53,17	2	4
1974-75	B.F. Davison	9	18	—	611	109	33,94	2	1
1971-72	B.D. Barbour	10	20	1	609	106	32,05	1	4

HIGHEST PARTNERSHIPS

BEST FIRST-WICKET STANDS

268	R.A. Gripper and J.K. Clarke v. Orange Free State at Bloemfontein	1967-68
140	D.B. O'Connell-Jones and J.M.S. Baldwin v. Griqualand West at Kimberley	1955-56
130	D.B. O'Connell-Jones and J.M.S. Baldwin v. North-Eastern Transvaal at Bulawayo	1955-56
129	R.A. Gripper and J.D. McPhun v. Worcestershire at Salisbury	1964-65
123	C.M. Harris and J.H.F. Fuller v. Western Province at Cape Town	1946-47

BEST SECOND-WICKET STANDS

281*	R.A. Gripper and R.B. Ullyett v. Orange Free State at Bloemfontein	1967-68
226	J.D. McPhun and R.B. Ullyett v. Border at Salisbury	1963-64
174	J.G. Heron and M.J. Procter v. Eastern Province at Port Elizabeth	1975-76
160	A.J. Pithey and K.C. Bland v. Griqualand West at Kimberley	1960-61
146	R.A. Gripper and R.B. Ullyett v. Transvaal B at Johannesburg	1963-64

BEST THIRD-WICKET STANDS

226	S.D. Robertson and M.J. Procter v. Eastern Province at Port Elizabeth	1975-76
211	J. Dell and D.J. Lewis v. Border at East London	1952-53
173	R.A. Gripper and A.J. Pithey v. Cavaliers at Salisbury	1962-63
169	J.H.A. Wallace and T.A. Chapman v. Griqualand West at Salisbury	1952-53
165*	R.A. Gripper and A.J. Pithey v. Natal at Salisbury	1964-65

BEST FOURTH-WICKET STANDS

210	A.J. Pithey and J.H. du Preez v. Eastern Province at Port Elizabeth	1966-67
187	B.J. Carew and D.J. Lewis v. North-Eastern Transvaal at Pretoria	1952-53
181	R.B. Ullyett and K.C. Bland v. Border at East London	1967-68
167	M.J. Procter and B.F. Davison v. Eastern Province at Bulawayo	1971-72
165	D.J. Lewis and P.N.F. Mansell v. Griqualand West at Kimberley	1955-56

NOTE: R.D. Brown and P.J. Allan added 300 for the Fourth Wicket for Rhodesia B against Eastern Province B at Salisbury in 1978-79.

BEST FIFTH-WICKET STANDS

203	P.N.F. Mansell and M.W. Davies v. Griqualand West at Bulawayo	1955-56
185	H. Campbell-Rodger and C.J.R. Hayward v. Transvaal at Johannesburg	1931-32
182	D.J. Lewis and M.W. Davies v. North-Eastern Transvaal at Bulawayo	1955-56
179	P.N.F. Mansell and M.W. Davies v. Griqualand West at Kimberley	1954-55
169	M.J. Procter and B.F. Davison v. International Wanderers at Salisbury	1972-73

BEST SIXTH-WICKET STANDS

193	R.B. Ullyett and D.B. Pithey v. Eastern Province at Salisbury	1965-66
166	M.J. Procter and H.A.B. Gardiner v. Western Province at Salisbury	1970-71
131	P.R. Carlstein and J.H. du Preez v. Transvaal B at Salisbury	1967-68
122	F. McDonald and E.S. Newson v. North-Eastern Transvaal at Brakpan	1946-47
116	R.D. Brown and D.A.G. Fletcher v. Northern Transvaal at Salisbury	1979-80

BEST SEVENTH-WICKET STANDS

144	D.B. Pithey and R.B. Ullyett v. North-Eastern Transvaal at Benoni	1957-58
131	B.J. Carew and C.D. Franklin v. Transvaal at Salisbury	1949-50
130	C.J. Pretorius and H.J. Tayfield v. Transvaal at Johannesburg	1947-48
126	B.F. Davison and D.A.G. Fletcher v. Transvaal at Johannesburg	1977-78
113	D.B. Pithey and J.H. du Preez v. Eastern Province at Salisbury	1965-66

BEST EIGHTH-WICKET STANDS

152	H.A.B. Gardiner and P.B. Clift v. Western Province at Salisbury	1974-75
112	C.J. Pretorius and D. Rees v. Griqualand West at Kimberley	1950-51
105	J.H. du Preez and D.A.G. Fletcher v. Transvaal at Johannesburg	1974-75
94	I.E. Haig and D.B. Arnott v. Eastern Province at Port Elizabeth	1960-61
79	J.H. du Preez and A.H. de Caila v. Transvaal at Johannesburg	1968-69
79	D.L. Houghton and R.M. Bentley v. Natal at Pietermaritzburg	1978-79

BEST NINTH-WICKET STANDS

119	P.B. Clift and R.D. Jackman v. Eastern Province at Bulawayo	1972-73
101	J.D. McPhun and H.A.B. Gardiner v. Western Province at Cape Town	1971-72
77	M.W. Davies and D.B. Arnott v. Border at East London	1955-56
74	D.B. Pithey and G.B. Lawrence v. Eastern Province at Port Elizabeth	1957-58
63	D. Rees and A.S. Carew v. Eastern Province at Port Elizabeth	1950-51
63	D.W. Townshend and A.H. de Caila v. Western Province at Cape Town	1967-68

BEST TENTH-WICKET STANDS

106	E. Sim and H.J. O'Reilly v. Griqualand West at Kimberley	1929-30
70	P.N.F. Mansell and A.S. Carew v. Griqualand West at Kimberley	1946-47
69	G.B. Lawrence and J.T. Partridge v. Worcestershire at Bulawayo	1964-65
59	D.A.G. Fletcher and R.H. Kaschula v. Natal at Durban	1971-72
58	J.H. du Preez and N.R. Williams v. Natal at Salisbury	1966-67

BOWLING

BEST INNINGS BOWLING ANALYSES

	O	M	R	W		
9 WICKETS						
M.J. Procter	36,1	17	71	9	v. Transvaal at Bulawayo	1972-73
8 WICKETS						
R.D. Jackman	17,4	7	40	8	v. Natal at Durban	1972-73
G.B. Lawrence	19,1	5	42	8	v. Western Province at Cape Town	1965-66
J.T. Partridge	19	2	69	8	v. Natal at Salisbury	1961-62
J.H. du Preez	49,1	18	92	8	v. Transvaal B at Salisbury	1967-68
J.T. Partridge	+34	6	124	8	v. Border at East London	1954-55

	O	M	R	W		
7 WICKETS FOR 50 OR LESS RUNS						
J.T. Partridge	12,1	8	9	7	v. Border at Bulawayo...............	1959-60
V.E.J. Dickinson	15,5	9	22	7	v. Eastern Province at Port Elizabeth ...	1960-61
M.J. Procter	16	2	32	7	v. Transvaal at Johannesburg	1971-72
P.B. Clift	15	4	38	7	v. Transvaal at Salisbury.............	1973-74
R.B. Ullyett	+17,6	3	42	7	v. N.E. Transvaal at Benoni..........	1957-58
G.B. Lawrence	25,1	8	43	7	v. Transvaal at Bulawayo	1959-60
P.N.F. Mansell	18,4	4	43	7	v. Surrey at Salisbury................	1959-60
6 WICKETS FOR 25 OR LESS RUNS						
J.T. Partridge	+11,4	5	13	6	v. N.E. Transvaal at Pretoria	1955-56
G.B. Lawrence	11,3	4	19	6	v. Transvaal at Bulawayo	1961-62
J.T. Partridge	12	7	20	6	v. Eastern Province at Port Elizabeth ...	1966-67
D.J. Beets	15,4	6	25	6	v. Griqualand West at Kimberley	1960-61
5 WICKETS FOR 15 OR LESS RUNS						
M.J. Procter	10	8	8	5	v. Border at Salisbury	1970-71
M.J. Procter	10,5	4	9	5	v. Western Province at Cape Town....	1971-72
R.H. Kaschula	11	7	13	5	v. Orange Free State at Bloemfontein...	1970-71
H.V. Paton	14,4	10	13	5	v. Western Province at Salisbury......	1958-59
G.B. Lawrence	17	8	14	5	v. N.E. Transvaal at Pretoria	1963-64

BEST MATCH BOWLING ANALYSES

	O	M	R	W		
14 WICKETS						
J.T. Partridge	32,4	6	101	14	v. Natal at Salisbury	1961-62
13 WICKETS						
P.N.F. Mansell	43,5	7	120	13	v. Surrey at Salisbury................	1959-60
P.N.F. Mansell	+66,5	10	205	13	v. Border at East London............	1951-52
11 WICKETS FOR 100 OR LESS RUNS						
P.N.F. Mansell	+30,7	6	84	11	v. Border at East London............	1955-56
D.A.G. Fletcher	36,4	7	92	11	v. Eastern Province at Bulawayo	1974-75
G.B. Lawrence	51,4	18	98	11	v. Western Province at Cape Town....	1965-66
10 WICKETS FOR 80 OR LESS RUNS						
D.J. Beets	39,4	18	59	10	v. Griqualand West at Kimberley	1960-61
J.T. Partridge	+29,4	8	80	10	v. N.E. Transvaal at Pretoria	1955-56

NOTE: + = 8-ball overs.

LOWEST AVERAGE EACH SEASON
(Qualification: 10 wickets)

		O	M	R	W	AV.	5WI	10WM
1922-23	P. Rabinson	48,3	13	112	10	11,20	1	—
1929-30	W. Wood	122,5	20	359	19	18,89	1	—
1931-32	M.H. Quinn	115,5	23	293	24	12,21	2	—
1946-47	L.S. Brown	+165	19	552	21	26,29	1	—
1947-48	A.P. Singleton	+ 50	11	148	12	12,33	1	—
1950-51	P. Johnson	+122	21	392	18	21,78	1	—
1951-52	P.N.F. Mansell	+245,5	41	802	49	16,37	6	2
1952-53	J.T. Partridge	+208,6	42	629	33	19,06	3	—
1954-55	B.J. McBride	+ 66	9	180	13	13,85	1	—
1955-56	P.N.F. Mansell	+206,3	57	518	36	14,39	2	1
1956-57	G.B. Lawrence	+ 91	22	260	12	21,67	2	—
1957-58	R.B. Ullyett	+ 91,6	31	193	15	12,87	1	—
1958-59	H.V. Paton	85,1	36	144	11	13,09	1	—

		O	M	R	W	AV.	5WI	10WM
1959-60	G.B. Lawrence	310,3	104	615	37	16,62	2	—
1960-61	D.J. Beets	69,3	26	129	12	10,75	1	1
1961-62	G.B. Lawrence	109,4	28	267	19	14,05	2	—
1962-63	J.T. Partridge	334,1	138	659	46	14,33	3	—
1963-64	G.B. Lawrence	190,1	71	299	27	11,07	2	—
1964-65	G.B. Lawrence	134,1	36	359	17	21,12	1	—
1965-66	G.B. Lawrence	219	73	451	28	16,11	2	—
1966-67	J.T. Partridge	90	28	266	13	20,46	1	—
1967-68	B.F. Davison	124,5	46	265	17	15,58	1	—
1968-69	A.J. Traicos	180,1	53	527	21	25,10	2	—
1969-70	J.H. du Preez	130,2	22	473	14	33,79	—	—
1970-71	M.J. Procter	188,4	69	350	26	13,46	1	—
1971-72	M.J. Procter	359,5	96	833	52	16,01	3	1
1972-73	M.J. Procter	393,2	103	1 006	56	17,96	4	2
1973-74	R.D. Jackman	272,4	61	685	32	21,40	2	—
1974-75	D.A.G. Fletcher	201	43	617	33	18,69	4	1
1975-76	P.B. Clift	361,2	92	847	37	22,89	1	—
1976-77	B. Horton	178,5	30	631	19	33,21	—	—
1977-78	V.R. Hogg	131	22	418	16	26,12	1	—
1978-79	V.R. Hogg	103,4	22	239	11	21,72	—	—
1979-80	D.A.G. Fletcher	139	26	465	18	25,83	—	—
1980-81	V.R. Hogg	150,3	43	328	19	17,26	—	—
1981-82	E.J. Hough	72	19	160	10	16,00	—	—

MOST WICKETS IN A SEASON: OVER 30 WICKETS

		O	M	R	W	AV.	5WI	10WM
M.J. Procter	1972-73	393,2	103	1 006	56	17,96	4	2
M.J. Procter	1971-72	359,5	96	833	52	16,01	3	1
P.N.F. Mansell	1951-52	+245,5	41	802	49	16,37	6	2
J.T. Partridge	1962-63	334,1	138	659	46	14,33	3	—
R.H. Kaschula	1980-81	395,3	104	1 099	45	24,42	—	—
G.B. Lawrence	1960-61	315	100	626	42	14,90	1	—
R.H. Kaschula	1970-71	308,1	143	608	41	14,83	3	—
R.D. Jackman	1972-73	282,5	64	725	39	18,59	1	1
J.T. Partridge	1961-62	201,4	46	537	38	14,13	3	1
M.J. Procter	1973-74	322,5	85	829	38	21,87	—	—
G.B. Lawrence	1959-60	310,3	104	615	37	16,62	2	—
P.B. Clift	1975-76	361,2	92	847	37	22,89	1	—
P.N.F. Mansell	1955-56	+206,3	57	518	36	14,39	2	1
J.T. Partridge	1954-55	+241,4	52	740	34	21,76	1	1
J.T. Partridge	1952-53	+208,6	42	629	33	19,06	3	—
D.A.G. Fletcher	1974-75	201	43	617	33	18,69	4	1
P.B. Clift	1978-79	274	56	720	33	21,81	1	—
J.T. Partridge	1959-60	299,4	86	637	32	19,91	3	—
R.H. Kaschula	1971-72	365,5	131	814	32	25,43	1	—
R.D. Jackman	1973-74	272,4	61	685	32	21,40	2	—
R.H. Kaschula	1979-80	311,2	89	852	32	26,62	—	—
A.J. Traicos	1980-81	272,2	59	624	32	19,50	—	—
D.S. Tomlinson	1946-47	+187	10	855	31	27,58	2	—

ALL-ROUND CRICKET

100 RUNS AND 10 WICKETS IN A MATCH

P.N.F. Mansell 94* and 13*, 7-71 and 3-79 v. North-Eastern Transvaal at Pretoria........ 1951

400 RUNS AND 20 WICKETS IN A SEASON

		R	H.S.	AV.	100	R	W	AV.
1951-52	P.N.F. Mansell	485	94+	48,50	—	802	49	16,37
1954-55	P.N.F. Mansell	427	131	61,00	2	447	27	16,56
1962-63	D.B. Pithey	428	166	30,57	1	511	24	21,29
1970-71	M.J. Procter	934	254	133,43	6	350	26	13,46
1971-72	M.J. Procter	695	107	40,88	1	833	52	16,01
1972-73	M.J. Procter	841	131	49,47	2	1 006	56	17,96
1973-74	M.J. Procter	563	110	33,12	1	829	38	21,87
1974-75	P.B. Clift	411	74+	29,35	—	684	25	27,36

WICKET-KEEPING

MOST DISMISSALS IN AN INNINGS

5	C.M. Harris	(3-2) v. M.C.C. at Salisbury	1948-49
		(4-1) v. Border at East London	1951-52
		(4-1) v. North-Eastern Transvaal at Pretoria	1951-52
5	H.A.B. Gardiner	(4-1) v. Griqualand West at Kimberley	1970-71
		(4-1) v. International Wanderers at Salisbury	1974-75
		(5-0) v. Natal at Durban	1975-76
5	S.D. Robertson	(5-0) v. Northern Transvaal at Pretoria	1973-74

MOST DISMISSALS IN A MATCH

8	C.M. Harris	(7-1) v. North-Eastern Transvaal at Pretoria	1951-52
7	T. Deftereos	(6-1) v. Transvaal B at Bulawayo	1960-61
7	C.M. Harris	(6-1) v. Border at East London	1951-52
7	S.D. Robertson	(7-0) v. Northern Transvaal at Pretoria	1973-74

MOST DISMISSALS IN A SEASON

32	(29-3)	H.A.B. Gardiner	1971-72
30	(25-5)	C.M. Harris	1951-52
30	(26-4)	H.A.B. Gardiner	1975-76
26	(25-1)	S.D. Robertson	1973-74
25	(24-1)	H.A.B. Gardiner	1974-75
24	(17-7)	H.A.B. Gardiner	1970-71
20	(20-0)	H.A.B. Gardiner	1972-73
20	(14-6)	R.D. Brown	1980-81

NOTE: Figures in parentheses represent (catches — stumpings).

FIELDING

MOST CATCHES IN AN INNINGS

4	J.H. du Preez	v. Eastern Province at Port Elizabeth	1965-66
4	G.B. Lawrence	v. North-Eastern Transvaal at Pretoria	1952-53
4	P.N.F. Mansell	v. North-Eastern Transvaal at Pretoria	1951-52
4	P.L. Winslow	v. Orange Free State at Bloemfontein	1957-58

MOST CATCHES IN A MATCH

6	J.H. du Preez	v. Eastern Province at Port Elizabeth	1965-66
		v. Transvaal at Johannesburg	1974-75
6	P.N.F. Mansell	v. North-Eastern Transvaal at Salisbury	1954-55

MOST CATCHES IN A SEASON

20	M.J. Procter	1972-73
14	P.N.F. Mansell	1946-47
13	R.A. Gripper	1960-61
12	J.H. du Preez	1974-75

CAREER RECORDS

50 OR MORE APPEARANCES

J.H. du Preez	112
D.A.G. Fletcher	101
B.F. Davison	90
R.A. Gripper	79
S.D. Robertson	77
D.J. Lewis	73
P.B. Clift	68
G.B. Lawrence	66
A.J. Pithey	65
A.J. Traicos	58
J.T. Partridge	56
K.C. Bland	55
P.N.F. Mansell	55
H.A.B. Gardiner	54
J.G. Heron	52
R.H. Kaschula	50

MOST CAPTAINCIES

D.J. Lewis	41
A.J. Pithey	34
M.J. Procter	25
B.F. Davison	25
D.A.G Fletcher	23
R.A. Gripper	18
K.C. Bland	13
D. Rees	11
S.D. Robertson	11

PLAYERS SCORING 3 000 OR MORE RUNS

B.F. Davison	4 480
S.D. Robertson	4 343
R.A. Gripper	4 107
J.H. du Preez	3 988
A.J. Pithey	3 987
D.A.G. Fletcher	3 719
M.J. Procter	3 662
D.J. Lewis	3 254
P.N.F. Mansell	3 027

PLAYERS TAKING 100 OR MORE WICKETS

G.B. Lawrence	296
J.T. Partridge	281
J.H. du Preez	277
R.H. Kaschula	208
D.A.G. Fletcher	207
P.B. Clift	205
P.N.F. Mansell	203
M.J. Procter	186
A.J. Traicos	152
R.D. Jackman	124

1 000 RUNS AND 50 WICKETS

	Runs	Wickets
P.B. Clift	1 943	205
J.H. du Preez	3 988	277
D.A.G. Fletcher	3 719	207
P.N.F. Mansell	3 027	203
D.B. Pithey	1 113	65
M.J. Procter	3 662	186

PLAYERS MAKING 40 OR MORE CATCHES

P.N.F. Mansell	84
J.H. du Preez	71
S.D. Robertson	69
D.A.G. Fletcher	66
B.F. Davison	64
R.A. Gripper	54
M.J. Procter	52
G.B. Lawrence	44
A.J. Traicos	42
R.B. Ullyett	40

WICKET-KEEPERS MAKING 50 OR MORE DISMISSALS

H.A.B. Gardiner	156	(137 cts. 19 sts.)
C.M. Harris	100	(77 cts. 23 sts.)
A.H. de Caila	70	(57 cts. 13 sts.)
D.B. Arnott	51	(40 cts. 11 sts.)

CAREER RECORDS

BATTING AND FIELDING

	Career	M	I	N.O.	Runs	H.S.	Av.	100	50	C	S
Adamson, J.A.	1931	5	8	2	48	24*	8,00	—	—	—	—
Anderson, G.	1904-09	2	3	1	3	2	1,50	—	—	2	—
Anderson, P.H.	1951	6	10	3	63	20*	9,00	—	—	2	—
Armstrong, A.	1938	1	1	—	5	5	5,00	—	—	—	—
Arnold, E.C.	1924-27	3	6	—	144	57	24,00	—	1	4	1
Arnott, D.B.	1954-61	28	39	8	458	58	14,77	—	1	40	11
Ashburner, R.W.	1947-50	7	13	—	170	46	13,08	—	—	7	5
Ashburnham, L.P.	1909	1	2	—	15	11	7,50	—	—	—	—
Austin, Q.A.	1927-46	5	8	—	65	25	8,13	—	—	3	—
Bain, J.	1922	1	1	—	6	6	6,00	—	—	—	—
Baldwin, J.M.S.	1949-56	19	33	—	639	65	19,36	—	4	11	—
Barber, G.M.H.	1956-59	2	4	—	10	8	2,50	—	—	2	—
Barbour, B.D.	1971-78	37	72	3	1 590	106	23,04	3	6	15	—
Bawden, D.B.E.	1975-79	6	10	—	152	42	15,20	—	—	1	—
Baxter, B.M.	1967	1	1	1	5	5*	—	—	—	1	—
Beets, D.J.	1960-61	4	6	1	41	19	8,20	—	—	3	—
Bell, A.J.	1938	1	1	1	1	1*	—	—	—	1	—
Benkenstein, M.M.	1970-75	15	27	3	550	84	22,92	—	3	6	—
Bennett, B.M.	1964-67	4	4	4	7	4*	—	—	—	2	—
Bentley R.M.	1977-80	16	30	4	937	122	36,04	1	7	7	—
Birrell, H.B.	1957-59	7	12	—	236	116	19,67	1	—	2	—
Blanckenberg, C.H.	1909	1	2	—	7	7	3,50	—	—	1	—
Blanckenberg, W.R.	1904	1	2	—	1	1	,50	—	—	—	—
Bland, K.C.	1956-68	55	97	10	2 751	197	31,62	4	13	22	—
Boast, N.I.	1930-36	2	3	1	47	33*	23,50	—	—	2	2
Bourdillon, T.E.	1909-24	5	9	—	78	24	8,67	—	—	3	—
Bowes, T.R.C.	1971-74	4	6	2	29	13	7,25	—	—	2	—
Boyd, B.B.	1975	1	2	—	45	27	22,50	—	—	1	—
Bradley, A.J.	1922-24	3	5	—	63	19	12,60	—	—	3	—
Brooks, F.B.	1909-22	2	3	—	43	28	14,33	—	—	—	—
Brooks, F.G.	1904-09	2	4	—	123	61	30,75	—	2	1	—
Brown, R.D.	1976-82	25	46	2	1 136	108	25,82	3	5	35	11
Brown, L.S.	1946-47	8	14	2	154	44*	12,83	—	—	5	—
Buchanan, J.M.	1945-53	10	16	6	64	18	6,40	—	—	3	—
Bunyard, G.S.	1962	1	2	1	26	24	26,00	—	—	2	—
Butchart, I.P.	1980-82	5	7	—	106	54	15,14	—	—	4	—
Cameron, D.P.	1968	1	2	—	28	25	14,00	—	—	2	—
Campbell, A.	1924-29	4	8	3	106	37	21,20	—	—	—	—
Campbell-Rodger, H.	1924-31	8	15	1	503	108	35,93	2	1	6	—
Catterall, R.H.	1924	1	2	—	48	38	24,00	—	—	2	—
Carew, A.S.	1946-50	12	19	3	160	29	10,00	—	—	9	—
Carew, B.J.	1948-53	11	19	2	499	179	29,35	2	—	1	—
Carlstein, P.R.	1967-76	38	69	1	2 017	125	29,66	2	15	18	—
Carse, J.A.	1977-79	10	16	4	137	44	11,42	—	—	2	—
Chapman, T.A.	1952	5	10	2	276	124*	34,50	1	—	2	—
Charsley, J.H.	1935-45	6	6	—	47	35	7,83	—	—	4	—
Chimowitz, B.L.	1945	1	2	—	53	49	26,50	—	—	—	—
Clarke, J.K.	1967-69	15	28	1	719	130	26,63	2	2	14	—
Clift, P.B.	1971-79	68	118	29	1 943	75*	21,83	—	7	38	—
Clinton, G.S.	1979	4	8	—	138	38	17,25	—	—	2	—

	Career	M	I	N.O.	Runs	H.S.	Av.	100	50	C	S
Coker, H.O.	1909	1	1	—	0	0	0,00	—	—	—	—
Cornish, D.J.	1946	1	1	—	3	3	3,00	—	—	—	—
Cornwall, D.J.L.	1960	1	2	—	15	12	7,50	—	—	—	—
Coventry, R.W.	1953-57	17	26	1	386	94	15,44	—	2	28	—
Cowper, S.A.	1922-24	3	5	1	46	18*	11,50	—	—	1	—
Crisp, R.J.	1929-30	2	3	—	7	4	2,33	—	—	—	—
Curle, A.C.	1922	1	2	—	42	34	21,00	—	—	—	—
Curran, K.M.	1980-82	11	13	5	228	56*	28,50	—	2	4	—
Curran, K.P.	1947-54	6	11	3	230	52*	28,75	—	1	5	—
Davidson, F.	1938	2	3	—	29	23	9,67	—	—	2	—
Davidson, T.	1938	1	1	—	17	17	17,00	—	—	—	—
Davies, M.W.	1950-56	20	31	3	1 096	133	39,14	3	6	6	—
Davison, B.F.	1967-78	90	158	9	4 480	137*	30,07	6	24	64	—
de Caila, A.H.	1961-73	34	44	13	483	42	15,58	—	—	57	13
Deftereos, T.	1957-60	4	7	1	30	19*	5,00	—	—	9	1
de Grandhomme, H.L.	1946-49	4	8	—	75	28	9,38	—	—	4	—
de Grandhomme, L.L.	1980-81	5	6	1	71	19	14,20	—	—	5	—
Dell, J.	1952	4	8	1	211	99	30,14	—	1	2	—
Den, A.M.	1935	1	—	—	—	—	—	—	—	—	—
Den, G.M.	1963	2	2	—	4	4	2,00	—	—	—	—
Deudney, N.A.	1966	3	6	—	61	27	10,17	—	—	1	—
de Villiers, R.F.	1961	1	—	—	—	—	—	—	—	—	—
Dickinson, R.H.J.	1929	4	8	2	93	26	15,50	—	—	5	1
Dickinson, V.E.J.	1955-64	20	30	2	308	30	11,00	—	—	12	—
Dinsdale, S.C.	1969	1	2	—	16	15	8,00	—	—	1	—
Dollar, F.	1927-29	4	8	3	16	10*	3,20	—	—	4	—
Downey, H.	1947	1	2	—	30	25	15,00	—	—	—	—
Duckworth, C.A.R.	1954-62	36	62	5	1 459	105	25,60	1	7	40	6
Dudhia, M.H.E.M.	1980-82	2	1	—	0	0	0,00	—	—	—	—
Dudleston, B.	1976-79	22	43	1	1 465	142	34,88	3	6	18	—
Duff, C.E.	1904-09	2	4	1	21	11*	7,00	—	—	2	—
Dunk, T.W.	1969-81	28	53	1	1 097	106	21,09	1	4	9	—
du Preez, J.H.	1961-79	112	185	23	3 988	112	24,62	1	19	71	—
Dyer, N.J.	1946	2	3	1	40	15	20,00	—	—	3	1
Elliott, D.G.	1922	1	1	—	23	23	23,00	—	—	1	—
Evans, D.H.	1972-73	4	4	1	11	8*	3,67	—	—	15	2
Evans, H.K.S.	1938-45	4	5	2	43	23*	14,33	—	—	8	1
Fletcher, A.W.R.	1976	4	7	2	94	39*	18,80	—	—	3	—
Fletcher, D.A.G.	1969-81	101	179	22	3 719	89	23,75	—	18	66	—
Fletcher, G.E.	1927	1	2	—	82	51	41,00	—	1	1	—
Forbes, R.	1931	1	2	1	7	6*	7,00	—	—	—	—
Fowler, D.	1929	1	2	—	4	3	2,00	—	—	1	1
Frangos, N.J.	1963-66	14	28	—	786	87	28,07	—	5	7	—
Franklin, C.D.	1948-50	5	10	3	187	101*	26,71	1	—	—	—
Freilinghaus, H.O.	1909	1	2	—	24	21	12,00	—	—	1	—
Fuller, J.H.F.	1935-47	14	26	2	560	107*	23,33	1	1	4	—
Gardiner, H.A.B.	1964-75	54	90	16	1 700	99	22,97	—	7	137	19
Geach, P.W.L.	1978	2	3	2	9	4	9,00	—	—	—	—
Gemmell, G.	1922-24	3	5	—	45	34	9,00	—	—	1	—
Gloak, R.D.	1924	1	2	—	11	8	5,50	—	—	1	—
Grant, G.C.	1931	5	9	—	215	68	23,89	—	1	7	—
Green, O.P.S.W.	1927	1	2	—	28	23	14,00	—	—	1	—
Griffin, G.M.	1961-62	5	9	1	180	51	22,50	—	1	3	—

	Career	M	I	N.O.	Runs	H.S.	Av.	100	50	C	S
Grimmer, I.	1950	1	1	1	2	2*	—	—	—	—	—
Gripper, R.A.	1957-71	79	147	11	4 107	279*	30,20	7	15	54	—
Haig, I.E.	1960-66	25	41	—	1 108	72	27,02	—	9	10	—
Halkett, P.A.C.	1961	1	1	—	8	8	8,00	—	—	—	—
Hancock, W.	1904	1	2	1	5	5*	5,00	—	—	—	—
Harris, C.M.	1946-54	32	56	4	933	114	17,94	1	1	77	23
Harris, M.	1949	1	2	—	26	25	13,00	—	—	1	—
Hayes, R.W.	1946-52	6	12	—	156	44	13,00	—	—	8	—
Hayward, C.J.R.	1927-38	16	28	5	851	95	37,00	—	7	13	—
Henderson, R.G.C.	1961	1	1	—	17	17	17,00	—	—	—	—
Henwood, N.	1909	1	2	—	4	4	2,00	—	—	—	—
Henwood, P.C.	1909	2	4	2	26	15	13,00	—	—	1	—
Heron, J.G.	1967-82	52	97	5	2 447	175	26,59	5	9	36	—
Hitzeroth, W.B.	1954-61	5	8	—	68	36	8,57	—	—	6	—
Hodgson, C.A.T.	1980-82	3	5	—	173	87	34,60	—	1	2	—
Hodnett, K.B.	1976	1	2	1	13	9*	13,00	—	—	1	—
Hodnett, W.H.	1962	1	2	—	6	6	3,00	—	—	2	—
Hogg, V.R.	1971-82	34	42	19	121	21	5,26	—	—	11	—
Hopley, G.C.	1922	1	2	—	39	22	19,50	—	—	—	—
Horton, B.	1975-77	16	23	10	82	16	6,31	—	—	9	—
Hough, E.J.	1982	3	1	—	4	4	4,00	—	—	—	—
Houghton, D.L.	1978-82	22	40	3	761	87	20,57	—	3	34	4
Huckle, M.R.G.	1966	1	2	1	18	14*	18,00	—	—	—	—
Hyde, A.	1927-46	19	30	2	543	80	19,39	—	4	6	—
Hyde, V.	1931	2	3	1	17	17*	8,50	—	—	1	—
Irvine, C.V.	1936	1	2	—	2	2	1,00	—	—	—	—
Jackman, R.D.	1972-79	35	56	14	523	50	12,45	—	1	16	—
Jarvis, M.	1980	2	2	1	7	7	7,00	—	—	—	—
Johnson, J.B.C.	1945	2	3	—	96	64	32,00	—	1	1	—
Johnson, P.	1946-52	14	21	8	133	25	10,23	—	—	5	—
Jones, J.G.	1975	3	5	—	33	25	6,60	—	—	3	—
Jonker, C.B.	1978-80	4	3	—	7	4	2,33	—	—	3	—
Kaschula, R.H.	1970-81	50	54	16	302	29	7,95	—	—	23	—
Keast, R.T.	1960-63	3	6	1	66	25	13,20	—	—	1	—
Keigwin, H.S.	1909	2	4	—	196	111	49,00	1	—	2	—
Kemp, C.B.	1955	6	7	2	87	34	17,40	—	—	3	—
Kennedy, R.	1945	1	1	—	1	1	1,00	—	—	—	—
Koch, L.B.	1958-60	6	11	1	219	63	21,90	—	1	3	—
Lang, E.	1922	1	2	—	41	29	20,50	—	—	—	—
Laughlin, E.	1969-70	10	14	—	178	47	12,71	—	—	4	—
Lawrence, G.B.	1952-65	66	95	23	908	60*	12,61	—	1	44	—
Leather, D.	1964	1	2	—	0	0	0,00	—	—	—	—
Lee, J.M.	1957	5	7	4	14	7	4,67	—	—	2	—
Lee, W.J.	1929	1	2	—	35	30	17,50	—	—	—	—
Lewis, D.J.	1945-63	73	119	13	3 254	170*	30,70	8	10	34	—
Leibbrandt, J.M.	1947-51	16	28	3	387	54	15,48	—	2	13	—
Linnell, M.G.	1904	1	2	—	21	15	10,50	—	—	—	—
Mansell, M.	1936	1	2	—	38	34	19,00	—	—	—	—
Mansell, P.N.F.	1936-59	55	91	8	3 027	154	36,47	5	22	84	—
Martin, S.H.	1947-49	9	17	1	468	87	29,25	—	3	1	—
McBride, B.J.	1952-54	7	9	1	70	28	8,75	—	—	3	—

	Career	M	I	N.O.	Runs	H.S.	Av.	100	50	C	S
McCallum, A.J.	1979-80	2	3	—	14	8	4,67	—	—	—	—
MacDonald, F.	1946-48	14	26	3	630	72	27,39	—	4	4	—
McKenzie, P.D.	1966-67	2	3	2	11	6	11,00	—	—	3	—
McLoughlin, P.R.	1967-70	7	8	2	114	37	19,00	—	—	2	—
McPhun, J.D.	1959-71	32	56	6	1 504	154	30,08	3	6	31	—
MacTavish, C.R.	1964	1	2	—	23	22	11,50	—	—	1	—
Meyer, J.	1980	2	2	1	46	40	46,00	—	—	—	—
Michell, R.R.	1935	1	—	—	—	—	—	—	—	1	—
Mitchell, J.C.	1969-78	47	89	5	2 115	77	25,18	—	13	27	—
Moll, H.D.	1930-36	7	10	2	84	45	10,50	—	—	8	—
Montgomery, H.H.	1950	1	1	1	12	12*	—	—	—	—	—
Morgan, F.H.	1922-29	6	11	1	174	50	17,40	—	1	2	—
Morris, D.J.	1936	1	2	—	0	0	0,00	—	—	1	—
Morris, E.D.	1945	2	3	1	51	30*	25,50	—	—	—	—
Murray, D.	1950	2	4	1	17	5*	5,67	—	—	—	—
Myles, H.	1936	1	2	—	12	12	6,00	—	—	—	—
Napier, D.C.	1954-66	18	28	12	75	15*	4,69	—	—	3	—
Napier, M.	1935-47	10	18	1	329	97*	19,35	—	1	4	—
Napier, W.A.	1929-30	2	3	—	61	38	20,33	—	—	2	—
Newson, E.S.	1945-49	10	17	—	361	114	21,24	1	2	2	—
Noble, R.J.	1938-46	10	18	2	287	84	17,94	—	2	6	—
O'Connell-Jones, D.B.	1947-57	14	23	—	763	148	33,17	2	3	7	—
Oldham, P.D.	1949-59	2	4	—	45	28	11,25	—	—	1	—
Oldreive, B.H.	1970-71	6	10	1	151	40	16,78	—	—	3	—
Oliver, R.J.	1927	1	2	—	13	11	6,50	—	—	—	—
Olver, S.	1946	1	2	—	21	15	10,50	—	—	1	—
O'Reilly, H.J.	1929-30	5	9	2	85	37*	12,14	—	—	1	—
Parker, E.F.	1958-69	38	61	9	887	83*	17,06	—	1	31	—
Parry, W.J.	1935	1	1	—	47	47	47,00	—	—	—	—
Partridge, J.T.	1951-66	56	72	26	419	29*	9,11	—	—	14	—
Passaportis, T.L.	1946-49	2	4	—	24	16	6,00	—	—	—	—
Paterson, G.	1981	3	5	1	66	43*	16,50	—	—	—	—
Paton, H.V.	1954-58	8	9	2	107	34	15,29	—	—	2	—
Pattinson, T.A.	1935	1	—	—	—	—	—	—	—	2	—
Pattison, A.H.	1931	5	9	1	291	128	36,38	1	1	5	—
Payne, G.	1909	1	1	—	9	9	9,00	—	—	—	—
Peck, G.N.C.	1968	3	5	2	32	17*	10,67	—	—	—	—
Peckover, G.E.	1977-79	12	21	2	351	93	18,47	—	1	24	3
Pfaff, C.	1909	1	1	—	0	0	0,00	—	—	—	—
Pithey, A.J.	1950-68	65	116	12	3 987	161*	38,34	7	24	27	—
Pithey, D.B.	1956-65	24	41	4	1 113	166	30,08	2	5	9	—
Pretorius, C.J.	1946-52	15	28	2	816	140*	31,38	2	4	2	—
Procter, M.J.	1970-75	46	81	6	3 662	254	48,83	11	17	52	—
Pycroft, A.J.	1979-82	20	35	7	1 421	133	50,75	4	10	18	—
Quinn, M.H.	1931	5	8	2	34	13	5,67	—	—	1	—
Rabinson, P.	1922	2	3	—	17	7	5,67	—	—	—	—
Rawson, P.W.	1982	2	2	1	15	13	7,50	—	—	1	—
Rees, D.	1950-52	16	30	1	723	105	24,93	1	3	12	—
Richardson, C.P.	1904	1	2	—	0	0	0,00	—	—	—	—
Ridgway, C.R.	1927	1	2	—	5	5	2,50	—	—	—	—
Roberts, C.L.	1929	1	2	—	13	12	6,50	—	—	—	—
Robertson, R.G.	1961	2	3	1	25	22	12,50	—	—	2	—

	Career	M	I	N.O.	Runs	H.S.	Av.	100	50	C	S
Robertson, S.D.	1968-79	77	143	12	4 343	136	33,15	3	28	110	1
Robinson, L.G.	1904-09	3	6	—	223	95	37,17	—	2	2	—
Robinson, V.L.	1922-31	7	12	—	257	59	21,42	—	1	1	—
Roothman, J.B.	1950-52	10	19	1	547	99	30,39	—	2	6	—
Saunders, E.M.	1927	1	1	—	2	2	2,00	—	—	1	—
Scott, G.M.	1982	1	—	—	—	—	—	—	—	—	—
Seagrave, D.G.	1970-71	5	3	2	5	3*	5,00	—	—	4	—
Shepherd, J.N.	1975	3	5	—	189	65	37,80	—	2	1	—
Sierra, J.P.	1950	5	9	—	154	62	17,11	—	1	4	—
Sim, E.S.	1929	5	10	—	132	61	13,20	—	1	—	—
Singleton, A.P.	1946-49	9	17	—	402	72	23,65	—	1	4	—
Slaven, M.D.	1953-55	5	6	3	11	4*	3,67	—	—	2	—
Speight, A.G.E.	1927-30	2	3	—	32	18	10,67	—	—	2	—
Stephenson, G.M.	1909	1	2	1	22	19*	22,00	—	—	—	—
Streak, D.H.	1976	2	3	1	44	22*	22,00	—	—	2	—
Stuart, C.T.	1904	1	2	—	17	12	8,50	—	—	1	—
Swart, P.D.	1965	1	1	—	0	0	0,00	—	—	—	—
Syminton, T.P.	1929-30	6	11	1	328	84	32,80	—	2	1	—
Taberer, W.S.	1904-09	3	6	1	165	45	33,00	—	—	1	—
Tattersall, K.	1973-76	14	27	—	457	70	16,93	—	1	15	—
Tayfield, H.J.	1947-48	7	14	1	139	48	10,69	—	—	6	—
Teague, D.	1949	1	2	—	37	23	18,50	—	—	2	—
Thompson, J.D.	1927-35	10	17	—	341	47	20,06	—	—	14	4
Thorn, B.	1976	2	4	—	69	66	17,25	—	1	—	—
Tomlinson, D.S.	1927-47	24	41	8	590	109	17,88	1	1	7	—
Tomlinson, R.N.	1927-29	3	6	2	121	44*	30,25	—	—	1	—
Tonkin, K.J.	1969	2	4	—	50	32	12,50	—	—	2	—
Townsend, F.H.	1922	1	1	1	22	22*	—	—	—	—	—
Townshend, D.W.	1967-68	5	5	2	75	35	25,00	—	—	1	—
Townshend, T.J.	1976-77	2	3	—	33	22	11,00	—	—	—	—
Traicos, A.J.	1967-82	58	86	38	584	38	12,17	—	—	42	—
Tummell, A.H.	1904	1	2	—	2	2	1,00	—	—	—	—
Ullyett, R.B.	1957-67	47	82	3	2 096	135	26,53	4	6	40	—
Walkden, T.L.	1946	1	2	1	28	16	28,00	—	—	1	—
Walker, R.	1946	1	1	—	7	7	7,00	—	—	1	—
Wallace, G.C.	1980-82	10	16	1	331	71	22,07	—	1	5	—
Wallace, J.H.A.	1949-54	19	36	1	1 256	138	35,89	4	5	11	—
Wallace, J.R.D.	1966	2	4	—	14	14	3,50	—	—	—	—
Wallace, P.D.	1977	1	2	—	2	2	1,00	—	—	—	—
Walters, D.	1951	1	2	—	14	9	7,00	—	—	—	—
Ward, A.S.	1936	1	2	—	2	2	1,00	—	—	—	—
Ward, J.H.	1957	2	4	1	156	69*	52,00	—	1	—	—
Williams, B.H.	1966-69	8	16	3	136	30	10,46	—	—	4	—
Williams, N.R.	1963-67	7	9	2	52	21	7,43	—	—	4	—
Willing, J.W.	1929	2	4	—	37	21	9,25	—	—	—	—
Willson, R.H.	1961	3	5	2	16	8*	5,33	—	—	2	—
Winslow, P.L.	1956-59	19	35	3	829	139	25,91	1	2	30	—
Wood, F.	1922	1	2	1	25	21*	25,00	—	—	1	—
Wood, W.	1924-29	8	16	2	306	60*	21,86	—	1	4	—
Wooler, C.R.D.	1951-56	8	15	2	144	24	11,08	—	—	1	—

BOWLING

	B	M	R	W	Av.	5WI	10WM
Adamson, J.A.	702	15	372	21	17,71	1	—
Anderson, G.	316	4	180	14	12,86	2	—
Anderson, P.H.	1 195	25	523	12	43,58	—	—
Armstrong, A.	128	4	41	1	41,00	—	—
Austin, Q.A.	314	2	197	4	49,25	—	—
Barber, G.M.H.	188	5	108	3	36,00	—	—
Barbour, B.D.	16	—	21	—	—	—	—
Baxter, B.M.	72	—	60	—	—	—	—
Beets, D.J.	519	30	170	12	14,17	1	1
Bell, A.J.	112	—	76	2	38,00	—	—
Bennett, B.M.	570	26	249	5	49,80	—	—
Bentley, R.M.	1 218	60	522	18	29,00	—	—
Birrell, H.B.	86	1	55	1	55,00	—	—
Blanckenberg, W.R.	24	1	27	—	—	—	—
Bland, K.C.	1 388	66	672	17	39,53	—	—
Bourdillon, T.E.	301	10	173	3	57,67	—	—
Bowes, T.R.C.	390	10	233	4	58,25	—	—
Brooks, F.G.	54	—	54	—	—	—	—
Brown, L.S.	1 944	34	800	25	32,00	1	—
Buchanan, J.M.	1 799	57	631	20	31,55	—	—
Bunyard, G.S.	132	—	102	3	34,00	—	—
Butchart, I.P.	162	8	76	4	19,00	—	—
Cameron, D.P.	144	6	80	2	40,00	—	—
Campbell, A.	102	2	68	1	68,00	—	—
Campbell-Rodger, H.	555	16	296	13	22,77	—	—
Catterall, R.H.	66	—	47	2	23,50	—	—
Carew, A.S.	2 779	71	934	32	29,19	—	—
Carew, B.J.	496	7	263	6	43,83	—	—
Carlstein, P.R.	30	—	15	—	—	—	—
Carse, J.A.	1 037	26	619	14	44,21	—	—
Chapman, T.A.	24	—	17	—	—	—	—
Charsley, J.H.	1 127	28	469	18	26,06	2	—
Chimowitz, B.L.	56	—	43	—	—	—	—
Clift, P.B.	13 020	521	5 562	205	27,13	5	—
Clinton, G.S.	6	1	—	—	—	—	—
Coker, H.O.	84	—	78	2	39,00	—	—
Cornish, D.J.	160	4	53	1	53,00	—	—
Coventry, R.W.	2 520	62	1 063	29	36,66	—	—
Cowper, S.A.	456	10	230	7	32,86	—	—
Crisp, R.J.	314	6	191	7	27,29	—	—
Curle, A.C.	6	—	14	—	—	—	—
Curran, K.M.	1 036	35	565	24	23,54	—	—
Davidson, T.	72	—	63	—	—	—	—
Davison, B.F.	2 135	101	998	38	26,26	1	—
de Grandhomme, H.L.	72	—	55	—	—	—	—
de Grandhomme, L.L.	600	19	353	7	50,43	—	—
Den, A.M.	54	1	40	—	—	—	—
Den, G.M.	276	16	110	9	11,11	1	—
Deudney, N.A.	654	25	267	8	33,38	—	—
de Villiers, R.F.	114	3	68	2	34,00	—	—
Dickinson, V.E.J.	3 460	189	1 338	54	24,78	4	1
Dinsdale, S.C.	42	—	24	1	24,00	—	—

	B	M	R	W	Av.	5WI	10WM
Dollar, F.	582	19	287	13	22,08	—	—
Dudhia, M.H.E.M.	156	7	71	5	14,20	—	—
Dudleston, B.	455	13	208	10	20,80	—	—
Duff, C.E.	366	7	210	7	30,00	—	—
du Preez, J.H.	16 822	603	8 689	277	31,37	10	1
Fletcher, A.W.R.	479	15	278	3	92,67	—	—
Fletcher, D.A.G.	11 706	406	5 718	207	27,62	5	1
Fletcher, G.E.	24	1	23	—	—	—	—
Freilinghaus, H.O.	18	1	12	—	—	—	—
Fuller, J.H.F.	32	—	13	—	—	—	—
Geach, P.W.L.	180	4	82	3	27,33	—	—
Gemmell, G.	138	5	51	1	51,00	—	—
Gloak, R.D.	97	2	45	1	45,00	—	—
Grant, G.C.	150	2	75	3	25,00	—	—
Green, O.P.S.W.	12	1	14	—	—	—	—
Griffin, G.M.	666	20	292	10	29,20	—	—
Grimmer, I.	152	1	69	1	69,00	—	—
Gripper, R.A.	222	6	120	3	40,00	—	—
Hayward, C.J.R.	107	1	62	4	15,50	—	—
Henwood, P.C.	204	6	119	1	119,00	—	—
Heron, J.G.	10	—	17	—	—	—	—
Hitzeroth, W.B.	300	4	147	—	—	—	—
Hogg, V.R.	5 151	178	2 356	90	26,18	2	—
Horton, B.	2 685	82	1 462	47	31,31	1	—
Hough, E.J.	594	27	233	12	19,42	—	—
Huckle, M.R.G.	54	—	44	1	44,00	—	—
Hyde, A.	594	11	329	14	23,50	—	—
Hyde, V.	96	1	79	2	39,50	—	—
Irvine, C.V.	42	1	52	—	—	—	—
Jackman, R.D.	6 196	210	2 875	124	23,18	5	1
Jarvis, M.	120	2	84	2	42,00	—	—
Johnson, J.B.C.	16	1	9	—	—	—	—
Johnson, P.	2 555	71	974	42	23,19	2	—
Jones, J.G.	6	—	5	—	—	—	—
Jonker, C.B.	453	17	250	8	31,25	—	—
Kaschula, R.H.	12 637	666	5 271	208	25,34	7	1
Keast, R.T.	474	19	162	9	18,00	—	—
Kemp, C.B.	472	8	260	8	32,50	—	—
Koch, L.B.	5	—	6	—	—	—	—
Laughlin, E.	42	3	24	—	—	—	—
Lawrence, G.B.	15 534	738	5 119	296	17,29	13	1
Lee, J.M.	848	24	300	12	25,00	—	—
Lee, W.J.	12	—	14	—	—	—	—
Lewis, D.J.	1 179	59	424	10	42,40	—	—
Leibbrandt, J.M.	3 720	99	1 337	47	28,45	3	—
Linnell, M.G.	18	—	24	—	—	—	—
Mansell, P.N.F.	10 607	259	4 467	203	22,00	18	5
Martin, S.H.	1 660	50	499	21	23,76	1	—
McBride, B.J.	1 285	19	533	30	17,77	2	—

	B	M	R	W	Av.	5WI	10WM
MacDonald, F.	103	2	51	—	—	—	—
McKenzie, P.D.	162	5	82	2	41,00	—	—
McLoughlin, P.R.	776	40	353	15	23,53	—	—
McPhun, J.D.	12	2	—	—	—	—	—
Michell, R.R.	18	—	19	—	—	—	—
Mitchell, J.C.	3 440	142	1 498	41	36,54	1	—
Moll, H.D.	852	24	384	8	48,00	—	—
Montgomery, H.H.	104	4	36	3	12,00	—	—
Morgan, F.H.	642	8	427	7	61,00	—	—
Morris, D.J.	48	1	22	—	—	—	—
Morris, E.D.	291	5	110	2	55,00	—	—
Murray, D.	208	3	86	—	—	—	—
Napier, D.C.	2 889	124	1 246	28	44,50	—	—
Napier, M.	92	1	62	—	—	—	—
Napier, W.A.	144	5	102	—	—	—	—
Newson, E.S.	1 736	34	666	27	24,67	1	—
Noble, R.J.	702	13	392	7	56,00	—	—
Oldham, P.D.	220	4	154	3	51,33	—	—
Oldreive, B.H.	13	—	8	—	—	—	—
O'Reilly, H.J.	997	22	572	23	24,87	2	—
Parker, E.F.	5 207	216	2 576	86	29,95	3	1
Partridge, J.T.	14 006	598	5 340	281	19,00	18	3
Passaportis, T.L.	152	2	101	1	101,00	—	—
Paton, H.V.	1 028	48	380	17	22,35	1	—
Pattinson, T.A.	84	2	33	—	—	—	—
Payne, G.	6	—	6	—	—	—	—
Peck, G.N.C.	320	8	225	8	28,13	—	—
Pithey, A.J.	10	—	12	—	—	—	—
Pithey, D.B.	4 753	248	1 709	65	26,29	3	1
Pretorius, C.J.	208	3	130	1	130,00	—	—
Procter, M.J.	8 381	378	3 445	186	18,52	8	3
Pycroft, A.J.	3	—	—	1	0,00	—	—
Quinn, M.H.	695	23	293	24	12,21	2	—
Rabinson, P.	291	13	112	10	11,20	1	—
Rawson, P.W.	366	12	177	7	25,28	1	—
Rees, D.	8	—	6	—	—	—	—
Richardson, C.P.	24	—	26	—	—	—	—
Robertson, S.D.	95	4	33	1	33,00	—	—
Robinson, L.G.	50	1	40	1	40,00	—	—
Robinson, V.L.	102	5	39	—	—	—	—
Roothman, J.B.	8	1	—	—	—	—	—
Saunders, E.M.	126	7	62	2	31,00	—	—
Seagrave, D.G.	569	21	297	14	21,21	—	—
Shepherd, J.N.	510	22	191	6	31,83	—	—
Sierra, J.P.	8	—	7	—	—	—	—
Sim, E.S.	686	20	400	15	26,67	—	—
Singleton, A.P.	908	22	400	25	16,00	1	—
Slaven, M.D.	1 075	31	432	19	22,74	—	—
Stephenson, G.M.	168	8	104	5	20,80	1	—
Streak, D.H.	138	2	79	2	39,50	—	—
Swart, P.D.	54	2	23	—	—	—	—

	B	M	R	W	Av.	5WI	10WM
Symington, T.P.	12	1	10	—	—	—	—
Taberer, W.S.	204	5	139	—	—	—	—
Tattersall, K.	42	3	13	1	13,00	—	—
Tayfield, H.J.	1 419	34	509	24	21,21	2	—
Thompson, J.D.	132	3	64	5	12,80	—	—
Tomlinson, D.S.	3 602	35	2 324	74	31,41	4	—
Tomlinson, R.N.	408	12	198	1	198,00	—	—
Tonkin, K.J.	198	7	96	4	24,00	—	—
Townshend, D.W.	1 120	48	444	6	74,00	—	—
Traicos, A.J.	11 247	525	4 683	152	30,81	6	1
Tummell, A.H.	12	—	13	—	—	—	—
Ullyett, R.B.	3 183	130	1 311	46	28,50	3	—
Wallace, G.C.	66	2	42	—	—	—	—
Wallace, J.H.A.	24	—	13	—	—	—	—
Walters, D.	104	1	51	2	25,50	—	—
Williams, B.H.	852	19	465	14	33,21	—	—
Williams, N.R.	834	39	420	12	35,00	—	—
Willing, J.W.	210	2	143	4	35,75	—	—
Willson, R.H.	444	20	231	3	77,00	—	—
Wood, F.	12	—	14	—	—	—	—
Wood, W.	1 067	34	482	24	20,08	1	—
Wooler, C.R.D.	1 824	45	744	23	32,35	—	—

RHODESIA B CAREER RECORDS

BATTING AND FIELDING

	Career	M	I	N.O.	Runs	H.S.	Av.	100	50	C	S
Allan, P.J.	1978	4	7	1	267	138	44,50	1	1	—	—
Arnott, K.J.	1979	3	6	—	40	35	6,66	—	—	2	—
Barbour, B.D.	1977	1	2	—	168	86	84,00	—	2	—	—
Bawden, D.B.E.	1977-79	5	10	—	162	64	16,20	—	1	4	—
Benkenstein, M.M.	1979	3	6	—	115	47	19,17	—	—	1	—
Bentley, R.M.	1978	2	3	1	56	39*	28,00	—	—	1	—
Brown, R.D.	1977-78	5	9	1	372	200*	46,50	1	—	4	—
Carlstein, P.R.	1977-79	6	12	—	255	75	21,25	—	3	6	—
Carse, J.A.	1977-79	3	4	—	14	7	3,50	—	—	1	—
Coughlan, T.D.	1979	4	5	2	16	13*	5,33	—	—	—	—
Daines, G.W.	1978	2	4	—	49	25	12,25	—	—	1	—
De Grandhomme, L.L.	1979	6	11	5	219	60	36,50	—	2	6	—
Desai, K.	1977	1	2	—	6	6	3,00	—	—	—	—
Dunk, T.W.	1977-78	4	7	—	232	74	33,14	—	2	1	—
Du Preez, J.H.	1977	1	2	—	49	36	24,50	—	—	—	—
Ervine, N.B.	1977	1	1	—	5	5	5,00	—	—	1	—
Ervine, R.M.	1977	3	6	2	61	33	15,25	—	—	—	—
Fletcher, A.W.R.	1977-78	3	4	—	56	22	14,00	—	—	1	—
Friend, I.S.	1978	2	4	2	5	3	2,50	—	—	2	—
Gibb, M.H.	1977-78	4	7	1	75	34	12,50	—	—	5	—
Heron, J.G.	1977-79	4	8	1	242	77	34,57	—	3	1	—
Hodgson, C.A.T.	1979	1	2	—	9	9	4,50	—	—	—	—
Hodnett, K.B.	1977-78	4	8	—	47	19	5,88	—	—	4	2
Hogg, V.R.	1977-79	6	7	1	45	30	7,50	—	—	3	—
Hogge, M.S.	1977	2	3	1	60	34	30,00	—	—	2	—
Houghton, D.L.	1978-79	4	7	—	215	72	30,71	—	1	14	3
Houghton, W.J.	1978	3	4	—	106	65	26,50	—	1	5	—
Jarvis, M.	1979	2	2	—	8	8	4,00	—	—	1	—
Jonker, C.B.	1978-79	8	10	3	89	37	12,71	—	—	4	—
Kuhn, S.	1979	3	6	1	93	22	18,60	—	—	9	—
McCallum, A.J.	1978-79	7	14	1	438	106*	33,69	1	—	1	—
Meyer, J.	1979	4	8	1	252	69	36,00	—	2	—	—
Mitchell, J.C.	1977	1	2	—	64	42	32,00	—	—	1	—
Nimr-Springer, M.C.	1977	1	1	—	15	15	15,00	—	—	1	—
Parker, E.F.	1978	10	17	5	496	82	41,33	—	5	2	—
Peake, M.C.	1977	1	2	2	15	15*	—	—	—	—	—
Peckover, G.E.	1978-79	2	4	1	127	71	42,33	—	2	3	1
Scott, G.M.	1979	1	2	—	31	21	15,50	—	—	2	—
Seager, M.R.J.	1978	1	2	—	48	41	24,00	—	—	—	—
Shah, A.	1979	1	1	—	2	2	2,00	—	—	—	—
Streak, D.H.	1977-78	6	8	2	84	22	14,00	—	—	1	—
Thorn, B.	1977	4	8	—	191	53	23,88	—	1	4	—
Townshend, T.J.	1977	1	2	—	37	21	18,50	—	—	—	—
Traicos, A.J.	1977	2	3	—	102	43	34,00	—	—	2	—
Wallace, G.C.	1978-79	8	16	1	493	111	32,87	1	1	5	—
Wallace, P.D.	1977	2	3	—	97	49	32,33	—	—	1	—
Watson, L.N.	1978	2	4	—	15	7	3,75	—	—	1	—

BOWLING

	O	M	R	W	Av.	5WI	10WM
Allan, P.J.	61,2	13	205	4	51,25	—	—
Bawden, D.B.E.	57	8	219	5	43,80	—	—
Benkenstein, M.M.	2	—	12	—	—	—	—
Bentley, R.M.	66	21	196	11	17,81	—	—
Carlstein, P.R.	1	—	3	—	—	—	—
Carse, J.A.	93,5	17	284	8	35,50	—	—
Coughlan, T.D.	55	17	150	8	18,75	1	—
De Grandhomme, L.L.	170	54	374	12	31,1	—	—
Desai, K.	9	—	47	—	—	—	—
Du Preez, J.H.	70,3	23	134	8	16,75	1	—
Ervine, N.B.	5	—	26	—	—	—	—
Ervine, R.M.	72	25	187	4	46,75	—	—
Fletcher, A.W.R.	16	—	77	—	—	—	—
Friend, I.S.	48	7	181	5	36,20	—	—
Gibb, M.H.	4	—	11	—	—	—	—
Hodnett, K.B.	46	8	134	3	44,66	—	—
Hogg, V.R.	265	80	652	27	24,14	—	—
Hogge, M.S.	2	6	69	—	—	—	—
Houghton, W.J.	66	18	188	9	20,88	1	—
Jarvis, M.	60	13	185	6	30,83	—	—
Jonker, C.B.	230	40	747	27	27,66	—	—
McCallum, A.J.	81,4	22	228	8	28,50	—	—
Mitchell, J.C.	60	17	147	6	24,50	1	—
Nimr-Springer, M.C.	19	1	80	—	—	—	—
Parker, E.F.	107,3	34	319	8	39,87	—	—
Peake, M.C.	19	1	61	—	—	—	—
Streak, D.H.	160,1	41	437	8	54,62	—	—
Traicos, A.J.	123	33	294	9	32,66	—	—
Wallace, G.C.	63	15	209	5	41,80	—	—
Watson, L.N.	47	12	142	2	71,00	—	—

ZIMBABWE'S MOST RENOWNED PLAYING-FIELDS

Photo: *The Chronicle. By courtesy of Queens Sports Club.*

Photos: *Duncan Hannay.*

Photo: *By courtesy L. Morgenrood.*

Top: The Queens Sports Club, Bulawayo, during the M.C.C. v. Rhodesia match, November 1956.
Centre: Two views of the Salisbury Sports Club, now renamed Harare Sports Club, taken during the game between Zimbabwe and West Indies, October 1981.
Bottom: A typical crowd at the Police ground, Harare.